Jason Lantzer
Dwight Eisenhower and the Holocaust

Jason Lantzer

Dwight Eisenhower and the Holocaust

—

A History

DE GRUYTER
OLDENBOURG

ISBN 978-3-11-221548-7
e-ISBN (PDF) 978-3-11-132711-2
e-ISBN (EPUB) 978-3-11-132761-7

Library of Congress Control Number: 2023941116

Bibliographic information published by the Deutsche Nationalbibliothek
The Deutsche Nationalbibliothek lists this publication in the Deutsche Nationalbibliografie;
detailed bibliographic data are available on the internet at http://dnb.dnb.de.

© 2025 Walter de Gruyter GmbH, Berlin/Boston
This volume is text- and page-identical with the hardback published in 2023.
Cover image: Charred Bodies of Prisoners Burned to Death by the Nazis in a Concentration Camp
at Gotha, Germany, National Archives Catalog, NAID: 276537087, Local ID: 111-SC-203547.
Typesetting: Integra Software Services Pvt. Ltd.
Printing and binding: CPI books GmbH, Leck

www.degruyter.com

Acknowledgements

Most authors agree with Dwight Eisenhower that teamwork is essential to complete tasks. I have been blessed with quite a team of colleagues, friends, and family who have helped make the writing of this book possible.

Butler University is where my academic home has been for more than a decade. Once again, I need to thank my colleagues. I am indebted to the library staff, especially to Sally Childs-Helton, Sarah Damery, and Josh Petrusa. Additionally, Melissa Etzler, who team taught an Honors course about Germany and the United States with me and has been my partner in taking students to Europe since 2018 via faculty led study abroad trips, is a wonderful collaborator, colleague, and friend. I am also very thankful for the support of the entire staff of the Center for Global Education (Jill, Callie, Dena, Bond, and Judy) who have helped us get to both France and Germany, as well as back home again several times now. I am also very appreciative of the assistance of Heather Ellis and the wonderful staff of IES Abroad in Berlin who have facilitated our study abroad trips And thank you as well to my former colleague, Melissa Friedman who offered both her support and proofreading skills to an early draft of this manuscript. My students deserve a good deal of thanks for inspiring and helping shape this project. Guy Preskill, Isaac Warshawsky, Addy McKown, Libbie Wight, Ali Kerby, Meg McFadden, Kate Nelson, Sarah Mahnesmith, Shelby Oberst, Olivia Danielson, Emma Edick, Luke Bunting, Nick Huang, Kyra Laubacher, Madison Pines, and Rachael Lewis are some of the wonderful students I have had the pleasure of teaching at Butler who all, whether they knew it at the time or not, made an impact on the work you now hold in your hands.

I continue to marvel and appreciate the fact that I am one of James Madison's former students. He was my mentor from my first day of graduate school at Indiana University, and his encouraging words early on, when I was vacillating over embarking on this project, were profound and inspiring. Speaking of IU, thank you to my old friend and fellow alumnus, Dr. Jason VanHorn of Calvin University, who provided essential geographic knowledge in seconds when I asked for help out of the blue.

The support of numerous archives and libraries showcase the very best side of the academic research process. I am particularly indebted to the staff at the Dwight Eisenhower Presidential Library, especially Mary Burtzloff, Kevin Bailey, and Timothy Rives. The entire staff at the United States Holocaust Museum were also extremely helpful. I also want to thank Colonel Ty Seidule and Suzanne Christoff of the United States Military Academy at West Point for their help in finding out what Eisenhower may have learned about the military treatment of civilians while at the academy. A special thank you is also owed to Felicia Williamson and Hannah Evans of the Dallas Holocaust Museum Center for Education and Tolerance for facilitating my use of their resources as part of this project. Dara Baker and the Franklin Roosevelt Presidential Library staff were also extremely helpful in tracking down sources and offering advice. Thomas Jander of the Documents Department at the German History Museum in Berlin, Germany also provided useful information, as did Johannes Tuchel of the German Resistance Memorial Center and Michael Noth of the German Federal Archives Division, Military Archives. I am also thankful to Dr. Robert Baumann of the U.S. Army's Command and General Staff College for his help. Thank you as well to the Michigan State Library system, who provided a key document to me digitally in a remarkably quick, and kind, gesture. I appreciate the help of Courtney Chartier of Emory University for her insight into their collections on the Holocaust as well as the staff at the National World War II Museum in New Orleans and the staff at the American Jewish Archives. And lastly, thank you to Amber Maze of the Indianapolis Jewish Community Relations Council who put me in touch with Tibor Klopfer, who shared his family's story with me.

My final professional thank you is due to Rabea Rittgerodt and all those she works with at De Gruyter Oldenbourg who have made this book a reality. Rabea was kind enough to take a meeting based off a Twitter interaction, listen to my pitch, and then believe in the project when others doubted. I am very grateful to her and to the press for all that they have done to bring this part of Eisenhower's story to you.

As always, I am thankful to my family. My parents, Jack and Juanita Lantzer, nurtured my love of American history at a young age—including on an out of the way, side trip to Fort Knox's Patton Museum during one of our summer vacations. My brother, Justin, sister-in-law Deanna, and niece Maisie, opened their doors to me in Dallas, so I could do research in Texas. I am thankful for my sister-in-law, Anne, for getting married to my brother-in-law, Kako, and thus giving us an excuse to make our first trip to Europe in 2015, which brought me face-to-face with so much of the history I had lectured on and read about, but had not experienced firsthand, including Omaha Beach. And I am grateful as well to my in-laws (James and Kathy Heuer and Susan and Bill Hebert), my brother-in-law Will, as well as my children, Kate and Nick, and wife Erin, for making that trip such a memorable one.

With the thank yous out of the way, allow me a moment of reflection: How can an American, Protestant, historian, born some thirty years after the end of

World War II connect to this story? How can that same person pass it and its significance on to the next generation, including to his own children? These were, and are, the questions that followed me as I journeyed alongside Eisenhower into the story of the Holocaust[1] and sought to understand what his encounter with it meant for him and the United States as a whole.

On the one hand, as an historian, I convey the past (all sorts of pasts) to my students every time I enter the classroom. But that does not explain my interest in writing this book adequately. First of all, there are many books on the topic, many of which are in the bibliography and notes of this one. Second, there are many topics I could write about, so why this one? In very real ways, this is not "my" story. And yet, it is. Much of my family is German in heritage, and though my ancestors immigrated to the United States before the Civil War, those roots are real. Being an historian has informed that feeling even more: Germany was no backwater. It was in the heart of Europe and had, since at least the mid-nineteenth century been one of the arbiters of the modern industrial age. It was, in other words, the product of many of the same forces that created the modern United States. If the Holocaust could happen in Germany, what does that tell us about America?

When an historian begins doing research, they never know what they will find. In the case of this book, that research led me to the Central Database of Shoah Victims. Here I found over 150 "Lantzers" listed simply as "murdered." Most were from Tomaszow and Lubaczow in what is today Poland. Many died at Belzec. I was left wondering a very simple question, largely impossible to answer: were we related? My family had come to the United States in the 1850s, and as far as I knew were a mixture of German Methodists, Mennonites, and Lutherans—not Jewish and not from Poland. But my own research had shown some members

---

[1] Throughout the pages that follow, I have opted to use the word "holocaust" to describe what the Nazis unleashed on the Jews of Europe. In English, the Greek word translates to "a great destruction resulting in extensive loss of life, often by fire." While it had been used since the eighteenth century, including in reference to the World War I era Armenian genocide, to describe large-scale murder, it did not become widely adopted until the 1950s and 1960s to describe the events of the Second World War. Prior to that, especially among Jews, the word most often used was "Shoah" which translates to "catastrophe." My decision stems chiefly from the present, twenty-first century, use and knowledge of the term holocaust amongst both the general and professional publics (even though there has been debate about its usage within the scholarly community) as well as its use in virtually all the secondary sources I consulted. See, "The Holocaust," https://cla.umn.edu/chgs/holocaust-genocide-education/resource-guides/holocaust, 20 June 2021; "What is the Shoah?," http://www.memorialdelashoah.org/en/archives-and-documentation/what-is-the-shoah.html, 20 June 2021.

of my father's family had lived in "the east"—in lands that became modern Poland following the Great War. Had some of them converted to Christianity during the imperial period? Was "Lantzer" (or one of its variant spellings) simply ubiquitous at some point in the past? I do not know the answers to those questions and may never know. But whether these names represent cousins of mine or not, this book is dedicated to their memory. May we never forget.

Contents

Acknowledgements —— V

Introduction —— XI

Chapter 1
The Quote and the Man behind It —— 1
    Ohrdruf —— 2
    The Man from Abilene —— 10
    The Thousand Year Reich —— 17
    The Depressing Question of Immigration —— 21
    Ike and the Jews of Manila —— 23
    A Second Time and a Second Chance —— 25

Chapter 2
Freedom Imperiled —— 28
    War in the East —— 33
    Finding the Final Solution —— 36
    The Konzentrationslager (KZ) System —— 40
    Awaiting Liberation —— 46

Chapter 3
Waging a War of Liberation —— 48
    Refugees and Liberation —— 52
    The Resistance and the Perils of Unconditional Surrender —— 63
    Letting Loose the Dogs of War —— 67
    The Red Army and the Camps —— 70

Chapter 4
"First Hand Evidence" —— 78
    The Horrors of Buchenwald —— 84
    Death at Dachau —— 88
    Liberation Continues —— 92
    Ike's Press Offensive —— 100

Chapter 5
Crimes Against Humanity —— 108
  On to Berlin? —— 108
  The Military Governor —— 114
  Denazification —— 119
  Displaced Persons and the Harrison Report —— 126
  War Crimes Trials —— 135

Chapter 6
Never Again —— 143
  Duty, Honor, Country —— 143
  We Like Ike —— 147
  Ike and the State of Israel —— 158
  The Lingering Nazi Stench —— 167

Epilogue: Never Forgetting —— 175

Bibliography —— 183

Index —— 199

Introduction

In July 2015, I had the opportunity to visit Normandy, France for the first time. For me, this was the fulfillment of a childhood dream, one that led me to becoming an historian. Next to Gettysburg, the American battlefield I most wanted to visit growing up was Omaha Beach. My wife, as she so often has, made this dream of mine a reality.

Standing at Point du Hoc is to be surrounded by history. The massive German fortifications, the power of naval artillery, the obstacles ahead for the U.S. Army Rangers, all these things still envelop visitors in the present. To stand where presidents have stood, including Ronald Reagan, whose stirring words about "the boys of Pointe du Hoc" first caused me to want to visit Normandy, is a powerful experience. Reagan's rhetoric at that spot hit just the right chord on the fortieth anniversary of D-Day.[2] "We're here," he said to the assembled veterans, their families, and government officials:

> To mark that day in history when the Allied armies joined in battle to reclaim this continent to liberty. For four long years, much of Europe had been under a terrible shadow. Free nations had fallen, Jews cried out in the camps, millions cried out for liberation. Europe was enslaved, and the world prayed for its rescue. Here in Normandy the rescue began. Here the Allies stood and fought against tyranny in a giant undertaking unparalleled in human history . . . The men of Normandy had faith that what they were doing was right, faith that they fought for all humanity, faith that a just God would grant them mercy on this beachhead or on the next. It was the deep knowledge—and pray God we have not lost it—that there is a profound, moral difference between the use of force for liberation and the use of force for conquest. You were here to liberate, not to conquer, and so you and those others did not doubt your cause. And you were right not to doubt . . . These are the boys of Pointe du Hoc. These are the men who took the cliffs. These are the champions who helped free a continent. These are the heroes who helped end a war."[3]

Walking the beach itself, to see and stand upon that long stretch of sand, to view where the German guns were – knowing they were raking the beach with murderous fire, is to better understand what those American boys turned soldiers had to do in order to get off the beach and into France. To be alone in the wind and surf, and to try and comprehend the chaos that was June 6, 1944, can only be attempted on the ground. To later drive among the hedgerows is to better grasp how dangerous the job ahead was going to be for the Allies. And to then visit the American Military Cemetery, with its over 9,000 graves, perfectly laid out in orderly, cascading

---

[2] Douglas Brinkley, *The Boys of Pointe Du Hoc: Ronald Reagan, D-Day, and the U.S. Army Second Ranger Battalion* (New York: Harper Perennial, 2005), 180–183.

[3] Brinkley, *The Boys of Pointe Du Hoc*, 225–231.

rows of crosses and Stars of David, interspersed by rose bush clusters (which highlight a portion of the German defenses) both stirs the soul and confirms that from time to time, the government does indeed spend tax dollars wisely.

If Normandy's beaches seem an odd place to start a reflection on the Holocaust, they should not. For Americans, this is exactly where our involvement with that noble endeavor to end the crime of the century begins. True, Britain and France had been at war with the Nazis since 1939. Russia, then known as the Soviet Union, had joined the conflict against Germany in 1941 – but only after the Nazis had negated a non-aggression pact between the two countries by invading Soviet territory. The United States, on the other hand, had only joined the war in December 1941, after Germany's Axis partner Japan attacked the U.S. Pacific fleet at Pearl Harbor. And while American forces waged war against them and had taken part in successful invasions in North Africa in 1942 and Italy in 1943, all while being the "arsenal of democracy" and joining the air war over Germany, by and large the Nazi crimes remained the stuff of "buried" news, mixed with disbelief and anxiety over the stories being or being seen as propaganda, which prompted little Allied action to stop it. During those years, Germany's European empire remained intact, and the killing continued.

From an American perspective, all that changed with D-Day. As President Franklin Roosevelt said in the prayer he offered as the country awoke to news of the invasion: "Almighty God: Our sons, pride of our Nation, this day have set upon a mighty endeavor, a struggle to preserve our Republic, our religion, and our civilization, and to set free a suffering humanity."[4] That was the mission of the American forces on D-Day, "to set free a suffering humanity," and it became a defining moment for the man who commanded the Allied forces that day, Dwight David Eisenhower.

Eisenhower's mission was more complex than merely defeating the German armed forces on Normandy's beaches and beyond. America and her allies had done that once before in his lifetime. It was also more than just liberating nations the Germans had occupied. As Roosevelt had prayed, Eisenhower was leading a mission to "preserve our Republic, our religion, and our civilization" against a brutal, totalitarian system that sought not just to forge an empire, but to eliminate whole groups of people in the process. While Eisenhower had little foreknowledge about what he was to encounter in the midst of liberating Western Europe from the Nazi grasp, the Holocaust, with its camps, victims, and perpetrators were destined to change him and the nation he led. And though the Holocaust has become

---

[4] "Franklin D. Roosevelt's D-Day Prayer," http://docs.fdrlibrary.marist.edu/odddayp.html, 3 December 2015.

an historical touchstone, and has been studied widely,[5] the act of liberation and its impact on those took part, even when it is mentioned and even when it is the focus, is often lost in the "frightening abyss" that was the ideology and end result of the camps that Nazi Germany built.[6]

Until now, despite the fact that Eisenhower "dominated American public life" from the D-Day landings in 1944 until his death in 1969, his encounter with the Holocaust has been little studied. Perhaps this is not surprising, as it took decades for historians to stop underestimating his role as both a general and as president, with authors seeing him as either incidental to the actual war effort or as a kindly "grandfather," who happened to serve as president.[7] For a very long time, he was viewed as an "enigma," some sort of benign figure looming indistinctly out of the mists of the past, an administrative general and a caretaker president who presided over eight years of international calm and domestic tranquility. And yet, as some authors have noted, there is a complexity to his character.[8] Family, including his beloved wife Mamie, believed that it was nearly impossible to really know Ike in full, as he compartmentalized his life. His son John, himself a West Point graduate, eventual general, ambassador, and author, once wryly noted that to understand his father, you needed to appreciate that Ike was 25 percent congenial and "75 percent cold-blooded."[9]

However, the real Ike was more than any of those images convey. His staff knew him to be a tireless taskmaster who worked with incredible subtlety to move events in the direction he wished them to go. As one commentator put it, "beneath

---

5 See, for example, Raul Hilberg, *The Destruction of the European Jews* (Chicago: Quadrangle Books, 1961), v; Theodore S. Hamerow, *Why We Watched: Europe, America, and the Holocaust* (New York: W. W. Norton & Company, 2008), xii-xiii; Alvin H. Rosenfeld, *The End of the Holocaust* (Indianapolis: Indiana University Press, 2011), 12; Yisrael Gutman and Michael Berenbaum, editors, *Anatomy of the Auschwitz Death Camp* (Indianapolis: Indiana University Press, 1994), ix; Timothy Snyder, *Black Earth: The Holocaust as History and Warning* (New York: Tim Duggan Books, 2015), xii.
6 John C. McManus, *Hell Before Their Very Eyes: American Soldiers Liberate Concentration Camps in Germany, April 1945* (Baltimore: Johns Hopkins University Press, 2015), 154.
7 Mary S. McAuliffe, "Eisenhower, the President," *Journal of American History*, 68(December 1981), 625–632; Stephen G. Rabe, "Eisenhower Revisionism: A Decade of Scholarship," *Diplomatic History*, 17(Winter 1993), 97–115; William I. Hitchcock, *The Age of Eisenhower: American and the World in the 1950s* (New York: Simon and Schuster, 2018), xii-xv; Fred I. Greenstein, *The Hidden-Hand Presidency: Eisenhower as Leader* (New York: Basic Books, 1982). As Greenstein points out, even when liberals noted that Ike accomplished things, they attributed it more to luck than skill. See, page 7.
8 Susan Eisenhower, *How Ike Led: The Principles Behind Eisenhower's Biggest Decisions* (New York: Thomas Dunne Books, 2020), 308.
9 Evan Thomas, *Ike's Bluff: President Eisenhower's Secret Battle to Save the World* (New York: Back Bay Books, 2012), 13, 38–42.

the cheery demeanor and the easy, jocular way Eisenhower interacted with people, there was a mind that worked like a steel trap. He was a man of deep conviction and a firm set of ideas honed during the 'crisis years' of World War II."[10] Most would agree he was a man of principle, decency, and common sense, whom the country could count on to do what was right. Few seemed to grasp that "in both war and peace he gave the world confidence" that what America was doing was often the right thing to do to begin with.[11]

Part of his own confidence in America's mission was shaped by witnessing the Holocaust for himself. While publicly, Ike did not often dwell on what he saw, learned, and heard about Nazi atrocities and their victims, the private Eisenhower was another matter. His wartime experience, including what he saw at a liberated camp named Ohrdruf, shaped not just his leadership style but perhaps more importantly, his moral sense. Considering how long it took historians to appreciate Ike, it is equally understandable as to why placing his encounter in a narrative involving the Holocaust has often seemed problematic.[12] As Mark Celinscak notes, "the story of a concentration camp fits awkwardly within the context of military affairs."[13] Furthermore, historian Max Hastings has pointed out that Holocaust scholarship and works on World War II while covering the same events and individuals are often written in isolation from one another.[14] Studying Eisenhower's encounter with Holocaust then, allows us to bridge these disciplinary genres. Doing so in a book that keeps its focus squarely on both topics gives a broader context than either alone can muster. Hopefully, other scholarship will follow in the years to come that will further bridge this divide. With Ike's journey, we take the first step in that direction.

What follows then, is not just another book about the Holocaust, nor a new biography of Ike. Rather it is the neglected story of Eisenhower and the Holocaust: It will argue that his witness of the crime of the century changed not only his understanding of the crusade he was leading, but also his eventual presidency. As

---

10 Eisenhower, *How Ike Led*, 11.
11 Jean Edward Smith, *Eisenhower in War and Peace* (New York: Random House, 2013), xi.
12 Like many Americans who grew up in the postwar world, my likely first encounter with the Ohrdruf camp was in the Time-Life books series on the Second World War. There, in the volume entitled *Victory in Europe*, can be found a passing description of the camp as but a foretaste to what was soon discovered at Buchenwald. And while General George Patton getting ill is mentioned, Ike is nowhere to be found. See, Gerald Simmons and the editors of Time-Life Books, *World War II: Victory in Europe* (Alexandria: Time-Life Books, 1982), 100.
13 Mark Celinscak, *Distance from the Belsen Heap: Allied Forces and the Liberation of a Nazi Concentration Camp* (Toronto: University of Toronto Press, 2015), 23.
14 Max Hastings, *Inferno: The World at War, 1939–1945* (New York: Alfred A. Kopf, 2011), 486. See also, Russell F. Weigley, *Eisenhower's Lieutenants: The Campaign of France and Germany, 1944–1945* (Bloomington: Indiana University Press, 1981), xv.

John C. McManus reminds us, liberating the camps was a "visceral experience," different from combat, and "life altering" for those who took part in it.[15] In the pages that follow, I will use one of those liberators, Eisenhower, as our focal point for better understanding McManus' statement.[16] Ike's story also sheds some light on why the Holocaust continues to be of such interest to Americans, to the point that it is invoked in our political discourse down to the present. Ike, after all, was among the first to call on the world to never forget what was done in the camps. In our subsequent use, and misuse, of the lessons learned from the events he took part in, Americans show they at least remember his charge.

Great events impact us far more than we often know or realize. As a result of his experiences during the war in general and his witness of the Holocaust in particular, Ike became a principled, if not perfect, consensus builder and a champion of democracy at home and abroad, standing against totalitarianism in both its Nazi and Communist manifestations. He was not just a professional soldier, but a crusader against forces of oppression, and a liberator of the oppressed. This part of his story began the moment he entered Ohrdruf.

---

15 McManus, *Hell Before Their Very Eyes*, xi, 3.
16 As I was writing this section, I took special heart from John D. Wilsey's recent biography of Ike's secretary of state, John Foster Dulles. In it, Wilsey notes that biographers know what their subjects will do because of subsequent events, unlike the subjects themselves. Historians have the gifts of time and contextual perspective that those they write about did not have because for them the past was the present. Remembering that they were not perfect requires a certain amount of grace then, because neither are we. See, John D. Wilsey, *God's Cold Warrior: The Life and Faith of John Foster Dulles* (Grand Rapids: William B. Eerdmans Publishing Company, 2021) 3–4.

Chapter 1
The Quote and the Man behind It

The German concentration camp at Ohrdruf, Germany was unknown to Americans before April 1945. However, today, when guests begin their journey through the permanent exhibit at the United States Holocaust Memorial Museum in Washington, D.C., the first thing they encounter after exiting the elevator is a quote and picture of Dwight Eisenhower discussing his time there:

> The things I saw beggar description . . . The visual evidence and the verbal testimony of starvation, cruelty and bestiality were . . . overpowering . . . I made the visit deliberately in order to be in a position to give FIRST HAND evidence of these things if ever, in the future, there develops a tendency to charge these allegations merely to 'propaganda.

The words were inspired by Eisenhower's trip to the first camp liberated by U.S. forces and taken from a secret letter he sent to his superior, General George Marshall. The letter was both a testimonial and a call to action. Enshrined now at the museum, Ike's words live on as a challenge to those who read them to never forget.[1] Though only a small sub camp of the soon to be liberated Buchenwald, Ike and his party were shaken to their core during their visit. He never forgot what he saw there. In the years that followed, he often talked and wrote about the experience. In 1948, Eisenhower's *Crusade in Europe* hit bookstores. His recollection of viewing the camp is worth quoting at length, as it amplifies what he wrote to Marshall three years before:

> The same day I saw my first horror camp. It was near the town of Gotha. I have never felt able to describe my emotional reactions when I first came face to face with indisputable evidence of Nazi brutality and ruthless disregard of every shred of decency. Up to that time I had known about it only generally or through secondary sources. I am certain, however, that I have never at any other time experience an equal sense of shock . . . I visited every nook and cranny of the camp because I felt it my duty to be in a position from then on to testify at firsthand about these things in case there ever grew up at home the belief or assumption that 'the stories of Nazi brutality were just propaganda.' Some members of the visiting party were unable to go through the ordeal. I not only did so but as soon as I returned to Patton's headquarters that evening, I sent communications to both Washington and London, urging the two governments to send instantly to Germany a random group of newspapers editors and representative groups from the national legislatures. I felt that the evidence should be imme-

---

[1] Letter, General Eisenhower to General Marshall, April 15, 1945, Dwight D. Eisenhower's Pre-Presidential Papers, Principal File, Box 80, Marshall, George C (6) NAID#12005700, C.D. Jackson Papers, Box 2 Atrocities-Paris (1); NAID#12005699, Dwight Eisenhower Presidential Library, Abilene, Kansas.

diately placed before the American and British publics in a fashion that would leave no room for cynical doubt.[2]

Here are powerful statements from one of the most influential men of the twentieth century about one of history's greatest horrors. And yet, few historians have opted to go beyond quoting the quote to look at how the Holocaust shaped Ike, if they discuss the encounter at all.[3] But they should, for at Ohrdruf, Ike's blood was boiling, and his life changed. What he saw there shaped how he came to see the warfare he was waging and, eventually, his presidency and leadership of the Free World.

Ohrdruf

Ike's encounter with the Holocaust began almost innocently. At 9am, on April 12, 1945, Generals Eisenhower, Omar Bradley, and George Patton visited a salt mine in Merkers, Germany where looted gold, money, and art had been found by advancing American forces. Ike's mood was rather lighthearted at the mine, as he and his entourage viewed the vast treasure horde the Nazis had stolen, and hidden, from around Europe. At Patton's suggestion, the party moved on to Ohrdruf, where American forces had reported liberating some kind of work camp, complete with prisoners.[4] The mood of the day very quickly changed, as Patton noted, it was "the first horror camp any of us had ever seen. It was the most appalling sight imaginable."[5]

Ohrdruf was a small, satellite camp of Buchenwald. In the grand scheme of things, it was rather insignificant, save for one thing: it was here that American soldiers first liberated surviving prisoners.[6] At its peak, the camp had perhaps

---

2 Dwight D. Eisenhower, *Crusade in Europe* (New York: Doubleday and Company, 1953), 408–409.
3 There is no mention of the Holocaust, for example in one of the first nor one of the more recent books on Eisenhower. See, Relman Morin, *Dwight D. Eisenhower: A Gauge of Greatness* (New York: The Associated Press, 1969); Louis Galambos, *Eisenhower: Becoming the Leader of the Free World* (Baltimore: Johns Hopkins University Press, 2018).
4 George S. Patton, Jr., *War as I Knew It* (Boston: Houghton Mifflin Company, 1947), 291–292; Robert M. Edsel, *The Monuments Men: Allied Heroes, Nazi Thieves, and the Greatest Treasure Hunt in History* (New York: Center Street, 2009), 293–296. The Nazi treasure horde was technically in the (future) Soviet zone of occupation. Ike ordered it removed to the American zone. See, D.K.R. Crosswell, *Beetle: The Life of General Walter Bedell Smith* (Lexington: The University Press of Kentucky, 2012), 899.
5 Patton, *War as I Knew It*, 292.
6 John C. McManus, *Hell Before Their Very Eyes: American Soldiers Liberate Concentration Camps in Germany, April 1945* (Baltimore: Johns Hopkins University Press, 2015), 7; Michael Hirsh, *The Liberators: America's Witnesses to the Holocaust* (New York: Bantam Books, 2010), 26; Richard Garrick, 15 May 1998, USC Shoah Foundation—41511, accessed on 13 September 2022.

10,000–12,000 inmates, whose main task was to dig underground tunnels and complexes for the Nazis. Prisoners were worked to death, not killed outright as in death camps like Auschwitz. Disposal of the bodies was simplistic, most were dumped into mass graves or taken some thirty miles away to be cremated at Buchenwald. However, as American forces arrived in the area, the Germans began following protocols first practiced on the Eastern Front: They ordered the bodies unearthed and burned on a pyre, or "griddle," as Patton eventually described it. American liberators later estimated that only about a third of those who died at the camp were disposed of in this fashion. Those still alive were either marched to Buchenwald, executed, or left for dead. The death march to the larger camp left the roadway littered with bodies, which is what led the oncoming Americans to the camp's gates.[7]

The very presence of these first American liberators was all because of happenstance. Ohrdruf was discovered because a German deserter told his American captors about the elaborate, secret underground headquarters just off the Autobahn, west of Weimar. Based on that intelligence, Eisenhower authorized Patton to send a flying column to try and capture any members of the German army high command—the Oberkommando der Wehrmacht or OKW—who might be there. While they just missed Field Marshal Albert Kesselring, the Americans did find the headquarters complex, and the 4th Armored seized it and the town of Gotha with minimal resistance on April 4. As American Fred Diamond noted, it was "a nice little town—one of those spared in the engulfment of the area by the roaring tide of allied armor."[8] While securing the area, Diamond's fellow soldiers started finding dead prisoners on the road. Their commander, Colonel Hayden Sears dispatched men of the 8th Tank Battalion to investigate. As the Americans

---

7 McManus, *Hell Before Their Very Eyes*, 9, 14; Hirsh, *The Liberators*, 31–32; Robert H. Abzug, *Inside the Vicious Heart: Americans and the Liberation of Nazi Concentration Camps* (New York: Oxford University Press, 1987), 23, 26–27; Peter Caddick-Adams, *Fire and Steel: The End of World War Two in the West* (New York: Oxford University Press, 2022), 321–327; Yehuda Bauer, "The Death-Marches, January-May, 1945,"*Modern Judaism*, 3(February 1983), 6; Patton, *War as I Knew It*, 293; Jacob Adler, 28 February 2014, USC Shoah Foundation—54870, accessed on 13 September 2022; Richard Garrick, 15 May 1998, USC Shoah Foundation—41511, accessed on 13 September 2022; Ernest Katz, 28 March 1995, USC Shoah Foundation—1733, accessed on 13 September 2022; Marcel Laoiselee, Ohrdruf, le camp oublie de Buchenwald: Un Survivant Temoigne (Madison: The University of Wisconsin Press, 2010); James Zuidema, 1 December 1996, USC Shoah Foundation—23096, accessed on 13 September 2022.
8 Fred I. Diamond letter, 13 April 1945, RG-04.055, United States Holocaust Memorial Museum, Washington, D.C.

made their way towards the camp, more bodies were discovered in the woods and scouts reported a barbed wire enclosure up ahead. One of the Sherman tanks had a bulldozer blade on it and pushed open the gate of what appeared to be a military barracks.[9]

What the GIs found instead was a typical Nazi concentration camp.[10] Ohrdruf reeked of death, from decomposing bodies, from the giant pyre where some of the dead had been burned, and from human excrement. Trenches were filled with partially burned corpses and human ash, dusted with lime, from which partially visible, emaciated, limbs protruded. There were also stacks of bodies that were waiting to be burned. The Americans found corpses in the camp's buildings and scattered on the ground, including around thirty bodies of those killed that very day. Sergeant David Cohen remembered that some of the dead were still warm when he arrived at the camp and the ground was stained red with blood. The GIs liberated over 3,000 prisoners who still clung to life. The prisoners mumbled *Polski* ("we are Poles") to the Americans and asked for *Kartoffel zoop* (potato soup).[11]

What the Americans saw at Ohrdruf was "a twisted mass of smoldering, charred bones."[12] Lieutenant Colonel Albin F. Irzyk arrived at the camp on April 5. Slowly, he began to piece together what had obviously happened here in the days, weeks, and years before his men had arrived: The Germans built a camp to house prisoners, and those prisoners died—whether from malnutrition or at the hands of the Nazis, and then the dead were cremated. He knew, because there was ash everywhere. In some places it was shin deep.[13] His colleague, Colonel William Scudder of the 89th Infantry Division, described the camp as "a hell worse than any of us could have imagined: bodies—hundreds of bodies—pieces of bodies" seemingly ev-

---

9 Rick Atkinson, *The Guns at Last Light: The War in Western Europe, 1944–1945* (New York: Henry Holt and Company, 2013), 589; Charles B. MacDonald, *United States Army in World War II: The European Theater of Operations, the Last Offensive* (Washington, D.C.: Center of Military History United States Army, 1984), 376–378; Abzug, *Inside the Vicious Heart*, 22; Hirsh, *The Liberators*, 23–26; Fred I. Diamond letter, 13 April 1945, RG-04.055, United States Holocaust Memorial Museum, Washington, D.C.
10 David Eisenhower, *Eisenhower: At War, 1943–1945* (New York: Random House, 1986), 762.
11 Zero Calabrase testimony, 23 October 1992, RG-09.019.01, United States Holocaust Memorial Museum, Washington, D.C; Hughes Family Dachau Trial Album Acc. 2016.24, Box 1, Dallas Holocaust Museum; Atkinson, *The Guns at Last Light*, 589–590; Hirsh, *The Liberators*, 26; Jon Bridgman, *The End of the Holocaust: The Liberation of the Camps* (Portland: Areopagitica Press, 1990), 79; David Cohen, Oral History, USC Shoah Foundation, Visual History Archive, accessed 2 August 2017.
12 William I. Hitchcock, *The Bitter Road to Freedom: A New History of the Liberation of Europe* (New York: Free Press, 2008), 295.
13 Hirsh, *The Liberators*, 28–30.

erywhere.[14] Neither calling it hell nor cold logic could overcome the sheer shock of what they and their fellow liberators were encountering.[15] For most, there was simple incomprehension. Bert Ezell of the 4th Armored could not understand why, with the war virtually over, the Germans continued to kill prisoners even as the Americans approached. The men in the field had never heard of or imagined such places existed. As David Andres, also of the 4th Armored, put it, they might as well have been told they were going to encounter a YMCA summer camp, as none of them knew what a concentration camp was.[16] Americans quickly doubted that the German civilians living nearby could claim a similar level of ignorance. For one, there was the smell. American soldiers also observed that Germans eschewed the use of government-issued soap, because they feared it was made from the bodies of the prisoners in the camp.[17]

The GIs thought they were battle hardened. They had, after all, seen death before. But encountering the camp showed them how wrong they were. The Americans grew quiet as they made their way through Ohrdruf.[18] They were in shock. They knew who Hitler and the Nazis were and that they had to be stopped. But none of the soldiers really understood just what the Germans were actually doing in the camps. They "had no reliable reports," according to the 89th Infantry's Joseph Simboli.[19]

Considering the discovery, it was hardly surprising that Ike agreed to visit Ohrdruf. He believed it important for his men to see their senior commanders in the field as much as possible. As historian Merle Miller noted, Eisenhower also "was a man of insatiable curiosity." Viewing the camp became "the worst shock of his life."[20] Immediately, Ike ordered photographers to start taking pictures and the

---

14 Leila Levinson, *Gated Grief: The Daughter of a GI Concentration Camp Liberator Discovers a Legacy of Trauma* (Brule, Wisconsin: Cable Publishing, 2011), 37.
15 "Holocaust Testimony of William McCool," 2002, Gratz College Holocaust Oral History Archive, accessed on 8 September 2022. McCool was part of the 89th Infantry.
16 David Andres and Bert Erzell, oral histories, Dallas Holocaust Museum; Hirsh, *The Liberators*, 35.
17 David Andres and Charles Brosseau, oral histories, Dallas Holocaust Museum.
18 "Recollections of a Liberator: The Liberation of Ohrdruf and Buchenwald," https://www.pattonsbestmedics.com/recollections-of-a-liberator-the-liberation-of-ohrdruf-and-buchenwald-part-1-ohrdruf/, 9 September 2022.
19 Richard Garrick, 15 May 1998, USC Shoah Foundation—41511, accessed on 13 September 2022; "We Trudged Through an Unknown, Unexperienced Evil—Unaware How that Evil Took Hold in Us," https://thewarhorse.org/nazi-concentration-camp-liberation-soldier-recalls-ohrdruf/, 9 September 2022.
20 Douglas E. Clark, *Eisenhower in Command at Columbia* (New York: Lexington Books, 2013), 31; Merle Miller, *Ike the Soldier: As They Knew Him* (New York: Perigee Books, 1987), 770.

photos are among our best evidence of the affect the visit had on the Supreme Allied Commander. Surrounded by soldiers, Ike stood with his hands on his hips looking at the bodies of prisoners laying on the ground. As he began to walk away, on to some other area of the camp, Ike, hands clasped behind his back, continued to stare at the bodies. In another photo, he, along with Bradley and Patton, watched as former prisoners demonstrated torture techniques—with a standing prisoner, bent over a table at the waist, while another pulled his arms across the table at a 90-degree angle as a means to put immense pressure on the back, waist, and shoulders. Once again, Ike stood watching, hands on hips, lips tightly pursed.[21] Because his official translator was still on a plane headed to meet up with him, Private Don Timmer of the 89th Infantry Division was assigned to serve that role during the tour. Timmer confessed to Eisenhower that his German was not very good. Ike replied, "Don't worry, I know German, but I need time to formulate my responses."[22]

What Eisenhower was doing, just like his men a few days before, was trying to understand what he saw. After two hours some of his aides tried to get him to leave. Ike replied: "Don't bother me. I have to *get* this."[23] His party saw instruments of terror and the inmates told them that at least 3,000 people had died since January.[24] After seeing Ohrdruf, Ike wrote his wife Mamie, that "I never dreamed that such cruelty, bestiality and savagery could really exist in this world!"[25]

Eisenhower, Bradley, and Patton's reactions to the camp ran the gambit from shock to incomprehension. Bradley was overcome by the smell. Patton vomited because of what he saw. Eisenhower's expression grew increasingly grimmer the longer he was at the camp.[26] Captain Harry G. Butcher, one of Eisenhower's aides, noted that Ike felt "overpowered" by the stories he heard from the prisoners at Ohrdruf, but unlike Patton, Butcher noted in his diary, the Supreme Allied Commander did not "upchuck."[27] As one of Patton's aides remembered it, Eisenhower was left in a state of contemplation after visiting the camp. "The evidence of inhuman treatment, starvation, beating, and killing of these prisoners . . . by the Ger-

---

21 Pictures from United States Holocaust Memorial Museum.
22 Hirsh, *The Liberators*, 98–99.
23 Hirsh, *The Liberators*, 99.
24 Patton, *War as I Knew It*, 292–293.
25 Michael Beschloss, *The Conquerors: Roosevelt, Truman and the Destruction of Hitler's Germany, 1941–1945* (New York: Simon and Schuster, 2002), 212.
26 McManus, *Hell Before Their Very Eyes*, 21–24; Abzug, *Inside the Vicious Heart*, 27.
27 Harry C. Butcher, *My Three Years with Eisenhower: The Personal Diary of Captain Harry C. Butcher, USNR, Naval Aide to General Eisenhower, 1942 to 1945* (New York: Simon and Schuster, 1946), 803.

mans was beyond the American mind to comprehend," Ike said.[28] To Bradley, who could not fathom what he saw at Ohrdruf, Eisenhower said "I can't understand the bestiality of the German people. What would compel them to do anything like that?"[29]

While Patton may have gotten sick at the sight of the bodies, his uneasy stomach did not stop him, according to some of the men present, from unleashing a tirade of profanity about what he had seen.[30] The general noted that the Germans had attempted to destroy "the evidence of their crime" by burning as many of the bodies as they could. Whether they were inept (as Patton believed) or simply rushed as the American forces drew closer to Ohrdruf, the pile of bones and half burned bodies left on the makeshift pyre were ample testament to what had happened here.[31] Patton later wrote:

> This was one of the most appalling sights I have ever seen. One of the former inmates acted as impresario and showed us first a gallows where men were hanged for attempting to escape. The hanging was done with a piece of piano wire, and the man being hanged was not dropped far enough to break his neck but simply strangled by the piano wire . . . the wire is so adjusted that after a drop of about two feet, the man's toes can just touch the ground, so death takes some time. Two prisoners next to be hanged are required to kick the plank from under him . . . Just beyond . . . was a pile of about 40 bodies, more or less naked, all of whom had been shot through the head at short range. The group was covered with dried blood. These men had become so exhausted as to be useless for labor and were disposed of . . . in a shed near this place was a pile of about 40 completely naked human bodies in the last stages of emaciation. These bodies were lightly sprinkled with lime, not for the purpose of destroying them but for the purpose of removing the stench. When the shed was full—I presume its capacity to be about 200, the bodies were taken to a pit a mile from camp where they were buried.[32]

---

28 Martin Blumenson, editor, *The Patton Papers, 1940–1945* (Boston: Houghton Mifflin Company, 1974), 684.
29 Jim DeFelice, *Omar Bradley: General at War* (Washington, D.C.: Regnery Publishing, 2014), 342.
30 David Cohen, Oral History, USC Shoah Foundation, Visual History Archive, accessed 2 August 2017. Whether this happened with Eisenhower present is in dispute among historians, and though it certainly fits with Patton's persona it may be a conflated memory in terms of words and place.
31 Blumenson, editor, *The Patton Papers, 1940–1945*, 684; Merle Miller, *Ike the Soldier: As They Knew Him* (New York: Perigee Books, 1987), 770.
32 Blumenson, editor, *The Patton Papers, 1940–1945*, 683–684. For all his bravado, according to Eisenhower biographer Merle Miller, unlike Ike, Patton never fully understood how evil the Nazis were. Even after seeing the camps, Patton was still willing to liken the Nazis to a political party, like the Democrats or Republicans. See, Miller, *Ike the Soldier*, 771.

On April 15, Patton relayed a report to Ike that the prisoner who had guided himself, Eisenhower and Bradley around was, in fact, a disguised camp guard. Ike perhaps suspected it, asking the "guide" at one point why he was so fat. The morning after the visit, Patton informed his commander, the man was found dead, killed by some of the actual prisoners.[33]

Being at the camp with Eisenhower left an impression on the American soldiers. Sergeant Cohen walked into one of the camp's buildings as Ike was walking out. Though "green" upon seeing the dead bodies, Eisenhower looked at Cohen and said "God, sergeant, you have to have a strong stomach to take this."[34] Before leaving the camp, Ike told the men, "I want every American unit not actually in the front lines to see this place. We are told that the American solider does not know what he is fighting for. Now, at least, he will know what he is fighting against."[35]

But that was not all. After leaving the camp Eisenhower ordered the mayor of Gotha, Albert Schneider, to bring the town's citizens to the camp to help with the burial of the dead. He wanted them to see the camp with their own eyes and what had been done in their name. U.S. Army Intelligence determined that Schneider had joined the Nazi Party in 1933, was considered an honest mayor, and was "never brutal." The mayor seemed shocked by his visit to the camp. He told the Americans that "I did not believe that Germans are capable of atrocities like these. We were told that the Russians are cruel and commit wholesale murder in a brutal manner. There were rumors in the town, but we did not believe them." The town had, after all, benefitted by its proximity to the camp. The mayor was very depressed after the visit, so much so that both he and his wife committed suicide after witnessing the camp—perhaps out of guilt for doing nothing to stop the horrors that had unfolded so nearby. Their suicide note read: "We didn't know! But *we* knew."[36] The Americans believed the suicide came about because Schneider "had accepted the atrocities in the concentration camp as his responsibility as mayor."[37]

---

33 Letter, General Patton to General Eisenhower, April 15, 1954, Dwight D. Eisenhower's Pre-Presidential Papers, Principal File, Box 91, Patton George S. Jr. (1): NAID#12007734, Dwight Eisenhower Presidential Library, Abilene, Kansas; Patton, *War as I Knew It*, 293; Blumenson, editor, *The Patton Papers, 1940–1945*, 683–684. Patton also mentioned that their guide "was such a well-fed looking man that I had an idea he may have been one of the executioners." Blumenson adds that "Two days later, this guide was torn limb from limb by returning inmates."
34 David Cohen, Oral History, USC Shoah Foundation, Visual History Archive, accessed 2 August 2017.
35 Hirsh, *The Liberators*, 100.
36 Evan Thomas, *Ike's Bluff: President Eisenhower's Secret Battle to Save the World* (New York: Back Bay Books, 2012), 6; McManus, *Hell Before Their Very Eyes*, 17–19; Hirsh, *The Liberators*, 101.
37 Jackson, C.D.: Papers, Box 7, Intelligence—Paris (7) [Ohrdruf German concentration camp].

When word reached Patton, the general simply noted "the mayor of the town, together with his wife, when confronted with the spectacle, went home and hanged themselves. There are several in the vicinity," Patton continued, "who I think will be found dead."[38] Colonel Sears, who was in charge of bringing Gotha's citizens to the camp to serve as both witnesses and burial detail, told them "We hold the entire German nation responsible for their support and toleration of the Nazi government."[39]

On April 15, Eisenhower wrote his famed note to General Marshall: *The most interesting—although horrible—sight that I encountered during the trip was a visit to a German internment camp near Gotha. The things I saw beggar description. While I was touring the camp, I encountered three men who had been inmates and by one ruse or another had made their escape. I interviewed them through an interpreter. The visual evidence and verbal testimony of starvation, cruelty and bestiality were so overpowering as to leave me a bit sick. In one room, where they [there] were piled up twenty or thirty naked men, killed by starvation, George Patton would not even enter. He said he would get sick if he did so. I made the visit deliberately, in order to be in a position to give first hand evidence of these things if ever, in the future, there develops a tendency to charge these allegations merely to "propaganda."*[40]

The men who witnessed the camp alongside Eisenhower certainly did not view what they encountered as fuel for propaganda. As Fred Diamond noted of Ohrdruf, "this is eugenics as practiced by the Master Race."[41] To Al Sommer, the camp "destroyed completely" the idea that the Germans had any sense of Western Civilization at all.[42] Andy Coffey of the 89th Infantry Division called Ohrdruf "quite a shock and horror."[43] And Chaplain James Burwell Ficklin told his wife the camp was the "worst thing I've ever seen."[44] Meyer Levin, a war correspondent, wrote of the camp: "We had known. The world had vaguely heard. But until now no one of us had looked on this. Even this morning we had not imagined we

---

38 Blumenson, editor, *The Patton Papers, 1940–1945*, 684.
39 Hirsh, *The Liberators*, 36.
40 Alfred D. Chandler, Jr., editor, *The Papers of Dwight David Eisenhower: The War Years IV* (Baltimore: The Johns Hopkins Press, 1970), 2615–2616.
41 Fred I. Diamond letter, 13 April 1945, RG-04-055, United States Holocaust Memorial Museum, Washington, D.C.
42 Al Sommer Jr., letter, 8 April 1945, RG-09.056, United States Holocaust Memorial Museum, Washington, D.C.
43 Andy Murray Coffey, letter, 3 December 1993, RG-09.040, United States Holocaust Memorial Museum, Washington, D.C.
44 "Americans and the Holocaust: Reverend James Burwell Ficklin," USHMM, 28 June 2018.

would look on this. It was as though we had penetrated at last to the center of the black heart, to the very crawling inside of the vicious heart."[45]

The experience clearly shook their commander.[46] Lester Stricoff told a postwar interviewer that it was clear to all who were present that Ike was repulsed by what he saw and learned about at Ohrdruf. Eisenhower ordered his men to bear witness so that these kinds of atrocities would never happen again.[47] After seeing the camp, Ike referred to the system the Germans had created as "hell camps" when talking to the press.[48] In the years to come, he did not dwell on the war very often. But his granddaughter Susan later wrote, Ike's trip to Ohrdruf "never left him."[49] Eisenhower would never be the same, nor would he ever forget.

The Man from Abilene

Ohrdruf was a turning point, perhaps the turning point, for Eisenhower when it came to how he understood the Second World War. No longer were the Nazis just an opponent to be defeated. Germany now represented a very real evil that needed to be uprooted.[50] To comprehend how the Holocaust affected him beyond the words he wrote in the wake of his visit to Ohrdruf, we must journey to Abilene, Kansas. Here in an agricultural community in the American Midwest was where Dwight David Eisenhower first defined himself. David A. Nichols notes that many biographers have missed out on the simple fact that Ike was reared in and absorbed a "heartland culture" that never left him.[51] To understand the man, we must know something of the culture that produced him.

Ike's parents, David and Ida (Stover) Eisenhower, met at Lane College, a Mennonite school in Kansas. David harbored dreams of becoming an engineer, rather

---

45 Abzug, *Inside the Vicious Heart*, 19.
46 Michael James McKeogh and Richard Lockridge, *Sergeant Mickey and General Ike* (San Francisco: Lucknow Books, 2016), 126.
47 Lester Stricoff, Oral History, USC Shoah Foundation, Visual History Archive, accessed 2 August 2017.
48 Butcher, *My Three Years with Eisenhower*, 816.
49 Susan Eisenhower, *How Ike Led: The Principles Behind Eisenhower's Biggest Decisions* (New York: Thomas Dunne Books, 2020), 60, 318.
50 William B. Pickett, *Dwight David Eisenhower and American Power* (Wheeling, IL: Harland Davidson, 1995), ix.
51 David A. Nichols, *A Matter of Justice: Eisenhower and the Beginning of the Civil Rights Revolution* (New York: Simon & Schuster Paperbacks, 2007), 2–3, 7. To his credit, Nichols points out that at least some of that has to do with partisanship.

than following in the family tradition of being a farmer, and further broke tradition by refusing to speak German to his wife and eventual children. Despite some hardships (a successful store the Eisenhowers owned was closed due to an economic downturn a few years before Ike was born, necessitating the move to Texas, where David found work), by the time the family resettled in Abilene, life proved to be stable. A guiding influence in the home was the religious faith of David and Ida, which stressed among other things, service to others.[52]

The future general and president was born October 14, 1890, in Dennison, Texas.[53] Ike was raised "to be honest, humble, and hardworking" in the words of author Bret Baier, and was shaped by both faith and small-town Middle America. As a boy, he gravitated towards stories about great leaders, especially generals, and enjoyed reading about American history, as well as ancient and modern European history. He may have wanted more than Abilene could offer, but he never forgot where he came from. Nor was he ashamed of his upbringing.[54] As Kasey S. Pipes further notes, "he had simple values . . . He believed that America was a place where ordinary people could do extraordinary things."[55] Ike also learned from his parents the value of work and an appreciation for people regardless of their background or occupation.[56]

It was the allure of a free education and a career that led Ike to leave Kansas. He was 20 years old when he accepted an appointment to the United States Military Academy at West Point, in New York. Ike's decision caused a dilemma for his parents. They had raised their children to be independent and make their own choices. Ike's choice not only reminded them that they did not have the financial resources to send their son to college, but also was a direct abandonment of the

---

[52] Susan Eisenhower, *Mrs. Ike: Memories and Reflections on the Life of Mamie Eisenhower* (New York: Farrar, Straus and Giroux, 1996), 24–28.

[53] Pickett, *Dwight David Eisenhower and American Power*, 1–2; Blaine T. Browne, *Mighty Endeavor: The American Nation and World War II* (New York: Rowman & Littlefield, 2019), 157.

[54] Dwight D. Eisenhower, *At Ease: Stories I tell to Friends* (New York: Doubleday and Company, 1967), 40–41; Bret Baier, *Three Days in January: Dwight Eisenhower's Final Mission* (New York: William Morrow, 2017), 15–19; Susan Eisenhower, *Mrs. Ike: Memories and Reflections on the Life of Mamie Eisenhower* (New York: Farrar, Straus and Giroux, 1996), 23; Jack M. Holl, *The Religious Journey of Dwight D. Eisenhower: Duty, Honor, Country* (Grand Rapids: William B. Eerdmans Publishing Company, 2021), 28–29, 39. David and Ida Eisenhower were River Brethren, a branch of Protestant Christianity that shared much with Mennonites and the Jehovah's Witnesses. Ike, who helped craft civic religion in the United States during his presidency, eventually became a Presbyterian. See also, Jean Edward Smith, *Eisenhower in War and Peace* (New York: Random House, 2013), 11.

[55] Kasey S. Pipes, *Ike's Final Battle: The Road to Little Rock and the Challenge of Equality* (Los Angeles: World Ahead Publishing, 2007), 4.

[56] Eisenhower, *How Ike Led*, 45.

pacifism of the faith he had been raised in.[57] Their acceptance of his decision made the journey east easier for Ike.

Eisenhower did not really enjoy the academics of West Point, nor did he care for all the rules of the academy. But he did love its athletics and was very popular with the other future officers. West Point cadets took a wide variety of courses, ranging from traditional academic subjects, to specialized military classes. However, there was very little elective choice, as the program of study was "prescribed." The cadets attended classes in small sections and were expected to be prepared. Failure in a course was not an option, as it was grounds for dismissal.[58] Despite his nonchalance towards the classwork, Eisenhower was a solid student—excelling in some subjects and more often than not soundly in the middle of even the courses he struggled with.[59]

Out of all his academic work at West Point, Eisenhower's classes in law had the most significant bearing on how he later reacted to the Holocaust. Ike's time at the Point corresponded to an exciting period in the field of American military jurisprudence. The Army was debating a proposed revision of the code of military law as it pertained to court martial. If it did not cast a shadow over instruction, it was something that West Point's faculty was aware of and keeping tabs on, as proposals were advanced and discussed in both the War Department and Congress, and the faculty struggled to incorporate the new changes with the existing curriculum as it evolved. Furthermore, the Department of Law was known to bring in distinguished speakers from Columbia and Yale universities, as well as former President (and future Supreme Court Chief Justice) William Howard Taft to talk to the cadets on current events.[60]

Most of West Point's law textbooks were written by members of the faculty. Legal instruction was drawn primarily from four text books: *The Elements of Law, Constitutional Law, International Law,* and *Military Law and the Procedure*

---

57 Eisenhower, *Mrs. Ike*, 29–39.
58 *Official Register of the Officers and Cadets of the United States Military Academy for 1911*, 60; Lance Betros, *Carved from Granite: West Point Since 1902* (College Station: Texas A & M Press, 2012), 111–112; Smith, *Eisenhower in War and Peace*, 20–21, 25.
59 *Official Register of the Officers and Cadets of the United States Military Academy for 1912*, 23; *Official Register of the Officers and Cadets of the United States Military Academy for 1913*, 24; *Official Register of the Officers and Cadets of the United States Military Academy for 1914*, 17; *Official Register of the Officers and Cadets of the United States Military Academy for 1915*, 15.
60 Betros, *Carved from Granite*, 117; *Annual Report of the Superintendent, United States Military Academy 1914*, 32; *Hearing Before the Committee on Military Affairs, House of Representatives, Sixty-Second Congress, Second Session on H.R. 23628: Being a Project for the Revision of the Articles of War* (Washington: Government Printing Office, 1912). The Army argued that its court martial procedures essentially had not changed since 1806 and needed to be updated.

of Court Martial.[61] Cadets received instruction in courses entitled "Elements of the Common Law," "Constitutional Law," "International Law," and "Military Law" as "a foundation in legal education . . . that with diligence on the part of graduates" could be used "to handle intelligently the ordinary legal questions they are apt to meet in actual service."[62] Several of the texts were authored by Major General George B. Davis, who had served as Judge Advocate General of the United States as well as an instructor at West Point. Indeed, he wrote the book most important for Eisenhower's future encounter with the Holocaust, *The Elements of International Law*. In its over 600 pages of text, Davis paid close attention to international agreements. At its core, he argued that "International law is a system formed of those principles and rules of action which are acknowledged by civilized states as controlling in their mutual relations." The assumption was that "civilized states" all agreed to continually live up to these agreements. There was no notion that a signatory state would ever deviate from these norms. The book further stipulated that soldiers could not steal from civilians, and that noncombatants, as well as prisoners, were to be protected.[63]

As important as these topics eventually were, they meant little for Ike's immediate career prospects. He knew that his grades destined him for the infantry after graduation in 1915. While stationed at Fort Sam Houston in Texas, Eisenhower met Mary "Mamie" Doud that October and the two were married the following July. Their marriage "was the union of two people from backgrounds of glaring contrasts," which according to Ike's granddaughter Susan, likely was part of the attraction. Army life was not easy for the couple, and Mamie, who came from a much more affluent background than did her husband, had to learn how to match Ike's "spirit of sacrifice" when it came to doing his, and their, duty to the country. The couple would be blessed with two children, Doud (known as Ikky) born in 1917 and John, born in 1922. Unfortunately, the two brothers never knew one another, as Ikky died in 1921. Ike and Mamie never fully recovered from his death.[64]

---

61 *Official Register of the Officers and Cadets of the United States Military Academy for 1914*, 78; *Official Register of the Officers and Cadets of the United States Military Academy for 1915*, 8. See also, George B. Davis, *A Treatise on the Military Law of United States Together with the Practice and Procedure Courts-Martial and Other Military Tribunals*, (1916).
62 *Annual Report of the Superintendent, United States Military Academy 1914*, 31–32.
63 George B. Davis, *The Elements of International Law* (New York: Harper and Brothers, 1915), 19, 297, 312–319.
64 Geoffrey Perret, *Eisenhower* (New York: Random House, 1999), 53; "Mamie Geneva Doud Eisenhower," https://www.whitehouse.gov/about-the-white-house/first-families/mamie-geneva-doud-eisenhower/, 31 January 2021; Eisenhower, *Mrs. Ike*, xviii, 22, 34–35, 40–47, 66–72, 85. Long after World War II, rumors emerged that Ike had engaged in an extramarital affair with his Brit-

After the United States entered World War I in April 1917, Ike received orders to train soldiers at Fort Oglethorpe in Georgia and then at Fort Leavenworth in Kansas. Although he was a gifted instructor, Eisenhower worried that his work would deal a death blow to his army career, as he was deemed too good at teaching to be sent to the frontlines in Europe. This frustrated him. As he put it, "I had missed the boat in the war we had been told would end all wars."[65] When the conflict ended in 1918, he was faced with the reality of the "collapse [of] an Army from millions to a peacetime core" and the prospect that his lack of battlefield experience would cost him promotion and advancement.[66] That he had also become enamored with the new weapon known as the tank also seemed a strike against his career. As an infantryman, Ike's argument that armor had a future as a branch of the service was considered "blasphemy" by many in the Army's establishment.[67]

If he did not see combat at least he had the good fortune to have a string of mentors who prepared him in countless other ways. As historian William Hitchcock notes, "Eisenhower had a way of being noticed by senior officers."[68] After taking a convoy from Maryland to San Francisco (and writing a report on needed transcontinental transportation improvements), Ike found himself in Panama, serving under General Fox Conner. Sometimes known as "the brains of Pershing's American Expeditionary Force," Conner became Eisenhower's mentor in military

---

ish driver, Kay Summersby. The allegations were initially sparked by memoirs Summersby wrote, followed by a second book attributed to Summersby, which was largely ghostwritten and then turned into a fictionalized television miniseries in the late 1970s. Aired shortly before Mamie's final illness, the program was blasted by one of its initial technical advisors, as well as many of Ike's surviving subordinates who had witnessed his interactions with Summersby. Their opinion was that the relationship was friendly but always professional. Ike's voluminous correspondence with Mamie during the war also seemingly undercuts the allegations. See, John S. D. Eisenhower, editor, *Letters to Mamie* (Garden City: Doubleday & Company, 1978) and Eisenhower, *Mrs. Ike*, xvii, 193–194, 205–209, 222–223, 240–242, 323–329.

65 Eisenhower, *At Ease*, 155; Smith, *Eisenhower in War and Peace*, 48; Thomas, *Ike's Bluff*, 5; Eisenhower, *Mrs. Ike*, 51–52.

66 Geoffrey Perret, *Eisenhower* (New York: Random House, 1999), 67; Eisenhower, *At Ease*, 133, 151–152.

67 Eisenhower, *How Ike Led*, 7273. It was not just a question of armor replacing cavalry that had many within the military establishment up in arms following the Great War. The United States military also had a difficult time with what role airpower might play in the future, as the case of Colonel William "Billy" Mitchell—including his court martial—proved. See, Marc G. Desantis, "The Court-Martial of Colonel Billy Mitchell," https://www.historynet.com/the-court-martial-of-colonel-bill-mitchell/, 20 November 2022.

68 William I. Hitchcock, *The Age of Eisenhower: American and the World in the 1950s* (New York: Simon and Schuster, 2018), 13.

history and tactics and served as a one-man graduate school for the young officer. Conner also helped Ike get into Command and General Staff School at Fort Leavenworth, Kansas and from there, the Army War College at Carlisle, Pennsylvania. Ike excelled at both, even graduating at the top of his class.[69]

Conner also worked to get Eisenhower assigned to General John "Black Jack" Pershing's American Battle Monuments Commission, which finally got Ike to France (as well as Germany) and brought him into the accomplished general's orbit. Ike studied and read a corpus of literature and churned out the initial report in six months.[70] After serving under Pershing, Ike was assigned to General George Van Horn Moseley on the Army General Staff. Here, he helped study what was needed to retool industry in case of another major war.[71] Ike's time on the General Staff brought him to the attention of General Douglas MacArthur, whom he worked with for nearly six years, both in Washington, D.C. (while MacArthur was Army Chief of Staff) and in the Philippines (after MacArthur was appointed U.S. Military Advisor to the Philippines). MacArthur influenced Ike's style of command and understanding of how to be an administrator, in particular the importance of issuing an order and letting subordinates do the work without micromanagement. Eisenhower also watched as his boss mixed military affairs with political activities, learning not just how to navigate political channels and public relations blunders (including the way the Army was used against the Bonus Marchers during the Great Depression), but also the dangers that could come from being an overtly political general.[72]

While he learned a great deal from the senior officers he worked under, one thing he did not absorb from them was anti-Semitism. As historian Joseph W. Bendersky has

---

69 Eisenhower, *At Ease*, 185–187, 201; Pickett, *Dwight David Eisenhower and American Power*, 13–17; Thomas, *Ike's Bluff*, 30; Perret, *Eisenhower*, 87–92, 99; Pipes, *Ike's Final Battle*, 33; Hitchcock, *The Age of Eisenhower*, 12; Holl, *The Religious Journey of Dwight D. Eisenhower*, 85–87.
70 Eisenhower, *At Ease*, 206–209; Pickett, *Dwight David Eisenhower and American Power*, 17; Eisenhower, *Mrs. Ike*, 90–91, 102. The report is part history of the Great War, part travel log to American war memorials on the Western Front.
71 Eisenhower, *At Ease*, 210–211; Smith, *Eisenhower in War and Peace*, 94–95; Eisenhower, *Mrs. Ike*, 109. Ike's future aide, Walter Bedell Smith, also spent time working under Moseley. See, D.K.R. Crosswell, *Beetle: The Life of General Walter Bedell Smith* (Lexington: The University Press of Kentucky, 2012), 146–147, 153.
72 Eisenhower, *At Ease*, 213; Pickett, *Dwight David Eisenhower and American Power*, 19, 24; D. Clayton James, *The Years of MacArthur: Volume I: 1880–1941* (Boston: Houghton Mifflin Company, 1970), 564; William Manchester, *American Caesar: Douglas MacArthur, 1880–1964* (New York: Little, Brown and Company, 1978), 148; Holl, *The Religious Journey of Dwight D. Eisenhower*, 93–95; Susan Eisenhower, *Mrs. Ike: Memories and Reflections on the Life of Mamie Eisenhower* (New York: Farrar, Straus and Giroux, 1996), 119.

shown, anti-Semitism was part and parcel of much of the U.S. Army officer corps in the early twentieth century. It commingled with wider currents of eugenic thought, nativist notions of what constituted "real" Americans, and broader worries about immigration.[73] Perhaps the most blatant anti-Semite Ike worked for was Moseley, who equated communism with Jewish intellectuals, believed pogroms were punishments meted out to Jews for the rejection of Christianity, and argued for the sterilization of Jewish immigrants. Ike seemed to be able to ignore such tirades, focus on other topics, and separate Mosley's rants from how the general conducted himself professionally.[74] As Bendersky notes, "there is nothing even suggesting that . . . Eisenhower ever resorted to vulgar references to Jews. Given their [Ike and Marshall] personalities and styles of command, it is unlikely that they would have treated Jewish officers or enlisted men with anything other than respect, dignity, and fairness."[75]

In the Philippines, such questions at first seemed far away. Ike became friends with former Indiana governor turned American High Commissioner for the territory, Paul McNutt. The men, and their wives, Kathleen and Mamie, enjoyed socializing with each other and the men's small talk often turned to discussions about governmental policy. Ike and McNutt both wondered about the future of the Philippines, which the United States had placed on a path to full independence after taking the island archipelago during the Spanish-American War. Both men came to like Filipino President Manuel Quezon. Indeed, Ike learned a good deal about politics and political power from Quezon.[76] Both Ike and McNutt also had a deteriorating relationship with MacArthur, driven in large part by the general's personality and style. Ike was more popular with many of the Americans in Manila than his boss was, leading to some jealousy on the part of MacArthur. The two soldiers ultimately had a falling out in January 1938, when MacArthur ordered a military parade in Manila that upset Filipino politicians and then blamed it on Eisenhower.[77] In addition to the parade fiasco, Ike was also turned off by MacArthur's decision to accept a demotion in his American rank (two stars down from four now that he was no longer Army Chief of Staff) in order to be named a

---

[73] Joseph W. Bendersky, *The "Jewish Threat": Anti-Semitic Politics of the U.S. Army* (New York: Basic Books, 2000), xv-xvii, 1, 5–7, 171, 260.
[74] Bendersky, *The "Jewish Threat"*, 21, 204, 212, 250–251, 256–258, 309, 311–312; Smith, *Eisenhower in War and Peace*, 94–95.
[75] Bendersky, *The "Jewish Threat"*, 309.
[76] Pickett, *Dwight David Eisenhower and American Power*, 26; Holl, *The Religious Journey of Dwight D. Eisenhower*, 111–112; Eisenhower, *Mrs. Ike*, 147, 157.
[77] Dean J. Kotlowski, *Paul V. McNutt and the Age of FDR* (Indianapolis: Indiana University Press, 2015), 227–228; Manchester, *American Caesar*, 166; James, *The Years of MacArthur: Volume I: 1880–1941*, 525–526; Eisenhower, *Mrs. Ike*, 130–131.

field marshal in the Philippine's army. MacArthur wanted Ike to take a demotion as well, which Eisenhower refused to do.[78]

Being in the Philippines did not insulate Eisenhower from global events. It was in Manila that Ike first had to deal with the rise of Nazi Germany and heard the first whispers of persecution against Jews. He interacted with German nationals infrequently, though he came to share McNutt's low opinion of the German consul in Manila, Gustav Sakowsky, who was trying to raise the profile of Nazi Germany globally. There were around 500 Germans living in the city as the Nazis came to power, some of whom where Jews. Prior to Sakowsky's arrival, both gentiles and Jews were members of Manila's German Club. With the Nazi victory in 1933, such intermingling began to vanish. It was a portent of things to come.[79]

The Thousand Year Reich

To understand why, we must turn our attention from Asia to Europe. Following the end of the First World War, Germany transformed itself from an empire into a democracy known as the Weimar Republic. The country suffered a series of economic crises during the 1920s and 1930s, which in turn, eroded the nation's citizens' confidence in democracy. By the early 1930s, most Germans were drifting towards radical political movements, including fascism and communism. Adolf Hitler and his fascist Nazi party won out.[80]

Austrian by birth, Hitler had served in the German Army during the Great War. When he learned of Germany's defeat in November 1918, he became convinced that a conspiracy was behind it. Staying in the army after the war, he worked to keep tabs on the political groups that emerged in the wake of the Kaiser's abdication. In 1919, he was ordered to infiltrate the National Socialist German Workers Party (or Nazis), he quickly became converted to a political program that explained that at the heart of the conspiracy to destroy Germany had been Jews and Communists. By 1921, Hitler was leading the party and two years later, he had

---

78 Eisenhower, *Mrs. Ike*, 141.
79 Frank Ephraim, *Escape to Manila: From Nazi Tyranny to Japanese Terror* (Chicago: University of Illinois Press, 2003), 15; Kotlowski, *Paul V. McNutt and the Age of FDR*, 240. Much to Sakowsky's consternation, not only did Manila's German Club have members who were Jewish, but many of the city's Germans had good relations with, and some had even married, Filipinos.
80 David S. Mason, *A Concise History of Modern Europe: Liberty, Equality, Solidarity* (New York: Rowman and Littlefield, 2011), 133; Robert Gellately, editor, *The Nuremberg Interviews: An American Psychiatrist's Conversations with the Defendants and Witnesses, Conducted by Leon Goldensohn* (New York: Vintage Books, 2005), 222–225.

assembled many of the core followers who later became fixtures of the Third Reich. As Winston Churchill noted in his multi-volume history of World War II, at no point did Hitler mince words about who he believed to be responsible for Germany's woes, what he hoped to do to them, nor his belief in Germany's destiny of expansion. In his speeches, in his book *Mein Kampf*, and in his actions, he made it quite clear that Jews must be eliminated and Germany must expand. Few, it seemed, actually took him seriously.[81]

Hitler tapped into Germany's belief in the concept of the *Volk*, which blended notions of people, nation, and race, into a popular form of ethnic chauvinism that emphasized German superiority. The Nazis offered those who would listen not only solace through the theory, but also the opportunity to enact revenge on Germany's enemies, whether they were ideological, foreign, or domestic. As Deborah Dwork and Robert Jan van Pelt note, "we may not take the Teutonic Order, Frederick the Great, Lebensraum, or the Volk seriously, but . . . millions of Germans did." It resonated with them. At the heart of National Socialism was the belief that "Germans were a superior race," whose enemies could also be described in racial and ethnic terms. And those enemies needed to be destroyed before they ruined Germany forever.[82]

The Nazis could not claim dominion over the theoretical underpinnings of their belief system. National exceptionalism, racism, colonialism, imperialism, anti-Semitism, social Darwinism, and eugenics, none of these things were unique to Germany. Indeed, in many ways Hitler was just like any other totalitarian leader, he and his movement "rejected the notions of individualism, natural rights, and common humanity" that had become hallmarks of Western Civilization over centuries. It was, however, the anti-Semitism the Nazis espoused that bound together the other aspects of their ideology and gave them meaning and a sense of urgency.[83]

---

[81] Winston S. Churchill, *The Second World War: Volume I, The Gathering Storm* (Boston: Houghton Mifflin, 1948), 47–51; Gellately, editor, *The Nuremberg Interviews*, 222–225.

[82] Timothy Snyder, *Bloodlands: Europe Between Hitler and Stalin* (New York: Basic Books, 2010), 130; Peter Fritzsche, *An Iron Wind: Europe Under Hitler* (New York: Basic Books, 2016), 242; Mark Roseman, *The Wannsee Conference and the Final Solution: A Reconsideration* (New York: Picador Press, 2002), 9–10; Peter Longerich, *The Unwritten Order: Hitler's Role in the Final Solution* (Stroud: The History Press, 2016), 124, 128–129. Laurence Rees, *The Holocaust: A New History* (New York: Viking, 2017), 1–2; Deborah Dwork and Robert Jan van Pelt, *Auschwitz* (New York: W.W. Norton and Company, 2008), 12.

[83] Johann Chapoutot, *The Law of Blood: Thinking and Acting as a Nazi* (Cambridge, Massachusetts: The Belknap Press of Harvard University Press, 2018), 5, 325; Longerich, *The Unwritten Order*, 28; Saul Friedlander, *Nazi Germany and the Jews, 1933–1945—Abridged Edition* (New York:

Hitler and the Nazis were able to come to political power by adding the promise of pulling Germany out of the economic pit of despair to their Volkish ideology. Hitler offered a blueprint for the restoration of national honor and a fatherland that was home only to Germans, with plenty of *Lebensraum*, or living space, for the future.[84] Once in power, the Nazis moved methodically, always aware of public opinion, as they disrupted and transformed German society. They first outlawed their chief political opposition, the Communists, initiated a sterilization law (aimed at wards of the state)—the first step towards the Final Solution, and then ended the citizenship rights of Jews via the Nuremburg laws.[85]

For five years, Germany's Jews had their rights stripped away. Most continued to believe they needed only to weather the present circumstances. However, the threat of violence always loomed over them until finally, in 1938, the Nazis unleashed it. On November 9, the murderous face of Nazi anti-Semitism was revealed at home and abroad. Known as Kristallnacht, or the night of broken glass, Nazis attacked, defaced, looted, and burned Jewish owned businesses, cemeteries, homes, and synagogues across Germany in a pogrom sparked by a speech given in Munich by the Nazi head of propaganda, Joseph Goebbels. Fire brigades were ordered to contain the spread of the fires, but to let the Jewish buildings burn. Jews also became subject to widespread arrest, with people being plucked from the streets or their homes with little warning. While we have no idea how many Jews were murdered as part of Kristallnacht, over 30,000 entered the concentration camp system, and an estimated 7,500 Jewish businesses were destroyed. In

---

Harper Perennial, 2009), 30, 46–47; Theodore S. Hamerow, *Why We Watched: Europe, America, and the Holocaust* (New York: W. W. Norton & Company, 2008), 24–27.

84 Norman M. Naimark, *Genocide: A World History* (New York: Oxford University Press, 2017), 77; Roseman, *The Wannsee Conference*, 11; Timothy Snyder, *Black Earth: The Holocaust as History and Warning* (New York: Tim Duggan Books, 2015), 1, 7, 16–17, 27; Mason, *A Concise History of Modern Europe*, 136; Yisrael Gutman and Michael Berenbaum, editors, *Anatomy of the Auschwitz Death Camp* (Indianapolis: Indiana University Press, 1994), 99; Joel Fishman, "The Postwar Career of Nazi Ideologue Johann von Leers, aka Omar Amin, the 'First Ranking German' in Nasser's Egypt," *Jewish Political Studies Review*, 26(Fall 2014), 59; Snyder, *Bloodlands*, 156–157, 213; Giles MacDonogh, *1938: Hitler's Gamble* (New York: Basic Books, 2009), 1, 164; Michael Wildt, *An Uncompromising Generation: The Nazi Leadership of the Reich Security Main Office* (Madison: University of Wisconsin Press, 2003), 48, 326–327; Joachim Fest, *Inside Hitler's Bunker: The Last Days of the Third Reich* (New York: Farrar, Straus and Giroux, 2002), 34–35; Walter Laqueur, *Out of the Ruins of Europe* (New York: Library Press, 1971), 414–421; Dwork and van Pelt, *Auschwitz*, 12, 186.

85 Chapoutot, *The Law of Blood*, 139, 232; Snyder, *Black Earth*, 82–83, 219; Isabel Vincent, *Hitler's Silent Partners: Swiss Banks, Nazi Gold, and the Pursuit of Justice* (New York: William Morrow and Company, Inc., 1997), 9; Mason, *A Concise History of Modern Europe*, 140–143; Raul Hilberg, *The Destruction of the European Jews* (Chicago: Quadrangle Books, 1961), 294–295; Neil MacGregor, *Germany: Memories of a Nation* (New York: Vintage Books, 2014), 439–440.

Berlin alone, thirty synagogues were set ablaze, including the city's largest.[86] Roughly 120,000 Jews fled Germany (the same as in the previous five years combined) in the wake of the pogrom. Most moved somewhere else in Europe, away from Germany, but not, as they would soon discover, out of harm's way.[87]

Kristallnacht's violence was a top-down affair. Nothing was done without the party's approval, and it started and stopped when the party ordered. Because it was government sanctioned, there was seemingly little outsiders could do to stop what one American newspaper called a "wild orgy."[88] The American consulate in Leipzig noted that "Jewish shop windows by the hundreds were systematically and wantonly smashed throughout the entire city." But all the American diplomats could do was report on what was happening. The British also felt powerless during Kristallnacht, as did the League of Nations, which the United States never joined and that Germany was soon to depart, who seemed helpless in the wake of the violence. Notions that what Germany did domestically was Germany's business cast a long shadow and persisted even once the Second World War started. Such a mindset contributed to the Holocaust.[89]

Until the pogrom, German Jews believed they had little to fear from Hitler and his followers. For one, Jews made up only about one percent of the total population of the country and were nearly all assimilated, with most seeing themselves as Germans who happened to be Jewish. For another, they had seen government persecution before, and it had always been temporary. They were confident, in other words, that the Nazi's rhetoric would fade or moderate over time. Simply put, that did not happen.[90]

---

86 "The Night of Broken Glass," https://encyclopedia.ushmm.org/content/en/article/the-night-of-broken-glass, 20 May 2023; Snyder, *Black Earth*, 88; John Mendelsohn, editor, *The Holocaust: Volume 3, The Crystal Night Pogrom* (New York: Garland Publishing, Incorporated, 1982), 173, 184, 186; Laurence Rees, *The Holocaust: A New History* (New York: Viking, 2017), 139; Eric A Johnson and Karl-Heinz Reuband, *What We Knew: Terror, Mass Murder, and Everyday Life in Nazi Germany, An Oral History* (New York: Basic Books, 2005), 49; Roseman, *The Wannsee Conference*, 35; MacDonogh, 1938: Hitler's Gamble, 221–222, 225–227, 230.
87 Dallas Holocaust and Human Rights Museum exhibit, 3 November 2022.
88 *Dallas Morning News*, 11 November 1938.
89 Longerich, *The Unwritten Order*, 31; Mendelsohn, editor, *The Holocaust: Volume 3*, 194; Kenneth Strong, *Intelligence at the Top: The Recollections of an Intelligence Officer* (Garden City: Doubleday and Company, 1969), 53; Richard Breitman, Barbara McDonald Stewart, and Severin Hochberg, editors, *Refugees and Rescue: The Diaries and Papers of James G. McDonald, 1935–1945* (Indianapolis: Indiana University Press, 2009), 83; Martin Gilbert, *Auschwitz and the Allies* (New York: Pimlico, 2001), 160; Joseph E. Persico, *Roosevelt's Secret War: FDR and World War II Espionage* (New York: Random House, 2001), 421.
90 Jessica C. E. Gienow-Hecht, *Transmission Impossible: American Journalism as Cultural Diplomacy in Postwar Germany, 1945–1955* (Baton Rouge: Louisiana State University Press, 1999), 26;

The Depressing Question of Immigration

Beyond intimidation, some of the Nazi leadership hoped that Kristallnacht's violence might spur Jews to leave Germany. There was just one problem: few nations were willing to accept them. It must be remembered that Kristallnacht took place during the Great Depression. Any immigration was viewed as problematic by other governments in Europe as well as the United States. Furthermore, anti-Semitism was hardly just a German prejudice. It was rampant in European capitals and could also be found in subtle (and not so subtle ways) in Washington, D.C. as well. As Hitler noted, for all their moralizing about what Germany was doing to the Jews, no country was willing to take them as refugees.[91]

The United States government, under the leadership of President Franklin Roosevelt, was no exception. To begin with, Roosevelt believed that the plight of Germany's Jews was a problem the European powers (in particular, Great Britain) could and should deal with.[92] The British, after all, had issued the Balfour Declaration in 1917, that promised support to the settlement of Jews in Palestine. For someone who was such a natural politician, Roosevelt seemed oblivious that his British counterparts might have agendas of their own, which did not align with the president's preferred solution. The British only wanted what they considered to be the "top tier" of Jews in the Isles, its dominions (such as Canada and Australia) wanted none, and as for resettlement in the Holy Land—the British worried that the arrival of Jewish refugees would upset local Arabs and the shaky stability of the British mandate in Palestine. In 1939, in the wake of Kristallnacht, the British government actually tightened its immigration policies towards Jews.[93]

The Roosevelt Administration and the U.S. State Department saw more drawbacks than rewards in reworking the immigration quota system to allow more Jews into the United States, even after Kristallnacht. Indeed, any hope Jews might

---

Marlis G. Steinert, *Hitler's War and the Germans: Public Mood and Attitude During the Second World War* (Athens, OH: Ohio University Press, 1977), 133, 136; Hamerow, *Why We Watched*, 186–189; Hilberg, *The Destruction of the European Jews*, 30; Isabel Vincent, *Hitler's Silent Partners: Swiss Banks, Nazi Gold, and the Pursuit of Justice* (New York: William Morrow and Company, Inc., 1997), 6; Snyder, *Black Earth*, 82–83.
91 MacDonogh, *1938: Hitler's Gamble*, 221–222, 225–227, 230; Hamerow, *Why We Watched*, 31, 58–59, 78, 88–89; Snyder, *Black Earth*, 88; Hilberg, *The Destruction of the European Jews*, 259.
92 Persico, *Roosevelt's Secret War*, 218.
93 Breitman, Stewart, and Hochberg, editors, *Refugees and Rescue*, 160; MacDonogh, *1938: Hitler's Gamble*, 42, 52, 82, 103, 144–146, 231, 250; Strong, *Intelligence at the Top*, 53; Jorn Leonhard, *Pandora's Box: A History of the First World War* (Cambridge, Massachusetts: The Belknap Press of Harvard University Press, 2018), 438, 644; Alex von Tunzelmann, *Blood and Sand: Suez, Hungary, and Eisenhower's Campaign for Peace* (New York: Harper, 2016), 51.

have had in coming to America was preemptively closed, long before Hitler even came to power, by the Great Depression. In 1938, the United States was still recovering from the depression, with a 19 percent unemployment rate. The severe economic downturn only exacerbated anti-Semitism in America and led to a further constriction of immigration policy. On top of that, Jews found it very difficult to leave Germany. The Nazi government refused to allow them to depart with any wealth they may have accumulated. In the American context, this meant two things. First, under immigration laws, only a certain number of Germans (there was no notion in the law for refugees, nor for Jews as a specific group) could enter the country each year, per the 1924 National Origins Act. Secondly, U.S. law precluded visas for those immigrants deemed as potential paupers, and in the midst of the Great Depression, this was an important factor in keeping Jews out of the United States. With no assets, and unless they had someone to vouch for them financially in the country, there was no entry possible.[94] Though Roosevelt ordered more liberal interpretations of the law as the 1930s went on, he also never attempted to use his Democratic majorities in Congress to change them either. When pressed by reporters in the wake of bi-partisan condemnation of Kristallnacht (which the president described as something he "could scarcely believe") if he would allow more Jews into the country, Roosevelt defended the quota system reiterating that religious faith was not a classification under U.S. immigration law.[95] In the meantime, American diplomats looked for ways to stretch and bend the rules as much as they thought they could to help as many refugees, including Jews, as possible.[96]

---

[94] David M Kennedy, *Freedom From Fear: The American People in Depression and War, 1929–1945* (New York: Oxford University Press, 1999), 413–415; Richard Breitman and Alan M. Kraut, *American Refugee Policy and European Jewry, 1933–1945* (Indianapolis: Indiana University Press, 1987), 56; Hamerow, *Why We Watched*, 120–121, 128–129, 132–141; Deborah E. Lipstadt, "America and the Holocaust," *Modern Judaism*, 10(October 1990), 283.

[95] Kennedy, *Freedom From Fear*, 416; Breitman and Kraut, *American Refugee Policy and European Jewry*, 248–249; David S. Wyman, *The Abandonment of the Jews: America and the Holocaust, 1941–1945* (New York: The New Press, 2007), 314; Persico, *Roosevelt's Secret War*, 215; Laurence Rees, *The Holocaust: A New History* (New York: Viking, 2017), 143; Letter, FDR to New York Governor Herbert Lehman, November 13, 1935, President's Official File 133; Immigration, 1933–1935, Box 1, Franklin D. Roosevelt Presidential Library, Hyde Park, New York; Breitman, Stewart, and Hochberg, editors, *Refugees and Rescue*, 45; Benjamin A. Lindsey, "Organized Crime Against Civilization: The Congressional Investigation of Liberated Concentration Camps in 1945," (Master's Thesis, University of Vermont, 2012), 22–23.

[96] "An American Diplomat in Vichy France," Association for Diplomatic Studies and Training, 18 July 2013; "Who May Enter?: Issuing Visas to Jewish Refugees," Association for Diplomatic Studies and Training, 8 July 2015; "Our Man in Cairo During World War II," Association for Diplomatic Studies and Training, 6 July 2017.

While it did not spur largescale Jewish migration, Kristallnacht did destroy German credibility in much of Europe and in the United States. No one believed that the violence was spontaneous. It "shocked the Western word" and even if it did not change attitudes about immigration, it solidified Roosevelt's view that the Nazis could not be trusted.[97] But in the end, Kristallnacht was an internal state matter. American policy makers were shocked and horrified to be sure, but did not see, in the ashes of burned-out synagogues and Jewish businesses, much they could either do nor any indication that the Nazis intended to carry out such actions on a larger scale.[98]

There was another element at play as the grand tragedy that became the Holocaust took shape: disbelief. In the early 1930s, even when newspapers covered reports of what the Nazis said they were going to do to Jews or to their political opponents, most Western Europeans and Americans (including many in both the press and halls of power) doubted that they really meant it. As historian Martin Gilbert notes, by the time the war started, Hitler had been speaking against the Jews for over a decade and yet the Holocaust still caught most policy makers by surprise.[99] In 1939, the U.S. government had intelligence that Hitler was openly proclaiming that the "enemies of the German people must be eliminated" —with Jews at the top of a long list. Within the next year, the British government knew of the existence of the concentration camp system where Jews and other political enemies were being systematically sent.[100] None of this knowledge stopped the Holocaust from happening. For most leaders in the Great Britain and the United States what the Nazis were doing to the Jews, ultimately, was just one crime among many—a list that only grew with each passing year.[101]

Ike and the Jews of Manila

If there was one place that might be singled out as reacting to Kristallnacht in a more appropriate way than any of the Great Powers, it was the Philippines. While

---

97 MacDonogh, *1938: Hitler's Gamble*, 230–233, 255; Draft Statement by the President, November 15, 1938, President's Secretary's Files; Diplomatic Correspondence; Germany, 1933–1938, Box 31, Franklin D. Roosevelt Presidential Library, Hyde Park, New York; Richard Breitman and Allan J. Lichtman, *FDR and the Jews* (Cambridge: Belknap Press, 2013), 114–116; Kennedy, *Freedom From Fear*, 412.
98 Bendersky, *The "Jewish Threat"*, 239, 269.
99 Lindsey, "Organized Crime Against Civilization", 17–18; Martin Gilbert, *Auschwitz and the Allies* (New York: Pimlico, 2001), 14–15, 46–47.
100 Persico, *Roosevelt's Secret War*, 216.
101 Hamerow, *Why We Watched*, xiv.

seemingly far removed from the events occurring in Europe and the power centers of London and Washington, the fledgling island nation was poised to take action in the wake of the pogrom. And it just so happened that the Philippines was where Dwight Eisenhower was in the late 1930s.

Half a world away from the events then unfolding in Europe, Eisenhower found himself in the midst of heated debates in Manilla over Germany's treatment of Jews. There were, he recalled, fist fights within the foreign consulate community over the Nazis and their increasingly aggressive policies, which, in addition to Kristallnacht, included the Anschluss with Austria and the dismemberment of Czechoslovakia. While most of the diplomats Eisenhower knew saw Hitler as "a deep-dyed villain" there were some who saw him as "a hero to a small though vociferous element."[102] As Ike put it:

> There was uneasiness about the possibility of war. The Nazis were in the saddle and riding hard in central Europe. Among other things, they were persecuting the Jews unmercifully and many of the Jewish faith were fleeing Germany, trying to find homes elsewhere in the world. In Manila, arguments started between those people who for some strange reason were supporters of Hitler, and the rest of us. It was difficult to keep the arguments, even in social gatherings at the Army-Navy Club, under control. The Philippines had undergone four hundred years of domination by Spain. The results were mixed. Almost without exception, though, the Spanish community was on Hitler's side, partly because they believed that Hitler supported the Franco Government to which most of them gave their support. Hirohito got little attention. There was a considerable Jewish community in the city, and I had good friends among them.[103]

Among those "good friends" were Alex and Philip Frieder and their siblings. The Frieders were American Jews who had moved their family's cigar manufacturing business to the Philippines in 1921. While the Frieders arrived only with American influence, Jews had been in the Philippines since the 1870s and Jewish immigration grew once the islands passed from Spanish to American hands. By 1936, there were some 500 Jews in the Philippines. Alex Frieder regularly played poker with Ike, McNutt, and President Quezon and entertained them at the family home at 44 Brixton Hill, Santa Mesa. As the Nazi threat grew, the Frieders worked to get Jews with skills out of Europe. To do so, they needed the help of their American friends and the leader of the Philippines.[104]

Kristallnacht, then, brought the Nazi agenda directly to Eisenhower's door. When news of what had happened reached Manila in November, a rally in opposition took place in the city with 2,000 people in attendance. In the coming months,

---

102 Eisenhower, *Crusade in Europe*, 5; Eisenhower, *Mrs. Ike*, 150.
103 Eisenhower, *At Ease*, 229.
104 Ephraim, *Escape to Manila*, 14, 34, 58; *New York Times*, 14 February 2005.

thanks in no small part to the efforts of the Frieders, Quezon ordered an open door for Jews fleeing the Nazis in 1939. American High Commissioner McNutt had considerable latitude in allowing immigrants into the Philippines and that included Jews fleeing Europe. McNutt worked with Philip Frieder and Quezon to make it happen. They drew-up a plan to bring 10,000 European Jews to Mindanao over the next ten years. By the start of the war, around 1,300 Jews had arrived in the Philippines under the program.[105] Alex Frieder went a step farther, blasting the Nazis in an address and calling Hitler "the blatant champion of rule by brute force." He told an audience that Germany had gone from a place "that formerly prided itself in its civilization and culture" into "an unhappy land." The German consul disliked all the work Ike's friends were undertaking. The words and actions coming out of what was still, technically, an American territory no doubt contributed to Hitler equating the United States with "world Jewry" in a January 1939 address.[106]

At about this same time, because of his connections with Manila's Jewish community, Eisenhower received an offer that would have taken him out of the Army. Shortly before getting orders to report back to the United States, he was offered a job by a Jewish refugee organization seeking someone who might help find Jewish refugees a home in Asia. The contract was for five years at $60,000 a year. The offer came shortly after Kristallnacht and a verbal altercation that involved Eisenhower, in which he defended the right of Jews to not be discriminated against or persecuted. Like his friends, Ike's comments drew the ire of the German consul. Like his friends, he thought it the right thing—the American thing—to do.[107]

A Second Time and a Second Chance

The job offer was tempting. However, instead of taking it, Eisenhower found himself headed back to the United States. His deteriorating personal relationship with MacArthur made staying in the Philippines difficult, if not impossible. Furthermore,

---

[105] Philippine Embassy to Israel, "History of the Jews in the Philippines," http://www.philippine-embassy.org.il/index.php?option=com_content&view=article&id=33:history-of-the-jews-in-the-philippines&catid=11:the-open-doors-monument&Itemid=29, 26 May 2017; Kotlowski, *Paul V. McNutt and the Age of FDR*, 240–251; Ephraim, *Escape to Manila*, 44–45, 48–51; "How Jews Found a Secret Home in the Philippines," https://cnnphilippines.com/life/culture/2019/6/10/jews-in-the-philippines.html, 19 June 2021.
[106] Ephraim, *Escape to Manila*, 68–69; MacDonogh, *1938: Hitler's Gamble*, 255.
[107] Smith, *Eisenhower in War and Peace*, 148; Eisenhower, *At Ease*, 229–230. In 2022 dollars, Eisenhower would have made $1.3 million a year had he taken the job.

Ike was convinced war was on the horizon. He did not want to miss another chance at battlefield glory. After discussing his options with both MacArthur and Quezon, Ike put in for a transfer. When his orders arrived in May 1939, he was told to return to the United States and report to the 15th Infantry Regiment at Fort Lewis, Washington. Though he would later disparage his protégé, at the time, even MacArthur was sad to see Ike leave.[108]

Ike's decision came in the midst of the Second World War breaking out across the globe. In Asia, Japan had been waging war on China since 1937. But neither Ike nor his boss was really focused on Japanese ambitions to create an empire of their own. MacArthur even discounted the potential of Japan as a threat to either the United States or the Philippines.[109] After Kristallnacht, events in Europe seemed to be moving at a breakneck speed: Germany's takeover of Czechoslovakia, demands on Polish territory, a non-aggression pact with the Soviet Union, and then, on September 1, 1939, Germany's invasion of Poland and the start of the war in Europe. The United States, of course, would not join the conflict as a combatant until Germany's Axis partner, Japan, launched an attack on Pearl Harbor, Hawaii and the U.S. Pacific Fleet on December 7, 1941—with follow up attacks on the Philippines and other targets.

Ike returned to a United States that while not at war, was slowly getting on a war footing. By 1940, President Roosevelt recognized Hitler as both evil and as a threat to the United States. While still overwhelmingly isolationist, most Americans also recognized the Nazis as a problem that might need to be addressed in the future.[110] And when war was thrust upon them, while they might have been surprised by who, when, and how (Eisenhower, for example, assumed Germany would attack the United States after they defeated Great Britain and France) they were not surprised that it happened. Bill Fitzgerald, who later served in the 20th Armored Division, pointed out in an interview after the war that every American knew conflict was coming. It had engulfed Europe, it was raging in Asia, and it was covered every day in the newspapers. Not unlike Eisenhower, Fitzgerald also

---

108 Eisenhower, *Crusade in Europe*, 5; Eisenhower, *How Ike Led*, 54; Eisenhower, *Mrs. Ike*, 159; "President John F. Kennedy Meeting with Douglas MacArthur, 16 August 1962," Presidential Recordings Digital Edition, https://pride.upress.virginia.edu, 19 October 2022.
109 Kotlowski, *Paul V. McNutt and the Age of FDR*, 228.
110 Richard Moe, *Roosevelt's Second Act: The Election of 1940 and the Politics of War* (New York: Oxford University Press, 2013), 177; Hamerow, *Why We Watched*, 198–200, 262–263.

believed that the United States was better at war than either the nation's adversaries or its own people believed themselves to be.[111]

One of Ike's mentors who did predict conflict with and between the United States and Germany, long before Pearl Harbor, was General John Pershing. In 1934, with the Nazis firmly in control of the nation, the aging general said that Germany would re-arm, attack France, and force America to return to Europe to fight. Pershing's prophetic voice was largely discounted until Kristallnacht.[112] By then, events made the prospect of war not professional, but personal for Eisenhower. While worried about "the terrible human cost" a conflict would cause, Ike was also prepared to do his part to win it.[113]

---

[111] Bill Fitzgerald, oral history, Dallas Holocaust Museum; Eisenhower, *Crusade in Europe*, 5; James Holland, *Together We Stand: America, Britain and the Forging of an Alliance* (New York: Hyperion, 2005), 18.
[112] Breitman, Stewart, and Hochberg, editors, *Advocate for the Doomed*, 589.
[113] Pipes, *Ike's Final Battle*, 4, 7; Holl, *The Religious Journey of Dwight D. Eisenhower*, 113.

Chapter 2
Freedom Imperiled

Eisenhower's star continued to rise even as war clouds grew on the horizon. Over the nearly two years he was stateside before Pearl Harbor, Ike went from the 15th Infantry Regiment to being named chief of staff of the Third Infantry Division, followed by becoming chief of staff of the newly organized IX Corps, and then chief of staff to General Walter Krueger of Third Army. Under Krueger, Eisenhower won credit for designing Third Army's decisive victory over Second Army in the Louisiana Maneuvers of 1941. This series of assignments came with promotion, at last to the rank of brigadier general, as well as insights into mobilization and the need to teach, and not just order, new recruits as they came into the regular Army.[1]

Then came a phone call that changed his life. Eisenhower was ordered to Washington, D.C. on December 12, 1941. He believed General George Marshall had summoned him because he had spent time in the Philippines, which were now under attack by Japan. He also believed the order meant he was doomed to miss out on another war. Instead, Marshall tasked Eisenhower with drafting a plan for a unified, American-led, command in Europe. "There was no precedent to follow," Eisenhower noted, "no chart by which to steer" when it came to forging such a structure. Ike's old mentor, Fox Conner, had called Marshall a genius. In Eisenhower's opinion, that was incredibly high praise. His working relationship with Marshall not only confirmed Conner's assessment but bred a loyalty that never wavered for the rest of their lives. Ike's eventual report ended up being his own job description: commander of American forces in Europe. It also garnered Ike his second star.[2]

From the moment he arrived in Washington in December 1941, Ike was at work. His view of the conflict the United States was now a part of was both overarching and rather limited. In creating a new command structure, tasked with defeating Germany, those early days were consumed with simply making sure

---

[1] "Dwight David Eisenhower: The Centennial," https://history.army.mil/brochures/Ike/ike.htm, 19 January 2021; Jack M. Holl, *The Religious Journey of Dwight D. Eisenhower: Duty, Honor, Country* (Grand Rapids: William B. Eerdmans Publishing Company, 2021), 116–120; Susan Eisenhower, *Mrs. Ike: Memories and Reflections on the Life of Mamie Eisenhower* (New York: Farrar, Straus and Giroux, 1996), 164–167, 171–172.

[2] Dwight D. Eisenhower, *Crusade in Europe* (New York: Doubleday and Company, 1953), 4, 14, 18–19, 50; William Bragg Ewald, Jr., *Eisenhower the President: Crucial Days, 1951–1960* (Englewood Cliffs: Prentice-Hall, 1981), 59; Eisenhower, *Mrs. Ike*, 180–181.

Americans could translate a declaration of war into a deadly reality. Despite what he might have heard while in the Philippines of the Nazis placing Jews and other opponents of their regime into camps, such knowledge was pushed to the side due to the enormity of his new job. So demanding was the work that when his father died in March 1942, Ike could not attend the funeral.[3]

His eventual report entered the debate over the war gripping the capital. Americans naturally wanted to strike back at Japan in the wake of Pearl Harbor. However, Germany had declared war on the U.S. Should America fight a two-front war? Concentrate on Japan? Or focus only on the Nazis? Eisenhower believed that winning in "Europe first" made a good deal of sense. The United States was the only nation that could pick who it fought. By opting to take on Germany and Italy primarily, America could bring its strength to bear alongside Great Britain and the Soviet Union, who were already at war with the European Axis members. If the United States opted to fight Japan instead, it would be leaving its European allies to combat the empire Hitler was creating alone, without much aid from them in fighting Japan. Considering in late 1941 and early 1942 there was no way of knowing how long either Britain or the Soviet Union could hold out against Germany, "Europe first" seemed to be the only logical course of action.[4]

It is easy today to assume that Germany and Japan never had a chance of winning the war. And yet, as historian Niall Fergusson reminds us, between 1937 and 1942, no one seemed able to stop the two Axis powers.[5] Nor should their initial victories be surprising. After all, as Eisenhower noted in his postwar memoir, *Crusade in Europe*, in September of 1939, Poland had a larger and better equipped army than did the United States.[6]

British Prime Minister Winston Churchill had rallied his nation in the dark days of 1940 and 1941 with the hope that "the New World, with all its power and might," would eventually step "forth to the rescue and the liberation of the old."[7] For most Europeans before the war, the United States was "a terribly distant and unimportant country" known almost exclusively through its movies."[8] Ike's army would change that. On June 25, 1942, Eisenhower was placed in charge of Ameri-

---

[3] Eisenhower, *Mrs. Ike*, 174, 178–179.
[4] Eisenhower, *Crusade in Europe*, 27. It is important to note that "Europe First" did not mean there was no fighting to be done in the Pacific, only that the United States would be focusing the majority of its resources on defeating Germany before Japan.
[5] Niall Ferguson, *The War of the World: Twentieth-Century Conflict and the Descent of the West* (New York: Penguin Press, 2006), 474.
[6] Eisenhower, *Crusade in Europe*, 2.
[7] "We shall fight on the beaches, 1940," https://www.nationalchurchillmuseum.org/we-shall-fight-on-the-beaches.html, 23 March 2018.
[8] Nerin E. Gun, *The Day of the Americans* (New York: Fleet Publishing, 1966), 17.

can forces destined for the European theater. As a child, Ike had daydreamed about what it would be like to lead armies. Now he was being given the chance to do so in the greatest war of the twentieth century.[9]

Where, exactly, his forces were going to step forth, to borrow Churchill's phrase, was a matter of some discussion. While "Europe first" had prevailed from an operational perspective, there was still debate over if U.S. forces should go to England, sail directly to France, or perhaps hit the Axis empire on its periphery. By April 1942, the Army convinced President Franklin Roosevelt that the best course of action was a two-part plan to open up the European front: The first phase, codenamed Bolero, was to be a buildup of forces and material in England. Next would be, Sledgehammer, an emergency contingency invasion of France in case the Soviet Union seemed on the verge of collapse. Preferably though, the Americans would launch Operation Roundup in 1943, a springtime invasion of France. But throughout the process, there was back and forth and even confusion between both the American and British governments and their respective service branches over which plan was or should be implemented.[10] Sorting out those discussions became one of Eisenhower's jobs.

However, once Bolero was underway and Eisenhower in command, attention shifted to North Africa. American military planners, meeting with their British counterparts, began developing Operation Torch as a means to take control of the German aligned French colonies in North Africa while also helping relieve British forces currently keeping Egypt (and the Suez Canal) out of Nazi hands.[11] The decision to focus on North Africa might be seen as a necessary part of the European Theater of Operations in 1942, but all were agreed that it was not going to be the same thing as landing in France.

Although he was still learning on the job, it was up to the recently promoted Eisenhower to forge the grand Anglo-American alliance. He became an expert at not just coordinating the various military branches, but also with dealing with the egos of a wide variety of military and political leaders from both the United States, Great Britain, and other allied nations. Ike was a team builder and a "no nonsense" leader by inclination, though his relative inexperience and "informal" manner raised some eyebrows. Still, several of his British colleagues were in-

---

9 John S. D. Eisenhower, editor, *Letters to Mamie* (Garden City: Doubleday & Company, 1978), 125.
10 D.K.R. Crosswell, *Beetle: The Life of General Walter Bedell Smith* (Lexington: The University Press of Kentucky, 2012), 262–265.
11 Eisenhower, editor, *Letters to Mamie*, 22.

stantly impressed with his personality and potential.¹² It helped that he built a very competent team around him, which complimented his leadership style. Perhaps his best choice was in selecting General Walter Bedell Smith as his chief of staff. A fellow Midwesterner, Smith was a protégé of Marshall's and worked well in making sure Eisenhower's often broad directives became concrete orders.¹³

Their first test came when Operation Torch's landings occurred between November 8 and 10, 1942, just eleven months after the U.S. entered the war. While the battle for North Africa was not without its setbacks, the decision to land an almost entirely inexperienced American force in a lightly held portion of the Nazi empire was quickly validated. As the operation unfolded, it also became a political test for Eisenhower even more than a military one. Officially, France had surrendered to German forces in 1941, with the Nazis taking control of a wide swath of the nation directly and putting the rest under the nominal control of a pro-Axis government based in Vichy. It was this technically neutral, rump government that administered France's North African colonies. American forces were not officially liberating places like Algeria and Tunisia, but rather, fighting German and Italian forces there. As he kept one eye on the progress at the front, Eisenhower also had to walk a delicate balance between learning who in the French colonial government could be trusted, and dealing with the demands of Free French forces, led by Charles de Gaulle, who wanted to be given control of the area.¹⁴ All this was exacerbated by the fear that the Vichy government might officially join the Axis (or simply be taken over by Germany), shift-

---

12 John S. D. Eisenhower, *Strictly Personal* (Garden City, NY: Doubleday and Company, 1974), 51; Kenneth Strong, *Intelligence at the Top: The Recollections of an Intelligence Officer* (Garden City: Doubleday and Company, 1969), 109; Douglas E. Clark, *Eisenhower in Command at Columbia* (New York: Lexington Books, 2013), 32; Eisenhower, editor, *Letters to Mamie*, 29–30; Eisenhower, *Mrs. Ike*, 188.

13 Crosswell, *Beetle*, 9–10, 165–167, 257, 287–289, 314–318, 722. Marshall may have harbored some hope in early 1942 that by sending both Ike and Smith to Europe, he was paving his own way to overall theater command.

14 Eisenhower, *Crusade in Europe*, 108, 128–129; Crosswell, *Beetle*, 331–347, 367. The Allies had negotiated a ceasefire agreement with the local French commander, Admiral Jean-Francois Darlan, which allowed them to land. The Free French saw Darlan as a collaborator and traitor. Additionally, the Free French were not entirely united under the leadership of de Gaulle, who had competition from General Henri H. Giraud. While the "Darlan Deal" was problematic, much of the issue went away when Darlan was assassinated in December 1942. Giraud fell out of favor in September 1943 after taking Corsica from the Vichy government and making common cause with local communists. For more, see, Eisenhower, *Mrs. Ike*, 188–189; Fred I. Greenstein, *The Hidden-Hand Presidency: Eisenhower as Leader* (New York: Basic Books, 1982), 25–26; Eisenhower, editor, *Letters to Mamie*, 56–57, 75, 95.

ing French military assets to the Nazis and imperiling the flow of supplies, like oil, via the Suez Canal.[15]

It was in North Africa that Ike first encountered the geopolitical realities of anti-Semitism, and vicariously the Holocaust. Eisenhower discovered that Vichy France had been buying Arab support in their North African colonies (and Nazi goodwill) by stripping Jews of their citizenship rights. Although Eisenhower privately fumed about the collaborationist French and their conduct, he could not do much to alleviate the situation for the Jews, as he was advised that reversing the policies would likely cause Vichy France to officially join the Axis as well as spur an Arab uprising, necessitating a longer American military presence in the area while diverting manpower from the frontlines. Still, his first inclination was to push "to stop immediately whatever persecutions of the Jews may have resulted from the laws passed in France under German pressure," as he related to Marshall in a December 1942 letter. He just could not make it happen on his own. While anti-Semitism within the Army, State and War departments may have played a role in shaping that decision, there is also little doubt that Ike faced a complex situation on the ground and had to balance a variety of interests with his main task of defeating the Germans. That being said, he took notes of how Jews were being treated by the Nazis and those under their influence as American and British forces pushed the Germans out of North Africa and then followed them to Italy in 1943. He also, eventually, got the French to agree to liberalize, if not immediately overturn, the Vichy decrees.[16]

None of Eisenhower's experiences to date prepared him for his eventual encounter with the Holocaust at Ohrdruf in 1945. While German persecution of Jews and others that the Nazis deemed to be inferior (in a multitude of ways) was well publicized in the United States, there was a gap between newspaper coverage and policy action. Furthermore, persecution of these groups, even of arrests and the

---

[15] "An American Diplomat in Vichy France," Association for Diplomatic Studies and Training, 18 July 2013. The diplomat in question giving this interview was Douglas MacArthur II, the nephew of General Douglas MacArthur, Ike's old boss.

[16] Alfred D. Chandler, Jr., editor, *The Papers of Dwight David Eisenhower: The War Years, Volume II* (Baltimore: The Johns Hopkins University Press, 1970), 738, 821, 1037; Joseph W. Bendersky, *The "Jewish Threat": Anti-Semitic Politics of the U.S. Army* (New York: Basic Books, 2000), 314, 433–434; Judah Nadich, *Eisenhower and the Jews* (New York: Twayne Publishers, 1953), 13; Eisenhower, *Crusade in Europe*, 108, 128–129; Crosswell, *Beetle*, 331–347, 367; Laurence Rees, *The Holocaust: A New History* (New York: Public Affairs, 2017), 187–189. It was Marshall who advised the State Department against issuing orders in November 1942 that might "alleviate the condition of the Free French and the Jews" in North Africa. See, "The Chief of Staff, United States Army to the Under Secretary of State," 16 November 1942, Foreign Relations of the United States, Diplomatic Papers, 1942, Europe, Volume II, accessed on 7 September 2022.

establishment of camps, did not yet indicate to those who read them what became known as the Holocaust as a proven fact. For Ike in the early months of the war, there was little time to ponder such stories – often times a mere paragraph rather than a fully formed narrative—buried in newspapers, and not always on the front page.[17] He had orders to complete, and they did not include liberating concentration camps.

War in the East

With American entry into the war, Germany faced the prospect of a vast conflict it might not be able to win. Ike's foe began to reassess and reorder its war aims. Nazi propaganda increasingly talked about the Jewish threat that had caused the war and threated to doom Germany once again to defeat. Destroying the Jews was now a top priority for Hitler's government—both to try and forestall this potential outcome and as revenge for it.[18]

The process started just a few months before Pearl Harbor. In March 1941, Hitler told his generals that the regular rules of warfare were not going to apply when it came to the invasion of the Soviet Union, calling the upcoming phase of the war a "fight to the death." The Nazi leader was convinced that the Soviets would crumble once Operation Barbarossa was unleashed in June 1941.[19] For their part, the Soviets did not take the growing Nazi threat seriously. Soviet leader Joseph Stalin believed he had an alliance with Hitler in place, an alliance that had netted the Soviets territory and peace—as the Nazi war machine conquered Po-

---

17 The United States Holocaust Memorial Museum is in the process, along with thousands of volunteers, of creating a database that demonstrates the breadth of coverage given to Nazi Germany's policies before and after the start of the war in American newspapers. As of this writing, over 54,000 accounts from all 50 states have been uploaded. For more, see, "History Unfolded: US Newspapers and the Holocaust," https://newspapers.ushmm.org/, 28 February 2023.
18 Timothy Snyder, *Bloodlands: Europe Between Hitler and Stalin* (New York: Basic Books, 2010), 214; Isabel V. Hull, *Absolute Destruction: Military Culture and the Practices of War in Imperial Germany* (Ithaca: Cornell University Press, 2005), 325.
19 Marlis G. Steinert, *Hitler's War and the Germans: Public Mood and Attitude During the Second World War* (Athens, OH: Ohio University Press,1977), 117; Mark Roseman, *The Wannsee Conference and the Final Solution: A Reconsideration* (New York: Picador Press, 2002), 39–42; Konrad H. Jarausch and Michael Geyer, *Shattered Past: Reconstructing German Histories* (Princeton: Princeton University Press, 2003), 145; Snyder, *Bloodlands*, 166; David Stahel, *Operation Barbarossa and Germany's Defeat in the East* (New York: Cambridge University Press, 2011), 1; Gerhard L. Weinberg, *World in the Balance: Behind the Scenes of World War II* (Hanover: University Press of New England, 1981), 19.

land and much of Western Europe. The Soviet leader did not believe Hitler actually meant Germany needed more territory in the East or that Slavic people were inferior to the German Aryans.[20]

He should have. By the summer of 1941, not only had the vast majority of Germans reconciled themselves to living under the Nazi government but they also believed it their patriotic duty to fight on behalf of the Fatherland, especially since Germany had known nothing but victory under Hitler. They were also willingly benefiting from, aiding, abetting, and often taking part in what we know as the Holocaust. Few Germans resisted the Nazis because most of them believed in the overarching goals, even if they quibbled with some of the details.[21]

Operation Barbarossa was to be the culminating act of creating *Lebensraum*, or living space, for generations of Germans to come. However, this new territory was not just going to be added to Germany's empire, it was going to become Germanized. In Nazi ideology that meant those ethnic and national groups who were not German either needed to be subjugated, removed, or eliminated, often in that order. Within this policy, Jews already held a special place. After taking Poland in 1939, the German government began removing Jews from Germany and shipping them East—with the goal of making Germany proper *Judenfrei* (free of Jews). The longer the Nazis controlled an area, the less its administrators wanted Jews in their territory—which meant that there was never going to be a place for Jews within the boundaries of the Reich and its possessions.[22] As historian Richard Overy noted, the Germans sought "an empire 'cleansed of Jews.'" And "for Hitler, the war and the subsequent steps to Jewish annihilation were inseparable."[23]

Ethnic cleansing, then, was the next development towards the Holocaust. Once the war against the Soviet Union started, German soldiers were ordered to kill with impunity. No one seemed to question the need to carry out a brutal

---

20 Weinberg, *World in the Balance*, 14.
21 Isabel Vincent, *Hitler's Silent Partners: Swiss Banks, Nazi Gold, and the Pursuit of Justice* (New York: William Morrow and Company, Inc., 1997), 10; Hannah Arendt, *Eichmann in Jerusalem: A Report on the Banality of Evil* (New York: Penguin, 2006), 100.
22 Johann Chapoutot, *The Law of Blood: Thinking and Acting as a Nazi* (Cambridge, Massachusetts: The Belknap Press of Harvard University Press, 2018), 337, 349, 352, 362–363; Deborah Dwork and Robert Jan van Pelt, *Auschwitz* (New York: W.W. Norton and Company, 2008), 120, 295; Mark Roseman, *The Wannsee Conference and the Final Solution: A Reconsideration* (New York: Picador Press, 2002), 61–62; Marlis G. Steinert, *Hitler's War and the Germans: Public Mood and Attitude During the Second World War* (Athens, OH: Ohio University Press,1977), 134.
23 Richard Overy, *Blood and Ruins: The Last Imperial War, 1931–1945* (New York: Viking, 2021), 217–218.

war.²⁴ Reichsfuhrer SS Heinrich Himmler argued that Germanization of an area should include the execution on sight of Jews. There was no need to wait for the end of the war. Hitler concurred. To provide a veneer of moral cover for those German soldiers who still might need it, by the end of 1941 Jews were officially classified as partisans and thus, killed as soon as they were identified.²⁵

While the policy may have originated within the Nazi Party, it was not just the SS who were involved in rounding up Jewish men, women, and children on the Eastern front and killing them. In addition to the cooperation of many ethnic groups within the Soviet Empire, who believed themselves liberated by the arrival of the Nazis, the German Army also took part in the massacres. Having accepted the Nazis as the legitimate government of Germany, with a leadership that was fearful of being supplanted by the Nazi Party's military wing, both the Wehrmacht (German military) and Heer (German Army) rank and file accepted the order to exterminate those deemed their enemies with little hesitation as part of the war effort. Killing all the Reich's enemies was the only way to protect Germany they believed.²⁶

To bolster their ability to ethnically cleanse the conquered territories *Einsatzgruppen*, or special action units, were created. Moving in the wake of the German invasion forces, the teams hunted down, rounded up, and killed Jews, largely by shooting them. The four *Einsatzgruppen* units were likely responsible for the deaths of between 1.5 to 2 million people. The Germans also experimented with special vans, in which captured Jews were killed by carbon monoxide poisoning. Though a means to conserve bullets and a precursor to the use of Zyklon-B in

---

24 Timothy Snyder, *Black Earth: The Holocaust as History and Warning* (New York: Tim Duggan Books, 2015), 178.
25 Max Hastings, *Inferno: The World at War, 1939–1945* (New York: Alfred A. Kopf, 2011), 492–496; Evelyn Le Chene, *Mauthausen: The History of a Death Camp* (London: Methuen and Company, 1971), 48; Deborah Dwork and Robert Jan van Pelt, *Auschwitz* (New York: W.W. Norton and Company, 2008), 258, 261, 267; Snyder, *Bloodlands*, 176–184, 198, 202–204; Michael Burleigh, *Moral Combat: Good and Evil in World War II* (New York: Harper Collins Publishers, 2011), 399–408; Snyder, *Black Earth*, 250; Ferguson, *The War of the World*, 447; Inga Clendinnen, *Reading the Holocaust* (New York: Cambridge University Press, 1999), 93; Roseman, *The Wannsee Conference*, 86–91.
26 Chapoutot, *The Law of Blood*, 168, 193; Ferguson, *The War of the World*, 450–451; Theodore S. Hamerow, *Why We Watched: Europe, America, and the Holocaust* (New York: W.W. Norton & Company, 2008), 327; Hastings, *Inferno*, 492–495, 503; Bradley F. Smith, *Sharing Secrets with Stalin: How the Allies Traded Intelligence, 1941–1945* (Lawrence: University Press of Kansas, 1996), 28; Snyder, *Black Earth*, 148–149, 158–159, 177, 184, 188, 193, 224; Ferguson, *The War of the World*, 447; Raul Hilberg, *The Destruction of the European Jews* (Chicago: Quadrangle Books, 1961), 203, 212–214; Peter Longerich, *The Unwritten Order: Hitler's Role in the Final Solution* (Stroud: The History Press, 2016), 50; Snyder, *Bloodlands*, 126–131, 160, 416.

later concentration camp gas chambers, the vans were far from efficient and like mass shootings carried with them a psychological toll on the Nazis involved.[27]

Indeed, German policy changed as the invasion of the Soviet Union faltered. The onslaught was supposed to lead to the starvation of millions of Soviet citizens. It was supposed to feed the German army and provide food for civilians living back in Germany. In this, the invasion failed even by the winter of 1941.[28] Indeed, as early as August, Hitler was talking about the need to wage a "war against the Jews" and Nazi thinking on the conflict officially shifted from grand postwar plans to what might be accomplished in the immediate future. The war was no longer about conquest, but rather extermination.[29]

The Nazi leadership determined that in this dangerous time, a final solution to the Jewish problem needed to be found. Though deportations and executions (often in large numbers) of Jews and other undesirables had already been happening, Hitler and his leadership came to believe that organized mass murder would be easier to conduct and be more efficient than either mass deportation or localized executions. Additionally, shooting Jews was not cost effective—the Nazis needed the bullets for their battlefield enemies. The killing had started. And no one, certainly none of the Nazi leadership in Berlin, was going to stop it.[30]

Finding the Final Solution

The creation of what we call the Holocaust, then, was a process, not just a single order. While there might have been a goal, even before the "final solution," there was no fixed, step-by-step agenda on the part of the Nazis from 1933 forward to get there. The evolution of thought about the Jews from being *a* problem to *the* problem, one that needed to be *eliminated* not just *expelled* is an important one.[31]

---

27 "Einsatzgruppen: An Overview," https://encyclopedia.ushmm.org/content/en/article/einsatzgruppen, 19 June 2021.
28 Snyder, *Black Earth*, 194; Hastings, *Inferno*, 487.
29 Snyder, *Bloodlands*, 185, 188; Snyder, *Black Earth*, 198; Hamerow, *Why We Watched*, 292–293; Deborah Dwork and Robert Jan van Pelt, *Auschwitz* (New York: W.W. Norton and Company, 2008), 328–329, 340.
30 Snyder, *Bloodlands*, 209, 215; Chapoutot, *The Law of Blood*, 162; Burleigh, *Moral Combat*, 409; Hastings, *Inferno*, 502; Overy, *Blood and Ruins*, 222.
31 Raul Hilberg, *The Destruction of the European Jews* (Chicago: Quadrangle Books, 1961), 31; Hamerow, *Why We Watched*, 6; Peter Longerich, *Holocaust: The Nazi Persecution and Murder of the Jews* (New York: Oxford University Press, 2010), 7.

The Nazis estimated the number of European Jews at the start of the war to be 11 million.[32] While Germany's Jewish population was subdued legally and through violence like Kristallnacht, until the invasion of Poland what became the Holocaust was little more than rhetoric. However, Hitler had created the tone for genocide, without needing to explicitly order it. And once the Holocaust started to happen, only he could have stopped it. That he did not is almost as telling as if a signed document had been found with him giving the order to carry it out.[33] For his devoted disciples, including Himmler, the "final solution" meant just that, the Jewish "problem" was about to be solved, forever. Hitler had once said that when he was done Jews would "stop laughing everywhere." The Nazi leadership felt now was the time to make that statement a reality.[34]

Rhetoric increasingly turned to action, chiefly deportations, after the conquest of Poland. Jews were rounded up and shipped out of Germany to the newly added areas of the Reich. Once there, they were either confined to ghettos or sent to concentration camps. In both places, German Jews were soon joined by Jews from other conquered territories. Regardless of destination, rounding up Jews for relocation was violent, both in terms of the brutality of simply forcing people out of their homes as well as the accompanying deaths that resulted before a single step was taken or a train had departed towards a camp.[35] All the talk of "relocation" was a device to keep panic at bay. The Nazis attempted, as best they could, to conceal via "verbal camouflage" what it was they were doing. Not only was this a balm for those who were relocated, such euphemisms also shielded German civilians from "knowing" what was going on as well. Those who worked in the camps were sworn to secrecy and encouraged not to talk or discuss about what they were doing. The misdirection betrayed that during the early days of what became the Holocaust, the Nazis were unsure of what they were doing as well.[36]

The Nazis simply knew they had to do something. The problem with deporting Jews from one area to another was that for the first three years of the war, Germany was continually adding territory. That territory was now administered

---

32 Mark Roseman, *The Wannsee Conference and the Final Solution: A Reconsideration* (New York: Picador Press, 2002), 162. Today, historians believe the actual number of Jews in Europe to be closer to 9.5 million. See, "Jewish Population in Europe in 1933," https://encyclopedia.ushmm.org/content/en/article/jewish-population-of-europe-in-1933-population-data-by-country, 22 September 2022.
33 Roseman, *The Wannsee Conference*, 17–18, 50–51, 70.
34 Hilberg, *The Destruction of the European Jews*, 177, 266, 654–655; Burleigh, *Moral Combat*, 409; Hamerow, *Why We Watched*, 290.
35 Peter Fritzsche, *An Iron Wind: Europe Under Hitler* (New York: Basic Books, 2016), 176.
36 Hilberg, *The Destruction of the European Jews*, 142, 208, 318–319, 621, 650; Alan E. Steinweis and Robert D. Rachlin, editors, *The Law in Nazi Germany: Ideology, Opportunism, and the Perversion of Justice* (New York: Berghahn, 2013), 51–52.

by Nazis steeped in anti-Semitic rhetoric and ideology who wanted to rid it of Jews as well. Relocation was only viable if there was somewhere that was beyond the scope and reach of Nazi power. Until 1942, that seemed nearly impossible to conceive.[37]

But the ground for genocide, not just deportations, had already been laid out. Nazi anti-Semitism was intertwined with cutting edge eugenic theories, including the advent of legal, state conducted sterilization programs.[38] The Nazis utilized eugenic labels such as "feebleminded" and parlayed it into discussions about quality of life and financial responsibilities of both the state and family to care for the individual. Sterilization and then the murder of "undesirables," starting with those in state run care facilities, was a reality in Germany after the Nazis came to power. The official causes of death given to family members varied, but also fell into broad medical categories. Known as T-4, for the Tiergartenstrasse 4 address of its office in Berlin where the euthanasia plan originated, the program was unleashed in the autumn of 1939. Once the Nazis had justified euthanizing a minority group or segment of society, the moral boundary of killing people by the state in large numbers had been crossed. While there was enough public backlash that the T-4 program was suspended for institutionalized patients, those that had worked as part of the program were transferred to the concentration camp system to continue their work. They now had a larger and growing population of inmates to study, torment, and kill.[39]

The war presented both opportunities and dilemmas for the Nazis when it came to dealing with Jews. On the one hand, the advent of Allied air raids gave the German government a pretext for "evacuating" Jews out of Germany proper (as opposed to relocation) and sending them to camps in the East where they would be either murdered or worked to death. But the war also created pressure to enact a "final solution" to the Jewish question as well.[40] Designating Jews on

---

[37] Roseman, *The Wannsee Conference*, 28–31, 37, 74–75; Saul Friedlander, *Nazi Germany and the Jews, 1933–1945—Abridged Edition* (New York: Harper Perennial, 2009), 272.

[38] Yisrael Gutman and Michael Berenbaum, editors, *Anatomy of the Auschwitz Death Camp* (Indianapolis: Indiana University Press, 1994), 269; Sheila Faith Weiss, *The Nazi Symbiosis: Human Genetics and Politics in the Third Reich* (Chicago: University of Chicago Press, 2010), 280; Laurence Rees, *The Holocaust: A New History* (New York: Viking, 2017), 98–99.

[39] "Euthanasia Program and Aktion T4," https://encyclopedia.ushmm.org/content/en/article/euthanasia-program, 19 June 2021; *Tiergartenstrasse 4: Memorial and Information Point For the Victims of National Socialist Euthanasia Killings* (Berlin: Foundation Memorial to the Murdered Jews of Europe, 2016); Hastings, *Inferno*, 491; Deborah Dwork and Robert Jan van Pelt, *Auschwitz* (New York: W.W. Norton and Company, 2008), 125; Ferguson, *The War of the World*, 412.

[40] Michael Wildt, *An Uncompromising Generation: The Nazi Leadership of the Reich Security Main Office* (Madison: University of Wisconsin Press, 2003), 311–312; Hilberg, *The Destruction of*

the Eastern front as "partisans" and making their liquidation a war aim was fine, but it only went so far. There were other Jews, not just in Germany but all-over Western Europe, who were now under Nazi rule. Partisan fighting could not always be used as an excuse. Like any bureaucratic state seeking to solve a problem, the Nazis decided to hold a conference.

On July 31, 1941, Hermann Goering, the second highest ranking Nazi official, sent a letter to SS Obergruppen Fuhrer Reinhard Heydrich. In it, he ordered the junior Nazi to move from the "emigration and evacuation" of Jews from Reich controlled territory, which Heydrich had been tasked with starting in January 1939, to "bringing about the final solution of the Jewish question in the German sphere of influence in Europe. Whenever other governmental agencies are involved, they are to co-operate with you."[41] Heydrich was a logical choice for the job. He was a member of the SS and confidant of its leader, Heinrich Himmler. He was also the former director of the Gestapo and current director of the Reich Main Security Office. A Nazi since 1931, he believed that all Jews, not just those in Germany or in German conquered territory, needed to be exterminated.[42]

On January 20, 1942, just outside of Berlin in the lake community of Wannsee, Heydrich convened a conference to determine the fate of the Jews. Present were representatives for a vast array of the German governmental offices Heydrich believed were necessary to solve the Jewish question. However, he was not there to seek advice but rather to present his plan and get the apparatus of government on board. As Heydrich laid it out, rather than focus on emigration, Jews were to be "evacuated" to the East where they would be used as slave labor and then "be dealt with appropriately, because otherwise, by natural selection, they would form the germ cell of a new Jewish revival."[43]

The conference was remarkable because those participating did not debate the morality nor the means, only how best to achieve the goal of destroying European Jewry. There was no need for an official recommendation to or from Hitler to proceed with what became known as the Holocaust. The destruction of European Jewry underpinned everything they did and the time to act was now. Heydrich made it clear that what they were doing at Wannsee was building on Hitler's ideas and on the Fuehrer's orders. The resulting Wannsee Protocol was filled with seemingly rational discussion and bureaucratic language. It was also

---

the *European Jews*, 656; Donald M. McKale, *Hitler's Shadow War: The Holocaust and World War II* (New York: Cooper Square Press, 2002), 8.
41 Hilberg, *The Destruction of the European Jews*, 262.
42 Anthony Read, *The Devil's Disciples: Hitler's Inner Circle* (New York: W.W. Norton & Company, 2003), 754; Roseman, *The Wannsee Conference*, 19–21, 122.
43 Roseman, *The Wannsee Conference*, 99–101.

the blueprint for the genocide that took place in the camps. Most historians, as Mark Roseman relates, believe that Wannsee is best understood as the moment the Third Reich went from approving mass murder to formally adopting a policy of genocide. The only point really debated by the Nazis gathered at Wannsee was to what degree future generations would or would not understand what they had done.[44]

After the conference, there was direction and purpose to what the Nazis were doing with the evacuees and those they conquered, especially in Eastern Europe. By 1942, it was obvious that in addition to providing slave labor, the camps were the easiest way to kill massive numbers of people and were more cost/time effective than rounding up Jews and executing them individually.[45] Wannsee led to the construction of Belzec—with six gas chambers, Sobibor and Treblinka—with thirty gas chambers, while existing camps at Majdanek, which was formerly known as Lublin, and Auschwitz-Birkenau also received gas chambers. The end result was the transformation of Poland into "one vast Jewish cemetery."[46] Later, when the war began to turn against them, the Nazis realized that the Allies would not understand or approve of the Holocaust, which led to one other related decision. In 1942, Action 1005 was instituted by the SS. Its goal was to eliminate traces of earlier mass murder in areas conquered by the Reich. Besides, there was no longer a need for pits full of bodies. By then, nearly all of the camps, but especially the death camps, came equipped with incinerator ovens to dispose of the dead.[47]

The Konzentrationslager (KZ) System

Of course, Nazi Germany's use of the concentration camp (*Konzentrationslager* or KZ) predated the Holocaust. Hermann Goering approved the creation of camps shortly after the Nazis came to power, as a means to incarcerate, re-educate, and rehabilitate the large number of people deemed as enemies of the state, in order

---

44 Longerich, *The Unwritten Order*, 97; Longerich, *Holocaust*, 410–411; Roseman, *The Wannsee Conference*, 2–8, 15–16, 105–106, 110–111; Hilberg, *The Destruction of the European Jews*, 628–629; Rees, *The Holocaust: A New History* (New York: Public Affairs, 2017), 248–254.
45 Burleigh, *Moral Combat*, 405; Snyder, *Black Earth*, 202; Read, *The Devil's Disciples*, 751; Hilberg, *The Destruction of the European Jews*, 264–265; Roseman, *The Wannsee Conference*, 72–73, 104.
46 Roseman, *The Wannsee Conference*, 154–155; Read, *The Devil's Disciples*, 755–756; Judah Nadich, *Eisenhower and the Jews* (New York: Twayne Publishers, 1953), 171.
47 Hilberg, *The Destruction of the European Jews*, 628–629; Longerich, *Holocaust*, 410–411; Burleigh, *Moral Combat*, 400.

to not overburden the regular prison system. Initially, most of the new prisoners were political prisoners of the Reich, not out of hand, Jews. But the notion that the camps would be violence free and that people who were sent there arrived only after a fair trial was rarely given more than lip service. The goal was to bring a coating of order to the systematic use of violence the Nazis were unleashing on their opposition within Germany.[48]

The war and Wannsee changed the camps fundamentally. The Nazis enlarged the KZ system as their boundaries expanded. The camps became symbols of German domination and rule of conquered areas, the very manifestation of totalitarianism. Some remained, at their core, for political prisoners and prisoners of war. Others became chiefly for slave labor. And a very few were death camps from their inception. But those lines were not hard and fast, and death was a reality in every camp.[49]

The SS administered the camps, and its leader, Heinrich Himmler, wanted them to be as efficient at their mission as possible. Even before the war began the KZ system was known for showing no mercy to its prisoner population. With the launch of the final solution, the camps harnessed the power of the bureaucratic state to operate at new levels of horror. The organization needed to administer the system created a "banality of evil" among those who were part of it—but those clerks, those administrators like Adolf Eichmann, knew exactly what they were doing. While the bureaucrats never had to see or smell the dead, they accepted the idea that to help Jews was "misplaced humanity." Bureaucrats thought in larger terms than an individual German civilian might: getting rid of all Jews was the goal—there was no room to consider "good" Jews in the equation. The German *Volk* was all that mattered. Being part of the bureaucracy made it easier to rationalize the final solution.[50]

---

[48] Giles MacDonogh, *1938: Hitler's Gamble* (New York: Basic Books, 2009), 102; Read, *The Devil's Disciples*, 301–303. Nazi brutality dates back to Hitler's rise to power and includes not just the Gestapo but also organizations like the SA, who ran their own makeshift prisons prior to the start of the war. As one example, see, "Papestrasse SA Memorial," https://www.museumsportal-berlin.de/en/museums/gedenkort-sa-gefangnis-papestrasse/, 22 September2022. The author visited the museum in May 2022.
[49] Edwin Black, *IBM and the Holocaust: The Strategic Alliance Between Nazi Germany and America's Most Powerful Corporation* (New York: Crown Publishers, 2001), 351; Donald M. McKale, *Nazis after Hitler: How Perpetrators of the Holocaust Cheated Justice and the Truth* (New York: Rowman and Littlefield Publishers, 2014), 20; Gutman and Berenbaum, editors, *Anatomy of the Auschwitz Death Camp*, 5; Hilberg, *The Destruction of the European Jews*, 296, 561; MacDonogh, *1938: Hitler's Gamble*, 102; Burleigh, *Moral Combat*, 411.
[50] Evelyn Le Chene, *Mauthausen: The History of a Death Camp* (London: Methuen and Company, 1971), 23; Burleigh, *Moral Combat*, 415; Hilberg, *The Destruction of the European Jews*, 658–661;

The Nazi bureaucrats spearheaded not just a eugenic quest to rid the Reich (and the world) of Jews, but also to "Aryanize" German society. The homes, housewares, clothes, jewelry, goods, everything that had belonged to those sent to the camps had to be warehoused, cataloged, and sold or donated for the relief of Germans. As the camps filled, there were additional possessions prisoners brought with them on their journey that needed to be distributed as well. But the property was not limited to what might be found in a suitcase: it also included things like the hair and gold extracted from teeth, of those who were murdered in the camps. The camps were merely the final place for the Nazis to enact the "systematic plunder" on their enemies.[51]

There was at least one other issue the bureaucrats had to work through as they administered the Holocaust. There was a fundamental tension between mobilizing the entire population to fight the war and taking people out of both the domestic and war labor force and diverting them to the camps. The SS attempted to find a balance by advocating for the creation of more slave labor camps, arguing that they could be sources of research, development, and even production of goods the German military and civilians needed. In order to "reconcile the short-range needs of the war with the long-range policy of destruction" of their enemies, the work camps like Ohrdruf were placed near industrial centers and cities that needed cheap labor. It took until nearly the end of the war for the Nazis to realize that their camps were good at killing prisoners—whether directly or through hard labor and starvation—but not at producing goods the German war economy needed.[52]

Actually, taking people out of the workforce in the middle of the war in order to kill them was problematic, to the point that even some senior Nazis questioned

---

Black, *IBM and the Holocaust*, 7–11, 97; Mark Mazower, *Hitler's Empire: How the Nazis Ruled Europe* (New York: Penguin Press, 2008), 310; McKale, *Nazis after Hitler*, 24–25; "Theodor Eicke," http://holocaustresearchproject.org/othercamps/eicke.html, 14 June 2021. As historian Isabel V. Hull noted, eventually the Holocaust "developed its own internal dynamic." See, Hull, *Absolute Destruction: Military Culture and the Practices of War in Imperial Germany* (Ithaca: Cornell University Press, 2005), 326.

51 Burleigh, *Moral Combat*, 418, 437; Hilberg, *The Destruction of the European Jews*, 268–77, 436, 579; Gutman and Berenbaum, editors, *Anatomy of the Auschwitz Death Camp*, 246, 248, 369; Vincent, *Hitler's Silent Partners*, 9; Saul Friedlander, *Nazi Germany and the Jews, 1933–1945—Abridged Edition* (New York: Harper Perennial, 2009), 333; Donald M. McKale, *Nazis after Hitler: How Perpetrators of the Holocaust Cheated Justice and the Truth* (New York: Rowman and Littlefield Publishers, 2014), 17.

52 Read, *The Devil's Disciples*, 752, 799; Hastings, *Inferno*, 494, 503; Hilberg, *The Destruction of the European Jews*, 336, 586–588, 605; Mazower, *Hitler's Empire*, 307–309; Gutman and Berenbaum, editors, *Anatomy of the Auschwitz Death Camp*, 4, 104–106, 262.

the necessity or practicality of the decision. Germany's labor sector contracted by some 10 million men, due to military conscription, while the SS labor camps made up less than a half million new workers. Furthermore, the expenditures in constructing, administering, and staffing the camp system, not to mention the time, personnel, and logistical/transportation requirements of rounding up prisoners, diverted resources Germany could have used to fight the war.[53] The Wannsee Protocol ultimately placed achievement of the final solution on par with, and perhaps even above, military victory in the war.

For Jewish prisoners, arriving at the camps was the culmination of a disorientating process that started when they were rounded up, transported, and plugged into the system—assuming they survived those precipitating events.[54] And it was the system that would decide their fate. People did not know what to expect, nor were they told. They were ordered to do things, and they obeyed. Starting at the railway siding ramps, the disorientated prisoners were quickly examined and evaluated by Nazi doctors and guards. Some were destined for execution, others were assigned to medical experimentation, and some headed off to become slave laborers.[55]

Those sent to the death camps, like Auschwitz, followed a routine designed to continue the confusion and deception. As Saul Friedlander relates: "Children, the elderly, the sick, and large numbers of men and women were selected for death and marched immediately to the gas chambers." Of course, to avoid panic, they were not told this. Rather, they were told they were being escorted to "showers" for "disinfection." In the "shower" building, the prisoners were instructed to take off their clothes, place them on numbered hooks, and sent into a room complete with shower heads. Once the door was shut, Zyklon-B gas was pumped into the room and all inside died.[56]

The use of gas chambers in the camps was a move of expediency on the part of the Germans. Most Jews who died in the Holocaust were shot and their bodies dropped into pits that they themselves had dug.[57] It is estimated that the Nazis eventually murdered nearly 3 million Jews via mass executions. As Michael Bur-

---

53 Mazower, *Hitler's Empire*, 312; Read, *The Devil's Disciples*, 752; Hastings, *Inferno*, 490, 494, 503; Hilberg, *The Destruction of the European Jews*, 336, 586–588; David S. Wyman, *The Abandonment of the Jews: America and the Holocaust, 1941–1945* (New York: The New Press, 2007), 5.
54 Laurence Rees, *The Holocaust: A New History* (New York: Viking, 2017), xiii.
55 Gutman and Berenbaum, editors, *Anatomy of the Auschwitz Death Camp*, 7, 31; Hilberg, *The Destruction of the European Jews*, 206–209, 596, 624–626; Deborah Dwork and Robert Jan van Pelt, *Auschwitz* (New York: W.W. Norton and Company, 2008), 403; Snyder, *Bloodlands*, xiii; Snyder, *Black Earth*, 252.
56 Friedlander, *Nazi Germany and the Jews*, 358–359.
57 McKale, *Hitler's Shadow War*, 10; Snyder, *Black Earth*, 209; Snyder, *Bloodlands*, xiv-xv.

leigh notes, "there was nothing 'factory like' or "industrial' about how these people were killed."[58] However, it was determined that the ammunition used in such mass executions could be put to better military use. When the Riga ghetto in Latvia was liquidated in November 1941, for example, some 14,000 Jews were marched to the woods and shot.[59] The death camps, or killing centers, all of which were in Poland, were incredibly more efficient by comparison. People might arrive in the morning and their bodies be incinerated by evening.[60]

The labor, or work camps, like Ohrdruf were only marginally better. The camps were harsh, and mortality was high. Diseases like dysentery and typhus ran rampant and largely unchecked. Overcrowding in the barracks was common and the latrines overflowed with human waste. Food rations were minimal, and clothing became ragged. Death was the norm.[61] As Yisrael Gutman and Michael Berenbaum note, "Jewish prisoners in particular lived in the shadow of certainty that their relatives had perished, that their own fate was sealed, and that their incarceration in the camp was but a reprieve granted by the Germans to drain them of their strength through slave labor before sending them to their deaths."[62] All the while, the guards taunted them that their relatives were now ash.

Such comments demonstrate the sadism prisoners had to endure. Whether the Germans were already sadists before they went to work at the camps, or if the power over human life they had there caused them to become sadistic is beside the point. What was even worse was that the SS put prisoners in charge of other prisoners, undermining and often destroying solidarity. The brutality of the kapos in the day to day lives of the prisoners is what broke many people's spirits.[63]

---

58 Burleigh, *Moral Combat*, 401.
59 Read, *The Devil's Disciples*, 752–753; Gutman and Berenbaum, editors, *Anatomy of the Auschwitz Death Camp*, 209; Hilberg, *The Destruction of the European Jews*, 561, 627–628; Burleigh, *Moral Combat*, 430; Heather Pringle, *The Master Plan: Himmler's Scholars and the Holocaust* (New York: Hyperion, 2006), 265.
60 Hilberg, *The Destruction of the European Jews*, 555; Snyder, *Bloodlands*, 253, 256, 274.
61 Hilberg, *The Destruction of the European Jews*, 581–582; Gutman and Berenbaum, editors, *Anatomy of the Auschwitz Death Camp*, 26–27, 44, 131; John C. McManus, *Hell Before Their Very Eyes: American Soldiers Liberate Concentration Camps in Germany, April 1945* (Baltimore: Johns Hopkins University Press, 2015), 71, 138; Deborah Dwork and Robert Jan van Pelt, *Auschwitz* (New York: W.W. Norton and Company, 2008), 173; Norman M. Naimark, *Genocide: A World History* (New York: Oxford University Press, 2017), 79.
62 Gutman and Berenbaum, editors, *Anatomy of the Auschwitz Death Camp*, 28.
63 Snyder, *Bloodlands*, 268; Inga Clendinnen, *Reading the Holocaust* (New York: Cambridge University Press, 1999), 36; Le Chene, *Mauthausen*, 57; Marcus J. Smith, *Dachau: The Harrowing of Hell* (Albuquerque: University of New Mexico Press, 1972), 115.

Sadism went to an entirely new level, however, if prisoners were assigned to medical experimentation. A prisoner could be destined for either regular or irregular medical testing. The former involved (at least on the surface) acceptable clinical practices. The latter did not. Both almost always insured the eventual deaths of their subjects. Himmler took a good deal of pride in having the SS associated with medical research, believing that working with doctors on such projects heightened his organization's prestige within the Reich. For doctors involved with experimenting on real people, there were two paths available. The first was the understanding that if an experiment went wrong in some manner; a human being would die, making the doctor, in the words of Raul Hilberg, "a killer." The second path might transform the physician "into an architect of mass destruction."[64] Regardless, there was no worry of violating the Hippocratic Oath. The doctors could legally claim that under German law they were not experimenting on people. Instead, they could view themselves on the cutting edge of science.[65]

Those who participated in carrying out the Holocaust, whether bureaucrats, guards, or doctors chose to do so. They opted to cross a moral line, and many who perpetrated it never looked back. Their descent into darkness, their embrace of the Nazi vision was total and permanent.[66] Millions died as a result. The Nazis had two thirds, nearly 1.5 million people, of all the Jews in Poland in death camps by the end of 1942. The process, throughout Europe, took longer than expected, but it also left very few Jews either not in camps or alive by 1944.[67] As Peter Fritzsche notes, "most of the Jews who would be murdered by the Germans were dead before the German surrender at Stalingrad in January 1943."[68] Even when the tide of war turned against them, even when Allied forces were driving into Ger-

---

64 Gutman and Berenbaum, editors, *Anatomy of the Auschwitz Death Camp*, 303, 310–313, 317; Marcus J. Smith, *Dachau: The Harrowing of Hell* (Albuquerque: University of New Mexico Press, 1972), 178–179; Heather Pringle, *The Master Plan: Himmler's Scholars and the Holocaust* (New York: Hyperion, 2006), 248–254, 260–264, 272–278; Hilberg, *The Destruction of the European Jews*, 600–607.
65 Smith, *Dachau*, 92. Jews and many other groups were eugenically declared to be non-human and had no legal rights or standing under German law by the time the war began.
66 Burleigh, *Moral Combat*, 403; Pringle, *The Master Plan*, 324–325; Gutman and Berenbaum, editors, *Anatomy of the Auschwitz Death Camp*, 285; Norbert Troller, *Theresienstadt: Hitler's Gift to the Jews* (Chapel Hill: The University of North Carolina Press, 1991), xix; Daniel Jonah Goldhagen, *Hitler's Willing Executioners: Ordinary Germans and the Holocaust* (New York: Vintage Books, 1997), 394.
67 Hilberg, *The Destruction of the European Jews*, 337, 376–377.
68 Peter Fritzsche, *An Iron Wind: Europe Under Hitler* (New York: Basic Books, 2016), 156.

many itself, the Nazis did not stop killing Jews. The dying did not end until the war was over. The camps had to be liberated for it to stop.[69]

Awaiting Liberation

Such was the institutionalized evil and the people responsible for it that awaited Eisenhower and the Allied army he led. The United States Holocaust Memorial Museum's research indicates there were "some 42,500 ghettos, slave labor sites, concentration camps, and killing centers" constructed by the Germans throughout Europe and Soviet Russia."[70] The scale of the Nazi undertaking is so vast that it was and is hard to fully comprehend.[71] Equally so was why the Allied nations did so little to stop it.

It is not because they were unaware of the camp system. As early as 1942, the Allies had evidence detailing German anti-Polish policies, designed to discriminate against the Poles as the Germans moved into the conquered territory. Included in these reports was information about policies aimed specifically at Jews, from their forced movement and confinement in ghettos to their shipment to concentration camps. The Allies also knew that torture occurred in such camps.[72] And yet the political leadership in Allied nations refused to either believe or act, on both the information they had before them nor on what the Nazis had proclaimed time and time again that they were going to do to their enemies. Indeed, the Germans did very little to actually conceal what they were doing from the outside world, unlike the deceptions they put in place to lull their victims towards their fate.[73] Yet, ending the horrors in the camps was not going to be a cornerstone of fighting the war for the Allies.[74]

Not that the Germans, in 1942, believed the Allies were going to stop them anytime soon. Hitler paid very little attention to the United States in his thinking, either about geo-politics or the conduct of the war. Like Great Britain and France, he believed the United States to be weak. He was confident that between the Great De-

---

69 Snyder, *Black Earth*, 241; Hilberg, *The Destruction of the European Jews*, 600; Read, *The Devil's Disciples*, 758–759.
70 McKale, *Nazis after Hitler*, 342.
71 Konrad H. Jarausch and Michael Geyer, *Shattered Past: Reconstructing German Histories* (Princeton: Princeton University Press, 2003), 131.
72 Report, "Economic Life in Poland," Paul Sturman Papers, Box 3, Poland (3), NAID#7330178, Dwight Eisenhower Presidential Library, Abilene, Kansas.
73 Hastings, *Inferno*, 497–499.
74 Overy, *Blood and Ruins*, 622–630.

pression and American neutrality laws, the U.S. would not be able to play a real role in the conflict. No one in the German high command challenged his thinking. Nor did American entry into the war in December 1941 change his opinion. Indeed, Hitler argued that Jews had likely convinced the Roosevelt Administration to join the conflict, a sure indication that they needed to be destroyed.[75]

Though it was impossible to know at the time, 1941 proved to be the year of Hitler's two largest mistakes: invading the Soviet Union before truly defeating Great Britain and preemptively declaring war on the United States. Eisenhower surely could not have foreseen this course of events, having been thrust into command in North Africa less than a year removed from being a staff officer. Nor is it likely, other than a chance newspaper story here and there, that Ike was privy to the Holocaust. By the time the Roosevelt Administration became officially and more fully aware of what was happening in the Nazi camp system, Eisenhower was focused on Operation Torch. Thus far, intelligence on the camps and the plight of the prisoners in them was above his pay grade.

In the meantime, thousands of Jews were being deported to extermination camps. One of those rounded up was twelve-year-old Judith Wishnyatskaya, who wrote her father in June 1942: "We would so love to live but they won't let us, and we will die." And that is exactly what happened in 1943 when Judith was murdered in Byten, Belarus, along with over 5,000 others.[76] Those in the camps, people like Wishnyatskaya, were praying for liberation. It was slow in coming. But, leading the way from the west, was Dwight Eisenhower.

---

75 MacDonogh, *1938: Hitler's Gamble*, xi; Gerhard L. Weinberg, *World in the Balance: Behind the Scenes of World War II* (Hanover: University Press of New England, 1981), 55–77; Wildt, *An Uncompromising Generation*, 316–317; Snyder, *Black Earth*, 114; Hamerow, *Why We Watched*, 287.
76 Memorial to the Murdered Jews of Europe, Berlin, Germany.

Chapter 3
Waging a War of Liberation

In retrospect, it is clear that Eisenhower was at the head of a fighting force destined to be viewed as an army of liberation. Susan Eisenhower, Ike's granddaughter, later surmised that the Normandy landings in June 1944 was not just about opening up a western front against Hitler's Fortress Europa, but also needed to be seen as a means to end Nazi research into atomic weapons, halting the launching and production of V-1 and V-2 bombs, and as a means to insure "the survival of the Jewish people."[1]

Such historical revisionism is not, out of hand, incorrect. Ike himself embraced the liberator moniker for the forces under his command even before he stepped into Ohrdruf. He had long viewed the Nazis as a threat to the American way of life. The more he encountered them, the surer he was that the Allies were on the side of right and that Germany must be stopped. In that way, we can view his campaign as a means to "win the war to stop the killing." But even that is a retrospective conclusion. By D-Day, Eisenhower might have seen his forces as liberating nations conquered by Germany, but his knowledge of the Holocaust was still far from complete. The moment his forces waded ashore in Normandy, however, they put him on a collision course to not just learn more but also to ending Hitler's final solution.

These realizations were still in the future, however. The first step was naming Eisenhower the Supreme Allied Commander in charge of the liberation of western Europe. The title was a new role, not just for Ike, but for the Western alliance.[2] It had no real precedent from either the Great War, or the Napoleonic wars of the previous century. And though it might be seen as an American innovation, it also lacked an American lineage as well. By 1943, Ike received yet another promotion, this time with permanent rank. His power and authority increasingly made him a peer to those he was working with.[3]

The United States had been pushing for a cross-channel invasion of Western Europe since 1942. The assault had been postponed due to inadequate supplies, manpower, and lingering debate over leadership. Unlike in the First World War,

---

[1] Susan Eisenhower, *How Ike Led: The Principles Behind Eisenhower's Biggest Decisions* (New York: Thomas Dunne Books, 2020), 20.
[2] Eisenhower, *How Ike Led*, 5.
[3] Susan Eisenhower, *Mrs. Ike: Memories and Reflections on the Life of Mamie Eisenhower* (New York: Farrar, Straus and Giroux, 1996), 202; John S. D. Eisenhower, editor, *Letters to Mamie* (Garden City: Doubleday & Company, 1978), 141.

where the United States had been an associated power and considered by many Allied leaders a junior one at that, this time the Americans were leading the Allied assault, a reality that not all of the British commanders (including Field Marshal Bernard Montgomery) easily accepted.[4] However, there was little doubt by 1943 that the Supreme Allied Commander was going to be an American. The question was who.

Dwight Eisenhower was not President Franklin Roosevelt's first choice for the job. Despite overseeing American forces and working with Allied leaders during Operations Torch and Husky, the president's top choice was Ike's boss, General George Marshall. There was certainly a part of Marshall that wanted the job, and, in many ways, he was the logical choice. Not only did he outrank Eisenhower, but Marshall's skills as a planner and organizer were legendary. However, there were those who were also firmly against the idea, including Marshall's old boss, General John Pershing. While Pershing had nothing against his protégé, he told the president that Marshall's skills were best utilized in Washington, where he could make sure that Congress continued to supply American forces with what they needed. Roosevelt eventually agreed.[5]

The president assessed Eisenhower for himself in November 1943 as he made his way to the Tehran Conference.[6] Part of what Ike had going for him was that he was already on the ground and in the field. Furthermore, he had built professional relationships with the British officers and politicians, including Winston Churchill, that the SAC would be working alongside. In December, Roosevelt officially named Eisenhower to the position, meaning he would be in command of Operation Overlord—the Allied assault on Hitler's Western Wall in France. Mar-

---

4 Richard Overy, *Blood and Ruins: The Last Imperial War, 1931–1945* (New York: Viking, 2021), 339; Eisenhower, editor, *Letters to Mamie*, 201; Peter Caddick-Adams, *Fire and Steel: The End of World War Two in the West* (New York: Oxford University Press, 2022),31–33.
5 Joseph E. Persico, *Roosevelt's Secret War: FDR and World War II Espionage* (New York: Random House, 2001), 280–283; Norman Gelb, *Ike and Monty: Generals at War* (New York: William Morrow and Company, 1994), 433; D.K.R. Crosswell, *Beetle: The Life of General Walter Bedell Smith* (Lexington: The University Press of Kentucky, 2012), 517.
6 Michael Beschloss, *The Conquerors: Roosevelt, Truman and the Destruction of Hitler's Germany, 1941–1945* (New York: Simon and Schuster, 2002), 9–10, 20, 29. Eisenhower was impressed with Roosevelt, especially his mastery of geography. He was less impressed with the president's belief in his ability to innately "understand" the European mind, particularly those of Germany's leaders. Ike noted Roosevelt was "almost an egomaniac in his belief in his own wisdom" because he had visited Germany as a child and was convinced that the six-week trip gave him special insight into the nation, buttressed by his time in the Wilson Administration. The latter resulted in Roosevelt continually conflating Nazism with Prussian militarism and Hitler with the Kaiser.

shall took the decision with grace and fully supported Eisenhower. For his part, Ike never forgot his superior's magnanimity. Eisenhower's moment had arrived.[7]

There was little doubt about Ike's zeal. Writing around the same time of his promotion to SAC, he jotted down "I want to get this d—war won!!"[8] He recognized the irony that he, a German-American was leading an allied army to defeat his ancestors' homeland. As the days ticked down to D-Day, Ike often thought about his previous trip to Germany, during his time on the American Battle Monuments Commission. Then entering "the Fatherland" was "exhilarating."[9] This time, the journey would be more dangerous than driving along the roads in the Black Forest. And it would also be much more transformative.

While the United States had been at war for nearly two years and had launched massive amphibious invasions in 1942 and 1943 in the European Theater of Operation, nothing compared to Overlord. Its scale was unprecedented, as was its stakes. Not only was the target France, but there was little doubt the Germans knew the Allies were coming—they just did not know where. In large part their ignorance was because of the massive disinformation campaign Eisenhower's staff orchestrated. Still, there was foreboding about the amphibious invasion within the Allied camp. Many junior officers speculated that the lead units might suffer 90 percent casualties. And to top it off, the tides and weather had to be perfect. Ike prepared for the possibility that the invasion might fail.[10]

Eisenhower did everything he could to tip the odds of a successful invasion in favor of the Allies. He selected Normandy because it was not the obvious choice. Hitler was sure that the real target was the Pas-de-Calais, thanks to Allied disinformation (Ike enjoyed the fact that the Germans were hoodwinked).[11] He made sure the invasion force enjoyed overwhelming air superiority from the start. But it was the weather reports that caused him the most consternation. The invasion force was set, only to have the operation postponed on June 5. Ike was told that if Overlord did not happen on June 6, the Allies would have to wait nearly two weeks for

---

7 Dwight D. Eisenhower, *Crusade in Europe* (New York: Doubleday and Company, 1953), 70–71, 208–209; James Holland, *Together We Stand: America, Britain and the Forging of an Alliance* (New York: Hyperion, 2005), 142; Beschloss, *The Conquerors*, 29; Eisenhower, *Mrs. Ike*, 208; Eisenhower, editor, *Letters to Mamie*, 102.
8 Eisenhower, editor, *Letters to Mamie*, 140.
9 Eisenhower, *How Ike Led*, 51–53.
10 Persico, *Roosevelt's Secret War*, 308; Robert M. Citino, *The Wehrmacht's Last Stand: The German Campaigns of 1944–1945* (Lawrence: University Press of Kansas, 2017), 137; Bret Baier, *Three Days in January: Dwight Eisenhower's Final Mission* (New York: William Morrow, 2017), 54.
11 Stephen E. Ambrose, *Ike's Spies: Eisenhower and the Espionage Establishment* (Jackson: University of Mississippi Press, 1999), 79, 99. Part of the disinformation campaign was the famed Operation Mincemeat.

the tides to be right—not to mention refuel the naval ships and off load the men, who could not stay aboard that long, whether because of keeping them fed or just the growing threat that the Germans would learn they were there. Ultimately, it was Eisenhower's decision alone to make. After talking with his generals, doing a good deal of pacing and thinking, he decided that June 6 was D-Day. He gave his approval with a simple "O.K, let's go." According to Eisenhower, making that decision was the last time in his life he worried about the weather.[12]

While Eisenhower was not part of the first wave, he visited with those who were the tip of the invasion spear. Before they boarded their planes, Ike met with members of the American 101st Airborne Division. He felt a need to be with the men. Walking among them, he looked for things to discuss, whether it was farming or fishing, that he had in common with those he was sending into harm's way. As his son John later recounted, it was Ike's way of both appearing human and reminding his men that they had something to look forward to (and even fight for) after the war.[13] As the planes took off, he turned to get back in his car and said quietly, "Well, it's on." Always, inescapably, Eisenhower felt the weight of command.[14] Perhaps this was never truer than as he stood watching the Screaming Eagles disappear into the darkness towards France.

D-Day was filled with enough drama and peril to warrant the eventual books and movies that depict it. Landing craft and paratroopers went off course, the Germans, though caught by surprise, offered fierce resistance, pre-invasion intelligence proved correct about some things and completely off about others. But despite it all, within twenty-four hours, the situation was much better. The Allies had landed, held, and were firmly entrenched in France. While causalities were large, some 10,000, they were not as high as Eisenhower had feared they would be. D-Day was historic: no cross-channel invasion had been successful since William the Conqueror had landed in England in 1066. However, it did not end the

---

12 Eisenhower, *Crusade in Europe*, 250; Stephen E. Ambrose, *D-Day June 6, 1944: The Climactic Battle of World War II* (New York: Simon and Schuster, 1994), 183–189; Stephen E. Ambrose, *The Supreme Commander: The War Years of General Dwight D. Eisenhower* (Jackson: University of Mississippi Press, 1999), 417; James Holland, *Normandy '44: D-Day and the Epic 77-Day Battle for France* (New York: Atlantic Monthly Press, 2019), 79; Blaine T. Browne, *Mighty Endeavor: The American Nation and World War II* (New York: Rowman & Littlefield, 2019), 155–156; Eisenhower, *How Ike Led*, 143.

13 Eisenhower, *How Ike Led*, 31–32. As we have seen, Ike similarly made small talk with the enlisted men when he visited Ohrdruf as well.

14 Ambrose, *D-Day June 6, 1944*, 193–195; Eisenhower, *Crusade in Europe*, 252; Evan Thomas, *Ike's Bluff: President Eisenhower's Secret Battle to Save the World* (New York: Back Bay Books, 2012), 6.

war by itself.[15] It was but the first step in what Ike called in his invasion proclamation a "great crusade." After France, he vowed to the rest of Western Europe, "their day [of liberation] will come."[16]

Of course, the Nazis still had to be defeated. As news of the landings made it back to Germany, there was an odd surge of relief—at last they no longer had to anticipate the Allied invasion of France! But that sense of contentment of the battle being joined faded in the months to come. Germany simply did not have enough manpower to fight a multi-front war.[17] While this realization caused the Nazi leadership to become more fanatical in their rhetoric and in their desire to kill as many Jews as possible in order to achieve some form of victory, it prodded many within the German High Command to begin contemplating the need to try for a negotiated end to the fighting—at least in the West—despite Allied demands for unconditional surrender.[18] However, the man leading the Allied advance was not looking to negotiate, but to liberate Europe and put an end to Nazi Germany. This was to be a war to the finish, with no doubt who won, who lost, and why.

Refugees and Liberation

Writing near the end of his life, Eisenhower said, "From the start of OVERLORD, we knew that we would win—but we knew it not factually but with faith."[19] There was still fighting to be done and a war to be won. Speaking twenty years after D-Day, Eisenhower told CBS News anchor Walter Cronkite during an interview on Omaha Beach that the men under his command had fought and died on the coast of France "so that the world could be free. It just shows what free men will do rather than be slaves."[20]

---

15 Persico, *Roosevelt's Secret War*, 286; Ambrose, *D-Day June 6, 1944*, 480; William I. Hitchcock, *The Bitter Road to Freedom: A New History of the Liberation of Europe* (New York: Free Press, 2008), 13–14; Kasey S. Pipes, *Ike's Final Battle: The Road to Little Rock and the Challenge of Equality* (Los Angeles: World Ahead Publishing, 2007), 10; Holland, *Normandy '44*, 229.
16 Baier, *Three Days in January*, 54; David Eisenhower, *Eisenhower: At War, 1943–1945* (New York: Random House, 1986), 256, 267.
17 Marlis G. Steinert, *Hitler's War and the Germans: Public Mood and Attitude During the Second World War* (Athens, OH: Ohio University Press, 1977), 258–261; Gelb, *Ike and Monty*, 337.
18 Johann Chapoutot, *The Law of Blood: Thinking and Acting as a Nazi* (Cambridge, Massachusetts: The Belknap Press of Harvard University Press, 2018), 179; Ambrose, *Ike's Spies*, 117; Eisenhower, *Eisenhower: At War, 1943–1945*, 326; Holland, *Normandy '44*, 484.
19 Dwight D. Eisenhower, *At Ease: Stories I tell to Friends* (New York: Doubleday and Company, 1967), 290.
20 Ambrose, *D-Day June 6, 1944*, 583.

In the Nazi camp system, many people remained enslaved and yearned to be free once again. While the Allied landings in France were an important moment in the war, and word spread throughout Europe, until Allied armies showed up, life in the camps continued to be about survival and death.[21] However, the Allies were pushing the Nazis back, which means it is worthwhile to consider what American leaders knew about the Holocaust, how that knowledge altered their war aims, and how or if it informed what Eisenhower and the men he commanded did.

When it comes to the United States and its reaction to the Holocaust, the story begins and ends with President Franklin D. Roosevelt. His legacy is complicated when it comes to the Holocaust, and he set the tone for the American wartime response.[22] Starting with Kristallnacht, Roosevelt had been both shocked by Germany's actions and reluctant to do anything concrete about them. Indeed, he did little directly to aid the attempts of Jews to leave Nazi Germany prior to the outbreak of the war.[23] And yet, his reluctance to speak or act carried little in the form of political ramifications. American Jews stuck with Roosevelt through the elections of 1940 and 1944, and national Jewish groups and their leaders were reluctant to push the president to do anything to overtly alleviate the plight of European Jews, fearing that it might hurt Roosevelt politically. The president was certainly opposed to the Holocaust, but he also recognized the anti-Semitism of many Americans, including himself at times, when it came to even the perception of Jewish influence on his administration.[24] When asked, for example, by the president of the American Jewish Congress, Rabbi Stephen Wise, for some statement condemning the Nazi's actions, Roosevelt preferred to stick to broad language that included, but did not specify Jews. And Wise, who admired and was "deferential" to the president, accepted it as the best Roosevelt could do.[25]

---

21 Sarah Helm, *Ravensbruck: Life and Death in Hitler's Concentration Camp for Women* (New York: Nan A. Talese Doubleday, 2014), 391.
22 Richard Breitman and Allan J. Lichtman, *FDR and the Jews* (Cambridge: Belknap Press, 2013), 2–5; "The Battle over FDR's Record on Saving Jews from the Nazis," https://www.haaretz.com/jewish/holocaust-remembrance-day/2019-01-06/ty-article/.premium/u-s-holocaust-museum-accused-of-whitewashing-fdrs-record-on-saving-jews/0000017f-e3e6-df7c-a5ff-e3fe137e0000, 31 August 2022.
23 Laurence Rees, *The Holocaust: A New History* (New York: Viking, 2017), 138.
24 Deborah E. Lipstadt, "America and the Holocaust," *Modern Judaism*, 10(October 1990), 285, 289, 291; Theodore S. Hamerow, *Why We Watched: Europe, America, and the Holocaust* (New York: W.W. Norton & Company, 2008), 236, 266, 343–349, 362–366.
25 Richard Breitman and Alan M. Kraut, *American Refugee Policy and European Jewry, 1933–1945* (Indianapolis: Indiana University Press, 1987), 243; Lawrence J. Epstein, *Americans and the Birth of Israel* (New York: Rowman and Littlefield, 2017), 22; Beschloss, *The Conquerors*, 38–39.

However, despite worries that public statements might make things worse for prisoners of the Nazis, Roosevelt did condemn what the Germans were doing.[26] Kristallnacht was one thing, but the camps, especially once the United States was in the war, were something else entirely. By early 1942, there was ample evidence of what the Nazis were doing in the camps. Jan Karski, a Polish underground worker, was smuggled into both the Warsaw ghetto and the transit ghetto of Izbica, where he learned not only of the horrific conditions facing Jews but also of the Belzec killing center. He reported what he found in London and in Washington, though he quickly discovered that few officials seemed to grasp what he was telling them.[27]

Confronted with evidence, not just what might be brushed off as "rumors" or propaganda, American officials were still reluctant to take action. They were very aware of how their view of Germany had been shaped by British propaganda during World War I about the "rape of Belgium." Still, they were willing to talk about what the Nazis were doing. Roosevelt condemned "barbaric crimes against civilization" being committed by Germany in an August 1942 press conference. He told the assembled journalists that he had hoped such "atrocities" would decrease after Germany had finalized conquest of a given occupied country but based on what evidence the Allies had that simply did not seem to be the case. He promised that when the war was over, the Nazis responsible would face courts of justice; he reiterated this point again in October 1942.[28]

Information about the camps also likely influenced the Allied declaration of December 17, 1942, which described the ongoing events of the Holocaust in Nazi occupied Europe as well as the subsequent Casablanca Conference in January 1943. At Roosevelt's insistence, the Allies adopted a policy of "unconditional surrender," in which they promised to "conclude no separate peace with such a criminal regime as the one ruling in Berlin." While vowing that the policy was not directed

---

26 Erik Larson, *In the Garden of Beasts: Love, Terror, and an American Family in Hitler's Berlin* (New York: Broadway Paperbacks, 2011), 28–29, 241.
27 Raul Hilberg, *The Destruction of the European Jews* (Chicago: Quadrangle Books, 1961), 718–719; Beschloss, *The Conquerors*, 38; Dan Plesch, *Human Rights After Hitler: The Lost History of Prosecuting Axis War Crimes* (Washington, D.C.: Georgetown University Press, 2017), 72–73; Max Hastings, *Inferno: The World at War, 1939–1945* (New York: Alfred A. Kopf, 2011), 500. Karski would later become a professor at Georgetown University.
28 "Press Conference #842," http://www.fdrlibrary.marist.edu/_resources/images/pc/pc0138.pdf, 27 June 2018; "Franklin D. Roosevelt: Statement on Axis Crimes in Occupied Countries," http://www.presidency.ucsb.edu/ws/index.php?pid=16293&st=&st1=; "Franklin D. Roosevelt: Statement on the Plan to Try Nazi War Criminals," http://www.presidency.ucsb.edu/ws/index.php?pid=16174&st=&st1=, 28 June 2018; Beschloss, *The Conquerors*, 40–42, 61.

against the people of the Axis nations, "but we do mean to impose punishment and retribution in full upon their guilty, barbaric leaders."[29]

What was missing, of course, was specific phrases about the camps. The rhetoric was a step, but a small one. Unconditional surrender, on the other hand, had immediate ramifications. It committed the Allies to a war without negotiation. Unconditional surrender served as cover of sorts for Roosevelt when it came to the Holocaust. Just a few weeks after getting home from the Casablanca Conference, the president received a top-secret report prepared by the Office of Strategic Services detailing what American intelligence knew about the "extermination of Jews." Roosevelt concluded that the best way to put an end to the camps was to win the war.[30] American policy was now set. There was no need to debate related issues concerning the existence of the camps and Nazi policies towards Jews. Winning the war negated the need for rescue missions, bombing raids, and whether Jewish refugees should be let into the British mandate of Palestine or not.[31]

One could argue that the policy made some sense. Winning the war *would* end the Nazis and their camps. And realistically, there was little that could actually be done for the prisoners so long as Hitler controlled the Reich. In the minds of many of the Allied leaders, small scale covert action was a not a serious argument when it came to dealing with disrupting the German war machine. Indeed, it could have unintended and disastrous consequences. When Reinhard Heydrich, who had convened the Wannsee Conference, was assassinated by British trained operatives in June 1942, Nazi retribution was swift and terrible. The Germans executed 5,000 Czechs, razed the villages of Lezaky and Lidice, and sent thousands more, including some 3,000 Jews, off to concentration camps.[32]

---

29 Richard Breitman, *U.S. Intelligence and the Nazis* (New York: Cambridge University Press, 2005), 45; Donald M. McKale, *Hitler's Shadow War: The Holocaust and World War II* (New York: Cooper Square Press, 2002), 396; "Casablanca Conference," https://avalon.law.yale.edu/wwii/casablan.asp, 15 December 2020; D.K.R. Crosswell, *Beetle: The Life of General Walter Bedell Smith* (Lexington: The University Press of Kentucky, 2012), 456–457, 493.
30 Map Room Papers; MR 203(12); Sec. 1; OSS Numbered Bulletins, March-May 1943, Box 72, Franklin D. Roosevelt Presidential Library, Hyde Park, New York; Michael Burleigh, *Moral Combat: Good and Evil in World War II* (New York: Harper Collins Publishers, 2011), 448; Plesch, *Human Rights After Hitler*, 73–74; Beschloss, *The Conquerors*, 38–40; Breitman and Kraut, *American Refugee Policy and European Jewry*, 242.
31 Robert H. Abzug, *Inside the Vicious Heart: Americans and the Liberation of Nazi Concentration Camps* (New York: Oxford University Press, 1987), 18; Richard Overy, *Blood and Ruins: The Last Imperial War, 1931–1945* (New York: Viking, 2021), 624–625; Dallas Holocaust and Human Rights Museum exhibit, 3 November 2022.
32 Anthony Read, *The Devil's Disciples: Hitler's Inner Circle* (New York: W.W. Norton & Company, 2003), 750–751; Burleigh, *Moral Combat*, 308. Codenamed Operation Anthropoid, the assassination of Heydrich was a joint British and Czech venture that was planned prior to American entry into

But after D-Day, there was no longer a reason to think in such small terms. There were now other options. One suggestion floated in the halls of government as the war progressed were bombing missions that specifically targeted the railroad lines that fed victims to the camps. The War Department concluded in 1944 that medium range bombers based in the United Kingdom, France, or Italy would not be able to make it to a camp like Auschwitz. Heavy bombers could, but would need to cover 2,000 miles, most of it through German controlled territories. The gains, which planners argued was symbolic rather than military, were not worth the risks. Those held in the camps might have disputed such a conclusion, as do virtually all historians today, especially since bombers flew near Auschwitz on missions, but they had no voice in the report.[33]

Nor did they have an advocate in Franklin Roosevelt. In retrospect, doing something, like bombing Auschwitz would have made the Allies record on the Holocaust look better. The president, however, had decided against the bombing mission. Historian Michael Beschloss is blunt: "Shockingly disengaged from the struggle to rescue Jewish refugees from Hitler, he [FDR] made no serious effort to explore whether bombing the death camps might save many lives."[34] Roosevelt's interest and support, or lack thereof, were crucial factors as it turned out in determining U.S. policy.

The Roosevelt Administration also was against trying to rescue Jews or other prisoners from the camps. The War Department had decided early on that "rescue was not to be a part of its mission," the military had a war to fight and win. The U.S. State Department and British Foreign Office also wanted nothing to do with such missions, despite the fact that smaller-scale ones had saved thousands of lives.[35] Both departments actually worried that such operations would work—requiring a diversion of military resources on the one hand, and the need to re-

---

the war in October 1941. For a variety of reasons, it was not carried out until May 1942—prior to Operation Torch, but after the Wannsee Conference.

33 Yisrael Gutman and Michael Berenbaum, editors, *Anatomy of the Auschwitz Death Camp* (Indianapolis: Indiana University Press, 1994), 562–563, 576–580; Beschloss, *The Conquerors*, 63–65; "Menashe and Leah Lorenzi" Auschwitz Twins, CANDLES, Inc., https://candlesolocaustmuseum.org, 7 December 2016; Richard Breitman and Allan J. Lichtman, *FDR and the Jews* (Cambridge: Belknap Press, 2013), 281–285; Walter Laqueur, *Out of the Ruins of Europe* (New York: Library Press, 1971), 501; David S. Wyman, *The Abandonment of the Jews: America and the Holocaust, 1941–1945* (New York: The New Press, 2007), xxi, 298–302; Burleigh, *Moral Combat*, 456; Martin Gilbert, *Auschwitz and the Allies* (New York: Pimlico, 2001), 220, 339–341; Deborah Dwork and Robert Jan van Pelt, *Auschwitz* (New York: W.W. Norton and Company, 2008), 348–349.

34 Beschloss, *The Conquerors*, ix–x, 65–67.

35 Gutman and Berenbaum, editors, *Anatomy of the Auschwitz Death Camp*, 582; Lipstadt, "America and the Holocaust," 286; Gilbert, *Auschwitz and the Allies*, 163.

settle refugees on the other. Not that anyone inside or outside of the government for that matter, including American Jewish leaders, formulated much in the way of concrete plans. Nor did it help that anti-Semitism was rampant in both the War and State departments.[36] For "a determined Allied rescue campaign" to have happened, it would have taken a "substantial commitment" and the leadership of the United States. Such will, in Washington, was lacking.[37]

There is also some evidence that the planners were right, that rescue operations in reality were far grimmer than on paper. In March 1945, for example, General George Patton dispatched a task force to liberate American prisoners of war (including his son-in-law) held by the Nazis in Hammelburg. Led by Major Abraham Baum, some 300 men were sent 50 miles behind German lines. They had little intelligence about the area, did not take enough fuel, and lacked sufficient maps. By the time they made it to the camp, they discovered that not only were there 1,500 POWs expecting liberation, but that a large German force had been alerted to their presence. Only twenty-five POWs reached American lines, and over 260 members of the raiding party were either killed or captured. The majority of their vehicles were destroyed or left by the roadside. When informed of what happened, Ike called Patton's decision one of the worst "crackpot actions" ever undertaken by the U.S. Army.[38]

Based on the available evidence, Eisenhower was likely not consulted about the policy decisions around either bombing camps or rescue operations. That in and of itself is not surprising, considering that his job was always to forge an alliance and defeat the Germans in the field.[39] Take, for example, the very public

---

36 Hamerow, *Why We Watched*, 303; Larson, *In the Garden of Beasts*, 31, 38–39; Wyman, *The Abandonment of the Jews*, 25, 189; Breitman and Kraut, *American Refugee Policy and European Jewry*, 234–235, 256, 286. Breitman and Kraut believe that we expect so much of FDR, because we were told (by FDR, by the press, and then by scholars) to expect him to solve problems, not act like other presidents who have limitations and act like politicians.
37 Wyman, *The Abandonment of the Jews*, xix; Joseph W. Bendersky, *The "Jewish Threat": Anti-Semitic Politics of the U.S. Army* (New York: Basic Books, 2000), 226, 286, 310.
38 Alfred D. Chandler, Jr, editor, *The Papers of Dwight David Eisenhower: The War Years, Volume IV* (Baltimore: The Johns Hopkins University Press, 1971), 2616–2617; Duane Schultz, *Patton's Last Gamble: The Disastrous Raid on POW Camp Hammelburg in World War II* (New York: Stackpole Books, 2018). Patton would later claim that the raid diverted German attention from his movements and punched a hole in the German lines that he could then exploit. He also denied publicly that the raid was an attempt to liberate his son-in-law, despite private statements at the time and evidence uncovered after the raid's top-secret classification was ended decades after the war.
39 Breitman, *U.S. Intelligence and the Nazis*, 27, 31; Joseph W. Bendersky, *The "Jewish Threat": Anti-Semitic Politics of the U.S. Army* (New York: Basic Books, 2000), 313; Persico, *Roosevelt's Secret War*, 219. Despite the fact that there was considerable newspaper coverage of reports and rumors about the camps as early as 1942 (documented by the USHMM), Persico could not find

58 —— Chapter 3 Waging a War of Liberation

Bermuda Conference in 1943. On March 23, the Archbishop of Canterbury, William Temple, gave a scathing speech in the House of Lords calling on the British government to act on information known publicly on both sides of the Atlantic since the end of 1942, to end the extermination of Jews. Thus, a joint U.S.-U.K. meeting was held in Bermuda, a location selected to avoid press coverage. The British Foreign Office instructed its delegation to remember that they were to avoid an outcome that would prove "embarrassing" – like if the Germans unleashed a flood of refugees on the Allies. The American delegation likewise arrived on the island with orders to offer no monetary support for either rescue operations or refugee relief, nor would the president seek to change immigration quotas by going to Congress with such a request.[40] Despite the conference running from April 19th to the 29th, the end result was more platitudes, some fine tuning of policies dealing with existing refugees (but not any person currently held in the Nazi camp system), and was quickly labeled a "cruel mockery" and "empty posturing" by the press and other observers once the report was released.[41] While we cannot know for certain when Eisenhower first learned of the Bermuda Conference, it would appear that he was not consulted about it beforehand. The only mention of Bermuda prior to the conference in his papers are to its importance to cross-Atlantic transport of supplies (in a February 1942 report to Marshall) and as part of a wider discussion of deployment of African-American soldiers to bases around the globe (in a March 1942 report). There is no mention of either the conference or the island in Eisenhower's collected papers in 1943.[42]

However, as Ike's armies advanced changing conditions on the ground forced the politicians to react, requiring leaders in Washington and London to formulate responses that did not always fit easily under the notion that "winning the war"

---

any mention of the Holocaust in the official cables exchanged between Roosevelt and Churchill during the early years of the war, despite Ultra intercepts and eyewitness accounts making their way into the intelligence pool.

[40] "The Bermuda Conference," https://www.pbs.org/wgbh/americanexperience/features/holocaust-bermuda/, 11 April 2023; "The United States and the Holocaust, 1942–45," https://encyclopedia.ushmm.org/content/en/article/the-united-states-and-the-holocaust-1942-45, 5 May 2023.

[41] "The Bermuda Conference," https://www.pbs.org/wgbh/americanexperience/features/holocaust-bermuda/, 11 April 2023; "The United States and the Holocaust, 1942–45," https://encyclopedia.ushmm.org/content/en/article/the-united-states-and-the-holocaust-1942-45, 5 May 2023; "Summary of Bermuda Conference Recommendations," https://perspectives.ushmm.org/item/summary-of-bermuda-conference-recommendations, 5 May 2023.

[42] Alfred D. Chandler, Jr., editor, *The Papers of Dwight David Eisenhower: The War Years, Volume I and Volume II* (Baltimore: The Johns Hopkins University Press, 1970). See Volume I for the two reports mentioned (pages 149–152, 208–211). Volume II contains the months before, during, and after the conference.

was enough. Liberating Nazi controlled areas generated more intelligence about the Holocaust, as well as creating refugees and displaced persons that the Allied armies had to deal with, whether officials wanted to do so or not.[43] Doing more militarily would have taken more planning and soldiers, both of which would have altered how Ike conducted the war.

Furthermore, even into 1944, the vast majority of Americans, including those in the field, knew very little of what they were about to discover in the camps. Part of that had to do with the sheer volume of war news. But there was also widespread refusal to believe earlier reports of extermination camps because Americans had a difficult time accepting the idea that a civilized people like the Germans would actually do such a thing. No one doubted that the Nazis had imprisoned their (long list of) opponents. What no one believed or conceived was that they were actively killing those prisoners.[44]

As Supreme Allied Commander, not only did Eisenhower have his own intelligence apparatus under the Supreme Headquarters Allied Expeditionary Force (SHAEF), but his office also received regular intelligence briefings from Washington and London. Ike believed Allied intelligence to be a real strength and that it greatly aided his prosecution of the war. Of course, for him to act on intelligence required not only the authorization to do so, but also that the reports he read actually carried information about the camps. As it turned out, there were blind spots in those reports. Because they were geared around topics such as the German forces in the path of Allied forces, other issues, including the camps, were not prioritized in the resulting intelligence reports. Even when, as historian Robert Sutton notes, many of those working as part of SHAEF's network to gather intelligence had family imprisoned by the Nazis.[45] As the war progressed, Ike came to believe that intelligence officers all too often became easily fixated on one thing, and then disregarded other information that did not fit their established narrative. Nowhere was this seen more clearly than with the Holocaust. Intelligence services might have known about the camps, but because knowing about what went on inside the camps or what the camps as a system might represent

---

43 Burleigh, *Moral Combat*, 438, 446–450.
44 Robert Moses Shapiro, editor, *Why Didn't the Press Shout? American and International Journalism During the Holocaust* (Newark: KTAV Publishing House, 1995), 4, 42.
45 Robert K. Sutton, *Nazis on the Potomac: The Top Secret Intelligence Operation that Helped Win World War II* (Philadelphia: Casemate, 2021), 171–172. Sutton highlights several Jewish Americans in the military intelligence apparatus who lost family members in the Holocaust and knew about the existence of the camps both personally and professionally by the time the United States was in the war, but who seemingly embraced the concept of winning the war to end the Holocaust, rather than seeking to make the camps themselves a war objective for the Allies.

was not considered a priority, they actually *knew* very little about the camps.⁴⁶ As Ike later put it, what he was told about the final solution prior to Ohrdruf was "only generally or through secondary sources . . . I have never at any other time experienced an equal sense of shock" as when he stepped into Ohrdruf, and the pieces all came together right in front of him.⁴⁷

Others had a fuller picture, earlier. As evidence of the Holocaust mounted, Henry Morgenthau, Jr., Roosevelt's Secretary of the Treasury, emerged as the leading voice for the United States to do something concrete to aid Nazi Germany's victims. A secular Jew, Morgenthau was an old friend and neighbor of President Roosevelt's. Starting in January 1944, Morgenthau began pushing the president to do more to help the Jews and end their slaughter, including condemning fellow Roosevelt appointees for their lack of action. Prodded by Morgenthau, the president eventually agreed to the creation of the War Refugee Board to help facilitate discussion about what to do with the displaced persons Eisenhower's armies were encountering as well as deal with issues relating to those in the Nazi camp system.⁴⁸ Headed by John Pehle at the outset, the WRB quickly expanded its original operational parameters. Authorized by Executive Order 9417, the board did not just resettle refugees, at places like Fort Oswego in New York, but also sought ways to preemptively save future refugees (i.e., Jews who were in German occupied Europe). While Pehle would later lament that the board's work was "little and late," they did likely save thousands of Jews from the Holocaust, financially supported Swedish diplomat Raoul Wallenberg in his efforts to do the same and prodded the Roosevelt Administration to do more than it had been doing previously.⁴⁹

Events were starting to outpace political discussion, however. As the WRB proposal was being formulated within the Treasury Department, a plan was made following the Bermuda Conference in 1943 to set up a Jewish refugee camp in North Africa. The question was, where. The British wanted to put camps in the

---

46 Kenneth Strong, *Intelligence at the Top: The Recollections of an Intelligence Officer* (Garden City: Doubleday and Company, 1969), 112, 179–180, 210, 324; Persico, *Roosevelt's Secret War*, 405–406; Ambrose, *Ike's Spies*, ix, 16–17; Wyman, *The Abandonment of the Jews*, 27, 321–323; "Transcript of Interview: Dwight D. Eisenhower and A. Ross Wallen, Friday 27 November 1964, for THE POINTER," DDE Post Presidential Papers, 1965 Signature File, Box 7, PR-3 Public Relations 3, Interview 11-27-64, NAID #12023937, Dwight D. Eisenhower Presidential Library, Abilene, Kansas.
47 Cornelius Ryan, *The Last Battle* (New York: Simon and Schuster, 1966), 329.
48 Beschloss, *The Conquerors*, 43, 56–58.
49 Rebecca Erbelding, *Rescue Board: The Untold Story of America's Efforts to Save the Jews of Europe* (New York: Anchor Books, 2018); "War Refugee Board," https://encyclopedia.ushmm.org/content/en/article/the-war-refugee-board, 7 September 2022. Pehle was one of the chief advocates for the War Department to authorize the bombing of Auschwitz.

American controlled sector, which included the French colonies of Morocco, Tunisia and Algeria. Though Eisenhower did not object to the idea, the War Department did. Officials expressed concern (shared by General George Patton) that Muslims in the area would rise up in protest if Jews were brought into the area. Eisenhower noted the objections, which were echoed by some French colonial officials. It took a year, but ultimately the camps were opened in 1944, though they only ever accommodated about 2,000 of the potential 5,000 refugees—and not all of those where Jews.[50]

Nor was the creation of the WRB without its critics. With the war turning in the Allies' favor, Congress, which was still controlled by Roosevelt's Democratic Party, began to issue statements about the Nazi camp system. With the 1944 general election looming, Republicans were prepared to make Hitler's treatment of Europe's Jews an election issue. After repeatedly being assured by the Roosevelt Administration that it had been doing everything in its power to save those in the camps, Congressman John Vorys of Ohio countered that if that were true, the War Refugee Board was an unnecessary expansion of the federal government. However, he continued, if the Board was indeed needed, then administration officials had been lying to Congress and the American people.[51] Members of the War and State departments, including some who sat on the Board, were also reluctant to see it actually do anything, whether because they embraced "winning the war solves the problem" thinking or because of anti-Semitism. And America's British allies saw the Board as merely an electoral move designed to shore up the Jewish vote for Roosevelt's attempted fourth term, all while putting pressure on London to open up Palestine to more Jewish immigration.[52]

Whether it was the progress of the war or the creation of the WRB, on March 24, 1944, Franklin Roosevelt was finally ready to issue a clear statement about the Holocaust. The president proclaimed: "In one of the blackest crimes of all history—begun by the Nazis in the day of peace and multiplied by them a hundred times in time of war—the wholesale, systematic murder of the Jews of Europe goes on unabated

---

50 Wyman, *The Abandonment of the Jews: America and the Holocaust*, 117; Breitman and Kraut, *American Refugee Policy and European Jewry*, 178; Ambrose, *Ike's Spies*, 39, 46–47; Breitman and Lichtman, *FDR and the Jews*, 247–249.
51 Hamerow, *Why We Watched*, 358–360; Jeffery C. Livingston, "Ohio Congressman John M. Vorys: A Republican Conservative Nationalist and Twentieth Century American Foreign Policy," (Doctoral Dissertation: University of Toledo, 1989), 143.
52 Wyman, *The Abandonment of the Jews: America and the Holocaust*, xi, 25, 206, 292–293; Gilbert, *Auschwitz and the Allies*, 173; Richard Breitman, Barbara McDonald Stewart, and Severin Hochberg, editors, *Refugees and Rescue: The Diaries and Papers of James G. McDonald, 1935–1945* (Indianapolis: Indiana University Press, 2009), 312; McKale, *Hitler's Shadow War*, 398–399; Hamerow, *Why We Watched*, 90–95, 110, 114, 158–159.

every hour . . . None who participate in these acts of savagery shall go unpunished." These were, the president said, "crimes against humanity." However, Roosevelt stopped far short of calling for direct action to save those in the camps. He still believed that the only way to stop the suffering, and try those guilty of crimes, was to win the war.[53]

A few months later, it was Eisenhower's turn to issue a statement. In September 1944, the Polish underground alerted the Allies that the Germans planned to slaughter those housed in the camps as they retreated. The War Refugee Board asked Eisenhower to make a statement warning the Nazis not to follow through on the threat. Pehle believed that if Ike issued the statement, not only would it be less "political" than if the president made it, but it would also have added weight because Eisenhower was both the Supreme Allied Commander and American forces would eventually be occupying a portion of Germany. The War Department initially denied the request, citing the fear that it would prompt the Nazis to actually kill Jews in the camps. It took five weeks to not only get the War Department to agree to allow Eisenhower to make the statement, after Roosevelt endorsed the idea, but also to work out the language used. An early draft warned the Nazis about harming "stateless persons 'whether they are Jewish or otherwise.'" The eventual wording, which Eisenhower approved, after consultation by both the State and War departments and the British, was not as precise, reading "without regard to their nationality or religious faith." To some critics the bureaucratic back and forth, as well as Ike's approval of the editing was proof that the SAC and those he reported to were complicit in the Holocaust. More likely it reflects a soldier being thrust into the politics of a war he was trying to fight, working within the chain of command, and the requisite bureaucratic hoops associated with both.[54]

---

[53] Statement by the President Regarding Atrocities of War, March 24, 1944, President's Personal File; 1-F; Press Releases-Drafts, 1944, Box 18, Franklin D. Roosevelt Presidential Library, Hyde Park, New York.; Wyman, *The Abandonment of the Jews: America and the Holocaust*, 58; Hamerow, *Why We Watched*, 319, 352–357; Beschloss, *The Conquerors*, 40–42, 59–63, 284.

[54] Rebecca Erbelding, *Rescue Board: The Untold Story of America's Efforts to Save the Jews of Europe* (New York: Anchor Books, 2018), 202; Wyman, *The Abandonment of the Jews: America and the Holocaust*, 257; Joseph W. Bendersky, *The "Jewish Threat": Anti-Semitic Politics of the U.S. Army* (New York: Basic Books, 2000), 340; Breitman and Lichtman, *FDR and the Jews*, 291; Breitman and Kraut, *American Refugee Policy and European Jewry*, 201; Breitman, Stewart, and Hochberg, editors, *Refugees and Rescue*, 323; "Folder 9, Statement by General Eisenhower," http://www.fdrlibrary.marist.edu/_resources/images/wrb/wrb1467.pdf, 26 June 2018. The Soviet Union was also asked to make a similar statement. See, "The Acting Secretary of State to the Charge in the Soviet Union," 30 October 1944, Foreign Relations of the United States, Diplomatic Papers, 1944, Europe, Volume I, accessed on 7 September 2022. The "charge" was diplomat George Kennan.

At last, on November 8, 1944, Eisenhower addressed the German people:

Germans! You have in your midst a great many men in concentration camps and forced labor battalions. Germans! Do not obey any orders, regardless of their source, urging you to molest, harm, or persecute them, no matter what their religion or nationality may be. The Allies, whose armies have already established a firm foot-hold in Germany, expect, on their advance, to find these people alive and unharmed. Heavy punishment awaits those who, directly or indirectly, and to whatever extent, bear any responsibility for the mistreatment of these people. May this serve as a warning to whoever at present has the power to issue orders.[55]

Saving the Jews was never a war aim. But Eisenhower's statement showed that it could work in tandem with winning the war. Even if more could and should have been done, ultimately, those around Roosevelt were correct that winning the war would end the Holocaust.[56] And winning the war was Ike's job.

The Resistance and the Perils of Unconditional Surrender

Eisenhower's statement expressed a hope that some Germans might be willing to resist the Nazi government, at the very least by refusing to murder Jews and other prisoners. Ike noted that during the Great War, the Kaiser had perhaps held out hope that President Woodrow Wilson's Fourteen Points might offer an easy peace. But by 1944, the Allies were clear that was not to be the case for Nazi Germany.[57] Ike's statement, as it turned out, came nearly four months too late and was hampered, in part, by both the actions of the German resistance itself and the Allies demand of unconditional surrender.

The Germany Eisenhower faced was a totalitarian dictatorship and a prime example of a functioning police state. However, Nazi domination of the nation took time to take root and both cultural and political opponents were eliminated or coopted from 1933 onward. By the dawn of 1939, Hitler had so consolidated power that viable opposition no longer existed, and the population of Germany was "obedient" to the Nazi government, having been trained and terrorized into compliance.[58]

---

55 *New York Times*, 8 November 1944.
56 Wyman, *The Abandonment of the Jews*, 353; Gilbert, *Auschwitz and the Allies*, viii.
57 Gunter Bischof and Stephen E. Ambrose, *Eisenhower and the German POWs: Facts Against Falsehood* (Baton Rouge: Louisiana State University Press, 1992), 32.
58 Dwork and van Pelt, *Auschwitz*, 171; Timothy Snyder, *Black Earth: The Holocaust as History and Warning* (New York: Tim Duggan Books, 2015), 290–291; Giles MacDonogh, *1938: Hitler's Gamble* (New York: Basic Books, 2009), ix, 78, 245. During the first six years of Hitler's rule, Germans doubled their alcohol consumption. The Nazi consolidation of power was stressful.

With the coming of the war, the only institution left that could openly challenge the Nazis was the Wehrmacht. The German military tradition was a formidable one and reached back to the rise of Prussia under leaders such as Frederick the Great and the wars of German unification between 1864 and 1871. The military had a history of defending the government and the social order, though during the interwar period, its loyalty was to the idea of the German Reich, not a particular style of government.[59] Elements of its ethos certainly fit nicely into the Nazi state—a return to military prominence and glory, the redemption of national honor from the Treaty of Versailles, even—to a degree—anti-Semitism.[60] And as long as Germany was winning the war, those feelings trumped latent qualms the high command might have about the particulars of Nazi policy, including the camps and the Holocaust. Indeed, when it came to killing Jews as partisans, the Wehrmacht were often willing accomplices.[61]

It was the impending reality of D-Day, even more than setbacks on the Eastern Front, that finally snapped some of the officer corps out of acquiescence with the regime. Few German officers believed they could hold the Atlantic Wall and most believed that the war was lost after June 1944. Simply put, the Wehrmacht could not stop the Allies.[62] While there had been talk of a military coup to save the nation, both in 1938 and again in 1940, it was the inevitability of defeat by 1944 that finally got a coherent conspiratorial ring together. Most of the members of what became known as the July 20th conspiracy were professional soldiers or intelligence officers, many of them were devout Christians, and some two-thirds had Prussian roots. In many ways, they were the remnants of a German military and cultural upper class that existed at the dawn of the twentieth century.[63] As Franz Halder, the Army chief of staff who was complicit in the plot, put it, "there was nobody in Germany who could liberate the German people except the military."[64]

The July 20th plotters, however, were just as divided as the resistance groups that had come before them. Many, though not all, were Western orientated, and

---

59 Christopher Clark, *Iron Kingdom: The Rise and Downfall of Prussia, 1600–1947* (Cambridge: Harvard University Press, 2006), 629.
60 Daniel J. Hughes and Richard L. Dinardo, *Imperial Germany and War, 1871–1918* (Lawrence: University Press of Kansas, 2018), xi, 2, 16, 30–31, 54–57, 65.
61 Peter Hoffmann, "Colonel Claus von Stauffenberg in the German Resistance to Hitler: Between East and West," *The Historical Journal*, 31(September 1988), 632; Hannah Arendt, *Eichmann in Jerusalem: A Report on the Banality of Evil* (New York: Penguin, 2006), 98.
62 Citino, *The Wehrmacht's Last Stand*, 7, 347–350.
63 Clark, *Iron Kingdom*, 667–670.
64 Robert Gellately, editor, *The Nuremberg Interviews: An American Psychiatrist's Conversations with the Defendants and Witnesses, Conducted by Leon Goldensohn* (New York: Vintage Books, 2005), 289.

advocated either outright surrender to the British and American forces or crafting a negotiated settlement that allowed them, and perhaps the Anglo-Americans, to continue the war against the Soviet Union. There were a few secret communists in their number, who doubted if the Western Allies would really accept such terms and preferred capitulation to the Soviets who were the more pressing military threat. Regardless, few of them seemed to appreciate or understand the notion of unconditional surrender and virtually all of them worried about being labeled as traitors to Germany—not to *Nazi* Germany but rather to the Fatherland—and thus violating their oaths as officers. They knew that killing Hitler would create a power vacuum that would need to be filled quickly by the armed forces, which meant Wehrmacht officers not in the circle needed to be brought in line as fast as possible.[65]

The plotters also realized they needed to acknowledge the crimes that the Nazi regime was committing in the name of the Germany people.[66] Some Germans who had seen or heard of the camps knew that in addition to the war now being lost, they had lost their honor as officers as well.[67] So, in their eventual proclamation, they said: "The persecution of Jews which has taken place in the most inhumane and ruthless, deeply shaming, and absolutely irredeemable forms shall be immediately ceased." As former Army Chief of Staff, and active July 20th plotter, Ludwig Beck had noted several years before, "final decisions about the nation's existence are at stake here; history will incriminate these leaders with bloodguilt."[68]

---

[65] Allen Welsh Dulles, *Germany's Underground* (New York: The Macmillan Company, 1947), 166–167; Peter M. Kaiser, "Uber die Wechselfeziehungen zwischen deutschem Widerstand und westlicher Alliierten-Politik order Warum der Zweite Weltkrieg nicht schon 1942/43 beendet wurde," in Georg Ahrweiler, Rainer Rilling, Rolf Schellhase, editors, *Soziologische Ausfluge: Festschrift fur Hans Jurgen Krysmanski zum 60. Geburtstag* (Westdeutscher Verlag, 1997), 148–168; Hoffmann, "Colonel Claus von Stauffenberg in the German Resistance to Hitler: Between East and West," 629–650; Arendt, *Eichmann in Jerusalem*, 98; Stephan Malinowski, *Nazis & Nobles: The History of a Misalliance* (New York: Oxford University Press, 2020), 337–342. Anglican Bishop George Bell, a friend of German anti-Nazi theologian Dietrich Bonhoeffer—who knew of the plot, attempted to get the British government to engage with the July 20 group—to no avail. See, Richard J. Evans, *The Third Reich at War* (New York: Penguin Press, 2010), 271.

[66] Elisabeth Wagner, editor, *Der General-Quartiermeister: Briefe und Tagebuchaufzeichnungen des General Quartiermeisters des Heeres General der Artillerie Eduard Wagner* (Munich: Gunter Olzog Verlag, 1963), 237; Steinert, *Hitler's War and the Germans*, 285.

[67] Bischof and Ambrose, *Eisenhower and the German POWs*, 17.

[68] The German Resistance Memorial Center has portions of the proclamation highlighted as part of its exhibit space. If you cannot visit Berlin, see https://www.gdw-berlin.de/en/home/, 17 December 2020.

However late they had come to it, and whether it was out of a sense of morality or patriotism, the July 20th plotters were ready to take the fateful step of trying to oust Hitler. Ultimately, their plan failed for several reasons. First and foremost, while Colonel Claus von Stauffenberg, who was one of the leaders of the plot, was successful in planting a bomb in Hitler's East Prussian headquarters, it did not kill the Nazi leader. As a result, the inner circle of the plot could not convince other officers to join them in a coup.[69] Further complicating the situation was Allied failure to "breakout" from Normandy, which had it occurred earlier, may have given the plotters extra leeway in convincing other military officers that a change in the government was needed.[70] As it turned out, the Nazis recovered quickly and brutally crushed the plotters. Several members of the Army General Staff were executed in the courtyard of the OKW headquarters in Berlin, while many more were arrested, tortured, and either killed outright or sent to concentration camps where most eventually died before the end of the war. All told, some 5,000 Germans were executed by the Nazis for connections, both real and imagined, to the July 20th plot.[71]

Another issue the plotters ran into was the Casablanca doctrine of 1943, which called upon Germany to unconditionally surrender to the Allies. While some in Washington thought the policy was problematic, President Roosevelt was firm in adhering to it. He believed there was no need to work with "Junkers" in order to defeat the Nazis. Germany would simply be crushed.[72] The degree to which the plotters, or even the average German, understood or appreciated what unconditional surrender as a doctrine was, is also important to note. Virtually no one, including some who worked within the German government, had reliable access to the outside world or to news that was not censored or controlled by the Nazis.[73] The doctrine likely precluded Field Marshal Erwin Rommel from seeking

---

[69] Ian Kershaw, *The End: Germany, 1944–1945* (New York: Penguin Books, 2011), 33–34.; Stephen G. Fritz, *Ostkrieg: Hitler's War of Extermination in the East* (Lexington: University Press of Kentucky, 2015), 470–472; Citino, *The Wehrmacht's Last Stand*, 205–207. See also, Antje Vollmer and Lars-Broder Keil, *Stauffenbergs Gefahrten: Das Schicksal der unbekannten Verschworer* (Berlin: Hanser, 2013).

[70] Crosswell, *Beetle*, 657–661.

[71] Joseph E. Persico, *Piercing the Reich: The Penetration of Nazi Germany by American Secret Agents during World War II* (New York: Viking Press, 1979), 78; *New York Times*, 19 July 1994; Steinert, *Hitler's War and the Germans*, 265; "The July 20, 1944 Plot to Assassinate Adolf Hitler," https://www.ushmm.org/wlc//en/article.php?ModuleId=10008294, 23 March 2018; Gerhard L. Weinberg, *World in the Balance: Behind the Scenes of World War II* (Hanover: University Press of New England, 1981), 145; Steinert, *Hitler's War and the Germans*, 273.

[72] Persico, *Roosevelt's Secret War*, 232–235.

[73] Persico, *Piercing the Reich*, 87.

a ceasefire with Eisenhower in the aftermath of the landings at Normandy. The July 20th plotters were equally frustrated by the doctrine when it came to attempting to make contact with Allied leaders, including Ike, in the lead up to the bomb plot.[74]

With their failure and the resulting crackdown, internal opposition was eliminated by the Nazis. Surviving the plot gave Hitler confidence that he could still turn the war around. Before the end of July, he became fixated on the Western front and began planning a counterattack he was sure would bring victory from defeat. The only way to end Hitler's rule, and the Holocaust, now was for the Allies to conquer Germany.[75] Winning the war to end the camps had become a self-fulfilling prophecy.

Letting Loose the Dogs of War

After the Normandy breakout and bringing General George Patton to command the Third Army in the south of France, Eisenhower adopted a broad front strategy for the Anglo-American forces. As Ike advanced across all of France, other Allied armies were fighting in Italy, where Rome was taken on June 5, just as the invasion of France had started. Additionally, new airfields were opening up, allowing for a growing bombing campaign over Germany itself. And then there were the advances the Red Army was making on the Eastern front. The Nazis were now seemingly pressed all around.[76]

---

74 Wagner, editor, *Der General-Quartiermeister: Briefe und Tagebuchaufzeichnungen des General Quartiermeisters des Heeres General der Artillerie Eduard Wagner* (Munich: Gunter Olzog Verlag, 1963), 234; Hoffmann, "Colonel Claus von Stauffenberg in the German Resistance to Hitler: Between East and West," 637–639; Kaiser, "Uber die Wechselfeziehungen zwischen deutschem Widerstand und westlicher Alliierten-Politik order Warum der Zweite Weltkrieg nicht schon 1942/43 beendet wurde," in Georg Ahrweiler, Rainer Rilling, Rolf Schellhase, editors, *Soziologische Ausflüge: Festschrift für Hans Jurgen Krysmanski zum 60. Geburtstag* (Westdeutscher Verlag, 1997), 168.
75 *New York Times*, 19 July 1994; Hoffmann, "Colonel Claus von Stauffenberg in the German Resistance to Hitler: Between East and West," 629–650; Persico, *Roosevelt's Secret War*, 413–419; Steinert, *Hitler's War and the Germans*, 265; "The July 20, 1944 Plot to Assassinate Adolf Hitler," https://www.ushmm.org/wlc//en/article.php?ModuleId=10008294, 23 March 2018; Weinberg, *World in the Balance*, 145.
76 Ambrose, *Ike's Spies*, 111. Allied arrival in Rome came too late for many of the city's Jews, with the population of the Jewish ghetto largely being rounded up and sent off to camps in October 1943—eight months before the city's capture. See, Overy, *Blood and Ruins*, 228–229.

Some Allied leaders were already thinking about the postwar world. Secretary of the Treasury Morgenthau got President Roosevelt's approval to make a trip to Europe in August 1944 to begin studying the situation in person. Morgenthau, of course, met with Eisenhower. The general, while seeing the delegation from Washington as something of a waste of his time, had little to say about the economics of a post-Nazi Europe. He did say "there must be no room for doubt as to who won the war. Germany must be occupied. More than this, the German people must not be allowed to escape a sense of guilt, of complicity in the tragedy that has engulfed the world. Prominent Nazis, along with certain industrialists must be tried and punished. Membership in the Gestapo and in the SS should be taken as prima facie evidence of guilt." Eisenhower knew that Morgenthau had criticized how he had handled Vichy France (and their treatment of Jews) in Northern Africa in 1942, and so his tough talk about Germany was both to blunt the Secretary's earlier comments as well as a growing anger at the mounting casualties his forces were taking. But the significance of Eisenhower's statement is that it was made prior to the discovery or liberation of any of the Nazi concentration camps.[77]

Ike's objective was not to meet with politicians, it was to fight and win the war. He knew that the fighting was not over even though the Allies were advancing.[78] For much of the late summer and into the fall, logistics was more a worry to the Anglo-Americans than the Germans were, as the Allies continually outran their supplies. After Paris was liberated in August 1944, the Allied advance stalled. The broad front strategy Ike had adopted was great for grinding the Germans down, but it did not offer a central point for the Allied armies to focus on and led to a diffusion of their supply lines that slowed the ultimate movement towards Germany.[79]

Eisenhower's strategy increasingly received criticism from his British allies. Field Marshall Bernard Montgomery believed he could win the war by Christmas if Eisenhower would simply follow his advice. At last, Eisenhower relented and authorized what became Operation Market Garden—a British led thrust into the Netherlands. Montgomery preferred to not debate "strategy with those who took

---

[77] Morgenthau Presidential Diaries (Digital) Volume 6, August 19, 1944, entry, Franklin D. Roosevelt Presidential Library, Hyde Park, New York; Rebecca Erbelding, *Rescue Board: The Untold Story of America's Efforts to Save the Jews of Europe* (New York: Anchor Books, 2018), 196; Beschloss, *The Conquerors*, 68–73.
[78] Eisenhower, editor, *Letters to Mamie*, 211.
[79] Citino, *The Wehrmacht's Last Stand*, 348, 440; Antony Beevor, *The Fall of Berlin 1945* (New York: Viking Press, 2002), 84, 203; Hitchcock, *The Bitter Road to Freedom*, 69; Pipes, *Ike's Final Battle*, 12–13.

exception to his views." He never understood the Americans he served with and under, in part because he believed himself their military superior in every way. He certainly failed to even attempt to cultivate a friendship with or to understand Ike. Montgomery's planning for Market Garden was off, and the operation failed as the Germans held. Once again, the Allied advance stalled. Many American commanders felt as though Montgomery accomplished little with what he had, while always demanding more, and diverted strength from American Generals George Patton and Omar Bradly where the extra men and supplies might have made more of a difference.[80]

Slowly but surely, the Allies regained their momentum. American forces even made it into Germany itself. After fighting in September and October of 1944, Aachen became the first German city to fall to the Allies. Here, Americans, including Eisenhower, learned new facets of the war. First, German civilians all denied membership in the Nazi Party or ever supporting Hitler. The GIs noted, however, that such statements came only after the city had been taken, block by block, and the Wehrmacht driven away. The Americans were no longer seen as liberators as they had been in France. Now, they were conquerors. As a result, both German civilians and military personnel had to be assured they would not be shot when they surrendered—showing how the citizens of the Reich had been conditioned both by the Nazis and the experiences of German forces on the Eastern front to what happened if one capitulated.[81]

Up until this time the Germans had largely failed to focus on what Ike was doing because of their need to stop the Soviets, which they were also failing to do.[82] All the evidence in front of Eisenhower seemed to indicate that the Germans were essentially defeated by the winter of 1944. More importantly, everyone, from Ike on down wanted to believe that assessment was true. Those beliefs are what made the Ardennes offensive, better known as the Battle of the Bulge, such a surprise.[83] The German assault might look like a desperate gamble, which it was, but it also made a good deal of sense for the Nazis to try something. By the

---

[80] Citino, *The Wehrmacht's Last Stand*, 340–344; James M. Gavin, *On To Berlin: Battles of an Airborne Commander, 1943–1945* (New York: The Viking Press, 1978), 257; Gelb, *Ike and Monty*, 358–359, 376–377, 390–391, 396–397, 420–429; Kershaw, *The End*, 58; S.M. Plokhy, *Yalta: The Price of Peace* (New York: Viking, 2010), 33. Historian Ian Kershaw blames Monty for the failure of the Anglo-American forces to win in the West earlier, see Kershaw, *The End*, 388.
[81] Merle Miller, *Ike the Soldier: As They Knew Him* (New York: Perigee Books, 1987), 704; Marcus J. Smith, *Dachau: The Harrowing of Hell* (Albuquerque: University of New Mexico Press, 1972), 30, 124.
[82] David Kahn, *Hitler's Spies: German Military Intelligence in World War II* (New York: Macmillan Publishing Company, 1978), 428.
[83] Citino, *The Wehrmacht's Last Stand*, 380.

end of 1944, they could not defeat the Soviets. The Eastern front was a holding action. The Nazis were actually in a stronger position on the Western front than Allied intelligence believed them to be, and Hitler thought that a counteroffensive might force Great Britain and the United States to accept a negotiated settlement short of total victory. The plan was built on the Wehrmacht's poor opinion of the American Army, whom they despised. Victory in the Ardennes was the last hope the Nazis had of achieving any sort of military victory or at least a negotiated stalemate.[84]

The reaction to the German assault showed Ike at his best. Next to D-Day, the opening days of the Bulge were likely the most stressful of the war for Eisenhower and his staff. The Americans were taken by surprise and were specifically targeted by the Germans. Many U.S. units were either new to the line or filled with replacements and were caught by surprise. Eisenhower felt that the Bulge was a major attack from the moment reports started to come in. He had always thought Hitler would not give up without a fight and saw no military utility in a feint. He skillfully moved men to the front to contain and then repel the German assault.[85] After the failure of the Bulge, while Hitler was still in charge, many within the Wehrmacht believed their only course of action was to hold off the Soviets in order to allow Germany to surrender to the Americans and British.[86] The Allied dagger was now prepared to plunge into the heart of the Third Reich, though Eisenhower was sure that as long as Hitler remained alive there was no possibility of an end to the war.[87]

The Red Army and the Camps

Eisenhower's experience at Ohrdruf was still some months away. However, his was not the first encounter the Allies had with the Holocaust in all its horror. That distinction belonged to the Red Army. The Soviet response as their forces

---

[84] Gavin, *On To Berlin*, 208; Ralph W. Hauenstein with Donald E. Markle, *Intelligence Was My Line: Inside Eisenhower's Other Command* (New York: Hippocrene Books, 2005), 114; Antony Beevor, *Ardennes 1944: Hitler's Last Gamble* (New York: Viking Press, 2015), 25, 369. By the Battle of the Bulge, the Nazis realized the threat that at least Eisenhower posed. Evidence was gathered that Ike was specifically targeted for assassination during the battle. See, Eisenhower, *How Ike Led*, 75–76.
[85] Eisenhower, *Crusade in Europe*, 342–343; Citino, *The Wehrmacht's Last Stand*, 394; Eisenhower, *Eisenhower: At War, 1943–1945*, xxv; Hauenstein and Markle, *Intelligence Was My Line*, 107; Ambrose, *Ike's Spies*, 129.
[86] Eisenhower, *Eisenhower: At War, 1943–1945*, 676.
[87] Eisenhower, *At Ease*, 312.

came upon camps in the East, was different in many respects and informed the shock and surprise that Eisenhower and other Allied leaders had when they encountered the Holocaust themselves. In some ways, the Soviet gulag system was similar to the Nazi concentration camps. Both Germany and the Soviet Union, after all, were police states. Whether under fascists or communists, "entire categories of people were removed from the orbit of reciprocal moral obligation," allowing the state to do whatever it wanted to them, and for citizens to turn a knowing blind eye towards the inhumanity which followed. It was through this lens that Soviet soldiers encountered the Holocaust.[88] If the American and British liberators thought they had seen the worst of the camps, they were wrong. Not only were the Soviets first to encounter the camp system, but they were also the ones who found the death camps. And they did it long before American troops stumbled into Ohrdruf.[89]

Getting to that point, however, was brutal. The war on the Eastern front was a ferocious contest for nearly four years. It was one "of annihilation, a war of scorched earth, mass deportation, and easy, public slaughter."[90] The Soviets were driven by a visceral hatred for the Germans and what they had done since the start of Operation Barbarossa. By the end of the war, over 27 million citizens of the Soviet Union were dead. More than two thirds of that total were civilians slain in the midst of a continent gone mad. Additionally, some three million Soviet prisoners of war died in Nazi German camps, largely on purpose.[91]

As the Soviets began to retake portions of their country, they heard stories of and saw for themselves what the Germans had done. "Their enemy," as historian Catherine Merridale notes, "seemed to rejoice in violence. Escaping refugees told

---

[88] Burleigh, *Moral Combat*, 80–81, 100–101; Timothy Snyder, *Bloodlands: Europe Between Hitler and Stalin* (New York: Basic Books, 2010), 403.

[89] Snyder, *Bloodlands*, 311–312; Catherine Merridale, *Ivan's War: Life and Death in the Red Army, 1939–1945* (New York: Metropolitan Books, 2006), 291. American forces had encountered a camp near Strasbourg, called Natzweiler, in November 1944—but they did not know exactly what they uncovered. The camp had been utilized not just for labor but also medical experimentation. The Americans were unsure of what to make of the hair collections, urns, preserved bodies, and skeletal specimens, alongside evidence of the execution and torture of prisoners. See, Rick Atkinson, *The Guns at Last Light: The War in Western Europe, 1944–1945* (New York: Henry Holt and Company, 2013), 371; Abzug, *Inside the Vicious Heart*, 3–9; Report, "Investigation Report on the Life in a German Extermination Camp (KZ Natzweilier) and the Atrocities Committed There, 1941–1944," C.D. Jackson Papers, Box 2 Atrocities-Paris (1); NAID#12005699, Dwight Eisenhower Presidential Library, Abilene, Kansas; Heather Pringle, *The Master Plan: Himmler's Scholars and the Holocaust* (New York: Hyperion, 2006), 265.

[90] Merridale, *Ivan's War*, 22, 133, 143. See also, Konrad H. Jarausch and Michael Geyer, *Shattered Past: Reconstructing German Histories* (Princeton: Princeton University Press, 2003), 142.

[91] Eisenhower, *Eisenhower: At War, 1943–1945*, 677; Merridale, *Ivan's War*, 4, 183, 290.

of mass shootings, the torturing of partisans. The Fascists drank and laughed as the corpses of their victims burned on gasoline-drenched pyres." Realizing that the Nazis sought their elimination, because of their ethnic heritage, was a revelation to many soldiers in the Red Army. The German atrocities "clarified" to Soviet citizens the concept of nationalism and of Mother Russia (now cloaked in communist red) for the first time since the Bolsheviks had seized power. The Red Army's soldiers were not interested in liberation, nor were they seen as liberators by many people in places like Ukraine or Poland, but increasingly they wanted retribution and revenge against the Nazis for what the Third Reich had done across Europe.[92]

By 1944, as the Germans retreated they started collapsing the camp system in an effort to both finish the final solution in fewer locations while also erasing evidence that places like Treblinka, Sobibor, and Belzec had ever existed as death camps.[93] As good as the Nazis often were at erasing evidence of their crimes, they were far from perfect at it and at times had been so successful in killing people that despite their best efforts, coupled with the advancing Soviet armies, evidence was uncovered. The Red Army, for example, found what was left of an estimated one hundred thousand bodies in the Babi Yar ravine near Kyiv.[94] Not long thereafter, they found Majdanek.

In July 1944, Soviet forces came upon the Majdanek concentration camp, near Lublin, Poland. They liberated less than 700 survivors. In existence since 1941, the extermination camp likely claimed around 100,000 victims directly, with an additional 100,000 dying in its sub-camp system. The Nazis used gas chambers to kill and then the crematorium to dispose of the bodies. The smell lingered in the air, causing "Lubliners to shut their windows. They could not breathe, and even with the windows shut they could not sleep," according to one account. The Soviets uncovered machines designed to grind bones into fertilizer, Zyklon B containers, and rooms full of shoes, spectacles, suitcases, toys, and other personal items. Realizing the potential propaganda value, the Soviets allowed reports about the camp's discovery to be broadcast back in the Soviet Union. While some Western reporters

---

[92] Merridale, *Ivan's War*, 128, 281–287, 380–381; Anita Kondoyanidi, "The Liberating Experience: War Correspondents Red Army Soldiers, and the Nazi Extermination Camps," *The Russian Review*, 69(July 2010), 443; Snyder, *Bloodlands*, 278, 284, 305–307.

[93] Merridale, *Ivan's War*, 232; Helm, *Ravensbruck*, 392, 490–491, 585; Hilberg, *The Destruction of the European Jews*, 630; Abzug, *Inside the Vicious Heart*, xi; Jon Bridgman, *The End of the Holocaust: The Liberation of the Camps* (Portland: Areopagitica Press, 1990), 11.

[94] Merridale, *Ivan's War*, 293. On September 29 and 30, 1941, the Nazis murdered nearly 34,000 of Kiev's Jews and dumped the bodies in the ravine. The Germans continued to kill and dump bodies into Babi Yar for much of the next two years.

picked up the story, few in the Allied nations actually grasped what the words and pictures of the former camp were telling them, and for the most part the story was either dismissed or forgotten in the avalanche of war news that summer. Minimal recognition in the western press remained the case even after the Soviets allowed American reporters to visit the camp a month after its liberation.[95]

At about the same time, Soviet forces came upon what was left of the Sobibor and Treblinka camps. Unlike at Majdanek, the SS were able to ship surviving prisoners to other camps ahead of the Red Army, with most ending up at Buchenwald. The Germans also systematically destroyed much of the evidence of what had happened there—the deaths of over 167,000 at Sobibor and over 800,000 at Treblinka.[96] However, the same was not true of the next major camp the Soviets uncovered: Auschwitz.

Founded in the 1200s on land that was at times Austrian and other times Polish, by the 1930s Auschwitz was a part of the mythic "German East" that the Nazis wanted to restore to the Reich. After the conquest of Poland, a camp was erected there that eventually became a complex of labor camps, medical experimentation programs, and extermination centers that covered some 25 square miles. If there was an example of industrialized death in the Holocaust, Auschwitz was it—over 1 million people died there during its few years of existence, most of whom were Jews. At its peak, the camp could exterminate and dispose of the corpses of 20,000 people per day.[97] By January 1945, the camp was in the line of the advancing Red Army. Some sixty thousand surviving inmates were ordered on a "death march" to other camps still safely in German hands; most of whom did not survive the

---

95 Atkinson, *The Guns at Last Light*, 184; Yehuda Bauer, "The Death-Marches, January-May, 1945,"*Modern Judaism*, 3(February 1983), 13; Frank Van Vree, *Performing the Past: Memory, History, and Identity in Modern Europe* (Amsterdam: Amsterdam University Press, 2010), 261; Merridale, *Ivan's War*, 294–295; Bridgman, *The End of the Holocaust*, 21; David A. Hackett, editor, *The Buchenwald Report* (Boulder: Westview Press, 1995), 1; Kondoyanidi, "The Liberating Experience: War Correspondents Red Army Soldiers, and the Nazi Extermination Camps," 444; Wyman, *The Abandonment of the Jews*, 324; Benjamin A. Lindsey, "Organized Crime Against Civilization: The Congressional Investigation of Liberated Concentration Camps in 1945," (Master's Thesis, University of Vermont, 2012), 15.
96 Hitchcock, *The Bitter Road to Freedom*, 288; Bridgman, *The End of the Holocaust*, 22, 28; Kondoyanidi, "The Liberating Experience: War Correspondents Red Army Soldiers, and the Nazi Extermination Camps," 453–454. See also, "Treblinka," https://muzeumtreblinka.eu/en/informacje/commemoration/, 22 September 2022.
97 Dwork and van Pelt, *Auschwitz*, 11, 169, 177, 401; Gellately, editor, *The Nuremberg Interviews*, 296–309; Hilberg, *The Destruction of the European Jews*, 578, 605–607; Read, *The Devil's Disciples*, 756, 798; Hitchcock, *The Bitter Road to Freedom*, 287; Saul Friedlander, *Nazi Germany and the Jews, 1933–1945—Abridged Edition* (New York: Harper Perennial, 2009), 360; Gutman and Berenbaum, editors, *Anatomy of the Auschwitz Death Camp*, vii–viii, 292, 540.

transport. The Germans attempted to then destroy the camp, but the Soviet advance was too swift. Rooms and boxcars full of shoes, clothes, and hair were found abandoned, though much of the records and the final crematorium were destroyed. On January 27, the 28th and 106th Corps of the First Ukrainian Front liberated the camp, finding less than 8,000 prisoners still alive. The Soviets labeled them "living skeletons" due to their physical appearance. The Red Army soldiers seemed "ashamed to be human" according to Primo Levi as they compared themselves to the newly liberated survivors.[98]

Until Ohrdruf in mid-April, the Americans and British had no firsthand experience with liberating the camps themselves. Their frame of reference tended to be what they knew of German prisoner of war camps, though of course, these two types of camps were quite different.[99] True, prisoners who attempted to escape faced the prospect of recapture and could be executed. Allied airmen were often killed either before they arrived or shortly after they came to camps and Jewish POWs were routinely executed. But by and large, unlike with Soviet POWs, Anglo-American prisoners were treated according to the rules of war.[100]

By the time Eisenhower visited and publicized Ohrdruf, the Soviets had found more camps: Sachsenhausen was liberated on April 22 and Ravensbruck eight days later. Both camps were about 50 miles from Berlin. Soviet forces also liberated Theresinstadt near Prague on May 8.[101] Like Ike and his men, the Soviets wrestled

---

[98] Donald M. McKale, *Nazis after Hitler: How Perpetrators of the Holocaust Cheated Justice and the Truth* (New York: Rowman and Littlefield Publishers, 2014), 38; Hilberg, *The Destruction of the European Jews*, 631–632; Dwork and van Pelt, *Auschwitz*, 9, 351; Gilbert, *Auschwitz and the Allies*, 337; Bridgman, *The of the Holocaust*, 26; Kondoyanidi, "The Liberating Experience: War Correspondents Red Army Soldiers, and the Nazi Extermination Camps," 455; Gutman and Berenbaum, editors, *Anatomy of the Auschwitz Death Camp*, 126; *Washington Post*, 27 January 2015; "The Soviet Liberation of Auschwitz: Firsthand Memories and Photos," https://www.rbth.com/history/331599-auschwitz-liberation-soviet, 18 June 2021.
[99] *Times of Israel*, 2 December 2015.
[100] Read, *The Devil's Disciples*, 822–823; Evelyn Le Chene, *Mauthausen: The History of a Death Camp* (London: Methuen and Company, 1971), 127; Beevor, *Ardennes 1944*, 368. Among those Americans who were captured by the Germans during the war was future author, Kurt Vonnegut. Taken prisoner during the Battle of the Bulge, like Eisenhower, Vonnegut came from a German-American family. When pressed by his captors about why he was making war on his "brothers," Vonnegut remembered thinking "he was a Hoosier, not a Kraut." Before he was eventually liberated, Vonnegut also survived the firebombing of Dresden. See, Ginger Strand, *The Brothers Vonnegut: Science and Fiction in the House of Magic* (New York: Farrar, Straus and Giroux, 2015), 3–13.
[101] Hackett, editor, *The Buchenwald Report*, 1; Edmund Szybicki, *To Hope or Die: From Warsaw Uprising to Sachsenhausen Concentration Camp and After, Memoirs of a Survivor* (London: Athena Press, 2007), 70–71; Helm, *Ravensbruck*, 19.

with the reality of what they found. One Soviet war correspondent who interviewed camp survivors noted that "they [the Germans] poured corpses like potatoes out of the trucks into the ditch. They fertilized fields with human ashes, walking like ploughmen and sowing ashes out of bags. This fertilizer stunk and contained small bits of human bones. When it rained, the fertilizer turned red." Like their American counterparts who also encountered the camps, Soviet soldiers found that their minds "refused to accept the reality" of what they were seeing and hearing. The camps were worse than what they had seen on the battlefields. One Russian soldier wrote his wife: "yesterday we examined a death camp . . . next to this exploded crematorium, there are bones, bones and piles of shoes several meters high. There are children's shoes in the pile. Total horror, impossible to describe."[102]

Seeing the camps caused the soldiers of the Red Army to hate the Nazis even more. The atrocities they learned of from camp survivors justified not liberation but retribution in their minds. Soviet commanders ordered their men to visit the camps as they marched west and expertly channeled "the solders' feelings of angst and revulsion at the camps . . . into military rage." A growing conviction amongst the Soviets was that all Germans, not just the Nazi leadership, were responsible for the camps. They saw themselves as fighting "fascist beasts." That notion pushed them forward into Germany itself. It turned them brutal, they knew it, and they allowed that feeling to consume the Third Reich and the territories they encountered. The orgy of destruction that followed, which included rape, murder, and looting, largely vanished from official Soviet records as the Great Patriotic War neared its conclusion.[103]

While Soviet officials used the camps to inspire the Red Army, they spent little time contemplating the suffering that happened there. The reason was simple enough: Soviet leader Joseph Stalin wanted no group, including Jews, to surpass his nation in the "hierarchy of suffering" caused by the Nazis. Furthermore, the Holocaust was a *European* tragedy that took the focus off of the very real death and destruction that occurred within the U.S.S.R. Stalin believed anything else was secondary.[104] Survivors might be helped, but they would not be celebrated or

---

[102] Kondoyanidi, "The Liberating Experience: War Correspondents Red Army Soldiers, and the Nazi Extermination Camps," 446, 457. See also V. Letnikov's quote on page 438 of the article.

[103] Merridale, *Ivan's War*, 295–296, 300–323; Kondoyanidi, "The Liberating Experience: War Correspondents Red Army Soldiers, and the Nazi Extermination Camps," 439–441, 445, 447, 451–452; Sean McMeekin, *Stalin's War: A New History of World War II* (New York: Basic Books, 2021), 628–629; Hitchcock, *The Bitter Road to Freedom*, 306–307; Snyder, *Bloodlands*, 316–318; Helm, *Ravensbruck*, 624–627; Beschloss, *The Conquerors*, 234.

[104] Merridale, *Ivan's War*, 289–293; McKale, *Nazis after Hitler*, 78; Snyder, *Bloodlands*, 341–342; Hamerow, *Why We Watched*, 372–373; Kondoyanidi, "The Liberating Experience: War Corre-

memorialized. Two Soviet journalists, Illya Ehrenburg and Vasily Grossman, attempted to do so, however. They compiled evidence about the Holocaust in the wake of the Red Army's advance. Their collected reports were published as *The Black Book of Soviet Jewry*. It was initially distributed to the Allies and within the Soviet Union. However, in Stalin's hierarchy of Nazi victims, the Soviets alone could dominate. *The Black Book* was purged from Eastern bloc libraries within a few years of the end of the war.[105]

Even though reports of camps and atrocities pre-date any camp being liberated, seeing them changed how the Allies viewed the war. However, the Soviets largely did not share information or intelligence about the camps with Eisenhower, despite Ike's "open-handed policy" with them. For all he gave the Soviets, he got very little information in return.[106] Nor did the Soviets go out of their way to include journalists in tours of the camps. Even when Western journalists were allowed to report on what the Soviets had uncovered, few had seen the camps for themselves meaning their stories were met with skepticism for fear that the Soviets were merely spinning anti-Nazi propaganda. What the Soviets did pass on failed to make an impression on their Western Allies. As Nikolaus Wachsmann notes, the Soviets made very little of the liberation of even Auschwitz, which is why the discovery of camps by the American and British were so monumental.[107]

Thus, the decisions Eisenhower made when he walked through Ohrdruf was shaped by both his war experience and lack of intelligence about the camps coming down from Washington and Moscow. He understood the suffering the Soviet Union had endured, as he eventually saw it for himself. In *Crusade in Europe*, he noted "the experience of Russia in World War II was a harsh one."[108] But Eisenhower, who was shocked by his encounter with the camps, did all he could to publicize the horrors he saw because they explained what was at stake in the war in a way mere propaganda and patriotic rhetoric never could. Soviet commanders, such as Mar-

---

spondents Red Army Soldiers, and the Nazi Extermination Camps," 461; Chris Bellamy, *Absolute War: Soviet Russia in the Second World War* (New York: Alfred A. Knopf, 2007), 644.
105 "The Black Book," https://collections.yadvashem.org/en/search-results/black%20book?page=1&subjects_search_en=The%20Black%20Book, 20 November 2022.
106 Bradley F. Smith, *Sharing Secrets with Stalin: How the Allies Traded Intelligence, 1941–1945* (Lawrence: University Press of Kansas, 1996), 170, 186–187, 234–235, 241.
107 Peter Caddick-Adams, *Fire and Steel: The End of World War Two in the West* (New York: Oxford University Press, 2022), 322; Mark Celinscak, *Distance from the Belsen Heap: Allied Forces and the Liberation of a Nazi Concentration Camp* (Toronto: University of Toronto Press, 2015), 41, 49–51; Merridale, *Ivan's War*, 294; Nikolaus Wachsmann, *KL: A History of the Nazi Concentration Camps* (New York: Farrar, Straus and Giroux, 2016), 10; Kondoyanidi, "The Liberating Experience: War Correspondents Red Army Soldiers, and the Nazi Extermination Camps," 453.
108 Eisenhower, *Crusade in Europe*, 469.

shal Ivan Konev, had neither the discretion nor the support in Moscow to make the world understand what they had discovered.[109] But Ike did.

Eisenhower's "zeal for waging a war for freedom never waned."[110] Nor did his days ever seem to end. He slept, on average, five hours a night, smoked up to four packs of cigarettes a day, and consumed copious amounts of coffee in between.[111] German intelligence during the war systematically misunderstood or was simply mistaken about the Supreme Allied Commander, much of it colored by their own racial propaganda that saw German-Americans like Ike as inferior to Aryans.[112] The reality was by the end of 1944, Ike was leading one of the greatest military alliances ever assembled. He was confident that 1945 would bring victory in Europe, and after the spring of that year, a place where the Nazi camp system was ended as an institution and its prisoners set free.[113]

---

[109] *Daily Mail*, 19 May 2010; *Washington Post*, 27 January 2015; "The Soviet Liberation of Auschwitz: Firsthand Memories and Photos," https://www.rbth.com/history/331599-auschwitz-liberation-soviet, 18 June 2021.
[110] William I. Hitchcock, *The Age of Eisenhower: American and the World in the 1950s* (New York: Simon and Schuster, 2018), 21.
[111] Pipes, *Ike's Final Battle*, 1–2.
[112] Richard Breitman, Norman J.W. Goda, Timothy Nafatli, and Robert Wolfe, *U.S. Intelligence and the Nazis* (New York: Cambridge University Press, 2005), 106; *Daily Mail*, 12 September 2019.
[113] Snyder, *Bloodlands*, 277.

Chapter 4
"First Hand Evidence"

In the aftermath of the Battle of Bulge, coupled with Soviet advances on the Eastern front, Nazi Germany entered its end game. Eisenhower's broad front strategy was working.[1] While politically Adolf Hitler was still firmly in control of the Third Reich, militarily Germany was on the verge of collapse. It would merely take a few, final pushes to topple Hitler's dictatorship. As this thought percolated through the Nazi hierarchy, German strategy continued to move from attempting to achieve victory from the jaws of defeat to vengeance. So, while the war staggered to an end, the Holocaust continued, making liberation even more important.

As Allied forces advanced, the Nazis scrambled to both conceal the existence of the camp system as well as finish the work of killing their enemies. However, the Germans soon realized that the camp network was too vast to erase in the time they had left. At the beginning of 1945, there were still roughly 700,000 prisoners in the concentration camp system—between 200,000 and 250,000 of whom were Jews—with 40,000 SS members keeping watch over them.[2] Many Nazis were proud of their work in the camps and did not want proof of what they had done destroyed. Furthermore, what was left of the Nazi war machine was increasingly reliant on the slave labor force the camps provided, meaning that not all the prisoners could be eliminated, nor the camps closed.[3] As historian Ian Kershaw notes, "It would be asking too much to look for coherence in Nazi policy in these weeks, even in the area of killing the defenseless, in which the regime excelled."[4]

What could be done, however, was to deny "the joy of liberation" to as many of the prisoners as possible. As Allied forces advanced in 1944, the Nazis began moving prisoners out of the Mittelraum camps, which were located in conquered territory, and back to camps closer to or even inside of Germany itself. While some

---

[1] Kenneth Strong, *Intelligence at the Top: The Recollections of an Intelligence Officer* (Garden City: Doubleday and Company, 1969), 198.

[2] Ian Kershaw, *The End: The Defiance and Destruction of Hitler's Germany, 1944–1945* (New York: The Penguin Press, 2011), 228. The resulting retraction of the camp system led to an interesting phenomenon—for the first time since 1940, there were suddenly large numbers of Jews inside of Germany again. The only difference being almost none of them were ethnically German. See, Peter Longerich, *Holocaust: The Nazi Persecution and Murder of the Jews* (New York: Oxford University Press, 2010), 416.

[3] Bradley Biggs, *Gavin* (Hamden, Connecticut: Archon Books, 1980), 60; Heather Pringle, *The Master Plan: Himmler's Scholars and the Holocaust* (New York: Hyperion, 2006), 276; Saul Friedlander, *Nazi Germany and the Jews, 1933–1945—Abridged Edition* (New York: Harper Perennial, 2009), 417–418.

[4] Kershaw, *The End*, 230, 330–331.

Nazi diehards may have believed they were preserving the labor force, others, including Heinrich Himmler, saw the prisoners as potential bargaining chips. And though some prisoners were transported by trains that were diverted from military purposes, many more were forced to march on foot in the middle of winter with little clothing or food to sustain them. Guards were told to kill any stragglers and increasingly there was little concern about what to do with the bodies. These were death marches.[5] As Yehuda Bauer notes, the marches "were intended to continue the mass murder in the concentration camp by other means."[6]

Indeed, the liquidation and evacuation of the camps unleashed a new wave of brutality among the Nazis. Whatever restraint had once existed was now gone. Whether on the march or in the bulging camps, prisoners were routinely beaten to death, shot, and in at least one instance, locked in a building and burned alive. Prior to the marches, the Nazis killed those they thought were unfit for continued labor. In some camps, this meant those in the hospitals were murdered as well—though in others, those too ill to march were simply left to die, ironically meaning they were among the first liberated. Until Allied soldiers appeared though, the Germans maintained their grip on the prisoners.[7]

The Reich was descending into chaos as spring 1945 approached. The death marches, fleeing German civilians and military personal clogged the roadways. Now the veil of what happened in the camps was brought forth for the German people to see in full. Prisoners were killed in front of civilians, who did nothing to

---

[5] Michael Beschloss, *The Conquerors: Roosevelt, Truman and the Destruction of Hitler's Germany, 1941–1945* (New York: Simon and Schuster, 2002), 203; Yehuda Bauer, "The Death-Marches, January-May, 1945,"*Modern Judaism*, 3(February 1983), 1, 5, 7; Max Hastings, *Inferno: The World at War, 1939–1945* (New York: Alfred A. Kopf, 2011), 600; Andre Seillier, *A History of the Dora Camp* (Chicago: Ivan R. Dee, 2003), 242; Sarah Helm, *Ravensbruck: Life and Death in Hitler's Concentration Camp for Women* (New York: Nan A. Talese Doubleday, 2014), 584; Evelyn Le Chene, *Mauthausen: The History of a Death Camp* (London: Methuen and Company, 1971), 149; Kershaw, *The End*, 229–230; William I. Hitchcock, *The Bitter Road to Freedom: A New History of the Liberation of Europe* (New York: Free Press, 2008), 293–295.
[6] Bauer, "The Death-Marches, January-May, 1945," 9.
[7] Nicholas Stargardt, *The German War: A Nation Under Arms, 1939–1945, Citizens and Soldiers* (New York: Basic Books, 2015), 516; Marcus J. Smith, *Dachau: The Harrowing of Hell* (Albuquerque: University of New Mexico Press, 1972), 94; Rick Atkinson, *The Guns at Last Light: The War in Western Europe, 1944–1945* (New York: Henry Holt and Company, 2013), 602; Kershaw, *The End*, 228, 332–335; Joseph E. Persico, *Piercing the Reich: The Penetration of Nazi Germany by American Secret Agents during World War II* (New York: Viking Press, 1979), 276, 314; Longerich, *Holocaust*, 414; David P. Boder, *I Did Not Interview the Dead* (Urbana, IL: The University of Illinois Press, 1949), 21; Bauer, "The Death-Marches, January-May, 1945," 6.

stop the executions.[8] Despite later denials, by 1945, the Holocaust was already an open secret within Germany. Soldiers home on leave from the Eastern Front brought with them news of the work of the Einsatzgruppen and the mass murders. Civilians, often wives, who visited husbands who worked in the camp system or knew the truth. The cities and towns near the camps had seen them as an economic stimulus when Germany was winning the war and had long known the conditions prisoners lived and died under. Residents who lived in the nearby communities knew that shifting winds brought ash clouds from the crematoriums into their communities, and they knew their children played games like "camp guards and prisoners" in the streets – streets that were often filled with prison work details who might be either on their way to or from factories, clearing rubble, or defusing Allied bombs that had failed to explode. All these things were proof of widespread knowledge of the Holocaust.[9]

It was the liberating Allied forces who did not know about the Holocaust. Few Americans had any idea what a concentration camp in the German context was—nor of the variety of the camps within the German system.[10] As historian David Kennedy noted, Americans "knew some facts, but facts did not necessarily mean understanding."[11] Even the facts they did know, such as after the Soviet discovery of the death camps, as we have seen, were disputed. For Americans, per-

---

8 Edmund Szybicki, *To Hope or Die: From Warsaw Uprising to Sachsenhausen Concentration Camp and After, Memoirs of a Survivor* (London: Athena Press, 2007), 80; Kershaw, *The End*, 334–336.
9 Michael Burleigh, *Moral Combat: Good and Evil in World War II* (New York: Harper Collins Publishers, 2011), 440; Friedlander, *Nazi Germany and the Jews*, 361–363; Robert Gellately, editor, *The Nuremberg Interviews: An American Psychiatrist's Conversations with the Defendants and Witnesses, Conducted by Leon Goldensohn* (New York: Vintage Books, 2005), 82; Eric A Johnson and Karl-Heinz Reuband, *What We Knew: Terror, Mass Murder, and Everyday Life in Nazi Germany, An Oral History* (New York: Basic Books, 2005), 316; Raul Hilberg, *The Destruction of the European Jews* (Chicago: Quadrangle Books, 1961), 624; Theodore S. Hamerow, *Why We Watched: Europe, America, and the Holocaust* (New York: W.W. Norton & Company, 2008), 295–296; Hastings, *Inferno*, 489; Marlis G. Steinert, *Hitler's War and the Germans: Public Mood and Attitude During the Second World War* (Athens, OH: Ohio University Press, 1977), 140–141; Persico, *Piercing the Reich*, 325–326.
10 John C. McManus, *Hell Before Their Very Eyes: American Soldiers Liberate Concentration Camps in Germany, April 1945* (Baltimore: Johns Hopkins University Press, 2015), 2–3. The German camps were not the same, for example, as the internment camps for Japanese-Americans the Roosevelt Administration created during the war. See, Joseph E. Persico, *Roosevelt's Secret War: FDR and World War II Espionage* (New York: Random House, 2001), 440; Leila Levinson, *Gated Grief: The Daughter of a GI Concentration Camp Liberator Discovers a Legacy of Trauma* (Brule, Wisconsin: Cable Publishing, 2011), 88.
11 David M. Kennedy, *Freedom From Fear: The American People in Depression and War, 1929–1945* (New York: Oxford University Press, 1999), 794.

haps especially, the idea that Jews were being killed just because they were Jews seemed hard to comprehend.[12]

Until he arrived in Ohrdruf, the picture remained hazy even for Eisenhower. With American forces inside Germany though, the pieces of information being put together by Allied intelligence was getting clearer. In addition to Army Intelligence (G-2) the evidence arriving on his desk was increasingly being provided by the Office of Strategic Services, the forerunner of the Central Intelligence Agency, as well as from Washington. Thanks to OSS agents, Ike knew that the Nazis were trying to keep a forced labor population out of Allied hands—so there was some knowledge of the death marches.[13] However, the OSS had significant blind spots including those created by focusing on information, and disruption of, the Nazi capacity to wage war. The OSS might know about prison labor, but it cared only about the labor—not about the camp system that provided it. Allied intelligence, in other words, was not looking for, and thus largely did not generate, reports on the Holocaust.[14] Even when some Nazis were explicit, such as when an offer was made to ransom Hungarian Jews in 1944 rather than have them face "extermination and deportation," Allied intelligence failed to understand the Germans meant exactly what they said. Intelligence officers focused instead on the goods the Nazis demanded – trucks, soap, and coffee – as proof that things were getting desperate inside of Germany.[15]

However, that is not to say that the OSS had no information about the Holocaust. It did gather intelligence about the camps and the organization documented how Germany looted the countries it had conquered. They also learned of operations the Nazis conducted to round up Jews and transport them to the camps. The OSS reports were passed up the chain of command, where they often met with skepticism in Washington. The Joint Chiefs of Staff, for example, did not believe a new intelligence organization was needed—and cast doubt on many of

---

12 Donald M. McKale, *Hitler's Shadow War: The Holocaust and World War II* (New York: Cooper Square Press, 2002), 400, 414.
13 Earl F. Ziemke, *The U.S. Army in the Occupation of Germany, 1944–1946: Army Historical Series* (Washington, D.C., Center of Military History United States Army, 1975), 168.
14 Persico, *Piercing the Reich*, 8; Neal H. Petersen, editor, *From Hitler's Doorstep: The Wartime Intelligence Reports of Allen Dulles, 1942–1945* (University Park, PA: The Pennsylvania State University Press, 1996), 296, 460, 570; Allen Welsh Dulles, *Germany's Underground* (New York: The Macmillan Company, 1947), 71; Stephen E. Ambrose, *Ike's Spies: Eisenhower and the Espionage Establishment* (Jackson: University of Mississippi Press, 1999), 143.
15 The Ambassador in Turkey to the Secretary of State, 25 May 1944, Foreign Relations of the United States, Diplomatic Papers, 1944, Europe, Volume I, accessed on 7 September 2022.

the OSS reports, meaning OSS information rarely garnered enough support to prompt an order to Eisenhower.[16]

So, it took Ohrdruf to change the narrative. Soldiers from Eisenhower on down to privates were seeing the camps for themselves. The Supreme Allied Commander knew that during the Great War propaganda had manufactured atrocities. What he and his men saw were real examples of inhumanity on a nearly unprecedented scale.[17] As future historians noted, "clearly Eisenhower was appalled by what he saw."[18] By the spring of 1945, Ike hated the Germans. He hated them for the war, for continuing to fight after it was clear they were defeated. He hated them for the destruction they had caused and for the destruction fighting them caused. And now he hated them for what he saw in the camps.[19] On April 15, Ike wrote to Mamie: "The other day I visited a German internment camp. I never dreamed that such cruelty, bestiality, and savagery could really exist in this world! It was horrible."[20] Until that day, Ike had largely seen the war in sports ("us vs. them") and nationalistic ("good vs. bad") terms. Ohrdruf gave his perspective on the war a new moral hue that never left him.

Repulsion over what was discovered in the camps carried over to others who now wished that they had known more earlier. U.S. Army Colonel Ralph Hauenstein, who served as chief of the intelligence branch for the European Theater of Operations noted after the war: "At no time during the war did ETOUSA G-2 receive any intelligence regarding the Holocaust activities in Europe. The British had gained some indications of these atrocities through their interception of ULTRA messages, but these reports were carefully censored before they were passed on to us." When Hauenstein viewed Dachau, he was "appalled" that it

---

16 Persico, *Piercing the Reich*, 22, 311, 318; David Kahn, *Hitler's Spies: German Military Intelligence in World War II* (New York: Macmillan Publishing Company, 1978), 300–301; Petersen, editor, *From Hitler's Doorstep*, 16–17, 50–51.

17 David Eisenhower, *Eisenhower: At War, 1943–1945* (New York: Random House, 1986), 761; Stephen E. Ambrose, *Citizen Soldiers: The U.S. Army from the Normandy Beaches to the Bulge to the Surrender of Germany, June 7, 1944–May 7, 1945* (New York: Simon & Schuster, 1997), 462.

18 Gunter Bischof and Stephen E. Ambrose, *Eisenhower and the German POWs: Facts Against Falsehood* (Baton Rouge: Louisiana State University Press, 1992), 16.

19 Bischof and Ambrose, *Eisenhower and the German POWs*, 33.

20 John S. D. Eisenhower, editor, *Letters to Mamie* (Garden City: Doubleday & Company, 1978), 248.

"could have existed beneath our American intelligence radar."[21] It was obvious the Allies had known the parts but not the whole.[22]

Murder on the scale Germany conducted via the camps was simply impossible for Americans, from Eisenhower on down, to comprehend in the abstract.[23] As General James Gavin noted, "we all read of conditions of these Axis controlled countries, but none of us really appreciated how deplorable things were until we encountered conditions here."[24] Once seen, the camps raised serious questions about what the Allies had known and what they should have done.[25] As David Eisenhower wrote of his grandfather, his "mind is unknown. With access to all the information at Allied disposal, few had yet been in closer touch than Eisenhower with the full extent of Europe's degradation in the grip of Nazism, so he knew Ohrdruf was just one of many such places. Eisenhower and his colleagues in the high command also knew that the mass killings and work-torture deaths had reached a peak in the winter of 1944–1945 . . . . Had enough been done?"[26] The answer was, in retrospect, no. It was also a moot question to ask, for by the time Eisenhower visited Ohrdruf, there was less than a month left in the war. Still, in the coming weeks, more camps were discovered, which meant the question continued to linger over Ike. "The illusions of a glorious finish," his grandson noted, "ended on April 12, 1945."[27]

---

21 Ralph W. Hauenstein with Donald E. Markle, *Intelligence Was My Line: Inside Eisenhower's Other Command* (New York: Hippocrene Books, 2005), 130–137. Though Hauenstein does not say when he visited Dachau specifically, his recollections of interactions with both prisoners and guards, as well as the pictures he took, indicate that it was very early on after the camp's liberation. Additionally, his comments about the British cast doubt on how comprehensive Kenneth Strong's reports to Eisenhower were when it came to the Holocaust.
22 Peter Novick, *The Holocaust in American Life* (New York: Houghton Mifflin, 1999), 64–65.
23 Russell F. Weigley, *Eisenhower's Lieutenants: The Campaign of France and Germany, 1944–1945* (Bloomington: Indiana University Press, 1981), 696; Ben Shephard, *After Daybreak: The Liberation of Bergen-Belsen, 1945* (New York: Schocken Books, 2005), 190–191; Robert H. Abzug, *Inside the Vicious Heart: Americans and the Liberation of Nazi Concentration Camps* (New York: Oxford University Press, 1987), 10, 15.
24 Michael Hirsh, *The Liberators: America's Witnesses to the Holocaust* (New York: Bantam Books, 2010), 105; Biggs, *Gavin*, 50.
25 Bauer, "The Death-Marches, January-May, 1945," 19; Szybicki, *To Hope or Die*, 49; Samantha Power, *"A Problem from Hell": America and the Age of Genocide* (New York: Basic Books, 2002), 35.
26 Eisenhower, *Eisenhower: At War, 1943–1945*, 762–763. As Laurence Rees notes, the Allied advance—rapid as it was in the final months/weeks of the war—only contracted the camp system, it did little to save the prisoners—even if it was often portrayed as the ultimate justification for "winning the war to stop the killing." See Rees, *The Holocaust: A New History* (New York: Public Affairs, 2017), 405–409.
27 Eisenhower, *Eisenhower: At War, 1943–1945*, 761; Ambrose, *Citizen Soldiers*, 462.

The Horrors of Buchenwald

The final month of the war was a blur of activity. Ohrdruf was liberated on April 4, 1945, and Eisenhower visited the camp just over a week later. At the same time, Ike was on his way to Ohrdruf, American forces were liberating the camp it was attached to: Buchenwald. The large camp near Weimar became "the first major concentration camp to fall into the hands of the Western Allies while it still had a full population of prisoners."[28]

Buchenwald was located in the woods outside of Weimar. But these were not just any German woods, they were the very forest where Goethe had walked. The camp was originally opened as a place for political reeducation and the SS used the different prisoners' political allegiances to control the population by pitting groups against one another.[29] Buchenwald was no death camp like Auschwitz, but it eventually became a labor and prison camp where inmates might be worked or tortured to death.[30]

The beginning of the end at Buchenwald started on March 30, when American units arrived in Nordhasuen, near the Harz Mountains. Their objective was to secure V-1 and V-2 rocket production facilities that were located in the area. What they did not expect to find was the slave labor that worked in those factories. The smell of death led them to the nearby town of Mittelbau-Dora, where a concentration camp was located.[31] Like Ohrdruf, Dora was merely a sub-camp within the Buchenwald camp network.[32]

Prisoners at Buchenwald first learned of Allied advances near them the next day, April 1, when reports arrived at the camp that American tanks were some 40 miles away. At least some of the prisoners knew that when the Soviets had approached Auschwitz, the Germans had killed, or at least attempted to kill,

---

[28] Hirsh, *The Liberators*, 97; Peter Caddick-Adams, *Fire and Steel: The End of World War Two in the West* (New York: Oxford University Press, 2022), 328; McManus, *Hell Before Their Very Eyes*, 25; David A. Hackett, editor, *The Buchenwald Report* (Boulder: Westview Press, 1995), 1.

[29] Abzug, *Inside the Vicious Heart*, 45–47; McManus, *Hell Before Their Very Eyes*, 28–29; Neil MacGregor, *Germany: Memories of a Nation* (New York: Vintage Books, 2014), 458–473.

[30] McManus, *Hell Before Their Very Eyes*, 41–42; Johnson and Reuband, *What We Knew*, 99; Ferenc Laczo, "'I could hardly wait to get out of this camp, even though I knew it could only get worse until liberation came': On Hungarian Jewish Accounts of the Buchenwald concentration Camp from 1945–1946," *The Hungarian Historical Review*, 2(Ethnicity, 2013), 617.

[31] Ambrose, *Citizen Soldiers*, 461–462; Dan Stone, *The Liberation of the Camps: The End of the Holocaust and Its Aftermath* (New Haven: Yale University Press, 2015), 67; Abzug, *Inside the Vicious Heart*, 30–31; Hirsh, *The Liberators*, 57.

[32] Buchenwald's network included over 100 forced labor camps spread out over central/southeastern Germany, of which Ohrdruf and Dora were but two.

those who were not healthy enough to be marched out. Resistance to orders began to stiffen. The prisoners had been organizing themselves since late 1944 for the possibility of liberation. In those months, as it became obvious that the war would end with Germany's defeat, they noticed a decline in the effectiveness of the SS as an organization. Even then, the Nazis were still more than capable of killing hundreds of prisoners at a time if they so desired, but their edge was now off.[33]

SS Colonel Hermann Pister, the German commandant at Buchenwald, was ordered to liquidate the camp in light of American advances. However, he feared both disobeying the Nazi hierarchy as well as his fate if he was captured by the Americans. He opted to ship some 20,000 prisoners to other camps, chiefly Dachau, Flossenburg, and Theresinstadt, in early April—many of them Jews, most of whom died on their way. He opted not to kill the remaining prisoners, nor did he order explosives planted to destroy the camp. He did authorize his men to murder the prisoners in the camp jail, had the camp's records destroyed, and ordered bloodstains scrubbed clean or painted over. Pister himself stayed busy making plans to escape before he could be captured.[34]

On April 11, Combat Team 9 of the 9th Armored Infantry Battalion, Sixth Armored Division of Third Army moved into the nearby town of Hottelstedt. Capturing several SS men, the Americans were surprised when a group of fifty former prisoners emerged from the woods and tried to seize the Germans themselves. A small detachment of Americans was sent with the prisoners to the location of a camp, some two miles away.[35] Knowing the Americans were near, most of the SS staff had already abandoned Buchenwald, running up a white flag, and fleeing into the nearby forest. Shortly after 4pm, the Americans arrived at the camp's gates. As U.S. forces entered Buchenwald, they came under sporadic sniper fire. After securing the camp, the liberators found 21,000 prisoners still alive—4,000 of whom were Jews, and 700 of whom were children. The prisoners were living on a diet of 600 calories a day. American soldiers had to remind themselves the living skeletons before them were "human beings."[36]

---

[33] Hackett, editor, *The Buchenwald Report*, 3, 96–99.
[34] McManus, *Hell Before Their Very Eyes*, 34–35; Hackett, editor, *The Buchenwald Report*, 3–4, 100–104; Laczo, "'I could hardly wait to get out of this camp, even though I knew it could only get worse until liberation came': On Hungarian Jewish Accounts of the Buchenwald concentration Camp from 1945–1946," 627–628.; Abzug, *Inside the Vicious Heart*, 48. Pister was eventually captured, tried, convicted, and sentenced to death. He died of a heart attack in 1948 before he could be executed.
[35] Abzug, *Inside the Vicious Heart*, 49.
[36] Hitchcock, *The Bitter Road to Freedom*, 296–297; Atkinson, *The Guns at Last Light*, 603; Wilson Canafax, oral history, Dallas Holocaust Museum; M/Sgt Hubert V. Cook, 555th Signal Battalion, Photo box 4 1995.28 Cook Photographs: Buchenwald 1945 file, Dallas Holocaust Museum.

It was only with the arrival of the Americans that the prisoners, who had been secretly arming themselves, "self-liberated," capturing many of their former tormentors. It was hardly surprising having seen "man's inhumanity to man," as Rudy Baum of the 6th Armored put it, that the prisoners killed some eighty camp guards and personnel. They did so with the tacit approval of their American liberators.[37] As the 6th Armored moved on, American intelligence officers arrived at the camp. But for two days, Buchenwald was administered by its former prisoners. Finally, on April 13, the Army took over the camp officially and provided prisoners with medicine and food as they also worked to assure the proper disposal of bodies. Some of the survivors were so delirious from the trauma they had endured, and the lack of food and rampant illnesses, that they were unsure what to make of the arrival of American soldiers and their generosity.[38]

General Patton's anger towards the Nazis grew as reports about Buchenwald made it to him. In a letter to Eisenhower dated just four days after the camp's liberation, Patton noted, "We have found at a place four miles north of Weimar a similar camp [to Ohrdruf], only much worse. The normal population was 25,000, and they died at the rate of about a hundred a day. The burning arrangements, according to General Gay and Colonel Codman who visited it yesterday, were far superior to those which they had at Ohrdruf." Patton went on to write that "honestly, words are inadequate to express the horror of those [camps] institutions." He described Buchenwald's liberated prisoners as "animated mummies" who were "too feeble" to cheer (though they tried) as the American forces came into the camp. Patton elaborated:

> The place where they [the Nazis] had apparently put the finishing touches on those who had died or were about to die. In a basement which was entered by a chute, they had a number of iron hooks on the wall like those you hang the side of beef on. To these hooks they had a short piece of stout cord with a loop spliced on each end. This was put around a man's neck. Two men then lifted him and the loops were placed over the hook. If anyone showed signs of life, they had a club with a potato masher with which they bashed in the brains. Upstairs there were six furnaces much like a baker's oven, connected with the basement by an elevator. Apparently, they put six bodies on the elevator at a time, hoisted them up to the furnaces, and put them in.[39]

---

37 Hackett, editor, *The Buchenwald Report*, 4; Abzug, *Inside the Vicious Heart*, 52; Rudy Baum, oral history, Dallas Holocaust Museum.
38 Hackett, editor, *The Buchenwald Report*, 5–6; Johnson and Reuband, *What We Knew*, 33.
39 Letter, General Patton to General Eisenhower, April 15, 1954, Dwight D. Eisenhower's Pre-Presidential Papers, Principal File, Box 91, Patton George S. Jr. (1): NAID#12007734, Dwight Eisenhower Presidential Library, Abilene, Kansas; George S. Patton, Jr., *War as I Knew It* (Boston: Houghton Mifflin Company, 1947), 299–301; Martin Blumenson, editor, *The Patton Papers, 1940–1945* (Boston: Houghton Mifflin Company, 1974), 686–687. Eisenhower agreed with Patton that people should see the camps. Alfred D. Chandler, Jr., editor, *The Papers of Dwight David Eisenhower: The War Years IV* (Baltimore: The Johns Hopkins Press, 1970), 2621.

As had already become the standard Eisenhower endorsed practice, the Americans forced area residents to tour Buchenwald. The Germans living near the camp claimed to know nothing of what happened there.[40] And of course, the Americans knew they were lying, and it left a lasting impression on many soldiers. As one of Patton's aide's put it: "No race except a people dominated by an ideology of sadism could have committed such gruesome crimes."[41]

Per Eisenhower's orders, American news reporters were brought to Buchenwald. The journalists found there were no words they could use to really describe what they saw. As Percy Knauth of *Time Magazine* put it after visiting the camp, "You just can't understand it, even when you've seen it." Knauth's sentiments were echoed by CBS's Edward R. Murrow, who told his radio listeners: "I pray you believe what I have said about Buchenwald." Murrow considered his report "mild" compared to what he saw at the camp, but he also recognized that it was impossible to actually convey what he had seen to those who had not witnessed it themselves.[42]

On April 16, SHAEF received a report about Buchenwald, authored by Brigadier General Eric F. Wood, Lt. Col. Charles H. Ott, and CWO S.M. Dye. The report called April 11 "a red-letter day for the surviving inmates." The Americans discovered that the "intelligentsia and 'leadership'" from across Europe were in the camp, as the Nazis had the goal of eliminating Europe's "best liberal or democratic" leaders. There was also direct evidence, based on documents recovered and survivor testimony, that Jews were treated worse than the rest of the camp population. The "body disposal plant" was an example of "German industrial efficiency," with the potential to incinerate 400 bodies a day. The Americans also found intact crematoriums, execution rooms, and a hospital used for medical experiments on prisoners."[43] The report made an important argument, one that Americans would latch on to in the years to come when thinking about the Holocaust. While it was true that Buchenwald was not a death camp the way Auschwitz was, it was still "an extermination factory," where "mere death was not bad enough for anti-Nazis." Here, inmates were starved, worked hard, abused, beaten,

---

40 McManus, *Hell Before Their Very Eyes*, 129; Giles MacDonogh, *After the Reich: The Brutal History of the Allied Occupation* (New York: Basic Books, 2007), 87.
41 Blumenson, editor, *The Patton Papers, 1940–1945*, 687.
42 McManus, *Hell Before Their Very Eyes*, 60–61; Abzug, *Inside the Vicious Heart*, 127; Beschloss, *The Conquerors*, 223; Michael Neiberg, *Potsdam: The End of World War II and the Remaking of Europe* (New York: Basic Books, 2015), 25.
43 Report, "Inspection of German Concentration Camp for Political Prisoners located at Buchenwald," Walter Bedell Smith Collection of World War II documents, Box 36, Inspection of German Concentration Camp at Buchenwald 4/16/45; NAID#12007803, Dwight Eisenhower Presidential Library, Abilene, Kansas; Hackett, editor, *The Buchenwald Report*, 1.

tortured, forced to live in cramped barracks, and suffer from camp diseases. As horrific as the gas chambers were, at camps like Buchenwald death came slowly. There was no hope for freedom, merely death by attrition. "This concentration camp was by no means unique, nor were its methods different from similar camps" the report concluded.[44] American forces were soon to prove this point at a place called Dachau.

Death at Dachau

Dachau was a market town of 15,000 people on the Amper River, with roots dating back to the 700s. It was filled with ancient homes and churches, with a castle at its center. Part of the Munich metropolitan area, Dachau morphed into a suburb, which eventually included factories of its own. For a time in the years before the Great War, it even enjoyed a reputation as a nice place to escape the pressures of day-to-day life in Munich.[45]

The town's reputation began to change once the Nazis came to power in 1933. Dachau was selected as a location for an early concentration camp, which soon became the model for the entire system.[46] Briefly staffed by Bavarian police, once Heinrich Himmler's SS took complete control of the site its very nature transformed from a political prisoner camp with at least, officially, the goals of reeducation and rehabilitation, to one of brutality. Dachau's first SS commandant, Hilmar Wackerle, issued orders allowing for the execution of any prisoners who were deemed to be causing trouble and Himmler insulated his men from non-SS oversight by crafting a position that they and their camps were outside of regular legal circles. With that edict, Dachau became one of the centers for the Ahnenerbe's medical experimentation program. Its creation and transformation were far from a secret to those who lived nearby. The camp even had its own road signs.[47]

---

[44] Report, "Inspection of German Concentration Camp for Political Prisoners located at Buchenwald," Walter Bedell Smith Collection of World War II documents, Box 36, Inspection of German Concentration Camp at Buchenwald 4/16/45; NAID#12007803, Dwight Eisenhower Presidential Library, Abilene, Kansas.
[45] Atkinson, *The Guns at Last Light*, 611; Smith, *Dachau*, 79–80; McManus, *Hell Before Their Very Eyes*, 65; Abzug, *Inside the Vicious Heart*, 87.
[46] Yisrael Gutman and Michael Berenbaum, editors, *Anatomy of the Auschwitz Death Camp* (Indianapolis: Indiana University Press, 1994), 10; Smith, *Dachau*, 234.
[47] McManus, *Hell Before Their Very Eyes*, 70; Anthony Read, *The Devil's Disciples: Hitler's Inner Circle* (New York: W.W. Norton & Company, 2003), 314; Pringle, *The Master Plan*, 272; Gutman and Berenbaum, editors, *Anatomy of the Auschwitz Death Camp*, 293.

Like Buchenwald, Dachau was not a "death factory," but it was a place where people were systematically killed.[48] That such a distinction could be made, let alone that it had to be made, simply to tell the differences between the camps, was something that Americans eventually wrestled with. During the war years, Nazi medical experiments at the camp were little more than "barbarism." Couple that with the existence of a gas chamber at Dachau, and there was a "pervasive fear of death" among the prisoners that permeated the camp. This of course, was on top of the fact that prisoners "could not keep clean, dry, or warm" for very long. Each prison barrack at Dachau was built to house 200 people. By the end of the war, there were close to 1,600 crammed into each one. Death rates, just of those expiring in their sleep, climbed to 200 a day.[49]

By late April 1945, Dachau was one of the final large camps still under Nazi control. As the war came to a close, the prisoners could sense the end was near. Every day they survived, was a day closer to possible liberation. Since the Germans could not evacuate the camp, every day that passed produced a fresh wave of possible hope.[50] The Nazi guards debated whether to continue the killings at the camp. They contemplated fleeing or taking the camp apart. The chaos and indecision of the final days likely saved the lives of many of the prisoners.[51]

Liberating Dachau was not part of Allied "grand strategy" at all.[52] On April 29th, the U.S. Army's 42nd and 45th Divisions arrived in the vicinity of the Munich and discovered the camp. Some of the SS guards opted to contest the liberation, meaning that instead of just walking into the camp, the first wave of Americans had to fight their way in and deal with snipers.[53] After overcoming the opposition, the Americans were left in a state of shock. There was an odor of death clinging to the area. The Americans had not taken a military factory, but rather a concentration camp—with between 31,000 to 35,000 prisoners still clinging to life inside it. The GIs also found thirty railroad boxcars with over 2,000 emaciated corpses stacked in them.[54] As one American soldier put it, such sights could not be explained as being part of "the twentieth century," since "even primitive, savage people give a decent burial to their own dead and the dead of their enemies."[55]

---

48 Smith, *Dachau*, 106–107.
49 Smith, *Dachau*, 108, 114; McManus, *Hell Before Their Very Eyes*, 72–74.
50 Smith, *Dachau*, 142, 146–147.
51 Smith, *Dachau*, 143–145. MacDonogh, *After the Reich*, 67.
52 Jon Bridgman, *The End of the Holocaust: The Liberation of the Camps* (Portland: Areopagitica Press, 1990), 61–63.
53 Abzug, *Inside the Vicious Heart*, 90.
54 Hirsh, *The Liberators*, 192; Smith, *Dachau*, 79–80; Hitchcock, *The Bitter Road to Freedom*, 297.
55 Smith, *Dachau*, 80.

American soldiers entering Dachau received no advanced warning about what they would find there. They had no idea what a concentration camp *was* in the Nazi context. Dachau itself had made the pre-war news, the camp was not a surprise in that sense, as even Sixth Army Group's intelligence branch knew they were coming up on it. But that information was not passed on to the men who were about to become the camp's liberators.[56] After the war, some of the former GI's came to believe that their officers, including Eisenhower had "deliberately downplayed the camps," to prevent the men from becoming vigilante assassins.[57] If that was the plan, it failed. Having first been fired upon by SS diehards and then witnessing the horrible reality of the camp, retribution was on the minds of many of the GIs. They allowed prisoners to kill some of the guards as they attempted to surrender. At least four Germans were killed by American soldiers, who wept at the sight of the dead and called the Germans "sons of bitches" as they opened fire, noting after the fact that the Germans "had it coming." One Army surgeon reportedly refused to treat a wounded SS guard. When some of the former guards were found dead, one U.S. soldier noted, "no one is interested in how these unarmed men got the weapon." Giles MacDonogh estimates that forty guards and kapos were killed by Americans and liberated prisoners at Dachau. While several Americans were initially brought up on charges, General Patton dismissed the legal proceedings before the adjudication process really got started, believing the men more than justified in their actions at the moment.[58] Eisenhower minced few words: "Our forces liberated and mopped up the infamous concentration camp at Dachau . . . 300 SS camp guards were quickly neutralized."[59]

Major General Robert T. Frederick, the 45th Division commander—a man awarded eight Purple Hearts—was unnerved by Dachau.[60] The liberated prisoners showed the Americans what the Germans had done to them. They had lived in thirty-two, single-story, barracks buildings. They did not have beds, just a por-

---

[56] Peter Caddick-Adams, *Fire and Steel: The End of World War Two in the West* (New York: Oxford University Press, 2022), 455.

[57] Hirsh, *The Liberators*, 191–192.

[58] Hughes Family Dachau Trial Album Acc. 2016.24, Box 1, Dallas Holocaust Museum; Bill Fitzgerald, oral history, Dallas Holocaust Museum; Fred I. Diamond letter, 13 April 1945, RG-04 Concentration and other camps, United States Holocaust Memorial and Museum, Washington, D.C.; McManus, *Hell Before Their Very Eyes*, 104; Hirsh, *The Liberators*, 210; Atkinson, *The Guns at Last Light*, 612; Steven Friess, "A Liberator, But Never Free," https://newrepublic.com/article/121779/liberator-never-free, 15 February 2016; Smith, *Dachau*, 80; MacDonogh, *After the Reich*, 67; Blaine T. Browne, *Mighty Endeavor: The American Nation and World War II* (New York: Rowman & Littlefield, 2019), 255; Abzug, *Inside the Vicious Heart*, 93–95.

[59] Stone, *The Liberation of the Camps*, 101.

[60] Atkinson, *The Guns at Last Light*, 613.

tion of a triple tiered shelving unit that ran through each building. Many of the former prisoners were battling a range of diseases, but all of them were overjoyed, to the degree that they could still muster such a feeling, at seeing the Americans, at seeing people who were not intent on killing them.[61] As Harold Porter, who was part of the 116th Evacuation Hospital, put it after witnessing the horrors of Dachau, "although I stood there looking at it, I couldn't believe it."[62]

Nearly as horrible in the minds of the Americans was the reaction of the local populace at the liberation of the camp. Dachau's neighbors "lived in a different universe" when compared to the prisoners. By not complaining about abuses they saw, local citizens were able to keep the SS out of their daily lives. When German civilians were forced to view the camp, they all claimed to know nothing about the atrocities committed there, even going so far as to claim that Hitler must not have known.[63] It took American intelligence officers little time to discover that the citizens knew a great deal about the camp and had made a good living supplying it and its staff, as well as enjoying the slave labor of its prisoners. The Seventh Army's eventual report about Dachau concluded that the residents "didn't give a tinker's damn what happened to the poor souls whom they saw pass through their streets for years—so long as business was good and the SS Hauptsturmfuhrer paid his handsome rent . . . Today they are the ones who plead, 'Ja—wir wussten uberhaupt nichts was passiert da draussen: (But we really didn't know what was going on out there!). "Da draussen—as if it were on another planet! They are liars, and guilty as sin—everyone." There was nothing "normal" about the society that developed in the camp, nor about the society that created the camp system the report concluded. "Dachau and death," the authors said, "were synonymous."[64]

The day after Dachau was liberated, German radio informed the world that Hitler had died fighting the Soviets in Berlin. In reality, he had committed suicide, "cowering" in his hidden bunker beneath the Reich Chancellery building, in fear that he might be captured, paraded through the streets of Moscow, and then face justice for the crimes committed by the Nazi war machine he had unleashed.

---

61 Smith, *Dachau*, 88–92.
62 Letters, Harold Porter to his Parents, May 7, 10, 13, and 15 1945, World War II Participants and Contemporaries Papers, Porter Harold; Memorabilia, NAID#1055429, 12009096, 12009107, 12009108, Dwight Eisenhower Presidential Library, Abilene, Kansas.
63 Stargardt, *The German War*, 534; Abzug, *Inside the Vicious Heart*, 100–103; Ambrose, *Citizen Soldiers*, 464; Smith, *Dachau,* 222.
64 Report, "Dachau," Prepared by the Office of Strategic Services Section, Seventh Army, World War II Participants and Contemporaries Papers, Hoffman Steve: Dachau and Porter Harold, Dachau; NAID#12009126, Dwight Eisenhower Library, Abilene, Kansas.

Some Americans found a connection between Hitler's death and liberation of Dachau. The game was up.[65]

Liberation Continues

The discovery of camps like Buchenwald and Dachau were a "jolt," not just because of the horrors that the Allies found there but also because what they saw seemingly confirmed that Western civilization was not as civilized as they assumed. The camps were a confirmation of evil.[66] Though ending the camp system was never a military objective,[67] it happened nevertheless, and it changed the nature and meaning of the war for the Allies in very real ways. When presented with evidence about the camps, the captured Hermann Goring, who once was second only to Hitler in running Germany, attempted to dismiss it as "propaganda."[68] The Allies, having seen with their own eyes, rejected such nonsense. The camps proved to Americans that they had, as Eisenhower had told them, been fighting a crusade. Ike believed that anyone who saw the camps could not doubt why the Americans were waging war against the Nazis. He believed that seeing the camps in person was the only way to truly grasp the evil Germany had unleashed upon the world.[69]

The concept of genocide was not foreign to the Allies. The Armenian Genocide during the Great War was something that Eisenhower, as well as every policy maker in Washington, including Franklin Roosevelt, were aware of. It had been condemned openly by former president Theodore Roosevelt in 1918, who had called for a declaration of war on the Ottoman Empire to halt it. While President Woodrow Wilson had opted not to follow the earlier Roosevelt's call to action, both of his immediate successors in the White House—Warren Harding and Calvin Coolidge—publicly condemned it.[70] The main difference between the Arme-

---

65 McKale, *Nazis after Hitler*, ix; Smith, *Dachau*, 221.
66 Abzug, *Inside the Vicious Heart*, x; Bauer, "The Death-Marches, January-May, 1945," 14.
67 Mark Celinscak, *Distance from the Belsen Heap: Allied Forces and the Liberation of a Nazi Concentration Camp* (Toronto: University of Toronto Press, 2015), 23.
68 Atkinson, *The Guns at Last Light*, 620.
69 Abzug, *Inside the Vicious Heart*, 30.
70 "Theodore Roosevelt—Statement on the Armenian Genocide," http://www.armenian-genocide.org/roosevelt.html, 6 March 2017; "The Frontier Between Armenia and Turkey as Decided by President Woodrow Wilson," http://asbarez.com/151022/the-frontier-between-armenia-and-turkey-as-decided-by-president-woodrow-wilson/, 6 March 2017; "Genocide 1915: Armenian Genocide Information: Popular Quotes," http://www.genocide1915.info/quotes/, 6 March 2017. The Armenian Genocide was certainly remembered in Germany. During the Great War, a member of the German diplomatic delegation was told by Talat Pasha that "Turkey is taking advantage of the war

nian genocide and the Holocaust was this time Americans were encountering it for themselves, not passively debating it. As Elmer Joachim, one of Ike's GI's put it: "We must see to believe. I have seen Dachau – I believe."[71]

The same was true for the British. The United States' chief ally in the West knew more about Nazi Germany, and what they were capable of, than the Americans did at the start of the war. Unlike his counterpart in Washington, British Prime Minister Winston Churchill was more active in trying to halt Nazi atrocities, having publicly discussed "the crime without name" and ways to stop or at least mitigate it, long before the term "holocaust" was commonplace. Churchill had vowed that "when the hour of liberation strikes Europe, as strike it will, it will also be the hour of retribution" for the crimes Germany was committing.[72] Still, like the Americans, the British were reluctant to single out what was happening to the Jews, even though they often did condemn specific Nazi atrocities.[73]

But the British also seemed incapable of grasping just how evil the Germans could be. Until, that is, they liberated a camp of their own. In April 1945, about the same time Ike was at Ohrdruf, the British came upon the Bergen-Belsen camp near Hanover. For most of its existence, Bergen-Belsen had a reputation as a rather lenient camp, comparatively speaking. Heinrich Himmler envisioned it as a place where Jews, and others of a certain status, could be held and then used as bargaining chips with Allied governments. As the war turned against Germany more prisoners were shipped to Bergen-Belsen. By the time the British arrived an estimated 35,000 prisoners had died at the camp, including Anne and Margot Frank, many of them since the start of the year.[74]

---

in order to thoroughly liquidate its internal foes, i.e., the indigenous Christians, without being thereby disturbed by foreign intervention." It is perhaps telling that Adolf Hitler told Nazi leaders that Germany could do the same to the Jews because, "who, after all, speaks today of the annihilation of the Armenians?".

71 "Americans and the Holocaust: American Soldier Elmer Joachim," USHMM, 28 June 2018.
72 Benjamin A. Lindsey, "Organized Crime Against Civilization: The Congressional Investigation of Liberated Concentration Camps in 1945," (Master's Thesis, University of Vermont, 2012), 6; Martin Gilbert, *Auschwitz and the Allies* (New York: Pimlico, 2001), 68; Beschloss, *The Conquerors*, 42. For more on Churchill, see, Martin Gilbert, *Churchill and the Jews: A Lifelong Friendship* (New York: Henry Holt and Company, 2007).
73 Hamerow, *Why We Watched*, 367, 410.
74 Joanne Reilly, *Belsen: The Liberation of a Concentration Camp* (New York: Routledge, 1998), 11–13, 25; Celinscak, *Distance from the Belsen Heap*, 42; Bridgman, *The End of the Holocaust*, 47; Hitchcock, *The Bitter Road to Freedom*, 297; Abzug, *Inside the Vicious Heart*, 83; Hamerow, *Why We Watched*, 367, 410. The Frank sisters, as well as the others captured with them, had only been discovered in their hiding place after D-Day.

On April 15, British forces belonging to the 63rd Anti-tank and 11th Armored Division liberated the camp. The surviving prisoners they found were starving and suffering from typhus and typhoid, which likely came to Bergen-Belsen with prisoners transferred there from Auschwitz. Within hours, Anglo-Canadian medical teams were dispatched to try and help the newly liberated survivors. The British also found some 10,000 corpses littered around the camp and survivors that "looked like polished skeletons." There was also an odor, that one British intelligence officer described as "like the smell of a monkey camp." Other liberators said the smell reminded them of a barnyard, an outhouse, or of hell itself. Surrendering Germans informed the British that all records about the prisoners had been destroyed.[75]

For the British and Canadians, Bergen-Belsen defined the Holocaust.[76] British officers wept at the sight of liberated prisoners and one survivor later recalled the horrified looks on the faces of the soldiers.[77] As one Canadian liberator put it, "you know, people who treat other people like that can't be human. They *can't* be human." He decided the Germans were "vermin" who need to be "exterminated."[78] A British soldier wrote to his wife after seeing the camp, saying, "If only for this alone the war has been just and worthwhile, and there must be others like it and worse. Every person in any way connected with it must be killed."[79]

Following in Ike's footsteps, Field Marshal Bernard Montgomery ordered camera crews and photographers into Belsen as soon as he was informed of the camp's discovery. He also ordered Germans living nearby to tour the camp.[80] As the official British report put it: "The idea of torture and mutilation is so abhorrent to the BRITISH mind that it is NOT easy to believe that practices which are associated say with the SPANISH inquisition could be carried out in the twentieth century by EUROPEANS."[81]

---

75 Atkinson, *The Guns at Last Light*, 601; Reilly, *Belsen: The Liberation of a Concentration Camp*, 1; Hackett, editor, *The Buchenwald Report*, 1; Celinscak, *Distance from the Belsen Heap*, 3, 54, 59; McKale, *Nazis after Hitler*, 65.
76 Celinscak, *Distance from the Belsen Heap*, xv; Peter Caddick-Adams, *Fire and Steel: The End of World War Two in the West* (New York: Oxford University Press, 2022), 376–377.
77 Reilly, *Belsen: The Liberation of a Concentration Camp*, 24; Celinscak, *Distance from the Belsen Heap*, 194.
78 Celinscak, *Distance from the Belsen Heap*, 71, 96.
79 As quoted in Shephard, *After Daybreak*, 190.
80 Nigel Hamilton, *Monty: The Battles of Field Marshal Bernard Montgomery* (New York: Random House, 1994), 608.
81 Report, "Report on Atrocities Committed by the Germans Against the Civilian Population of Belgium, February 1945 by Headquarters 21st Army Group," C.D. Jackson Papers, Box 2 Atrocities-Paris (4); NAID#12005700, Dwight Eisenhower Presidential Library, Abilene, Kansas. The emphasis is in the original.

While each camp offered its own story to the larger Holocaust narrative, all were disturbing and tragic in their own rights, mixing joy on the part of the liberated with shock on the part of the liberators.[82] On April 19, for example, the American 90th Infantry liberated Flossenberg in Bavaria. They were a week too late to save the great German theologian Dietrich Bonhoeffer, as well as many of the other July 20th plotters incarcerated at the camp, and most of the other inmates. In March, the camp's estimated population was over 53,000 prisoners. The Germans had placed 15,000 (relatively) healthy prisoners on a death march ahead of the American advance. By the time the 90th Infantry arrived, the Americans found just over 1,500 prisoners deemed too sick to transport in the camp. They also found mass graves containing what was left of some of the camp's victims.[83]

On May 1st, General James Gavin of the 82nd Airborne was informed that the mayor of Ludwigslust, his wife and their daughter all had committed suicide. The general was surprised at the news, as American commanders had worked hard to make sure that the soldiers under their command behaved properly and German civilians knew that they had little to fear if they surrendered. The 82nd had crossed the Elbe River just a few days before and managed to take 150,000 German prisoners. Two days after the report about the mayor's death, Gavin learned why the family had taken their lives. The answer was the Wobbelin concentration camp. The general recalled in his memoirs that the smell reached him long before he saw the camp, but once he did, "it was more than a human being could stand. Even after three years of war it brought tears to my eyes. Living skeletons were scattered about, the dead distinguishable from the living only by the blue-black color of their skin compared to the somewhat greenish skin, taut over the bony frames of the living." After Gavin toured Wobbelin, he ordered all citizens ten years and older of Ludwigslust to visit the camp and forced them to bury the dead in a park in the center of town. One soldier of the 82nd Airborne said, "We were united in a bond of shame that we had ever seen such things." Another said,

---

82 Hitchcock, *The Bitter Road to Freedom*, 308.
83 G-2 Report No. 307, "The Hasag Panzerfaust Factory and Concentration Camp, " April 28, 1945, U.S. Army: Unit Records, Box 759, G-2 Periodic Reports April 1945, NAID#17368741, Dwight Eisenhower Presidential Library, Abilene, Kansas; "Flossenburg," https://encyclopedia.ushmm.org/content/en/article/flossenbuerg, 25 September 2022; Richard J. Evans, *The Third Reich at War* (New York: Penguin Press, 2010), 271. Bonhoeffer, who was a leader in the anti-Nazi Confessing Church, had been arrested in 1943 and had connections to the July 20th plotters. He was ordered executed as part of Hitler's decision to seek both retribution against as many of his opponents as possible as well as to deny them the chance to help rebuild Germany after the war. See, Dietrich Bonhoeffer, *The Cost of Discipleship* (New York: Touchstone, 1995), 13–33.

"it was a defining moment in our lives, who we were, what we believed in, and what we stood for."[84]

The largest camp left to be liberated was Mauthausen. Located in Austria, it was built in 1938, after Himmler visited the area to find a place for a concentration camp that would utilize slave labor to work in the nearby Linz quarries. Over the years, the camp grew to include sub-camps at Gusen, Ebensee, and Gunskirchen. The death rates from working in the Mauthausen quarries were high—so much so that it garnered a reputation within the camp system: If you were a prisoner, you did not want to be transferred there. It had its own gas chamber, which was used, and the camp's geographic location gave it a role during the final liquidation of Hungarian Jews. According to Robert Abzug, Mauthausen "was the stuff of which nightmares are made."[85]

However, by April 1945, Mauthausen was in a state of near collapse. Prisoners were being shipped to it, putting stress on the facilities, and increasing the daily death rate. The SS debated destroying camp (and all who still lived) or abandoning it ahead of the American advance. In the end, they ran out of time to decide, with the Germans fleeing just ahead of American forces.[86] Arriving at the camp on May 8, the GIs were shocked by what they saw, even though many other camps had been liberated during the previous month. The 11th Armored took control of the main camp with the 71st Division liberating Gunskirchen Lager. It had once held 17,000 Hungarian Jews. At the time of liberation, there were only 2,600 people left alive in the compound.[87]

The goal Americans set for themselves was to make the liberated prisoners "people again." One challenge the liberators faced was that they could not easily feed the survivors, as former prisoners were not prepared to eat caloric meals at regular levels—giving them too much food, or something like chocolate, caused even more sickness. Many of the people who were liberated could not, in the end, be saved. Medics and doctors had to deal with a host of diseases: typhus, dysentery, tuberculosis, and scurvy to name a few. Treating those illnesses, as well as physical injuries was one thing. Healing the liberated prisoners' damaged psyches

---

[84] Abzug, *Inside the Vicious Heart*, 62, 68; Atkinson, *The Guns at Last Light*, 601; James M. Gavin, *On To Berlin: Battles of an Airborne Commander, 1943–1945* (New York: The Viking Press, 1978), 288–289, 320.

[85] Chene, *Mauthausen*, 19; Abzug, *Inside the Vicious Heart*, 64, 106–107, 118; "Mauthausen," https://encyclopedia.ushmm.org/content/en/article/mauthausen, 25 September 2022.

[86] Chene, *Mauthausen*, 172, 234; Abzug, *Inside the Vicious Heart*, 108; Bridgman, *The End of the Holocaust*, 88.

[87] Abzug, *Inside the Vicious Heart*, 111, 118; Chene, *Mauthausen*, 162, 166; Hackett, editor, *The Buchenwald Report*, 1.

was something else entirely. Still, the living could be cared for, but the liberators also had to deal with the dead—and try to avoid a health crisis. To ensure the safety of those who survived, bodies had to be buried as quickly as possible. Supplies were diverted and rushed to camps.[88] Liberation became a logistical task, on top of its humanitarian, military, and medical aspects.

Making German civilians visit the camps was a means to remind the loyal citizens of the Reich that these things had been done in their name and with their consent. It was also a form of reeducation. Ike's Ohrdruf order was implemented at each subsequently liberated camp, with German citizens forced to clean and view the camps as well as bury the dead. The GIs, who expressed anger, rage, and disgust towards Germans after seeing the camps, saw the tours as a means of retribution and retaliation.[89] When the Third Armored and the 104th Infantry liberated Nordhausen, General Joe Collins ordered German civilians to help bury the dead, saying "there is no greater shame for any German than to be a citizen of this town."[90]

What Americans often noted, after the extremes of the camps (in terms of the crematoriums and the rampant disease) was the degree to which the Nazis had effectively dehumanized so many of their prisoners. The Germans wanted the prisoners to "lose their identities," while "survival depended on absolute obedience, but was not guaranteed by it." The prisoners in the camps lived, at least in part, because they daily denied the reality of their situation. The camps inhabited their own universe according to Robert Abzug.[91] The arrival of liberating soldiers radically upended the prisoner's world view. As Zwi Steintz, who was liberated by the Soviets at Sachsenhausen put it, "It is impossible to grasp that you are suddenly free."[92]

---

[88] Abzug, *Inside the Vicious Heart*, 33; Cornelius Ryan, *The Last Battle* (New York: Simon and Schuster, 1966),328; Levinson, *Gated Grief*, 88; McManus, *Hell Before Their Very Eyes*, 55–56, 135; Lindsey, "Organized Crime Against Civilization: The Congressional Investigation of Liberated Concentration Camps in 1945," (Master's Thesis, University of Vermont, 2012), 54, 65; "Isaak and Tzvi Klein," Auschwitz Twins, CANDLES, Inc., https://candlesolocaustmuseum.org, 7 December 2016; "Esther and Malka Deutch," Auschwitz Twins, CANDLES, Inc., https://candlesolocaustmuseum.org, 7 December 2016; Smith, *Dachau*, 138; Johnson and Reuband, *What We Knew*, 34; Eisenhower, *Eisenhower: At War, 1943–1945*, 765.

[89] Frank Van Vree, *Performing the Past: Memory, History, and Identity in Modern Europe* (Amsterdam: Amsterdam University Press, 2010), 265; Levinson, *Gated Grief*, 111; Eisenhower, *Eisenhower: At War, 1943–1945*, 766; Lindsey, "Organized Crime Against Civilization: The Congressional Investigation of Liberated Concentration Camps in 1945," (Master's Thesis, University of Vermont, 2012), 4.

[90] Atkinson, *The Guns at Last Light*, 600–601.

[91] Hackett, editor, *The Buchenwald Report*, 7; Smith, *Dachau*, 129–130; Gutman and Berenbaum, editors, *Anatomy of the Auschwitz Death Camp*, 476; Abzug, *Inside the Vicious Heart*, 44.

[92] Signage at Sachsenhausen KZ, Oranienburg, Germany.

Liberation also changed the soldiers who took part in it. On some level, it hardened them. American Al Sommer had read of the camps the Soviets had encountered. It all sounded "awful." But to witness it for yourself was something else, and difficult to describe. As he relayed it to his parents, Ohrdruf consisted of "one story, ramshackle barracks" that had once packed in more prisoners "much more tightly than any pinch-penny farmer would dare pack cattle in his barn." He concluded by writing, "I want to remember because in remembering in years to come I shall better be able to control any inclination towards softening the peace given a bastard people." Until he saw the camp, he had assumed he was fighting "some semblance of Roman civilization, an enemy with some standard of decency which might be remotely compared to ours. That feeling was destroyed completely" upon entering the camp.[93]

Eisenhower ordered units to view the camps as they moved forward, meaning that even soldiers who did not actively liberate the camps themselves still bore witness to what Nazi Germany had done. As Ike noted, "We are told that the American soldier does not know what he is fighting for. Now, at least, he will know what he is fighting *against*." The result, during the last month of the war, was an army that had a new mission. Soldiers noted that after they saw camps like Ohrdruf and Dachau, they fought harder—in part because now they knew why they were fighting. The more camps that were discovered, the more the "indescribable horror" of the camps became ingrained in how the Americans saw the Germans. Ike was sure that the camps (and their liberation) justified American involvement in the war. Seeing Ohrdruf intensified his hatred for the Nazis and shaped his attitude about the eventual German surrender.[94]

But liberating the camps also traumatized many of the soldiers. As historian Antony Beevor points out, "Like many others, Eisenhower was totally unprepared for the full horror of the concentration camps. Seeing such unbelievable suffering at first hand affected many for years afterwards in a liberator's version of survivor guilt."[95] Captain David Wilsey, for example, upon seeing Dachau, went from a "loving, joking, open, and optimistic husband" and father, to a guarded and gruff man. Only later did families such as Wilsey's realize that encountering the camps

---

[93] Al Sommer, Jr., letter, 8 April 1945, RG-09, Concentration and other camps, United States Holocaust Memorial and Museum, Washington, D.C.
[94] Harry C. Butcher, *My Three Years with Eisenhower* (New York: Simon and Schuster: 1946), 815; Levinson, *Gated Grief*, 39–40; Ambrose, *Citizen Soldiers*, 464; Stone, *The Liberation of the Camps*, 67; Stephen E. Ambrose, *The Supreme Commander: The War Years of General Dwight D. Eisenhower* (Jackson: University of Mississippi Press, 1999), 659.
[95] Antony Beevor, *The Fall of Berlin 1945* (New York: Viking Press, 2002), 203.

produced these personality traits as defense mechanisms. Seeing the camps never left the liberators and haunted many of them until their dying day.[96]

It is important, then, to note what liberation meant. It meant an end to the killing, but not the dying. It also meant an end to the camp system, but not the horrors that occurred within their walls. The war was still raging. Furthermore, many of the prisoners were hundreds, if not thousands of miles away from homes that may or may not have been standing. Liberation did not mean an instant return to where they came from or a return to their pre-war lives. Until the fighting was over, most of the former prisoners stayed in or near the camps. The difference was that people were now helping them rather than killing them. Food, medicine, and clothing were all diverted to aid the newly freed people of Europe.[97]

Those who survived the camps never forgot what the liberators did for them. Elements of the Ninth Army liberated Anna Kovitzka and other prisoners near Lippstadt in the spring of 1945, as they were being prepared for further evacuation. As she remembered it, the soldiers gave the prisoners food, but above all, they embraced them: "They were kissing us. Us dirty and lousy one! 'Do not weep,' they would say. But we wept more and again. And incessantly the tears ran." The soldiers also assured them that other Jews had survived the war. Jorn Gastfreund said "the Americans cared for us very, very well. The medical treatment was excellent."[98] These reactions undercut notions that Allied soldiers looked on prisoners only with a combination of "pity and disgust" or that they moved simply from the camps back to the front.[99] The men who ended the Nazi camp system may have been battle hardened, but what they saw there left a lasting impression.[100] And as both they and Eisenhower knew, there was still work to be done to make sure that the Holocaust never happened again.

---

96 Friess, "A Liberator, But Never Free," https://newrepublic.com/article/121779/liberator-never-free, 15 February 2016; Ben Logan, *Lest We Forget: Ben Harrison Logan, Jr.: An American Soldier in World War II* (Independently Published, 2021); James Zuidema, 1 December 1996, USC Shoah Foundation—23096, accessed on 13 September 2022.
97 Smith, *Dachau*, 93, 106; Friess, "A Liberator, But Never Free," https://newrepublic.com/article/121779/liberator-never-free, 15 February 2016.
98 Hitchcock, *The Bitter Road to Freedom*, 106–107; Boder, *I Did Not Interview the Dead*, 22, 49.
99 Hitchcock, *The Bitter Road to Freedom*, 298–304.
100 Hitchcock, *The Bitter Road to Freedom*, 284; McManus, *Hell Before Their Very Eyes*, 10–11, 15, 40, 43; Nerin E. Gun, *The Day of the Americans* (New York: Fleet Publishing Corporation, 1966), 17–19; Celinscak, *Distance from the Belsen Heap*, 77; Reilly, *Belsen: The Liberation of a Concentration Camp*, 24.

Ike's Press Offensive

Encountering the Holocaust did not snap Eisenhower out of isolationism, make him suddenly pro-war with Germany, nor a newly minted anti-Nazi. He was those things before April 1945. But it brought an edge to what he was doing, and it made him want to insure it never happened again. While others, including Patton, were willing to leave the camps behind them to a degree, Ike understood that what he witnessed at Ohrdruf was the central event of the war in Europe. It was for this reason that he eventually unleashed a press offensive about the camps even as victory approached.[101]

At Ohrdruf, Ike "forced himself" to see all of the camp and wanted no one to claim it was merely "propaganda."[102] As John Eisenhower, who visited his father soon after Ike was at Ohrdruf, recalled: "But the thing most on his mind was the horror camp near Gotha that he had gone through only the day before. The scene of atrocities had left him visibly shaken and he had not yet adjusted the entire episode in his mind . . . 'Well, the only speck of optimism I can see,' Dad said that evening, 'is that I really don't think the bulk of the Germans knew what was going on. When I saw that camp yesterday, I ordered the mayor of Gotha to turn out the townspeople and make them clean up the mess. Last night he and his wife went home and hanged themselves. Maybe there's some hope after all.'"[103]

Like his father, John Eisenhower visited a camp, in his case, Buchenwald, a few days after it was liberated. Despite the efforts of American soldiers, he knew many of the former inmates were likely going to perish and that no amount of cleaning was going to erase the crimes that took place there. Writing nearly thirty years later, the younger Eisenhower reflected on talking to Germans from Weimar: "I still have no idea how much those civilians knew about this camp." He also noted, "It took months after witnessing this scene before I could think of the Germans, viscerally, as human beings."[104]

It seemed as though a new camp was liberated nearly every day in April and May of 1945. Believing that the world needed to know what his men were finding, on April 19, Eisenhower wrote General George Marshall urging him to

---

101 Douglas E. Clark, *Eisenhower in Command at Columbia* (New York: Lexington Books, 2013), 33–34; Peter Caddick-Adams, *Fire and Steel: The End of World War Two in the West* (New York: Oxford University Press, 2022), 329–330.
102 Butcher, *My Three Years with Eisenhower,* 803; Norman Gelb, *Ike and Monty: Generals at War* (New York: William Morrow and Company, 1994), 421.
103 John S. D. Eisenhower, *Strictly Personal* (Garden City, NY: Doubleday and Company, 1974), 86–87.
104 Eisenhower, *Strictly Personal,* 88–90.

find a way to send reporters and members of Congress to Europe to see the camps and report back to the American people. "Conditions," Eisenhower said, "of indescribable horror prevail. I have visited one of these myself and I assure you that whatever has been printed on them to date has been understatement." He vowed to make all the arrangements for the trip and hoped the British government would also send a delegation. The "evidence," Ike continued, "of bestiality and cruelty is so overpowering as to leave no doubt in their minds about the normal practices of the Germans in these camps."[105] Eisenhower's decision to document and publicize the horrors of the camps contrasted with how the Soviets had handled the discovery of the extermination centers in Poland just a few months before.[106]

Within hours of receiving Eisenhower's cable, Marshall was meeting with representatives from Senate Majority Leader Alben Barkley and Speaker of the House Sam Rayburn's offices to figure out who from Congress were going to Europe. Six people from each house of Congress, evenly split between Republicans and Democrats, were selected. The Republicans were C. Wayland Brooks (Senate, Illinois) who had been a pre-war isolationist, Leverett Saltonstall (Senate, Massachusetts), Kenneth S. Wherry (Senate, Nebraska), James W. Mott (House, Oregon), Dewey Short (House, Missouri) who had studied in Germany and been a pre-war isolationist, and John M. Vorys (House, Ohio). The Democrats were Edouard Izac (House, California) who had been a POW held by the Germans during World War I, Robert E. Thomason (House, Texas), Walter F. George (Senate, Georgia), Elbert D. Thomas (Senate, Utah), as well as Majority Leader Barkley (Kentucky). Several senators were upset that they were not selected to go. The group left Washington, D.C. on April 22, per Ike's request that they get to Europe as quickly as possible.[107]

---

105 Chandler, editor, *The Papers of Dwight David Eisenhower: The War Years IV*, 2623; Cable, General Eisenhower to General Marshall, April 19, 1945, Dwight D. Eisenhower's Pre-Presidential Papers, Principal File, Box 134, Cables Off (GCM/DDE), 19 apri-10 Nov 45 (4), NAID#120038, Dwight Eisenhower Presidential Library, Abilene, Kansas.

106 "How the World Discovered Nazi Death Camps," https://news.yahoo.com/world-discovered-nazi-death-camps-020933983.html?guccounter=1&guce_referrer=aHR0cHM6Ly9kdWNrZHVja2dvLmNvbS8&guce_referrer_sig=AQAAAGX8LgECX5YQonmt1TB5eJJu7vf5EvuiqVoR3wmdEDdhRXnPrC2E8WeaPDpDwJqAPpu87GFxaro-aOTb8C_qIneKSKdTBVo_bjiQ_-UN6YnHdjR0ykmCumRKDx37FvOZLfUHuVG3YdGp9UnK-ZlH2J172Krdf_TJtZZ3u8bj-geP, 18 June 2021.

107 Cable, General Marshall to General Eisenhower, April 19, 1945, Dwight D. Eisenhower's Pre-Presidential Papers, Principal File, Box 134, Cables Off (GCM.DDE), 19 Apr-10 Nov 45(4) NAID#12009063, Dwight Eisenhower Presidential Library, Abilene, Kansas; Lindsey, "Organized Crime Against Civilization: The Congressional Investigation of Liberated Concentration Camps in 1945," (Master's Thesis, University of Vermont, 2012), 21, 28–31; Robert S. Wiley, *Dewey Short: Orator of the Ozarks* (Cassville, MO: Litho Printers and Bindery, 1985), 255; Marvin E. Stromer, *The Making of a Political Leader: Kenneth S. Wherry and the United States Senate* (Lincoln: University of Nebraska Press, 1969), 135.

What makes this mobilization of resources to publicly document the camps even more astounding is the context of exactly when Ike visited Ohrdruf and then made his request of Marshall. April 12, 1945 was not just the date by which, as one later German history of Ohrdruf noted, the area became "a synonym for cruelty,"[108] it was also the date upon which President Franklin Roosevelt died. Leading the nation for twelve years, through the Great Depression and the Second World War, Roosevelt, who had survived a crippling battle with polio as a young man and kept up a rigorous presidential schedule (including multiple wartime conferences around the globe), died while trying to rest and recuperate in Warm Springs, Georgia. Eisenhower was notified in the middle of the night, just hours after returning to Patton's headquarters at Herzfelde from his visit to Ohrdruf. His decision to request a congressional delegation during the nation's mourning period shows not just his own shock at what he had seen but also his determination to see the war come to a just conclusion—one that he surely believed Roosevelt also would have desired.[109]

The U.S. Congressional delegation arrived in Paris on April 23 and remained in Europe for several weeks. They met with Eisenhower and visited Nordhausen (Dora), where the V-1 and V-2 plants were before journeying to Buchenwald. There, the congressmen and senators got a full tour, including talking with some of the former prisoners. The group then decided to stay and visit other camps, so that no one at home would think Buchenwald was an exception or a hoax. And that is how they found themselves at Dachau. There the delegation started their tour with the crematoria and became so revolted at what they viewed, that they decided to leave after about thirty minutes. The Congressional delegation and other groups who toured the camps after them believed in talking about what they saw—as both a moral duty and good politics. Nearly all of them also contrasted what they saw and learned in the camps with the local German civilian population, who claimed ignorance about the camps and were seemingly little affected by the end of the Nazi regime.[110]

According to Benjamin Lindsey, the Congressional delegation's report to the nation changed how many Americans viewed the war and Germany. The delegation described what they saw as nothing short of "a systematic form of torture and death."[111] They labeled what the Nazis had done as "no less than organized crime

---

108 Manfred Stander, *Ohrdruf im Dritten Reich* (Sutton Verlag, 2012).
109 David Eisenhower, Eisenhower at War: 1943–1945 (New York: Random House, 1986), 763.
110 Abzug, *Inside the Vicious Heart*, 130–132; Lindsey, "Organized Crime Against Civilization: The Congressional Investigation of Liberated Concentration Camps in 1945," (Master's Thesis, University of Vermont, 2012), 35–37, 41–43, 58–59.
111 Lindsey, "Organized Crime Against Civilization: The Congressional Investigation of Liberated Concentration Camps in 1945," (Master's Thesis, University of Vermont, 2012), ix, 1.

against civilization and humanity."[112] There was a debate within the Congressional delegation about using the word "Nazi" as opposed to "German" to describe the perpetrators. When Senator Barkley presented his report to the Senate, "a grim, absolute silence reigned" in the chamber and his statement on the camps was endorsed by every senator from both parties.[113] Senator Wherry was shocked by what he saw. In a report of his own, he called Buchenwald "an extermination factory. The means of extermination included starvation, complicated by hard work, abuse, beatings, tortures, incredibly crowded sleeping conditions, causing sickness—especially typhus, dysentery, and tuberculosis." Wherry wanted "justice" for those who had perished at the camps.[114] Representative Vorys struggled to come to grips with what he saw. He also refused to believe German civilians who said they knew nothing about the Holocaust.[115] His colleague, Representative Short, told reporters that the final report "was understatement . . . rather than exaggeration." The Congressional delegation pushed for pictures taken in the camps to be made public. They wanted people to see the horrors for themselves.[116]

The official U.S. Congressional delegation was not the only group of politicians to visit the camps. Eisenhower urged British Prime Minister Winston Churchill to send a delegation from Parliament to tour the camps as well. Fifty MPs put their names forward, with ten ultimately selected to take part. The Prime Minister also had pictures of Bergen-Belsen made available to the House of Commons. On April 21, the group from Parliament visited Buchenwald, where they were joined by three members of the U.S. Congress who happened to be visiting the front, Representatives Clare Booth Luce of Connecticut, Leonard Hall of New York, and John Kunkel of Pennsylvania. The following day another Congressional group arrived that included Representatives Gordon Canfield of New Jersey, Carter Manasco of Alabama, and Senator Henry M. Jackson of Washington, also joined the growing tour group. The eventual British report made clear what they saw were not prisoner of war camps.[117] Luce, who was

---

112 Stromer, *The Making of a Political Leader*, 137.
113 James K. Libbey, *Alben Barkley: A Life in Politics* (Lexington: University Press of Kentucky, 2016), 237–238.
114 Stromer, *The Making of a Political Leader*, 136–138.
115 Jeffery C. Livingston, "Ohio Congressman John M. Vorys: A Republican Conservative Nationalist and Twentieth Century American Foreign Policy," (Doctoral Dissertation: University of Toledo, 1989), 142–147.
116 Lindsey, "Organized Crime Against Civilization: The Congressional Investigation of Liberated Concentration Camps in 1945," (Master's Thesis, University of Vermont, 2012), 76–80.
117 Reilly, *Belsen: The Liberation of a Concentration Camp*, 62–63; Stone, *The Liberation of the Camps*, 74; Lindsey, "Organized Crime Against Civilization: The Congressional Investigation of Liberated Concentration Camps in 1945," (Master's Thesis, University of Vermont, 2012), 47; Susan

the only female member of the House Armed Services Committee and later served as Ambassador to Italy during the Eisenhower Administration, gave an impassioned radio address from London in late April after visiting the camps, admonished cameramen who did not believe their movies and pictures should be made public because of the graphic scenes, and was adamant that nothing like the Holocaust should ever be allowed to happen again. Like Luce, the other Americans also echoed the official Congressional delegation report as well.[118]

Eisenhower wanted not only politicians but also newspaper editors to witness the horrors of the camps. He understood that Americans were having a difficult time grasping the news about what the Nazis had done and that they might need to hear it from voices outside of the government to truly believe what he had seen firsthand at Ohrdruf. General Patton fully supported the idea of sending the press to the camps.[119] At Ike's suggestion, Marshall selected eighteen editors from across the nation to travel to Europe alongside the Congressional delegation. The group was comprised of Julius Ochs Adler of the *New York Times*, Malcolm Bingay of the *Detroit Free Press*, Amon Carter of the *Fort Worth Star-Telegram*, Norman Chandler of the *Los Angeles Times*, William L. Chenery of *Collier's*, E.Z. Dimitman of the *Chicago Sun*, John Randolph Hearst of Hearst Newspapers, Ben Hibbs of the *Saturday Evening Post*, Stanley High of *Reader's Digest*, Ben McKelway of the *Washington Star*, William I. Nicholson of the *New Orleans Times-Picayune*, Joseph Pulitzer Jr. of the *St. Louis Post-Dispatch*, Gideon Seymour of the *Minneapolis Star Journal*, Duke Shoop of the *Kansas City Star*, Beverly W. Smith of *American Magazine*, Walker Stone of the Scripps-Howard Newspaper Alliance and *Washington Daily News*, and M E. Walter of the *Houston Chronicle*. Eisenhower met with the editors and spoke with them off the record. After their trip to Europe, Norman Chandler of the *Los Angeles Times*, said that every American should see what the Nazis had done, so that they would understand what the stakes of the war had been. Joseph Pulitzer, Jr. told a rally at Carnegie Hall after his return to the United States that "every member of the Gestapo, every member of the S.S., all German industrialists and financiers, and the entire Germany gen-

---

Eisenhower, *How Ike Led: The Principles Behind Eisenhower's Biggest Decisions* (New York: Thomas Dunne Books, 2020), 59.

118 Sylvia Jukes Morris, *The Price of Fame: The Honorable Clare Boothe Luce* (New York: Random House, 2014), 126–134.

119 Letter, General Patton to General Eisenhower, April 15, 1945, Dwight D. Eisenhower's Pre-Presidential Papers, Principal File, Box 91, Patton George S. Jr. (1): NAID#12007734 and Letter, General Eisenhower to General Patton, April 18, 1945, Dwight D. Eisenhower's Pre-Presidential Papers, Principal File, Box 91, Patton George S Jr. (1); NAID#12007733, Dwight Eisenhower Presidential Library, Abilene, Kansas; David S. Wyman, *The Abandonment of the Jews: America and the Holocaust, 1941–1945* (New York: The New Press, 2007), 325.

eral staff should be shot." He estimated that up to 1.5 million Germans would need to be executed "with Army bullets through their heads," but believed the Holocaust warranted such action.[120]

While Pulitzer's bombastic comments might have been brasher than what Eisenhower was prepared to say in public, they did meet Ike's goal of publicizing what his men had found. More politicians, reporters, and even a delegation of ministers wanted to come to Europe and visit the camps as well. Newspapers, newsreels, and radio broadcasts along with eyewitnesses were now spreading the word about the camps.[121] The requests for official tours and the sheer number of camps liberated came as the war was ending and proved to be increasingly difficult to coordinate as new demands on Ike's time grew with the prospect of victory. On May 4, Eisenhower messaged Marshall saying, "If America is not now convinced, in view of the disinterested witnesses we have already brought over, it would be almost hopeless to attempt to convince them through bringing anyone else." Other official delegations and tours could wait. Ike's goal of publicizing the camps had been achieved.[122]

In the midst of facilitating and meeting with the various delegations, Eisenhower had General Walter Bedell Smith, his chief of staff, hold a press conference in his place on April 21, 1945. Smith was asked several questions about the camps, his responses, which Captain Harry Butcher labeled as a "bang-up job," were to the point: German civilians were being tasked with burying "all these poor wretched people who were killed." When asked if the Allies were feeding the civilian burial details, Smith responded curtly "they feed themselves," assuming that "they can still stomach their food" after seeing the dead bodies in the camps. Smith urged the press to go and visit the camps. He also told the gathered reporters that "some of our generals are making civilians come in and look, and they all cover up their faces and won't look. Sometimes their hands have to be removed by force and pulled down and made to look." The final question in Butcher's transcript of Smith's press conference was:

Question: And they say they didn't know about it?

Answer: Yes—they all didn't know about it.[123]

---

120 Lindsey, "Organized Crime Against Civilization: The Congressional Investigation of Liberated Concentration Camps in 1945," (Master's Thesis, University of Vermont, 2012), 13, 32–33, 39, 98.
121 Robert Moses Shapiro, editor, *Why Didn't the Press Shout?: American and International Journalism During the Holocaust* (Newark: KTAV Publishing House, 1995), 109–114, 130.
122 Chandler, editor, *The Papers of Dwight David Eisenhower: The War Years IV*, 2679.
123 Butcher, *My Three Years with Eisenhower*, 815. See also, D.K.R. Crosswell, *Beetle: The Life of General Walter Bedell Smith* (Lexington: University of Kentucky Press, 2010), 900–902.

The delegations and press conferences all served a larger point Eisenhower was trying to make. The camps were not a propaganda story, embellished or manufactured to rile the public on behalf of the war effort. The evidence of the Holocaust was shocking and there was worry among the soldiers, generals, politicians, and members of the press that Americans back home would not believe them about the camps. Even some people in the government, after hearing delegation testimony and reading the reports, still referred to what happened in the camps as "so-called atrocities." But Ike's intuition was correct—people wanted to see the camps and the horrors that happened there. The official visits served another purpose as well, they added more "factual evidence" to what the Soviets had uncovered. And it was needed. The sheer amount of war news had often buried earlier reporting, which had always seemed secondary (at best) considering how low a priority government officials, from the president on down, had given discussing the camps. Ohrdruf, and Ike's reaction to his visit, changed the narrative.[124]

When reporters asked Ike on June 18, 1945, if publishing stories about the atrocities that had occurred in the camps was a good idea, the general replied, "I think I was largely responsible for it, so I must have thought it useful . . . I think people ought to know about such things. It explains something of my attitude toward the German war criminal. I believe he must be punished, and I will hold out for that forever." He also told the press that he did not believe Germans who said they did not know about the Holocaust. If it was true, it was because they opted not to know. The evidence to the contrary was overwhelming.[125]

Eisenhower's decision to publicize the liberation of the camps was a masterstroke. By doing so, he gave the world "devastating public evidence" of what the Nazis had done in the camps. This included, eventually a War Department documentary called "Death Mills" that was shown in theaters throughout occupied Germany.[126] Alexander Frieder, his old friend from the Philippines wrote to

---

124 Ambrose, *Citizen Soldiers*, 463; Beschloss, *The Conquerors*, 224; Helm, *Ravensbruck*, 588; Celinscak, *Distance from the Belsen Heap*, 78; Lindsey, "Organized Crime Against Civilization: The Congressional Investigation of Liberated Concentration Camps in 1945," (Master's Thesis, University of Vermont, 2012), 15; Reilly, *Belsen: The Liberation of a Concentration Camp*, 63; Hamerow, *Why We Watched*, 452–453; Hitchcock, *The Bitter Road to Freedom*, 298; Bettina Stangneth, *Eichmann Before Jerusalem: The Unexamined Life of a Mass Murderer* (New York: Vintage Books, 2015), 31.
125 Press Conference, General Eisenhower at the Pentagon, June 18, 1945, Dwight D. Eisenhower's Pre-Presidential Papers, Principal File, Box 156, Press Statements and Releases 1944–46 (1) NAID#120007716, Dwight Eisenhower Presidential Library, Abilene, Kansas.
126 Rebecca Erbelding, *Rescue Board: The Untold Story of America's Efforts to Save the Jews of Europe* (New York: Anchor Books, 2018), 260; Shapiro, editor, *Why Didn't the Press Shout?*, 130; "Death Mills," http://www.camps.bbk.ac.uk/testimonies/death-mills.html, 20 May 2023.

praise his efforts at allowing others "to witness the horrible stench and the utter cruelty that those thugs practiced upon innocent and defenseless people in those medieval internment dungeons. Never in history could there have been more vile, more inhuman, more cruel barbarity!"[127] Soldiers who took part in the liberation of the camps did not believe that the public should be spared any of the details. Those who saw the camps wanted others to know and to believe what had happened in places like Buchenwald and Dachau. George Sakheim, who helped liberate Nordhausen, told a postwar interviewer that he was saddened by what he saw at the camp, but also angered that Germans could do such things. It justified why the U.S. had to fight the war.[128] Seeing the camps transformed the American understanding of the conflict, providing "moral clarity." It also transformed the Allied forces into liberators, not just in word, but in fact.[129] Among their number was their leader, Dwight Eisenhower.

---

[127] Letter, Alexander Frieder to General Eisenhower, June 1, 1945, Dwight D. Eisenhower's Pre-Presidential Papers, Principal File, Box 43, Frieder Alex, NAID#12007723, Dwight Eisenhower Presidential Library, Abilene, Kansas.
[128] Reilly, *Belsen: The Liberation of a Concentration Camp*, 61; Celinscak, *Distance from the Belsen Heap*, 84–85, 106–107; Timothy Snyder, *Bloodlands: Europe Between Hitler and Stalin* (New York: Basic Books, 2010), 412–413; George Sakheim, Oral History, USC Shoah Foundation, Visual History Archive, accessed 2 August 2017.
[129] Hitchcock, *The Bitter Road to Freedom*, 308; Atkinson, *The Guns at Last Light*, 604.

Chapter 5
Crimes Against Humanity

What Dwight Eisenhower and others saw starting in April 1945 were merely pieces of the Nazi camp puzzle. Ohrdruf was but a slice of the Holocaust, amplified by some 600 other camps. All of them testament not only to the dehumanization of prisoners and Nazi alike, but also of bureaucratic, industrialized, efficient, modern barbarity unleashed by Germany.[1] Ike's encounter changed him, and the nation he represented. No longer would American government officials say of each other "he hates the Nazis too much."[2] But there was still a war to win and a peace to secure. The discovery of the camps, however, changed what Americans thought might and even should happen in postwar Europe.[3]

On to Berlin?

The looming question, as it had been for close to a year, was which of the Allied powers was going to take Berlin. At the Yalta conference in February 1945, President Franklin Roosevelt, British Prime Minister Winston Churchill, and Soviet Premier Josef Stalin had discussed the looming defeat of Germany and where the Allied armies would meet. Berlin, of course, was also a topic. Stalin made it seem to Churchill that the Red Army would soon be encircling the German capital. To Roosevelt, he conveyed a different image – of a siege that might last months. Armed with that information, and in the wake of the Battle of the Bulge, Roosevelt agreed to a division of Germany at the Elbe River and lines that gave the Red Army the responsibility of liberating most of eastern and central Europe. If the Elbe was the demarcation line, there was no point in the Western Allies going very far past it, nor was there a need for them to help with the encirclement of

---

[1] Donald M. McKale, *Hitler's Shadow War: The Holocaust and World War II* (New York: Cooper Square Press, 2002), 416; John C. McManus, *Hell Before Their Very Eyes: American Soldiers Liberate Concentration Camps in Germany, April 1945* (Baltimore: Johns Hopkins University Press, 2015), 41.
[2] Erik Larson, *In the Garden of Beasts: Love, Terror, and an American Family in Hitler's Berlin* (New York: Broadway Paperbacks, 2011), 342.
[3] Michael Neiberg, *Potsdam: The End of World War II and the Remaking of Europe* (New York: Basic Books, 2015), 24.

the German capital. Indeed, Roosevelt became convinced that the Soviets deserved the honor of taking Berlin.[4]

For all intents and purposes then, Yalta settled the issue of who was going to take the German capital. Sentiment within American military circles had never been that adamant about capturing the city and though Eisenhower had always considered it a target, it was not the only one on SHAEF's list. His main goal was to make sure that Germany knew they were defeated—so that there would be no sequel to the post-World War I stabbed in the back myth.[5] Ike also believed that forestalling a Nazi last stand in the Alps was imperative. The intelligence before him offered conflicting reports of Nazi plans, but the fear of a redoubt and of Hitler creating his own Wagnerian Götterdämmerung, simply could not be ignored by the Supreme Allied Commander. While the rapid American advance contributed to stopping such a final stand, the uncertainty diverted Eisenhower's attention away from the discussion over Berlin.[6] Ike prioritized seizing the Ruhr Valley—one of Germany's industrial centers, and with it, large numbers of German prisoners. Doing so would further cripple Nazi industrial output and help insure an Alpine last stand did not happen.[7]

Thanks to Yalta, Ike had his orders: press to the Elbe River. Any American gains beyond that line would be turned over to the Soviets. As for Berlin, in Eisen-

---

[4] Antony Beevor, *The Fall of Berlin 1945* (New York: Viking Press, 2002), 78; S.M. Plokhy, *Yalta: The Price of Peace* (New York: Viking, 2010), 90; Norman Gelb, *Ike and Monty: Generals at War* (New York: William Morrow and Company, 1994), 337; Chris Bellamy, *Absolute War: Soviet Russia in the Second World War* (New York: Alfred A. Knopf, 2007), 648, 654; D.K.R. Crosswell, *Beetle: The Life of General Walter Bedell Smith* (Lexington: The University Press of Kentucky, 2012), 884.

[5] David Eisenhower, *Eisenhower: At War, 1943–1945* (New York: Random House, 1986), 761; Kenneth Strong, *Intelligence at the Top: The Recollections of an Intelligence Officer* (Garden, City, NY: Doubleday and Company, 1969), 260, 264.

[6] Strong, *Intelligence at the Top*, 255–256; Joseph E. Persico, *Piercing the Reich: The Penetration of Nazi Germany by American Secret Agents during World War II* (New York: Viking Press, 1979), 289–290; Kenneth O. McCreedy, "Planning the Peace: Operation Eclipse and the Occupation of Germany," *Journal of Military History*, 65(July 2001), 728; Neal H. Petersen, editor, *From Hitler's Doorstep: The Wartime Intelligence Reports of Allen Dulles, 1942–1945* (University Park, PA: The Pennsylvania State University Press, 1996), 15; Stephen E. Ambrose, *Ike's Spies: Eisenhower and the Espionage Establishment* (Jackson: University of Mississippi Press, 1999), 151–152; Gelb, *Ike and Monty: Generals at War*, 410; Beevor, *The Fall of Berlin 1945*, 141; Gerald Simmons and the editors of Time-Life Books, *World War II: Victory in Europe* (Alexandria: Time-Life Books, 1982), 92–93.

[7] D.K.R. Crosswell, *Beetle: The Life of General Walter Bedell Smith* (Lexington: The University Press of Kentucky, 2012), 901–905; Russell F. Weigley, *Eisenhower's Lieutenants: The Campaign of France and Germany, 1944–1945* (Bloomington: Indiana University Press, 1981), 674–680, 686. The Americans estimated some 150,000 German soldiers were in and around the Ruhr Pocket. The actual number of prisoners taken was over 317,000.

hower's estimation it was now a mere "geographical location" with political importance, as opposed to "the most important objective in Germany" since it lay nearly 200 miles beyond the Elbe. Furthermore, his fellow American generals were divided over whether it was worth taking the Nazi capital or not. While George Patton thought it would be easy to make a lightning strike to seize the city, Omar Bradley believed it would cost at least 100,000 U.S. casualties.[8] Eisenhower decided that the best course of action would be for the Americans to continue bombing Berlin to aid in the Soviet advance.[9] And while Ike would further argue that with the city being destroyed it was a less desirable objective, historian Russell Weigley contends that Hitler's desire to hold his capital showed just how important a military objective the city actually was. The Soviets understood that in a way Eisenhower did not.[10]

Of course, Eisenhower was not really a part of this decision-making process.[11] As Ike put it, he was "a field commander," not a chief of staff when it came to discussing the political situation of postwar Europe. Simply put, he was not consulted.[12] Ike would also remind a friend after the war, that generals must obey the civilian leadership. "My single job was to bring victory in Europe as quickly

---

[8] Joseph C. Harsch, "Why Eisenhower Halted at the Elbe," *Christian Science Monitor*, 10 April 1995; Gelb, *Ike and Monty: Generals at War*, 407; Beevor, *The Fall of Berlin 1945*, 203; Harry C. Butcher, *My Three Years with Eisenhower* (New York: Simon and Schuster: 1946), 804; Cornelius Ryan, *The Last Battle* (New York: Simon and Schuster, 1966), 202–203; Stephen E. Ambrose, *The Supreme Commander: The War Years of General Dwight D. Eisenhower* (Jackson: University of Mississippi Press, 1999), 630–631, 636; Jean Edward Smith, *Eisenhower in War and Peace* (New York: Random House, 2013), 431; Gelb, *Ike and Monty: Generals at War*, 410. The Soviets suffered over 300,000 casualties in the process of attacking and taking the city. "The Battle for Berlin," https://www.historylearningsite.co.uk/world-war-two/world-war-two-and-eastern-europe/the-battle-for-berlin/, 8 April 2018. Additionally, Eisenhower was cognizant that the war with Japan was still ongoing—and it was expected that many of the men in Europe would be sent to fight in the Pacific Theater of Operation once Germany was defeated. See, Neiberg, *Potsdam*, 43.

[9] Allen Welsh Dulles, *Germany's Underground* (New York: The Macmillan Company, 1947), 168–169. Intelligence analysts after the war doubted the utility of outright destruction of cities when it came to shortening the war, but one of the dogmas that emerged during the war was that victory (not just the importance of air supremacy) through airpower was possible.

[10] Russell F. Weigley, *Eisenhower's Lieutenants: The Campaign of France and Germany, 1944–1945* (Bloomington: Indiana University Press, 1981), 698–699; Richard Overy, *Blood and Ruins: The Last Imperial War, 1931–1945* (New York: Viking, 2021), 346.

[11] Gunter Bischof and Stephen E. Ambrose, *Eisenhower and the German POWs: Facts Against Falsehood* (Baton Rouge: Louisiana State University Press, 1992), 57.

[12] Dwight Eisenhower to Fred I Kent, 17 April 1952, Louis Galambos, Editor, *The Papers of Dwight David Eisenhower: NATO and the Campaign of 1952, XIII* (Baltimore: The Johns Hopkins University Press, 1989), 1182–1184.

as possible, with minimum loss in lives."[13] When it came to Berlin, Yalta placed a premium on political considerations over the purely military question of if the Americans could take the city.[14] The driving force behind agreeing to Soviet requests to allow the Red Army alone to capture Berlin rested on President Roosevelt's belief that he had a special relationship with Stalin, something he often reiterated to Ike.[15] At this time, both Americans trusted Stalin as a man of his word. The problem, as the British were quick to point out, was that no one knew what the Soviets really planned on doing either about Berlin or after the war. Churchill believed the Western allies should go as far east as possible, and that included taking Berlin. In their opinion, Roosevelt, Eisenhower, and other American leaders clearly underestimated how important the city actually was. Churchill did not want the Soviets to have Berlin, but he could not get the terminally ill Roosevelt to change his mind. Nor could the British Prime Minister order Eisenhower, or George Marshall, Ike's superior, to change course from Yalta. Churchill might worry about the postwar world, but few Americans seemed to care.[16]

In Eisenhower's estimation the British were part of the calculus as to why he could not take Berlin in the first place. Field Marshal Bernard Montgomery constantly requested more men and supplies, which undercut General Omar Bradley, whose advancing forces were in a better place to drive for the German capital. The seemingly glacial pace of British advances after D-Day and the near disaster of Operation Market Garden, which Montgomery had insisted upon and led, were on Eisenhower's mind.[17] Additionally, the doctrine of unconditional surrender also came into play for the Supreme Allied Commander when it came to Berlin. While many German officers were, by the spring of 1945, interested in surrender-

---

13 Dwight Eisenhower to Julius Earl Schaefer, 27 December 1951, Louis Galambos, Editor, *The Papers of Dwight David Eisenhower: NATO and the Campaign of 1952, XII* (Baltimore: The Johns Hopkins University Press, 1989), 819–821.
14 Weigley, *Eisenhower's Lieutenants*, 685, 687.
15 "President John F. Kennedy Meeting with Dwight Eisenhower, 10 September 1962," Presidential Recordings Digital Edition, https://pride.upress.virginia.edu, 19 October 2022.
16 Robert M. Citino, *The Wehrmacht's Last Stand: The German Campaigns of 1944–1945* (Lawrence: University Press of Kansas, 2017), 453–454; Beevor, *The Fall of Berlin 1945*, 144, 194; Strong, *Intelligence at the Top*, 248, 260–265; Persico, *Roosevelt's Secret War*, 423; Gelb, *Ike and Monty: Generals at War*, 411–413; Bradley F. Smith, *Sharing Secrets with Stalin: How the Allies Traded Intelligence, 1941–1945* (Lawrence: University Press of Kansas, 1996), 242; Harsch, "Why Eisenhower Halted at the Elbe," *Christian Science Monitor*, 10 April 1995; Crosswell, *Beetle*, 862.
17 Eisenhower, *Eisenhower: At War, 1943–1945*, xxiv.

ing to the Western Allies, few wanted to do so to the Soviets and fewer still had the authority to offer a complete capitulation.[18]

No sooner had Eisenhower accepted the Yalta agreement as the proper course of action, than the flow of events changed his perspective. Eisenhower's broad front strategy in Western Europe broke the back of the Nazis by the spring of 1945.[19] Suddenly, American commanders began thinking about going for Berlin after all. By mid-April, American forces were deep inside Germany—some units over 100 miles deep into what would become the Soviet zone of occupation, well across the Elbe River. The Americans were on the verge of taking Leipzig and elements of the Ninth Army were just 50 to 60 miles away from Berlin. Ike's men were mechanized, while the Soviets were largely using foot and horsepower to push forward. Some in SHAEF's headquarters even sketched out a plan to use airborne forces to seize the city.[20]

Ike was willing to go beyond Leipzig and onto Berlin if he could do so "cheaply" in terms of casualties and "if resistance is light and the Russians do not advance in that sector."[21] The plan that was drawn up called for the American 101st Airborne to land at Tempelhof airport, the 82nd Airborne to take Gatow airport, and British airborne units to land in Oranienburg. These operations would be quickly followed up by rapid advances by Allied mechanized units. Though there was some enthusiasm for the idea, eventually Eisenhower opted not to execute the

---

18 Ian Kershaw, *The End: The Defiance and Destruction of Hitler's Germany, 1944–1945* (New York: The Penguin Press, 2011), 369–376, 386–387; Beevor, *The Fall of Berlin 1945*, 142, 144; Butcher, *My Three Years with Eisenhower*, 827, 844; Earl F. Ziemke, *The U.S. Army in the Occupation of Germany, 1944–1946: Army Historical Series* (Washington, D.C., Center of Military History United States Army, 1975), 61, 162.
19 William B. Pickett, *Dwight David Eisenhower and American Power* (Wheeling, IL: Harland Davidson, 1995), 55; Gerald Simmons and the editors of Time-Life Books, *World War II: Victory in Europe* (Alexandria: Time-Life Books, 1982), 92–93; Crosswell, *Beetle*, 876, 894–897. The Soviets grew concerned about American gains, believing that the Nazis (who were still resisting the Red Army) had cut some sort of deal with the Western Allies as they surrendered or that the United States and United Kingdom were about to conclude a separate peace with Germany.
20 Beevor, *The Fall of Berlin 1945*, 194; Michael Beschloss, *The Conquerors: Roosevelt, Truman and the Destruction of Hitler's Germany, 1941–1945* (New York: Simon and Schuster, 2002), 222–223; Weigley, *Eisenhower's Lieutenants*, 681–684; James M. Gavin, *On To Berlin: Battles of an Airborne Commander, 1943–1945* (New York: The Viking Press, 1978), 298–301, 317; Peter Caddick-Adams, *Fire and Steel: The End of World War Two in the West* (New York: Oxford University Press, 2022), 399.
21 Alfred D. Chandler, Jr, editor, *The Papers of Dwight David Eisenhower: The War Years, Volume IV* (Baltimore: The Johns Hopkins University Press, 1971), 2592–2594, 2615; "Last Stand at Volkerschlachtdenkmal: The Battle of Leipzig, 1945," https://warfarehistorynetwork.com/article/last-stand-at-volkerschlachtdenkmal-battle-of-leipzig-1945/, 7 September 2022. See also, Stephen E. Ambrose, *Eisenhower and Berlin, 1945: The Decision to Halt at the Elbe* (New York: W.W. Norton, 2000).

plan and his decision was partially influenced by what he witnessed at Ohrdruf. As Americans liberated concentration camps their desire to make the Nazis pay for their crimes grew. While such sentiment helped fuel the desire to take Berlin, Ike now knew that it paled in comparison to what the Soviets had endured and discovered. Eisenhower's contacts with the Soviets had convinced him that the Red Army was coming for retribution, not liberation. He knew that they would be brutal in ways his men likely would not.[22] And perhaps he believed the Germans deserved it.

Ultimately, it was the Red Army that captured Berlin. Between Allied bombing and the Soviet artillery bombardment, the city was "cloaked in haze and smoke" and continued to smolder days after the fighting actually ended. The Soviet's final offensive started on April 16. Five days later, they were inside the city itself. Within days they were across the Teltow Canal and fighting their way towards the Tiergarten area of the city—the locus of Nazi power. On April 30, Hitler committed suicide, though fighting continued to rage until May 2, when the last of the Berlin garrison finally surrendered. By then, the city was destroyed and virtually unrecognizable to those who had known it before the war.[23]

The collapse of the Third Reich during the first week of May was swift.[24] In the early morning hours of May 7, 1945, German Army Chief of Staff, General Alfred Jodl, as the designee of the new German leader, Admiral Karl Doenitz, arrived at Eisenhower's headquarters in Reims, France to sign surrender documents. Eisenhower refused to meet with the German delegation, in part because he viewed the German leaders as complicit in the horrors he had witnessed at Ohrdruf, until after the signing ceremony took place. Ike then ordered Jodl into his office, where the German was given a pointed lecture about what unconditional surrender meant. Shortly after the ceremony, Soviet officials demanded that the Germans surrender again, this time in Berlin, an event that was accomplished the following day.[25]

---

22 Michael Hirsh, *The Liberators: America's Witnesses to the Holocaust* (New York: Bantam Books, 2010), 56; Robert M. Edsel, *The Monuments Men: Allied Heroes, Nazi Thieves, and the Greatest Treasure Hunt in History* (New York: Center Street, 2009), 307–308.
23 William I. Hitchcock, *The Bitter Road to Freedom: A New History of the Liberation of Europe* (New York: Free Press, 2008), 128; Citino, *The Wehrmacht's Last Stand*, 3; Butcher, *My Three Years with Eisenhower,* 838; Catherine Merridale, *Ivan's War: Life and Death in the Red Army, 1939–1945* (New York: Metropolitan Books, 2006), 327–331; Strong, *Intelligence at the Top*, 290–291.
24 Richard Overy, *Blood and Ruins: The Last Imperial War, 1931–1945* (New York: Viking, 2021), 345.
25 "Surrender of Germany (1945)," https://www.archives.gov/milestone-documents/surrender-of-germany, 25 February 2023; Susan Eisenhower, *How Ike Led: The Principles Behind Eisenhower's Biggest Decisions* (New York: Thomas Dunne Books, 2020), 56, 61–62; Crosswell, *Beetle*, 919–923; "Museum Berlin-Karlshorst," https://www.museum-karlshorst.de/en/, 5 May 2023. Field Marshal Wilhelm Keitel was the German representative at the surrender ceremony in Berlin. Both he and Jodl were eventually executed for their crimes.

Though he expressed interest in seeing Berlin nearly as soon as the fighting ended, Ike was not part of second signing ceremony. He eventually made it to the German capital in the summer of 1945.[26] It was only then, with the Nazis defeated, that he came to better appreciate the "enormous political and diplomatic consequences" of allowing the Soviets to take Berlin. He had been focused on winning the war and had trusted President Roosevelt to make those decisions, and now Roosevelt was dead.[27] Eisenhower quickly regretted both his blind trust in the president and letting the Soviets capture the city. In retrospect, he said "I always felt that the Western Allies could probably have secured an agreement to occupy more of Germany than we actually did."[28] The loss of Berlin was something he did not plan on repeating in the future.[29]

The Military Governor

By the end of the war, Eisenhower had become the symbol of Allied victory to Americans. His boss, General George Marshall told him, "you have made history, great history for the good of mankind and you have stood for all we hope and admire in an officer of the United States Army."[30] While SHAEF's job ended with the collapse of the Nazi regime, the Army's work continued after the war. It was hardly a surprise that Ike was named the American military governor of Germany, a position he held until November 11, 1945.[31] It was fitting that the man

---

[26] Butcher, *My Three Years with Eisenhower*, 835; John S. D. Eisenhower, *Strictly Personal* (Garden City, NY: Doubleday and Company, 1974), 100–111.

[27] Gelb, *Ike and Monty: Generals at War*, 409; Beevor, *The Fall of Berlin 1945*, 203.

[28] Dwight D. Eisenhower, *Crusade in Europe* (New York: Doubleday and Company, 1953), 474–475; Gavin, *On To Berlin*, 312; Eisenhower, *Eisenhower: At War, 1943–1945*, 714–715.

[29] Dwight Eisenhower to Forrest Carlisle Pogue, 20 February 1952, Louis Galambos, Editor, *The Papers of Dwight David Eisenhower: NATO and the Campaign of 1952, XIII* (Baltimore: The Johns Hopkins University Press, 1989), 1001. While Ike had not been involved with Yalta and accepted both it and the Potsdam agreement that set the inner German border, with the dawn of the Cold War anyone viewing a map of central Europe could see the difference between where the American advance had ended and where the Iron Curtain had actually descended. The fact that even portions of what was now East Germany had been taken by his men and then turned over to the Soviets likely gnawed at Eisenhower.

[30] Stephen E. Ambrose, *Eisenhower: Soldier and President* (New York: A Touchstone Book, 1990), 202–204.

[31] Ralph W. Hauenstein with Donald E. Markle, *Intelligence Was My Line: Inside Eisenhower's Other Command* (New York: Hippocrene Books, 2005), 75; Gelb, *Ike and Monty: Generals at War*, 433; Crosswell, *Beetle*, 12.

most Americans saw as responsible for victory in Europe would now lead the American zone of occupation.

His new title was nearly as important as his old one. As military governor, he helped set the tone, not just for the Allied occupation of Germany, but for Germany's future as well—launching the rebuilding efforts and meting out punishment to Nazi war criminals. The first step on Ike's agenda was to ensure that the Germans understood, unlike after the First World War, that they had been completely defeated. When Allied forces made it into Germany, Eisenhower's Proclamation Number One said, "We come as conquerors, but not as oppressors." He was angry that the Germans had continued to resist Allied forces for as long as they had and the images of what he had seen in Ohrdruf were burned into his mind. He believed that Germans needed to listen to what Americans had to say. Now was not the time for dialogue.[32]

With the war over, Ike's headquarters moved to Frankfurt, in the American Zone of occupied Germany. His new office was located in the I.G. Farben building, which had suffered almost no damage during the war. As he pondered his new duties, he wrestled not only with the task before him, but also a desire to have his wife join him in Germany. In the end, he wrote to Mamie that "with destruction, disorder and disease all rampant in Germany" he did not think it a good idea for her to come to Frankfurt. Furthermore, be believed it would smack of favoritism—considering that so many of those under his command were also going to remain separated from those they loved.[33]

Everywhere there was destruction. And while the Nazis were the proximate cause, Ike knew that much of the rubble was the product of American and British weapons he had commanded in ending the Third Reich. He spent time trying to better understand why Germany had become so enamored with Hitler, why they had fought the war to the bitter end, and why they had willingly killed so many in the camps his men had helped to liberate.[34] He found no easy answers to these questions, only a determination that they would not be repeated.

---

[32] Jessica C. E. Gienow-Hecht, *Transmission Impossible: American Journalism as Cultural Diplomacy in Postwar Germany, 1945–1955* (Baton Rouge: Louisiana State University Press, 1999), 29, 48, 89; Jack M. Holl, *The Religious Journey of Dwight D. Eisenhower: Duty, Honor, Country* (Grand Rapids: William B. Eerdmans Publishing Company, 2021), 147.

[33] John S. D. Eisenhower, editor, *Letters to Mamie* (Garden City: Doubleday & Company, 1978), 256; Susan Eisenhower, *Mrs. Ike: Memories and Reflections on the Life of Mamie Eisenhower* (New York: Farrar, Straus and Giroux, 1996), 229. As Peter Caddick-Adams notes, I.G. Farben had a long history of working with the Nazi Party, benefited directly from the use of slave-labor via the concentration camps, and helped produce (via one of its subsidiaries) Zyklon-B. Executives "burned fifteen tons of paperwork prior to the arrival of the Americans in Frankfort. See his *Fire and Steel*, 321.

[34] Susan Eisenhower, *How Ike Led: The Principles Behind Eisenhower's Biggest Decisions* (New York: Thomas Dunne Books, 2020), 57, 95; Eisenhower, editor, *Letters to Mamie*, 256.

Part of his mission then, became to transform Germany's very culture—in particular, the militarism that had defined, in the minds of many Americans, both Imperial and Nazi Germany.[35] However, Eisenhower was trapped between hardliners in Washington, D.C., led by Secretary of the Treasury Henry Morgenthau and the realities of administering a now occupied Germany. Morgenthau was an early advocate of a harsh peace—one that reverted Germany (split into two, smaller states—with large portions of its pre-Nazi territory given to France, Poland, and the Soviet Union) to a pre-industrial, agricultural economy, with a school system administered by the Allies, no military, and an Allied court system that would spend the foreseeable future prosecuting and executing former Nazis. While the Morgenthau Plan had significant detractors, including Secretary of War Henry Stimson and British Prime Minister Winston Churchill, it also influenced the discussion of what a postwar Germany should look like and even found some support from Franklin Roosevelt. The president, as Eisenhower knew firsthand from their conversations, had long associated the Nazis with the Prussians he had encountered during a trip to Europe in his youth. Facing a second war against them in his lifetime, Roosevelt no longer counted Germany as part of the civilized world. At Yalta, while not advocating the Morgenthau Plan in its entirety, he did discuss the "dismemberment" of Germany to ensure that it was never a threat to world peace again—and found a willing conversationalist along those lines in Josef Stalin.[36]

Ultimately, the Morgenthau Plan shaped the document that guided Eisenhower through the end of the war and into his term as military governor: JCS 1067. Crafted by the Joint Chiefs of Staff in Washington, the document directed Eisenhower to insure that "the Germans cannot escape responsibility for what they have brought upon themselves" and it reminded him that "Germany will not be occupied for the purpose of liberation but as a defeated enemy nation." In its language, JCS 1067 sounded like the Morgenthau Plan, but its fine print gave Ei-

---

35 Gienow-Hecht, *Transmission Impossible*, 28, 54.
36 Beschloss, *The Conquerors*, x, 115–117, 125; Hitchcock, *The Bitter Road to Freedom*, 129, 171–175; Persico, *Roosevelt's Secret War*, 348–349; Plokhy, *Yalta: The Price of Peace*, 94; Ian Ousby, *The Road to Verdun: World War I's Most Momentous Battle and the Folly of Nationalism* (New York: Doubleday, 2002), 201; Christopher Clark, *Iron Kingdom: The Rise and Downfall of Prussia, 1600–1947* (Cambridge: Harvard University Press, 2006), 664–679. At the 1943 Tehran Conference, Stalin had (jokingly, or so he said later) called for the execution of 50,000 Germans at the end of the war. Roosevelt had quipped that the United States could only approve 49,000. Churchill got up and left the room in disgust. See, Robert Gellately, editor, *The Nuremberg Interviews: An American Psychiatrist's Conversations with the Defendants and Witnesses, Conducted by Leon Goldensohn* (New York: Vintage Books, 2005), viii–ix; Nigel Hamilton, *War and Peace: FDR's Final Odyssey, D-Day to Yalta: 1943–1945* (New York: Houghton Mifflin Harcourt, 2019), 422.

senhower freedom of action in determining exactly how to implement its larger objectives. While his hatred of the Nazis never abated, Eisenhower was also never as vindictive in victory as some of the plan's strongest advocates. With Roosevelt's death, implementing the harshest aspects of the plan lost a good deal of momentum, giving Eisenhower even greater leeway to strike a balance between retribution and rehabilitation.[37]

He was, after all, governor of not just a portion of a defeated nation, but one that had been destroyed. Amid rubble were millions of refugees, millions of former slave laborers, and millions of former Nazis—all of whom had to be provided for in terms of food and (as winter approached) coal. The whole situation was "bleak" he wrote to his wife, Mamie.[38] Aiding all of these defeated enemies and the former prisoners, as well as overseeing German agriculture, housing, justice, education, and industry were now Ike's responsibility—on top of watching over his own men in the Army of Occupation. While he ultimately was on the job for just six months, every day he spent as military governor set a precedent for what nearly everyone assumed was going to be a long-term Allied occupation of Germany. Thankfully, in addition to JCS 1067, Eisenhower had other resources to help him in the practical administration of Germany. The U.S. Army had pondered what occupation forces should do throughout the 1930s and early 1940s, and SHAEF had started work on a *Handbook for Military Government in Germany*, designed to be a blueprint of sorts for how the Allies would deal with a conquered Germany, before the end of the war.[39] Now it was up to Eisenhower to figure out how to make all these theoretical documents work in reality.

It was not an easy task. Most experts understood that the brief American military occupation of portions of Germany after World War I had been "impromptu."[40] That being said, the military's main task was to fight and win the war and there was an expectation that the civilian leadership (the White House, State, War, and Treasury departments) would do most of the planning concerning any future occupation. Indeed, some of those around Roosevelt did not want the military involved in the

---

37 Directive to the Commander in Chief of the U.S. Occupation Forces (JCS 1067), April 1945; Beschloss, *The Conquerors*, 169, 207; Hitchcock, *The Bitter Road to Freedom*, 109, 170; Eisenhower, *Eisenhower: At War, 1943–1945*, 403; Aaron Rapport, *Waging War, Planning Peace: U.S. Noncombat Operations and Major Wars* (Ithaca: Cornell University Press, 2015), 57; Kenneth O. McCreedy, "Planning the Peace: Operation Eclipse and the Occupation of Germany," *Journal of Military History*, 65(July 2001), 736; Aaron Rapport, *Waging War, Planning Peace: U.S. Noncombat Operations and Major Wars* (Ithaca: Cornell University Press, 2015), 51–52, 79.
38 William I. Hitchcock, *The Age of Eisenhower: American and the World in the 1950s* (New York: Simon and Schuster, 2018), 29.
39 Ziemke, *The U.S. Army in the Occupation of Germany*, iv, 59, 274–279; Beschloss, *The Conquerors*, 71.
40 Harold Zink, "American Occupation Policies in Germany," *The Review of Politics*, 9(July 1947), 285.

occupation planning at all, even though Ike cautioned that civilian agencies could not operate "independently" in a warzone. Many within the White House assumed the occupation would be quick. President Roosevelt said American involvement would be one to two years, with the British then taking over responsibility for Europe while the United States focused on the Pacific. In reality, the military would not conclude official occupation until 1949.[41] In part, this was because the Roosevelt Administration "tended to think about the future in abstract rather than concrete terms." As it turned out, other than Secretary Morgenthau, no one in the administration spent much time thinking about what postwar Germany might look like. Furthermore, working on guidelines for occupation while fighting still raged seemed somewhat out of place to many in Washington, including the president.[42]

Ike found the plans coming out of Washington regarding occupation somewhat "utopian" according to historian Aaron Rapport. Eisenhower believed "that he and the Army [were] the instruments and not the makers of policy." That said, what he was seeing as his men marched into Germany was a Europe that was devastated and "a shell of its former self."[43] While the occupation plans were being debated and finalized, Ike and the Army utilized Operation Eclipse as a framework. Eclipse was instituted in territory that the Allied armies liberated from German control and had been designed to work in tandem with Operation Overlord. It provided a means for the eventual return of local, civilian government. However, it was not drafted with Germany itself in mind, especially as the enormity of the Holocaust became evident. Ike saw his job becoming one of convincing the politicians that European society was on the verge of collapse and needed to be rebuilt along American lines and principles.[44] And he believed that in the near term, the Army was the best way to make that happen.

Of course, making that argument, as well as figuring out the nuances of occupation, meant Ike had to draw on what he had learned during the war about inter-

---

41 Kenneth O. McCreedy, "Planning the Peace: Operation Eclipse and the Occupation of Germany," *Journal of Military History*, 65(July 2001), 713–720, 737; Aaron Rapport, *Waging War, Planning Peace: U.S. Noncombat Operations and Major Wars* (Ithaca: Cornell University Press, 2015), 48, 62–63; Harold Zink, "American Occupation Policies in Germany," *The Review of Politics*, 9 (July 1947), 287. And of course, the United States continues to have military bases in Germany and Europe down to the present.
42 Rapport, *Waging War, Planning Peace*, 47–49, 58–59, 67–69, 73–74.
43 John J. McCloy, "American Occupation Policies in Germany," *Proceedings of the Academy of Political Science*, 21(January 1946), 80; Rapport, *Waging War, Planning Peace*, 65.
44 Kenneth O. McCreedy, "Planning the Peace: Operation Eclipse and the Occupation of Germany," *Journal of Military History*, 65(July 2001), 721, 725, 729; Rapport, *Waging War, Planning Peace*, 48, 60–61, 66–67, 77–78; Harold Zink, "American Occupation Policies in Germany," *The Review of Politics*, 9(July 1947), 284.

national diplomacy. Those lessons served him well during his term as military governor. Eisenhower had a team in place to help him with the American sector, including his ultimate successor as governor, General Lucius Clay. Both men had initial high hopes that the wartime cooperation between the Allies would continue. Indeed, Ike believed he could work with the Soviets—a feeling that was affirmed when he was a guest at the Moscow victory parade in Red Square in June 1945. However, he also did not believe that the United States needed to follow the desires of Stalin when it came to both Germany and the progress of the war in the Pacific. He told the new U.S. president, Harry S. Truman during the Potsdam Conference in the summer of 1945, that in his estimation, the United States did not need Soviet help in defeating Japan—with or without a nuclear bomb.[45] Eisenhower was comfortable advising the new president and looked forward to the end of the war in the Pacific. But for now, he had the administration of Germany to deal with.

Denazification

Eisenhower believed his main task as military governor was the denazification of Germany. He sought to purge Nazism from the very fabric of German culture. His zeal for doing so stemmed in large part from what he saw at Ohrdruf.[46] However, achieving this goal proved to be more problematic than many, including policymakers back in Washington, initially concluded it would be. Ordering the destruction of Nazi emblems and statues or changing street names was one thing. Purging Germany, in its cities, villages, and very soul, of Nazism was something else entirely.

At the outset of occupation, official American policy was to arrest, try, and (potentially) convict all former Nazis that came into their custody.[47] However, Eisenhower had to first determine just who, exactly was a Nazi. Did that mean all party members? Those who fought in the armed forces? Only the leadership in Berlin? Or was "Nazi" merely shorthand for "German" at this point—thus making all Germans collectively guilty? After all, the German civilian population had embraced the war effort, including parroting official government propaganda about why Jews needed

---

[45] Neiberg, *Potsdam*, 59, 96, 108; "Cecilienhof," https://en.potsdam.de/content/cecilienhof-palace, 17 September 2022. Author visit, 18 May 2022; Tim Weiner, *The Folly and the Glory: America, Russia, and Political Warfare, 1945–2020* (New York: Henry Holt & Company, 2020), 28; Crosswell, *Beetle*, 18–19.

[46] Gienow-Hecht, *Transmission Impossible*, 28; "Runde Ecke," https://www.runde-ecke-leipzig.de/, 17 September2022; Author visit, 20 May 2022; Susan Eisenhower, *How Ike Led: The Principles Behind Eisenhower's Biggest Decisions* (New York: Thomas Dunne Books, 2020), 64.

[47] Bischof and Ambrose, *Eisenhower and the German POWs*, 66–67.

to be relocated to camps and why Germany was justified in conquering so much of Europe. Much of the Nazi ideology, let alone feelings of patriotism, were borrowed from German culture and society that predated the party.[48] Ultimately, Eisenhower led the Americans much further into trying to answer those questions and to purge Nazism from the German psyche than the other Allied powers.[49]

No matter how difficult the challenge, there was never any doubt to Eisenhower's commitment to the denazification process. As early as 1944, he had concluded that the General Staff of the German Army needed to share the blame for the war and had even mused about the possibility of liquidating the entire military command structure, or possibly exiling them. As military governor, Ike wanted people who held power in Nazi Germany, down to the mayoral level, tried before military courts of law, believing that justice would be best meted out by the occupying Allied powers.[50] While he slowly came to realize just how difficult total denazification could be, Eisenhower rejected notions of compromising the goal. If that meant starting at the top and working downward, that is what he and those under his command would do.[51]

The Nazi leadership was one thing, but what of the German people themselves? Ike's friend from the Philippines, Alexander Frieder, urged him to be wary, as people "will try to paint a picture of the guiltlessness of the German people ... and thereby soften in your whole German rehabilitation program. Twice in a generation those bastards upset the world with their warped mentality and barbarous ideology. Only for the grace of God and the strength of American arms and superb leadership were they stopped dead in their tracks from spreading

---

[48] Peter Fritzsche, *An Iron Wind: Europe Under Hitler* (New York: Basic Books, 2016), 137–144; Beschloss, *The Conquerors*, 51; Marcus J. Smith, *Dachau: The Harrowing of Hell* (Albuquerque: University of New Mexico Press, 1972), 152; Walter Laqueur, *Out of the Ruins of Europe* (New York: Library Press, 1971), 327–345, 440; Gellately, editor, *The Nuremberg Interviews*, 271; Deborah Dwork and Robert Jan van Pelt, *Auschwitz* (New York: W.W. Norton and Company, 2008), 154; Alan E. Steinweis and Robert D. Rachlin, editors, *The Law in Nazi Germany: Ideology, Opportunism, and the Perversion of Justice* (New York: Berghahn, 2013), 16–17; Ziemke, *The U.S. Army in the Occupation of Germany*, 380–381; Joachim Fest, *Inside Hitler's Bunker: The Last Days of the Third Reich* (New York: Farrar, Straus and Giroux, 2002), x.
[49] John J. McCloy, "American Occupation Policies in Germany," *Proceedings of the Academy of Political Science*, 21(January 1946), 84. President Franklin Roosevelt believed it would take two generations to get rid of both Prussianism and Nazism from the German system. See, Rapport, *Waging War, Planning Peace*, 56.
[50] Telford Taylor, *The Anatomy of the Nuremberg Trials: A Personal Memoir* (Boston: Back Bay Books, 1992), 107–108.
[51] Ziemke, *The U.S. Army in the Occupation of Germany*, 384–385; Ambrose, *Eisenhower: Soldier and President*, 213; Harold Zink, "American Occupation Policies in Germany," *The Review of Politics*, 9(July 1947), 294.

their hatred and barbarity over the rest of the world."[52] Ike kept those words in mind as he began his new duties.

Many of the Germans Eisenhower encountered in the wake of the war certainly fit Frieder's description. The nation's population, whether from war weariness, desire to survive and rebuild, or having been conditioned to accept authority and orders, adapted remarkably quickly to occupation—even if they, like the American occupiers, at least initially, were not sure what to expect. There was no large-scale resistance, no guerilla warfare. There was, however, a rapid disassociation with the Nazi regime. While the Allies recognized that the Germans were emerging from a totalitarian government, they were shocked at how many claimed to have never supported Hitler, never wanted to wage war, and how quick Germans were to claim that others (not them) were "real" Nazis. Many Germans, as it turned out, "had no desire to accept responsibility for the war or its consequences."[53] Obviously, Eisenhower had work to do.

In the months after the final collapse, the Allies attempted to judge German public opinion. What they found was a nation that if it no longer supported Nazism, still found a good deal of patriotic pride in their Fatherland. Many Germans felt the Third Reich had been justified in fighting Great Britain, France, and the hated Russians. They also told American pollsters that the only reason the United States had gotten involved in the conflict was because of the power of world Jewry. The bombing of German cities was referred to as the "revenge" of the Jews. Well into 1946, over a third of Germans polled believed they had fought a war of "legitimate national defense" —including the killing of Jews, Poles, and non-Aryan civilians, and around half were prepared to endorse the idea that National Socialism was a "good idea carried out badly."[54] Most Germans wanted to move on, to "let the grass grow over" what had happened during the Nazi period. The war's outcome, including the occupation, was viewed as atonement enough.

---

[52] Letter, Alexander Frieder to General Eisenhower, June 1, 1945, Dwight D. Eisenhower's Pre-Presidential Papers, Principal File, Box 43, Frieder Alex, NAID#12007723, Dwight Eisenhower Presidential Library, Abilene, Kansas.
[53] Kershaw, *The End*, 380–381; Hitchcock, *The Bitter Road to Freedom*, 202; Smith, *Dachau*, 223; Ziemke, *The U.S. Army in the Occupation of Germany*, 280; Laurence Rees, *The Holocaust: A New History* (New York: Viking, 2017), 414–417. By the 1990s, it became common for Germans to see the Allies as having liberated them from Nazism. See the Memorial in the New Townhall in Munich as an example.
[54] Nicholas Stargardt, *The German War: A Nation Under Arms, 1939–1945, Citizens and Soldiers* (New York: Basic Books, 2015), 563–564; Michael Burleigh, *Moral Combat: Good and Evil in World War II* (New York: Harper Collins Publishers, 2011), 440–441; "Exit the Fatherland," https://aeon.co/essays/germany-became-a-tolerant-nation-only-by-painful-small-steps, 7 June 2021.

Nowhere was Germanic rationalization seen more clearly than when the topic turned to the camp system. Germans interviewed by the Allies said that if people were imprisoned in concentration camps, they must have committed some sort of crime and so, should have expected punishment.[55] But the rationalization did not end there. Acknowledging that people had suffered in the camps, Germans who survived Allied air raids began to not just compare their suffering with those in the camps but claim that they had it worse than prisoners. According to Otto Ohlendorf, the former head of Einsatzgruppe D, "the treatment of the Germans by the Allies was at least as bad as the shooting of those Jews. The bombing of cities with men, women, and children burning with phosphorus—these things were done by the Allies." The air war, Germans asserted, was "sadistic" and made the horrors of the camps pale in comparison.[56]

Obviously, it was difficult for some Germans to reconcile what they had done (or had been done in their name) and the horrors they had endured between Allied bombing, invasion and postwar expulsion of ethnic Germans from places like Poland, with the fact that the Holocaust meant their issues were always going to be secondary to the Allies, including Eisenhower.[57] Americans recognized that the Germans had suffered during the war. But to compare what they went through to Jews, who had been forced from their homes, lost all their possessions, sent to ghettos, then to concentration camps—including death camps—seemed ridiculous.[58] As the Allies discovered for themselves, not only did Germans claim to have never supported the Nazi Party, but they also said they had no knowledge of either the camp system or the Holocaust. It was nothing short of national amnesia. American journalist Martha Gellhorn reported that if the Germans had hid-

---

55 Rees, *The Holocaust: A New History*, 414–417.
56 Gellately, editor, *The Nuremberg Interviews*, 390, 427; Fest, *Inside Hitler's Bunker*, vii–ix, 127–130; Stargardt, *The German War: A Nation Under Arms*, 541; Merridale, *Ivan's War*, 347; Antony Beevor, *Ardennes 1944: Hitler's Last Gamble* (New York: Viking Press, 2015), 43; McKale, *Nazis after Hitler*, 167; W.G. Sebald, *On the Natural History of Destruction* (New York: Modern Library Classics, 2004); Hitchcock, *The Bitter Road to Freedom*, 189; Judah Nadich, *Eisenhower and the Jews* (New York: Twayne Publishers, 1953), 28–29.
57 R.M. Douglas, *Orderly and Humane: The Expulsion of the Germans after the Second World War* (New Have: Yale University Press, 2012), 128, 149–150, 156; Neiberg, *Potsdam*, 132; McManus, *Hell Before Their Very Eyes*, 20, 130.
58 Robert H. Abzug, *Inside the Vicious Heart: Americans and the Liberation of Nazi Concentration Camps* (New York: Oxford University Press, 1987), 156; Daniel Jonah Goldhagen, *Hitler's Willing Executioners: Ordinary Germans and the Holocaust* (New York: Vintage Books, 1997), 8–11; Konrad H. Jarausch and Michael Geyer, *Shattered Past: Reconstructing German Histories* (Princeton: Princeton University Press, 2003), 8.

den as many Jews as they claimed, the camps she had visited should never have been full.[59]

Survivors of the camps found the German mindset inexplicable, but also not surprising.[60] Armin Hertz, who was a prisoner at both Auschwitz and Buchenwald, noted that the citizens of Weimar all "claimed they didn't know there was such a camp. Nobody knew what went on. But we knew that throughout the years the prisoners from Buchenwald went into the city of Weimar and cleaned the streets, dug ditches there, did excavations, and whatever. If they dropped a bomb, they took them out there to defuse the bombs. So, they must have seen them because they also were wearing these striped uniforms. But they claimed they did not know." Other survivors gave allowances for not knowing the scale of the Holocaust but believed Germans who claimed to know nothing about the camps were lying both to those asking and to themselves. The sheer number of camps and guards made it an impossible position to believe.[61]

The American occupiers found the German refusal to admit what had happened in their country arrogant. They were also shocked at the "apparent indifference to the suffering" of those the Nazis had placed in jails and camps.[62] American soldiers continued to ponder just how much the German people knew and were complicit in the crimes the Nazi's committed. As Major Richard J. Eaton put it, "if they did know and approved of them, then they are more consummate and artful deceivers than seems humanly possible."[63] One of Eisenhower's goals was to require Germans to feed, clothe, and care for former workers and prisoners in the camps. He also wanted to force Germans to take responsibility for what their leaders and military had done during the war. He was pleased that on at least some occasions, citizens exhibited real remorse for having not helped Jews and other prisoners.[64]

---

59 Heather Pringle, *The Master Plan: Himmler's Scholars and the Holocaust* (New York: Hyperion, 2006), 291–292; Eric A Johnson and Karl-Heinz Reuband, *What We Knew: Terror, Mass Murder, and Everyday Life in Nazi Germany, An Oral History* (New York: Basic Books, 2005), 150; Yisrael Gutman and Michael Berenbaum, editors, *Anatomy of the Auschwitz Death Camp* (Indianapolis: Indiana University Press, 1994), 536.
60 David P. Boder, *I Did Not Interview the Dead* (Urbana, IL: The University of Illinois Press, 1949), 56.
61 Johnson and Reuband, *What We Knew*, 34, 107.
62 Ziemke, *The U.S. Army in the Occupation of Germany*, 281; Smith, *Dachau*, 41.
63 "Runde Ecke," https://www.runde-ecke-leipzig.de/, 17 September2022; Author visit, 20 May 2022.
64 Smith, *Dachau*, 47; Raul Hilberg, *The Destruction of the European Jews* (Chicago: Quadrangle Books, 1961), 202.

In seeking justice and an accounting, Ike attempted to walk a fine line of not being seen as vengeful, but rather fair, to the average German.[65] Before the end of the war, Eisenhower's men had captured 3 million German POWs. In addition to insuring that these men were both cared for and participated in the denazification process, Ike had to show the German civilian population that he was also policing his own men. He ordered an investigation into if any American soldiers had committed war crimes. Some 75 allegations were made, of which only five rose to what was considered "serious incidents" in need of further action. He also had to ensure that both German POWs and civilians alike had enough food and coal for the coming winter, a task he accomplished thanks to American resources, logistics, and the fact that the winter of 1945–1946 was largely mild. While food scarcity would plague all Europe for several more years, the American zone began its recovery under Ike.[66]

It was hardly surprising that Germans preferred the occupation forces of the U.S., Great Britain, and even the French over that of the Soviet Union.[67] However, the stirrings of rapprochement also complicated denazification. One of the regulations that Eisenhower was instructed by Washington to enforce was a strict policy of no fraternization between U.S. soldiers and German civilians. Like many of the occupation guidelines that eventually made their way to Eisenhower's desk, the policy was largely conceived before the war had ended and the horrors of the camps were made public. While no one disagreed with the idea that the Nazis had created a "nation of sinners against peace and human decency," German civilians were still people who might be "sick, hungry, and frightened, old and young, pretty and pitiable, guilty and innocent." As official U.S. Army historian Earl Ziemke pointed out, "even though they might accept the idea of German collective guilt, the American soldiers did not feel at ease as agents of collective retribution." It was a policy almost impossible to enforce, and Eisenhower eventually let it lapse.[68]

---

65 Joseph W. Bendersky, *The "Jewish Threat": Anti-Semitic Politics of the U.S. Army* (New York: Basic Books, 2000), 367.
66 Eisenhower, *How Ike Led*, 93; Bischof and Ambrose, *Eisenhower and the German POWs*, 5, 57, 105–107. Despite some specious allegations otherwise, the work of Bischof and Ambrose shows conclusively that there was no systematic killing, starvation, or mistreatment of German POWs under Eisenhower.
67 Marlis G. Steinert, *Hitler's War and the Germans: Public Mood and Attitude During the Second World War* (Athens, OH: Ohio University Press, 1977), 314; Merridale, *Ivan's War*, 349; Hitchcock, *The Bitter Road to Freedom*, 199; "Denazification," http://www.alliiertenmuseum.de/en/topics/denazification.html, 18 June 2021.
68 Ziemke, *The U.S. Army in the Occupation of Germany*, 160–161; Ambrose, *Eisenhower: Soldier and President*, 213; Hitchcock, *The Bitter Road to Freedom*, 179–181, 196–198.

He also understood that denazification risked being sacrificed because of postwar politics. While the Allies had a common foe in Germany, they were able to work together. In occupying Germany there continued to be a need for good relations between the Western Allies and the Soviet Union and that job fell on Eisenhower to manage. It was complicated by the Soviet adherence to communism and the fact that the U.S.S.R. was essentially a totalitarian dictatorship, which was antithetical to American values. Additionally, many senior officers in the Army, including General George Patton were vocally anti-communist and willing to halt denazification to shore-up the rebuilding of the western portion of Germany into a democracy. Ike noted with increasing dismay as the press wondered less about denazification and focused instead on the economic rebuilding of the Allied zones and as Patton's statements about the evils of communism morphed into anti-Semitic conspiracies between international Jewry and Bolshevism. While Ike hoped the postwar world would adhere to American values it was obvious to him that the horrors of the concentration camps had left a more vivid stamp on him than on Patton.[69]

One area of denazification that Eisenhower held firm on, however, was on arresting, imprisoning, and prosecuting verified Nazis. He refused a blanket amnesty for German prisoners of war in U.S. custody until their identities could be checked. Doing so was not just a matter of justice, it also eased the strain placed on destroyed German cities the prisoners might want to return to. Of the three million German POWs in American custody, some two million eventually had some form of charge levied against them by the Americans, though only about 100,000 were brought to formal trial. The U.S. also fired officials, including teachers, with strong Nazi ties, renamed streets, and destroyed statues, monuments, and emblems left over from Hitler's Third Reich.[70] In a stroke of retribution that Eisenhower likely enjoyed, about 25,000 of the suspected Nazi criminals were housed at the former concentration camp at Dachau. All of them were forced to tour the gas chambers and crematorium as well as view pictures taken during the camp's liberation.[71] While his successors later modified these policies, especially as the Cold War

---

69 Alfred D. Chandler, Jr. and Louis Galambos, editors, *The Papers of Dwight David Eisenhower: Occupation, 1945, Volume VI* (Baltimore: The Johns Hopkins University Press, 1971), 375–376; Joseph W. Bendersky, *The "Jewish Threat": Anti-Semitic Politics of the U.S. Army* (New York: Basic Books, 2000), 315–316, 352, 356–358, 368; Ira Chernus, "Eisenhower and the Soviets, 1945–1947: Rhetoric and Policy," *Rhetoric and Public Affairs*, 2(Spring 1999), 61–67, 74.
70 Eisenhower, *Crusade in Europe*, 434; Ziemke, *The U.S. Army in the Occupation of Germany*, 290–293; Perry Biddiscombe, *Denazification: A History, 1945–1950* (Stroud, UK: Tempus Press, 2007), 9; Jean Edward Smith, editor, *The Papers of General Lucius D. Clay: Germany, 1945–1949, Volume I* (Bloomington: Indiana University Press, 1974), 46, 60–61, 130; McKale, *Nazis after Hitler*, 99; Ambrose, *Eisenhower: Soldier and President*, 215; Pringle, *The Master Plan*, 299.
71 McManus, *Hell Before Their Very Eyes*, 144.

emerged, Eisenhower gave the American Zone a start at leaving the Third Reich behind.[72]

Displaced Persons and the Harrison Report

Denazification, Eisenhower realized early on, was going to be a long process. If that was the only issue he had to work on as military governor, it would have been nearly a fulltime job in and of itself. However, in addition to purging Germany of Nazi influence, Eisenhower was also tasked with starting its rebuilding and administering the American zone of occupation. Part of his time was thusly devoted to taking care of the people who lived within the zone, and none more specifically than a group known as "displaced persons" or DPs.

Wars create refugees. As the official U.S. Army history of the occupation put it: "One of the familiar human products of war is the refugee, the resident of a combat zone set adrift either by anticipated or actual destruction of his home and means of livelihood. An object of pity as an individual, in the mass he becomes a menace, clogs roads, imposes potentially ruinous burdens on already strained civilian services, and spreads panic."[73] In World War II, the refugee issue was compounded by the problem of the displaced person, which was a direct result of the Nazi camp system. These were not just refugees, but people the Nazis had seized in countries outside of Germany (or from within Germany), and then placed in camps. They were victims of the Nazis, often hundreds of miles away from their homes and families—assuming those homes and families still existed. All told, there were some 30 million DPs by May 1945.[74] Many of them were now Eisenhower's responsibility. Caring for them became part of the final chapter of the war.[75]

Even before the conflict ended, SHAEF had recognized that refugees, if not DPs, were going to be part of their mission planning. But they did not realize the scope of the problem until well after D-Day, and even then, did not really include in their planning the liberation of the concentration camps nor for how to care for the DPs during the occupation of Germany.[76] The lack of time devoted to planning, coupled with the lack of intelligence about both the camp system and the Holocaust

---

72 Bendersky, *The "Jewish Threat"*, 358. As Peter Caddick-Adams notes, an additional reason for lack of prosecution was that many Nazis died in the final months of fighting, committed suicide rather than surrender, or fled. See his *Fire and Steel*, 517.
73 Ziemke, *The U.S. Army in the Occupation of Germany*, 52.
74 Ziemke, *The U.S. Army in the Occupation of Germany*, 52; Abzug, *Inside the Vicious Heart*, 147.
75 Peter Novick, *The Holocaust in American Life* (New York: Houghton Mifflin, 1999), 84.
76 Ziemke, *The U.S. Army in the Occupation of Germany*, 53, 167.

helps to explain Eisenhower's worry about "the dangerous chaos of liberation" getting out of hand and the decision to keep the now freed former prisoners in the camps while the Allies marched on towards ultimate victory over the Nazis. Simply put, the initial theorizing about DPs, either by SHAEF or by the United Nations Relief and Rehabilitation Administration (UNRRA) was not enough.[77]

So, who were these DPs? It was Eisenhower's call for politicians, newspaper editors, and clergy members to come and visit the camps that gave him (and us) some real insight into both their identity and plight. One of those who answered Ike's call was Professor David P. Boder of the Illinois Institute of Technology in Chicago. Broder did some of the first systematic interviews of DPs and noted "the displaced persons, in spite of their sorry state today, are not riffraff, not the scum of the earth, not the poor devils who suffer because they don't know their rights, not idlers who declaim that the world owes them a living. They are uprooted people. They represent the members of all classes of society – farmers, industrial workers, teachers, lawyers, engineers, merchants, artists, housewives – who have been dislocated by a world catastrophe."[78] As he and others soon discovered, the DP population also contained virtually all the remaining Jews in Europe.

The DPs who survived internment, war, and liberation tended to enter the postwar world with just their lives. Far from home, often with no knowledge of if their families had survived the Nazis or not, many went from the joy of liberation to feelings of anxiety about the future. Some wanted revenge on Germans and held strong resentment towards the German communities near the camps.[79] Many of the surviving Jews now considered themselves stateless and did not want to return to their home countries. Nor, as it turned out, did all the survivors like one another—which surprised the Americans, who just assumed everyone would be happy to have made it through the war. Even if the DPs had been al-

---

[77] Chandler and Galambos, editors, *The Papers of Dwight David Eisenhower: Occupation, 1945, Volume VI*, 416–418; "United Nations Relief and Rehabilitation Administration," https://encyclopedia.ushmm.org/content/en/article/united-nations-relief-and-rehabilitation-administration, 18 September 2022; Beevor, *Ardennes 1944*, 2; McManus, *Hell Before Their Very Eyes*, 109; Smith, *Dachau*, 129; Bendersky, *The "Jewish Threat"*, 350–351; Judah Nadich, *Eisenhower and the Jews* (New York: Twayne Publishers, 1953), 33. SHAEF issued Memo 39 about DPs on 16 April 1945, roughly at the same time that the first camps, including Ohrdruf, were being liberated.

[78] Boder, *I Did Not Interview the Dead*, xi–xii, xvii. See also, "Home," http://voices.iit.edu/, 22 May 2018.

[79] Isabel Vincent, *Hitler's Silent Partners: Swiss Banks, Nazi Gold, and the Pursuit of Justice* (New York: William Morrow and Company, Inc., 1997), 2–4; Richard Overy, *Blood and Ruins: The Last Imperial War, 1931–1945* (New York: Viking, 2021), 759.

lowed to leave the camps, adjusting to freedom took time, especially in the condition Europe was in post-May 1945.[80]

Not surprisingly many of the DPs were frustrated. Having survived the camps and the war, they were ready to get on with their lives—indeed, to live. They did not want to be in camps anymore, nor to abide by someone else's rules.[81] As Eisenhower noted, "even food, clothes, and decent treatment could not immediately enable them to shake off their hopelessness and apathy."[82] While the camps under the Americans were a vast improvement over the German system, they were still camps. The Army believed that it was providing the DPs with a secure, clean, well-administered environment. But to Jewish DPs, especially, who had no homeland, who were not welcome in Germany, and had no place waiting for them, there was an unbearable "staleness" of being unwanted and still in a camp.[83]

Their displeasure was heard back in Washington, D.C. Secretary of the Treasury Henry Morgenthau decided to demand action to remedy the situation. The secretary had developed a dislike of Eisenhower, blaming the general for not prioritizing helping Jews rather than winning the war. Because saving Jews from the camps had not been a war aim, Morgenthau believed they were being treated poorly, or at best, just like other DPs. The secretary wanted the policy changed. He demanded that President Harry Truman send a fact-finding delegation to Europe to see about the condition of the DP camps.[84] Though the new president did not particularly care for Morgenthau, he did agree to send Earl G. Harrison to lead the investigative commission. A Philadelphia lawyer, former commissioner of immigration and naturalization in the Roosevelt Administration, and newly named dean of the University of Pennsylvania law school, Harrison agreed to investigate the conditions facing Jewish DPs. His mission was authorized by the president on June 22, 1945 and by early July, Harrison arrived in Germany.[85]

---

80 Eisenhower, *Crusade in Europe*, 439; McManus, *Hell Before Their Very Eyes*, 46–47, 109; Johnson and Reuband, *What We Knew:*, 18; Nadich, *Eisenhower and the Jews*, 41, 45; David A. Hackett, editor, *The Buchenwald Report* (Boulder: Westview Press, 1995), 98; Gutman and Berenbaum, editors, *Anatomy of the Auschwitz Death Camp*, 477; Hitchcock, *The Bitter Road to Freedom*, 284; Abzug, *Inside the Vicious Heart*, 145; Beevor, *Ardennes 1944*, 2; Smith, *Dachau*, 129.
81 Hitchcock, *The Bitter Road to Freedom*, 323, 332.
82 Eisenhower, *Crusade in Europe*, 439–440.
83 Hitchcock, *The Bitter Road to Freedom*, 320, 332–337; Atina Grossmann, *Jews, Germans and Allies: Close Encounters in Occupied Germany* (Princeton, N.J.: Princeton University Press, 2007), 163–164; Abzug, *Inside the Vicious Heart*, 138–139. Munich became a hub of DP camps in the American sector.
84 Hitchcock, *The Bitter Road to Freedom*, 5, 318; Beschloss, *The Conquerors*, 54.
85 Abzug, *Inside the Vicious Heart*, 162; Grossmann, *Jews, Germans and Allies*, 138; *Washington Post*, 11 July 2003; Nadich, *Eisenhower and the Jews*, 33, 196.

In some respects, Harrison discovered, the Army was both the best and worst possible organization to deal with the DP issue. Obviously, it was on the ground, had an in place logistical and organizational network, and the means to carry out the administration of camps. On the other hand, its men had virtually no training in such matters, it was a force designed for winning a war (which had only recently ended), and the DPs were hardly uniform either in terms of their nationality/language/cultural backgrounds or towards their desire to return home. Layered on top of that was a German populace who seemed, despite the recent past, so very similar and like the American occupiers. Harrison observed that American empathy for the DPs, whether because of latent anti-Semitism, ignorance of all they had been through, or because of the influence of other factors like homesickness, was on the wane.[86]

Harrison issued his report shortly after the conclusion of the Potsdam Conference.[87] In it, he noted the "appreciation" of the "victims of Nazi persecution for the interest of the United States Government in them," but "they have been 'liberated' more in a military sense than actually." He found it intolerable that the victims of the Nazis were still being housed in the former Nazi camps. "Beyond knowing that they are no longer in danger of the gas chambers, torture, and other forms of violent death, they see—and there is—little change." Meanwhile, many Germans are back to living a "normal" life. He urged consideration for the Jews above all other DPs. Not doing so was the same as "closing one's eyes to their former and more barbaric persecution, which has already made them a separate group with greater needs." He concluded that the Germans do not feel guilt for what happened and that many of the survivors wanted to leave Germany and Austria and go to Palestine. "As matters now stand, we appear to be treating the Jews as the Nazis treated them except that we do not exterminate them. They are in concentration camps in large numbers under our military guard instead of SS troops. One is led to wonder whether the German people, seeing this, are not supposing that we are following or at least condoning Nazi policy." Harrison wanted immigration opened and improvements made, including better food and new officers assigned to administer the camps, immediately.[88]

---

[86] Bendersky, *The "Jewish Threat"*, 349–360.
[87] Neiberg, *Potsdam*, 254.
[88] "Harrison Report," https://www.ushmm.org/exhibition/displaced-persons/resourc1.htm, 29 June 2017; Jon Bridgman, *The End of the Holocaust: The Liberation of the Camps* (Portland: Areopagitica Press, 1990), 115; Abzug, *Inside the Vicious Heart*, 162; Grossmann, *Jews, Germans and Allies*, 138.

The report was a bombshell when it began circulating in Washington in August. As historian William Hitchcock notes, while not entirely critical of the Army considering the task at hand, the report "dealt a shattering blow to the reputation of the occupation army, and clearly wounded Eisenhower personally."[89] Not surprisingly, Ike came to different conclusions and believed the report was fundamentally unfair to the military and its (and thus his) efforts to date.[90] While he found some of the report's details enlightening, particularly about the feelings of Jewish DPs in regards to staying in Europe, he was irked by those who let "their humanitarian impulses outraged by conditions that were frequently beyond help, began carrying to America tales of indifference, negligence, and callousness on the part of the troops. Generally, these stories were lies."[91] Furthermore, what he saw in the summary report sent to him was fundamentally different than what Harrison had "verbally" reported to his office.[92]

Part of Ike's defensiveness came from the fact that he had started to deal with some of the issues Harrison's report publicized prior to the report even being issued. On August 10, while also responding to inquirers from both President Truman and other White House officials, Eisenhower decided to create a special advisor to assess the conditions of Jewish DPs. The officer selected was Major (later Lieutenant Colonel) Judah Nadich, a rabbi and senior Jewish chaplain in the ETO. Nadich launched his own inspection tours of the camps. And while his report was more positive than Harrison's, it also confirmed one aspect of the Harrison Report that particularly galled Eisenhower: While his orders on how to care for DPs were clear and consistent, they were not always being followed.[93]

---

[89] Nadich, *Eisenhower and the Jews*, 34–35; Hitchcock, *The Bitter Road to Freedom*, 319; Harry S. Truman, *Memoirs: Volume 2, Years of Trial and Hope* (Garden City: Doubleday & Company, 1956), 137–138. See also, Chandler and Galambos, editors, *The Papers of Dwight David Eisenhower: Occupation, 1945, Volume VI*, 268.
[90] Mark Wyman, *DPs: Europe's Displaced Persons, 1945–1951* (Ithaca: Cornell University Press, 1998), 136; Joanne Reilly, *Belsen: The Liberation of a Concentration Camp* (New York: Routledge, 1998), 90.
[91] Eisenhower, *Crusade in Europe*, 440.
[92] Chandler and Galambos, editors, *The Papers of Dwight David Eisenhower: Occupation, 1945, Volume VI*, 266.
[93] Chandler and Galambos, editors, *The Papers of Dwight David Eisenhower: Occupation, 1945, Volume VI*, 353–354; "Headquarters, United States Forces, European Theater, to the Commanding Generals, Western Military and Eastern Military Districts," 22 August 1945, Foreign Relations of the United States: Diplomatic Papers, 1945, General: Political and Economic Matters, Volume II, accessed on 7 September 2022; Bischof and Ambrose, *Eisenhower and the German POWs*, 207–209; Nadich, *Eisenhower and the Jews*, 37–49, 63–78, 113–117, 123–130; *New York Times*, 2 September 2007. Nadich became one of Ike's staunchest defenders against charges that he was either anti-Semitic or uncaring towards the plight of Jews, whether DPs or those who established Israel.

Ike had expected his orders to be carried out and had initially agreed to the policy of treating all the DPs, including Jews, the same. He was quite upset to discover that his orders were being disregarded, particularly in the area under occupation by General George Patton's Third Army. A pattern emerged of Ike issuing directives and Patton opting not to issue appropriate orders to his command to put them into effect. Third Army's position, for example, was that if a DP was housed in a private home and not in a camp then they were no longer DPs and were not the concern of American forces. Eisenhower issued new orders when it came to DPs in late September. When Patton drug his feet even on these directives of clarification, Ike sent out another round of orders in mid-October. He also took the difficult step of relieving Patton of command of Third Army and replacing him with General Lucian Truscott. Ike charged Truscott with being "ruthless" in terms of denazification and to give priority to the "victims of Nazi persecution." No American soldier in Germany was going to be able to say they did not understand the position of the commanding general when it came to DPs.[94]

To hammer home how important he held the issue, Eisenhower decided to visit some of the DP camps himself. All told, he made unannounced tours of five camps, two of which, the Bismarck Strasse housing block in Stuttgart and the Feldafing camp near Munich were home to Jewish DPs.[95] At Feldafing, the former Supreme Allied Commander took part in Yom Kippur services, which "electrified the large congregation" of 5,000. He listened as the Klausenberger rabbi, Yekusiel Yehudah Halberstam, relayed his experience in the Holocaust, including rhetorically asking Eisenhower why the Americans had not intervened earlier and why they had not bombed Auschwitz to stop the killing. By the end of the Halberstam's talk, Ike had tears in his eyes. Speaking after the address, Eisenhower asked the Jewish DPs to be patient, but promised them that one day they would have homes of their own again and vowed that the U.S. Army was there to help.[96]

---

[94] Nadich, *Eisenhower and the Jews*, 120–121, 130–133, 153–154, 203, 206, 221; Bendersky, *The "Jewish Threat"*, 355. Wilson Allen Heefner, *Dogface Soldier: The Life of General Lucian K. Truscott, Jr.*(Columbia: University of Missouri Press, 2010), 253–254; Eisenhower, editor, *Letters to Mamie*, 272; Eisenhower, *How Ike Led*, 91; Bischof and Ambrose, *Eisenhower and the German POWs*, 3. Patton's obstruction and his terming of Jewish DPs as being "lower than animals," prompted Ike's decision to relieve him of his command. See, Ziemke, *The U.S. Army in the Occupation of Germany*, 384–385. The controversial American general died after a car accident in December 1945.

[95] Nadich, *Eisenhower and the Jews*, 129–130; Chandler and Galambos, editors, *The Papers of Dwight David Eisenhower: Occupation, 1945, Volume VI*, 358–359; Geoffrey Perret, *Eisenhower* (New York: Random House, 1999), 357; Hitchcock, *The Bitter Road to Freedom*, 321.

[96] "Confronting General Eisenhower Over Allies Refusal to Bomb Auschwitz," http://www.aish.com/ho/i/Confronting-General-Eisenhower-Over-Allies-Refusal-to-Bomb-Auschwitz.html, 5 July 2018; "Sermon on Yom Kippur by the Klausenberger Rebbe," https://www.yadvashem.org/yv/en/exhibitions/rosh_hashana/rabbi_yekutiel_yehuda_halberstam.asp, 16 June 2021.

Ike's visit to Feldafing caused a sensation in the international Jewish community. Holocaust survivors long remembered their encounter with the American military governor. Rose Kohn said it was "a beautiful thing" for Eisenhower to have come to the camp and spend time with the Jewish DPs. Mina Moszenberg said, "he looked like God to me," and praised him for ordering Germans out of their homes, so that DPs would have better places to live shortly after his visit. Sam Wise remembered that when Ike arrived at the camp, he ordered his guards to take down machine gun positions placed for his security, telling them "I haven't any enemies here." And Larry Flynn recalled that Ike listened to the camp's rabbi, and then ordered changes immediately to how the camp was administered.[97] His visit to the DP camps was hailed by David Ben-Gurion as well.[98] At least some Jewish DPs eventually came to the United States over Palestine because of their interaction with American GIs—including Eisenhower.[99]

Obviously, Eisenhower took the Harrison Report seriously. He poured over it, making notations on his copy. And he mentally compared the DP camps under his purview with what he had seen at Ohrdruf. On September 14, 1945 he sent a preliminary response to President Truman. While "concerned" about the letter the president had sent him about the report and conceding that some of "my subordinates in the field are not carrying out my policies," Harrison's story did not ring entirely true to Ike. He told Truman that "in the United States Zone . . . no official complaints" had been lodged, and "in the United States Zone in Germany no possible effort is being spared to give these people every consideration toward better living conditions, better morale and a visible goal." Eisenhower followed this up with a letter on September 18, commenting on his recently completed trips to the DP camps. The general noted that "the hopelessness of the ordinary displaced person comes about from fear of the future." Those from the Baltic States, Poland, and Romania, did not want to return to their nations, now under the control of the Soviet Union. And when it came to the Jews, most expressed an interest in leaving Europe for Palestine. He "found no instances of displaced persons still living in the old 'horror' camps." Ike also noted that it was far easier to

---

[97] Larry Flynn, Oral History, USC Shoah Foundation, Visual History Archive, accessed 2 August 2017; Rose Kohn, Oral History, USC Shoah Foundation, Visual History Archive, accessed 2 August 2017; Mina Moszenberg, Oral History, USC Shoah Foundation, Visual History Archive, accessed 2 August 2017; Sam Wise, Oral History, USC Shoah Foundation, Visual History Archive, accessed 2 August 2017.

[98] Nadich, *Eisenhower and the Jews*, 233, 239.; Isaac Alteras, *Eisenhower and Israel: U.S.-Israeli Relations, 1953–1960* (Gainesville: University Press of Florida, 1993), 29; Grossmann, *Jews, Germans and Allies*, 163–164; Bridgman, *The End of the Holocaust*, 73.

[99] Eisenhower, *How Ike Led*, 92.

care for the DPs in camps, than it would be to release them into the general population. As he worked to improve their situation, he told the president that he believed Harrison had missed the larger picture of what he and the Army were doing when it came to not just the DPs but with the American occupation zone of Germany overall.[100]

And then came his final response to the report. Dated October 8, 1945, Eisenhower began by noting that Harrison's trip had been made in July, just two months after the end of the war. Many things had changed since then and his efforts to "improve" the conditions that DPs found themselves in continued. Ike reminded the president that the U.S. Zone was absorbing more than double of its war time population, as Germans returned home, ethnic Germans were expelled from lands beyond Germany's postwar borders, and the addition of both the American forces and DPs themselves. He assured Truman that "displaced persons have absolute preference over Germans for housing" and that Jewish DPs had their own centers. While some Jewish DPs had been formerly housed in old concentration camps, none of them remained "longer than was absolutely necessary for medical quarantine and recovery from acute illness." Furthermore, Ike tactically pointed out that all this was largely being done by the military mere months after it had been fighting a war, in a role it was not accustomed to. While they may have "fallen below standard" from time to time, and had not attained "perfection," "real and honest efforts are being made to provide suitable living conditions for these persecuted people until they can be permanently resettled in other areas." Harrison's report, in Ike's opinion, "gives little regard to the problems faced, the real success attained in saving the lives of thousands of Jewish and other concentration camp victims, and repatriating those who could and wished to be repatriated, and the progress made in the two months to bring these unfortunates who remained under our jurisdiction from the depths of physical degeneration to a condition of health and essential comfort."[101] What the Allies had achieved in the housing, care, and movement of some 8 million DPs in Germany,

---

100 Report, Earl G. Harrison's "Mission," August 1945, Dwight D. Eisenhower's Pre-Presidential Papers, Principal File, Box 116, Truman Harry S. (4) NAID#12007695, Dwight Eisenhower Presidential Library, Abilene, Kansas; Telegram, General Eisenhower to President Truman, September 14, 1945, Dwight D. Eisenhower's Pre-Presidential Papers, Principal File, Box 116, Truman Harry S. (4) NAID#12007865, Dwight Eisenhower Presidential Library, Abilene, Kansas; Letter, General Eisenhower to President Truman, September 18, 1945, Dwight D. Eisenhower's Pre-Presidential Papers, Principal File, Box 116, Truman Harry S. (4) NAID#12007674, Dwight Eisenhower Presidential Library, Abilene, Kansas; Hitchcock, *The Bitter Road to Freedom*, 322.
101 Letter, General Eisenhower to President Truman, October 8, 1945, Dwight D. Eisenhower's Pre-Presidential Papers, Truman Harry S. (4) NAID#1200766, Dwight Eisenhower Presidential Library, Abilene, Kansas; Nadich, *Eisenhower and the Jews*, 116. For more on the reparation of DPs,

including the 300,000 Jews found in German, Austrian, and Italian camps, was miraculous in many ways.[102] And Ike believed those efforts needed to be celebrated, not condemned.

While Harrison thought Eisenhower's characterization of his report was "misleading," its existence and Ike's reaction to it kept the issue of both the DPs and the Holocaust at the forefront of postwar newspapers. The discussion showcased not just the overall improving conditions the DPs had as the winter of 1945 approached, but it also prompted Truman to formally request the British to allow more Jews to immigrate to the Palestine protectorate, which they continued to resist doing.[103] In many ways, that had been among Harrison's chief goals, having noted that: "The civilized world owes it to this handful of survivors to provide them with a home where they can again settle down and begin to live as human beings."[104]

Interestingly, one of Ike's final decisions about DPs spoke not just to what had happened during the war but the approaching confrontation with America's former Soviet allies. In late 1945, Eisenhower approved the request of some Polish Jews to come into the American Zone, rather than be returned to Poland. The decision was officially against regulations. However, Ike and his subordinates defended the decision on "humanitarian grounds." As a result, the policy was granted temporary approval and Jews who had survived Nazism were allowed to stay in a place free from communism as well.[105]

---

see, Hitchcock, *The Bitter Road to Freedom*, 259, and 285; Hauenstein, *Intelligence Was My Line*, 127–129.

102 Grossmann, *Jews, Germans and Allies*, 131–132; Eisenhower, *Eisenhower: At War, 1943–1945*, 810.

103 Ziemke, *The U.S. Army in the Occupation of Germany*, 416–417; Barry Trachtenberg, *The United States and the Nazi Holocaust: Race, Refuge and Remembrance* (New York: Bloomsbury, 2018), 97; Hitchcock, *The Bitter Road to Freedom*, 319, 348–351; Mark Celinscak, *Distance from the Belsen Heap: Allied Forces and the Liberation of a Nazi Concentration Camp* (Toronto: University of Toronto Press, 2015), 114–115; Tuvia Friling and Moshe Tlamin, "The New Historians and the Failure of Rescue Operations during the Holocaust," *Israel Studies*, 8(Fall 2003), 35; Grossmann, *Jews, Germans and Allies*, 134–141; Joseph W. Bendersky, *The "Jewish Threat": Anti-Semitic Politics of the U.S. Army* (New York: Basic Books, 2000), 356; Chandler and Galambos, editors, *The Papers of Dwight David Eisenhower: Occupation, 1945, Volume VI*, 354.

104 Grossmann, *Jews, Germans and Allies*, 138.

105 "Memorandum of Conversation, by the Adviser on Refugees and Displaced Persons," 21 December 1945, Foreign Relations of the United States: Diplomatic Papers, 1945, General: Political and Economic Matters, Volume II, accessed on 7 September 2022.

War Crimes Trials

The last component of Eisenhower's time as military governor of the American zone of occupied Germany was getting everything in place for the war crimes trials. Discussion of war crimes, how judgement might be passed on the Germans by Allies, and what such trials would mean for postwar Germany and the world were all things Eisenhower considered in the six months he remained in command. While he left before the trials truly got underway, Ike set the stage for what most Americans came to know as the Nuremberg Trials.

Starting in 1942, Allied leaders began discussing the need to punish the Germans for crimes being committed during the war. The European governments-in-exile truly began the conversation, knowing what was happening in their own nations now under Nazi rule. Of course, gathering evidence beyond eyewitness accounts, such as documents, was difficult during the war.[106] By October 1943, the United States, Great Britain, and Soviet Union were prepared to make a statement of their own, via the Moscow Declaration. In it, the Big Three warned the Nazis that they knew that Germany was committing "abominable deeds" and taking part in "atrocities and crimes" that would result in prosecution—either in the countries in which the crimes occurred or by the Allies themselves. In January 1944, the Allies created the United Nations War Crimes Commission.[107] All that was needed was for Germany to be defeated.

These developments had repercussions for Eisenhower as Supreme Allied Commander. In 1943, the War Department instructed him to discontinue any discussion by SHAEF about war crimes, criminals, or potential punishments—fearing that the Nazis might make reprisals against Allied POWs—and preferring that the Allied governments make such statements. At the same time, the War Department was busy researching and updating what a war crime and related punishments were in the wake of World War II.[108] American doctrine largely still adhered to the Second Hague Convention (1899), which talked of the need to treat prisoners of war "humanely," with no loss of personal articles, save for "arms, horses, and military papers." Furthermore, POWs were to be cared for by the "hostile Government," and while prisoners of war could be employed for labor

---

106 Ziemke, *The U.S. Army in the Occupation of Germany*, 219–220; Dan Plesch, *Human Rights After Hitler: The Lost History of Prosecuting Axis War Crimes* (Washington, D.C.: Georgetown University Press, 2017), 70–71, 79.
107 Ziemke, *The U.S. Army in the Occupation of Germany*, 169; *Nazi Conspiracy and Aggression: Volume 1* (Washington, D. C.: United States Government Printing Office, 1946), 1, 143; Plesch, *Human Rights After Hitler*, 81; Beschloss, *The Conquerors*, 22.
108 Ziemke, *The U.S. Army in the Occupation of Germany*, 170–172.

purposes, though not for military reasons, they were to be paid, with the money used to improve their condition, with the balance paid to them upon their release.[109] The convention was something Eisenhower was aware of, and that the Nazis had often disregarded when it came to POWs. However, the crimes the Nazis were accused of went beyond the scope of the convention. As the War Department continued its revision work, it also drew upon another legal doctrine that Eisenhower had known since his days at West Point: the Lieber Code, which had guided American military law since the Civil War.[110] The new American policy would not be completed until well after the war, so, for the time being, old policies would have to be bent towards dealing with new realities.

Those realities, of course, were the atrocities committed at the camps, which were so horrific that a whole new category or terminology needed to be created. The enormity of the concentration camp system, the deaths that occurred there, and the bodies of the living and the dead, cried out for retribution and justice. Suddenly, the discussion amongst the Allies switched from generic "war crimes" to much more specific, horrific, actions. Denazification was no longer going to be just about an ideology, but about punishing those accountable for killing millions away from the battlefield.[111]

Not surprisingly, one of the leading advocates for trials and punishing those responsible for the crimes that occurred in the camps was Eisenhower. While some Americans in the military, and the eventual war crimes prosecutorial staff, had doubts about the concept of guilt by association, Eisenhower did not. Still reeling from what he saw at Ohrdruf, Ike had refused to be generous towards Jodl at the surrender ceremony—setting the tone for how the Allies would treat their German peers. Having seen the camps, Eisenhower doubted if anyone in the service of Hitler's regime had any honor at all. He expressed his belief in organizational guilt at a press conference in June 1945, specifically mentioning the SS and the OKW. The following month, during the Potsdam Conference, Ike expanded his thoughts further while talking to President Truman—advocating that all leading politicians, members of the German military (with the General Staff

---

[109] "Treaties, States Parties and Commentaries: Hague Convention (II)," https://ihl-databases.icrc.org/applic/ihl/ihl.nsf/Treaty.xsp?documentId=CD0F6C83F96FB459C12563CD002D66A1&action=openDocument, 12 July 2017.

[110] Taylor, *The Anatomy of the Nuremberg Trials*, 5; John Fabian Witt, *Lincoln's Code: The Laws of War in American History* (New York: Free Press, 2012), 3.

[111] McKale, *Nazis after Hitler*, 5; Taylor, *The Anatomy of the Nuremberg Trials*, 52; *Indianapolis News*, 12 April 1945.

permanently dissolved), the SS, and Gestapo by virtue of their affiliation with the Nazi Party should be arrested and put on trial.[112]

Nor did he stop there. Ike worked hard to get the Joint Chiefs of Staff to authorize war crimes trials for concentration camp commandants and guards as war criminals. He believed that the "abominable deeds" done in the camps, whether inside or outside of Germany had to be punished. Under the Moscow Declaration, such war criminals were to be sent to the country in which the crimes were committed for trial. Eisenhower noted that such a reading of the law did not consider crimes committed against United Nations nationals inside of Germany. Eisenhower was using a conspiracy module to construct a rationale for the trials. His reasoning helped get the charges changed to crimes against humanity.[113]

For Eisenhower, "World War II was far too personal a thing to entertain" feelings of "professional soldiers" being "comrades in arms." Not when it came to the Nazis. Not after he came face to face with the Holocaust. Eisenhower wrote a friend that "I am well acquainted with their [Germans] history." There was no way to see Germans as blameless for either the world war or for the horrors of the concentration camps.[114]

Now, with the war over, it was time to seek justice.[115] The war crimes trials represented "the first time in history that legal proceedings have been instituted against leaders of an enemy nation." There was "no exact precedents for the charges" that were being made against the Nazi leadership, and "a heavy burden was laid on the accusing nations to make sure that their proof measured up to the magnitude of the accusations."[116] At the end of May, Eisenhower met with U.-S. Supreme Court Justice Robert Jackson, who had been appointed by President Truman as the lead American prosecutor to the International Military Tribunal. They discussed the best way to hold the Nazi prisoners, with Eisenhower telling

---

112 McKale, *Nazis after Hitler*, 5; Taylor, *The Anatomy of the Nuremberg Trials*, 52, 108–111, 238–239; Kasey S. Pipes, *Ike's Final Battle: The Road to Little Rock and the Challenge of Equality* (Los Angeles: World Ahead Publishing, 2007), 55–56; Beevor, *The Fall of Berlin 1945*, 205. Jodl would eventually be convicted of war crimes and executed in 1946.
113 Ziemke, *The U.S. Army in the Occupation of Germany*, 391–392; Taylor, *The Anatomy of the Nuremberg Trials*, 270.
114 Eisenhower, *Crusade in Europe*, 157; Chandler and Galambos, editors, *The Papers of Dwight David Eisenhower: Occupation, 1945: VI*, 153–154; Holl, *The Religious Journey of Dwight D. Eisenhower*, 144–145.
115 Ziemke, *The U.S. Army in the Occupation of Germany*, 215–216.
116 *Nazi Conspiracy and Aggression: Volume 1* (Washington, D. C.: United States Government Printing Office, 1946), v. See also, Graham B. Cox, *Seeking Justice for the Holocaust: Herbert C. Pell, Franklin D. Roosevelt, and the Limits of International Law* (Norman: University of Oklahoma Press, 2019).

Jackson that the Army would do everything possible to aid his work. Ike also approved of Jackson's plan to try the Gestapo as a criminal organization.[117]

Gathering that evidence fell, in part, on Eisenhower. As he discovered, the job was far easier than many expected. Despite orders to do so, many of the Nazis hated to destroy their records and often boasted of what they were doing, or planned to do, to prisoners in general and Jews in particular. While there was hardly a complete archive from every camp or every governmental building, there was so much paper and other material evidence that eventually Justice Jackson, ordered an end to discovery because the legal team had more than they needed or could use.[118]

The charges Jackson and the other prosecutors were about to bring against the Nazi defendants were crafted as part of the London Agreement of August 1945, which created the International Military Tribunal. Broadly speaking, the criminal charges fell under four groupings:

(a) Atrocities and offenses against person on property constituting violations of international law, including the rules and customs of land and naval warfare.
(b) Initiation of invasions of other countries and of wars of aggression in violation of international laws and treaties.
(c) Other atrocities and offenses, including atrocities and persecutions on racial, religious, or political grounds, committed since 30 January 1933.
(d) Membership in groups such as the SS or Gestapo that the IMT determined to be "criminal" in nature.

Much like with evidence gathering, Eisenhower was ordered, this time via JCS 1023/10, to begin the assessment of German prisoners in American custody that fit these criteria, and to assist the other Allies in doing the same for their prisoners. He likely took note of the specific use of January 1933 in the IMT proclamation.

---

[117] John Q. Barrett, "Meeting Ike (May 1945," https://thejacksonlist.com/wp-content/uploads/2015/07/20150526-Jackson-List-Eisenhower.pdf, 8 January 2021.
[118] Brian E. Crim, *Our Germans: Operation Paperclip and the National Security State* (Baltimore: Johns Hopkins University Press, 2018), 53; Pringle, *The Master Plan*, 292–294; Taylor, *The Anatomy of the Nuremberg Trials*, 135, 169; Smith, *Dachau*, 233; John Mendelsohn, editor, *The Holocaust: Volume 3, The Crystal Night Pogrom* (New York: Garland Publishing, Incorporated, 1982), 149, 383; Adolf Hitler's Private Will, Marriage Certificates and Political Testament, April 1945, Harry S. Truman Library, HST-WWII; World War II Collection, 1932–1996, Subject Files, Documents Relating to the Last Will of Adolf Hitler (MHDC350), copy provided by the Dwight Eisenhower Presidential Library, Abilene, Kansas.

That meant the IMT was going to be prosecuting Nazis not just for the crimes that occurred during the war, but for the entire period of Hitler's rule.[119]

Rather than hold the trials in Berlin, the decision was made to conduct them in Nuremburg. There were several reasons for the city's selection. For one, it was heavily symbolic. The Nazis had held some of their largest rallies in the Bavarian city. For another, it was not as destroyed as Berlin was. And lastly, it was in the American occupation sector. Placing the trials there allowed the United States to coordinate the proceedings and help ensure that the proceedings' appearance shied away from a Nazi, or Soviet, style "show trial." Like many other aspects, preparation of the site fell to Eisenhower. In addition to readying lodgings, court, and conference rooms, Ike ordered a plane be made available to fly the French and Russian judges from Berlin to Nuremberg in October, as well as making sure that the German defense consuls were provided with food, housing, and payment.[120]

Making the proceedings legitimate in the eyes of the world was necessary, not just because of the novelty of the IMT. One goal of the trials was to aid in denazification, meaning part of the target audience was the German public. Many Germans doubted the legitimacy of the proceedings and just as many seemed indifferent to the need for them. They saw no reason to take responsibility for what had been done in their name by the Nazi government. The Allies viewed the trials as a means to bring about both punishment for the guilty and justice for the dead, as well as a way to confront the "national amnesia" that seemed to have set in across Germany.[121]

Justice Jackson believed what Germany had done was violate everyone's rights, on an international scale. His opening statement to the IMT was a historical treatise on the Nazi regime. He made pointed remarks about the liberation of the Belsen, Buchenwald, and Dachau concentration camps—the camps liberated by the British and Americans. The prosecutors wanted to "show why and how these things happened," that the war and the Holocaust went hand-in-hand with the looting of nations, cities, and individuals and that the disease of Nazism and the genocide it had unleashed had permeated every aspect of German society to the point that Germans had turned their back on higher, moral law, causing "a

---

[119] Ziemke, *The U.S. Army in the Occupation of Germany*, 393; Taylor, *The Anatomy of the Nuremberg Trials*, 272; Dean J. Kotlowski, *Paul V. McNutt and the Age of FDR* (Indianapolis: Indiana University Press, 2015), 372; Hilberg, *The Destruction of the European Jews*, 687.
[120] Taylor, *The Anatomy of the Nuremberg Trials*, 131, 144; Gellately, editor, *The Nuremberg Interviews*, x–xi; Hilberg, *The Destruction of the European Jews*, 684; Pringle, *The Master Plan*, 292.
[121] Gienow-Hecht, *Transmission Impossible*, 61; Ziemke, *The U.S. Army in the Occupation of Germany*, 281; Smith, *Dachau*, 47; Hilberg, *The Destruction of the European Jews*, 202; Steinert, *Hitler's War and the Germans*, 315.

rupture in Western Civilization" as more than one observer described it, while embracing and blindly obeying a criminal undertaking in the form of the Third Reich.[122]

The Nazis on trial harbored a "hideous self-pity" about the postwar legal proceedings. Hermann Goering, for example, most often blamed his fellow Nazi leaders, such as Joseph Goebbels, Heinrich Himmler, Reinhard Heydrich, and Martin Bormann, who were either dead or missing, for the charges levied against him. Others, like Walther Funk, the Reich Minister for Economic Affairs, claimed to be filled with regret for what had happened in Germany, while also believing he had a sacred duty to fulfill his oath to the Nazi state. There was also a good deal of pride in what they had done and having been part of an undertaking so historic. Hans Frank, who had served as the head of the General Government in Poland, rationalized that killing millions was the bargain he had to pay to hold his position. Except for Albert Speer, none of the chief defendants expressed regret at the plan the Nazis had carried out. Indeed, some Nazis, like Alfred Rosenberg, who was the head of the Reich Ministry for the Occupied Eastern Territories and a Nazi theorist, remained unrepentant to the end, arguing that the Jews needed to be destroyed.[123]

Most Germans did not deal with the Nuremburg trials or discussion about the Holocaust very well. They wanted to move on from the war and rebuild their lives, towns, cities, and eventually their nation. If the IMT succeeded, it was in documenting the crime of the century in what many deemed the trial of the cen-

---

[122] "Opening Statement Before the International Military Tribunal," https://www.roberthjackson.org/speech-and-writing/opening-statement-before-the-international-military-tribunal/, 8 January 2021; Hilberg, *The Destruction of the European Jews*, 685; Taylor, *The Anatomy of the Nuremberg Trials*, 135, 169; Pringle, *The Master Plan*, 296; Plesch, *Human Rights After Hitler*, 61; Edsel, *The Monuments Men*, 396–397; Dwork and van Pelt, *Auschwitz*, 198; Sarah Helm, *Ravensbruck: Life and Death in Hitler's Concentration Camp for Women* (New York: Nan A. Talese Doubleday, 2014), 20; Stargardt, *The German War: A Nation Under Arms*, 517; Richard Breitman, Barbara McDonald Stewart, and Severin Hochberg, editors, *Refugees and Rescue: The Diaries and Papers of James G. McDonald, 1935–1945* (Indianapolis: Indiana University Press, 2009), 336; Dietrich Von Hildebrand, *My Battle Against Hitler: Faith, Truth, and Defiance in the Shadow of the Third Reich* (New York: Image Books, 2014), 297.

[123] Theodore S. Hamerow, *Why We Watched: Europe, America, and the Holocaust* (New York: W.W. Norton & Company, 2008), 324; Pringle, *The Master Plan*, 323; Steinweis and Rachlin, editors, *The Law in Nazi Germany*, 26–27, 38–39, 172; McKale, *Nazis after Hitler*, 130, 157, 160, 238–241; Evelyn Le Chene, *Mauthausen: The History of a Death Camp* (London: Methuen and Company, 1971), 78; Gellately, editor, *The Nuremberg Interviews*, xxvii, 5, 11, 14, 19–25, 39, 44, 63, 84–85, 111–117, 145, 188, 197–198, 205, 210–211, 215, 233, 246, 251, 267, 315, 339, 357–359, 364, 368, 387–391, 405, 408; Hilberg, *The Destruction of the European Jews*, 695; Burleigh, *Moral Combat*, 401; Steinert, *Hitler's War and the Germans*, 143.

tury. Still, Allied prosecutors never quite grasped or were willing to admit that millions of people had been slaughtered because of their race, ethnic, cultural, sexual orientation, or religious identities. The seriousness with which the Nazis had pursued their eugenic agenda—and the lengths to which that had taken sterilization and murder—were also difficult to accept. After all, eugenic sterilization was not unique to Germany and had originated in the United States. Furthermore, many of the chief culprits, like Hitler and Goebbels, were never put on trial. Even Goering escaped the hangman's noose by committing suicide shortly after the conclusion of closing arguments. Thousands of other, lesser-known Nazis, escaped trial altogether.[124]

Beyond the documentation of the Holocaust, the IMT did accomplish some other goals. For one, the fact that governmental officials were tried for war crimes by an international body is not without significance. It helped give focus to the work of Ralph Lemkin, who was among the first to describe the Holocaust by the phrase "genocide" and gave impetus to the December 1947 declaration by the United Nations of labeling genocide as a crime against humanity.[125] Furthermore, while we tend to focus on the "main event" trial at Nuremberg, with Jackson's historic opening argument and Goering and other top Nazis in the docket, there were some 2,000 trials in total heard as a result of war crimes committed during the Second World War, with cases heard by the IMT from November 1945 until October 1946. While justice in this world did not come for all Nazis, some justice on behalf of the victims was served.[126]

One of the Americans responsible for the success of the trials was Dwight Eisenhower. However, he was not in Germany for most of the Nuremberg court proceedings. Having fought and won the war, and helped established the peace, Ike was ready to come home. Though he was good at it, he did not enjoy the bureaucratic nature of his assignment.[127] While denazification continued under his deputies-turned-successors, Generals Joseph T. McNarney and Lucius D. Clay, Ei-

---

124 Alvin H. Rosenfeld, *The End of the Holocaust* (Indianapolis: Indiana University Press, 2011), 122–123; John Mendelsohn, editor, *The Holocaust: Selected Documents, Volume 9, Medical Experiments on Jewish Inmates of Concentration Camps* (Clark, New Jersey: The Lawbook Exchange, Ltd., 2010), Introduction and 168–173; Dwork and van Pelt, *Auschwitz*, 65, 77; Johann Chapoutot, *The Law of Blood: Thinking and Acting as a Nazi* (Cambridge, Massachusetts: The Belknap Press of Harvard University Press, 2018), 1–6, 146; *Tiergartenstrasse 4: Memorial and Information Point for the Victims of National Socialist Euthanasia Killings* (Berlin: The Foundation Memorial to the Murdered Jews of Europe, 2016), 11–12, 74–75; McKale, *Nazis after Hitler*, x–xi, 129, 186, 216–217.
125 Samantha Power, *"A Problem from Hell": America and the Age of Genocide* (New York: Basic Books, 2002), 17–29, 38–43, 47–50, 60–63.
126 Beschloss, *The Conquerors*, 274–275; Plesch, *Human Rights After Hitler*, 1.
127 Gienow-Hecht, *Transmission Impossible*, 28.

senhower's contributions were both foundational and fundamental to the success of the program.[128] Even then, Ike said that it would likely take fifty years to see if the occupation of Germany was a success or not.[129]

As far as the Army was concerned, Ike and the men under him handled the occupation quite well. Unlike in liberated parts of Europe, the Americans had to rebuild not just German cities but German society itself. Every level of German life was tainted by the Nazis.[130] As Assistant Secretary of the Army John J. McCloy put it, "I think it is safe to say that no zone commander was faced with as many diverse and heavy problems as was General Eisenhower. It is difficult for anyone who has not observed conditions in Germany during the last stages of the war and after the defeat to begin to appreciate the complexity of the task of reconstituting the functions of government in the conquered area . . . the conditions were literally indescribable."[131] Whatever success the American sector of western Germany enjoyed, much of it had to do with how Ike structured the administration of the occupation.[132]

However, denazification had a short shelf life—not because the Nazis made a comeback, nor because the Allies did not try. Rather, the grand alliance that had defeated Hitler's Third Reich, having lost the opponent that brought it together, divided between the communist Soviet Union and the Western democracies of the United States, Great Britain, and France. As 1948 gave way to 1949, Europe, like Germany, was quite divided, between East and West, between totalitarianism and freedom. And just as it had during World War II, the United States eventually turned to Eisenhower for leadership during the Cold War.[133]

---

128 Taylor, *The Anatomy of the Nuremberg Trials*, 235; Smith, editor, *The Papers of General Lucius D. Clay: Germany, 1945–1949, Volume I*, xxxiv, 14–15, 658–661; Beschloss, *The Conquerors*, 272–273.
129 Eisenhower, *How Ike Led*, 67.
130 John J. McCloy, "American Occupation Policies in Germany," *Proceedings of the Academy of Political Science*, 21(January 1946), 81–82, 84; Harold Zink, "American Occupation Policies in Germany," *The Review of Politics*, 9(July 1947), 284–285.
131 McCloy, "American Occupation Policies in Germany," 83.
132 McCloy, "American Occupation Policies in Germany," 90; Kenneth O. McCreedy, "Planning the Peace: Operation Eclipse and the Occupation of Germany," *Journal of Military History*, 65 (July 2001), 738.
133 McKale, *Nazis after Hitler*, 9; Plesch, *Human Rights After Hitler*, 48; Gienow-Hecht, *Transmission Impossible*, 147; Hitchcock, *The Bitter Road to Freedom*, 369; Neiberg, *Potsdam*, 106; "Denazification," http://www.alliiertenmuseum.de/en/topics/denazification.html, 18 June 2021.

Chapter 6
Never Again

On May 15, 1948, the *New York Times* reported:

> The Jewish state, the world's newest sovereignty, to be known as the State of Israel, came into being in Palestine at midnight upon termination of the British mandate. Recognition of the state by the United States, which had opposed its establishment at this time, came as a complete surprise to the people, who were tense and ready for the threatened invasion by Arab forces and appealed for help by the United Nations. In one of the most hopeful periods of their troubled history the Jewish people here gave a sigh of relief and took a new hold on life when they learned that the greatest national power had accepted them into the international fraternity.[1]

As the newspaper noted, American recognition had not been guaranteed at the moment David Ben-Gurion announced Israel's creation. Among those who were initially reluctant to support the creation of the new Jewish state was Dwight Eisenhower. However, in the years to come not only did the former Supreme Allied Commander change his mind but he became one of Israel's staunchest supporters. One reason for the shift in his opinion was the memory of what he had seen at Ohrdruf and his vow to never allow something like the Holocaust to happen again.

But memories of the Second World War and Holocaust did not just shape Ike's eventual stance on Israel. They also helped propel him to become president of the United States, shaping his administration in ways both overtly and, at times, in ways that the public (and even historians) did not at first recognize.

Duty, Honor, Country

The price to defeat Hitler had been high. The price of not defeating him would have been even higher. As historian Timothy Snyder points out, what we know about "the Holocaust overshadows German plans that envisioned even more killing." In other words, a Nazi victory would have meant even more deaths on an even larger scale.[2] Dwight Eisenhower was determined that the United States would never again come late to a challenge with such stakes. As such, the war and the Holocaust were never far from his mind. While publicly, Eisenhower did not seem to dwell on the Holocaust, the private Eisenhower was another matter.

---

[1] *New York Times*, 15 May 1948.
[2] Timothy Snyder, *Bloodlands: Europe Between Hitler and Stalin* (New York: Basic Books, 2010), ix.

His wartime experiences, including what he saw at Ohrdruf, shaped not just his leadership style but perhaps more importantly, his moral sense.

Initially, Eisenhower said that what he wanted to do after victory in Europe was to return to the United States and go fishing. Ike's desire to come home was evident in his letters.[3] Of course, he ended up being the first military governor of the American occupation zone instead. His decision to leave Germany in November 1945 had little to do with wanting another new assignment, this time as Army Chief of Staff, and more to do with wanting to be back in the United States, having spent most of the past two decades abroad.[4]

It was, however, duty calling him back to the United States. Not only did the country still need him it seemed, but so too did President Harry Truman. Less than a year on the job and having already seen the country to victory over Germany and Japan—including the use of the atomic bomb—Truman wanted Eisenhower's expertise as the Cold War began. Ike watched with pride as his old boss, George Marshall, became Secretary of State and the architect of American commitment to rebuilding Europe. Eisenhower also had a front row seat to the creation of the Truman Doctrine—which committed the United States to containing the spread of communism in Europe.[5]

But then, in May 1948, Eisenhower announced he was leaving the active service to become the president of Columbia University in New York. Ike saw education as a central tenant that made American different than its totalitarian adversaries. "A dictatorial government cannot abide free universities as America understands them," Ike said. "Hitler's Germany found it necessary to replace regular teachers with men controlled by a central government, who were told what they were to teach. It seems to me that there are two ways for a government to become a dictatorship; one is to slide into it, and the other is to be enslaved by a stronger military power. The United States must be vigilant against both dangers."[6] For Eisenhower, "the principal purpose of education is to prepare the student for effective personal and social life in a free society." While some of the faculty at Columbia never got past the fact he was from the Midwest and educated at West Point, believing he

---

[3] Rick Atkinson, *The Guns at Last Light: The War in Western Europe, 1944–1945* (New York: Henry Holt and Company, 2013), 635; Susan Eisenhower, *Mrs. Ike: Memories and Reflections on the Life of Mamie Eisenhower* (New York: Farrar, Straus and Giroux, 1996), 236.

[4] William I. Hitchcock, *The Age of Eisenhower: American and the World in the 1950s* (New York: Simon and Schuster, 2018), 31, 49.

[5] "The Truman Doctrine, 1947," https://history.state.gov/milestones/1945-1952/truman-doctrine, 9 January 2021. See also David McCullough's *Truman* (New York: Simon & Schuster, 1992).

[6] "Dwight Eisenhower to Alumni and Friends of Columbia University," 24 February 1949, Louis Galambos, Editor, *The Papers of Dwight David Eisenhower, Columbia University, XI* (Baltimore: The Johns Hopkins University Press, 1984), 505–508.

was only "engaged" by the school's athletic programs, Ike's personal prestige raised the status of the university merely by his presence and many students found it inspiring to be able to see him in person. He seemingly enjoyed his time as a university president, though his time on campus was often limited by continually being called back to national service and his eventual decision to run for president.[7]

Because he was at Columbia, Ike officially missed out on the Berlin Crisis. In 1947, the British and Americans started unifying their zones administratively, a process joined by the French in March 1948, which angered the Soviet Union. No sooner had Ike started his job at Columbia, than Josef Stalin decided to blockade Berlin as a means to force the Western Allies to abandon the old German capital entirely to the Soviets. From June 24, 1948 until May 12, 1949, West Berlin's lifeline was maintained by an airlift orchestrated by Eisenhower's former deputy, General Lucius Clay. Later in 1949, having withstood the blockade and maintained their claim to Berlin, the Allies officially merged their zones to create West Germany, with the Soviets launching East Germany that October. The crisis also prompted the formation of the North Atlantic Treaty Organization (NATO) which pledged the United States to defend Western Europe militarily. The Alliance was more than just a paper decree, as it came with the commitment of U.S. forces to bases in Europe.[8]

Soon enough, Eisenhower was brought back into the active service. In February 1949, Truman asked him to become the informal head of the Joint Chiefs of Staff and reactivated his military service. In December 1950, the president nominated him to become the Supreme Allied Commander-Europe of NATO, a post Ike ascended to in early 1951. Taking a leave of absence from Columbia, Eisenhower

---

7 Douglas E. Clark, *Eisenhower in Command at Columbia* (New York: Lexington Books, 2013), 63, 89, 93; Hitchcock, *The Age of Eisenhower*, 49; Eisenhower, *Mrs. Ike*, 41, 251; "Dwight D. Eisenhower," http://c250.columbia.edu/c250_celebrates/remarkable_columbians/dwight_d_eisenhower.html, 9 January 2021. Ike also dealt with the emerging Cold War on campus—vowing to fire any faculty member who was a communist, while also accepting money from the communist government in Poland to establish a Polish studies chair. Those experiences informed, and help explain, how he later handled Senator Joseph McCarthy. See, Herbert Brownell, *Advising Ike: The Memoirs of Attorney General Herbert Brownell* (Lawrence: University of Kansas Press, 1993), 258, 262; Fred I. Greenstein, *The Hidden-Hand Presidency: Eisenhower as Leader* (New York: Basic Books, 1982), 155–227; Matthew Continetti, *The Right: The Hundred-Year War for American Conservatism* (New York: Basic Books, 2022), 104–109; Susan Eisenhower, *How Ike Led: The Principles Behind Eisenhower's Biggest Decisions* (New York: Thomas Dunne Books, 2020), 181–201.
8 "The Berlin Airlift, 1948–1949," https://history.state.gov/milestones/1945-1952/berlin-airlift; 9 January 2021; "Dwight Eisenhower," https://www.nato.int/cps/en/natohq/declassified_137961.htm, 9 January 2021; Ira Chernus, "Eisenhower and the Soviets, 1945–1947: Rhetoric and Policy," *Rhetoric and Public Affairs*, 2(Spring 1999), 69.

was now back in a military uniform full-time, traveling throughout Western Europe to solidify European support and making the case for the new alliance before Congress. Ike's presence was needed, not just because of the newness of the American commitment but because it came during the Korean War—including Truman's deteriorating relationship with Eisenhower's old commander, General Douglas MacArthur. With NATO established, Eisenhower left his post in the summer of 1952—just in time to accept the Republican Party's nomination for president of the United States.[9]

On the one hand, agreeing to the NATO job allowed Ike to disentangle himself from domestic political discussion and consideration.[10] On the other, the Army he rejoined and soon became the commander-in-chief of had been transformed by the Second World War and the Holocaust. For one, the rules of conventional war were now different. The First Geneva Convention (1949) made clear that not only wounded and sick soldiers, but also civilians were now to be considered "outside the struggle and enjoying general immunity" in its Article 13.[11] Additional commentary on the Third Geneva Convention (1949) clarified the revamped Article 13 further, stating its intention was to "abolish forever the criminal practices inflicted on thousands of persons during the Second World War."[12] The postwar period also saw revision of how the Army taught soldiers to treat enemy prisoners of war. In November 1952, as the former Supreme Allied Commander was planning his presidential administration, the Department of the Army released FM 19-40, "Handling Prisoners of War." While noting the Army doctrine adhered to the Geneva Convention of 1949, the document stressed, among other things, that "commanders exercise supervision over prisoners of war on behalf of the United

---

[9] Tim Weiner, *The Folly and the Glory: America, Russia, and Political Warfare, 1945–2020* (New York: Henry Holt & Company, 2020), 29; Hitchcock, *The Age of Eisenhower*, 49; "Dwight Eisenhower," https://www.nato.int/cps/en/natohq/declassified_137961.htm, 9 January 2021; Isaac Alteras, *Eisenhower and Israel: U.S.-Israeli Relations, 1953–1960* (Gainesville: University Press of Florida, 1993), 25; Gary A. Donaldson, *When America Liked Ike: How Moderates Won the 1952 Presidential Election and Reshaped American Politics* (New York: Rowman & Littlefield, 2017), 29.
[10] Dwight Eisenhower to Forrest Carlisle Pogue, 20 February 1952, Louis Galambos, Editor, *The Papers of Dwight David Eisenhower: NATO and the Campaign of 1952, XII* (Baltimore: The Johns Hopkins University Press, 1989), 602–605.
[11] "Treaties, States Parties and Commentaries: Geneva Convention I, Commentary 1952," https://ihl-databases.icrc.org/applic/ihl/ihl.nsf/Comment.xsp?action=openDocument&documentId=24EDDBDE44E33800C12563CD00420907, 12 July 2017.
[12] "Treaties, States Parties and Commentaries: Geneva Convention III, Commentary 1960," https://ihl-databases.icrc.org/applic/ihl/ihl.nsf/Comment.xsp?action=openDocument&documentId=E34CAB7D3C60B986C12563CD00425C11, 12 July 2017. Similar sentiment can also be found about Geneva Convention IV as well.

States, and are responsible for their custody, administration, and treatment."[13] There is little doubt the new wording was a response to defiant Nazi claims that they were either following orders when killing so-called "partisans" nor that they did not know what was happening to prisoners in the camps. There is also little doubt that Eisenhower approved of the new doctrine.

We Like Ike

By the time he ran for president, Eisenhower wanted to lead the nation because he knew he could do the job and do it well. His wife, Mamie, had noticed when Ike was Army Chief of Staff that he had changed. He was used to giving orders and making decisions.[14] During the war, many of his subordinates noted how Ike inspired confidence in those who encountered him.[15] Perhaps one of the key factors compelling him to run for the presidency was that he knew how to make decisions. While many would point to his authorization of the Normandy landings in June 1944, a better example, especially in terms of long term consequences, can be seen at Ohrdruf. Ike's decision to not just document, but to both see for himself and publicize what he saw altered forever how the Holocaust would be remembered.[16] He was now prepared to take those skills to the entire nation and Western world.

There was a groundswell of support for an Eisenhower candidacy in both political parties—as neither knew where his allegiance was. Indeed, in October 1944, Ike noted that he had no political party as a soldier. And as late 1950, Eisenhower said he had no real interest in politics.[17] Though he had worked well with both Franklin Roosevelt and Harry Truman, Ike announced he was a Republican ahead of the 1952 election cycle. After securing the GOP nomination, he launched a campaign that saw him cross the nation—always to the acclaim of large crowds. People wanted to see the man Americans credited with defeating the Nazis. His perceived foreign policy expertise all but sealed his election when he vowed to journey to Korea and find a way to end the stalemated war himself.[18]

---

13 *Department of the Army Field Manual, FM 19–40: Handling Prisoners of War* (Washington: United States Government Printing Office, 1952), 2.
14 Eisenhower, *Mrs. Ike*, 215.
15 Susan Eisenhower, *How Ike Led: The Principles Behind Eisenhower's Biggest Decisions* (New York: Thomas Dunne Books, 2020), 81.
16 Eisenhower, *How Ike Led*, 14.
17 Eisenhower, *How Ike Led*, 104; John S. D. Eisenhower, editor, *Letters to Mamie* (Garden City: Doubleday & Company, 1978), 216; Eisenhower, *Mrs. Ike*, 212–213.
18 Lewis L. Gould, *Grand Old Party: A History of the Republicans* (New York: Random House, 2003), 326–339; Evan Thomas, *Ike's Bluff: President Eisenhower's Secret Battle to Save the World*

It should be noted that Eisenhower had very little to gain by running for elective office. He was already immensely popular with the American people and entering partisan politics held the potential to dull his lustrous reputation.[19] It should also be noted that many of his former subordinates helped convince him to run. They were sure of his abilities.[20] His decision to enter the race was compounded by the estimation that he was the best available candidate when compared to the other possibilities. Eisenhower was unsure of not just who the Democratic nominee would be (and the party of Roosevelt and Truman had controlled the White House for two decades at this point), but he was equally unsure about the leading candidate of his own party—Senator Robert Taft of Ohio. Taft was the son of a former president and was a political power both in his home state and in the Senate. He was also, as Eisenhower surmised after a meeting in January 1951, an isolationist despite the lessons Ike believed the Second World War and emerging Cold War should have made evident.[21] The general felt he had a duty to run.[22]

Becoming a political nominee was a new experience for Ike.[23] In both the Republican primary and general election cycles, he was accused by his opponents as being a communist agent, of being both a Jew and at other times a Catholic (while also having it be alleged that he was anti-Semitic and anti-Catholic), and even that he was too ill to actually serve as president.[24] From nowhere was the mudslinging worse or the partisan rift deeper than with the White House. The general-turned-candidate had some initial misgivings about the president, nearly from their first meeting. It was not personal, or even stylistic, the rift was professional. Ike believed Truman had been unprepared to assume the mantle of leadership in April of 1945—but he did not blame Truman for that, it was clearly the now dead Roo-

---

(New York: Back Bay Books, 2012), 26; Donaldson, *When America Liked Ike*, 92–94; James T. Patterson, *Mr. Republican: A Biography of Robert A. Taft* (Boston: Houghton Mifflin Company, 1972), 504, 512–523, 546, 560–561; Continetti, *The Right*, 87; Herbert Brownell, *Advising Ike: The Memoirs of Attorney General Herbert Brownell* (Lawrence: University of Kansas Press, 1993), 128; Eisenhower, *How Ike Led*, 162–163. Eisenhower's campaign enjoyed wide support—including a campaign song penned by Irving Berlin and a commercial animated by the Walt Disney Studios.
19 Brownell, *Advising Ike*, 300.
20 Brownell, *Advising Ike*, 102.
21 Fred I. Greenstein, *The Hidden-Hand Presidency: Eisenhower as Leader* (New York: Basic Books, 1982), 49. Robert Taft understood that foreign affairs could impact domestic concerns, but believed that the job of Congress, in particular the Senate, was to focus on home not abroad. This even applied to the Second World War. To Ike's chagrin, Taft had even gone so far as to say, "I feel very strongly that Hitler's defeat is not vital to us," back in 1941. See, Patterson, *Mr. Republican*, 240–249.
22 Eisenhower, *Mrs. Ike*, 264, 275.
23 Continetti, *The Right*, 88–89.
24 Eisenhower, *Mrs. Ike*, 269.

sevelt's fault for selecting the Senator from Missouri and then keeping his new vice president largely in the dark on major policy decisions, including the atomic bomb. For his part, Truman may have felt more personally betrayed by Ike's decision to run as a Republican after all but offering him the Democratic nomination a few years before. The campaign season made things worse, when Truman approved Democratic charges in 1952 that claimed Eisenhower, even more so than Roosevelt, had "been politically involved with Yalta and Potsdam deals that gave East Germany and Poland . . . to the Communists." The two men did not reconcile until after the death of John F. Kennedy over a decade later.[25]

In the end, none of the attacks mattered. Ike's popularity and the trust the American people had in his leadership, coupled with a desire for political change swept him into office in both 1952 and 1956. As Robert Wuthnow notes, Ike's 1952 victory in the electoral college was nearly by the same margin as FDR's twenty years before (83 percent for Ike, compared to 89 percent for Roosevelt) and Roosevelt had the help of running against incumbent Herbert Hoover in the midst of the Great Depression. And though Roosevelt's reelection in 1936 was nearly total (98 percent of the electoral college), Ike still managed to extend his percentage of the electoral college in 1956 to 86 percent. Simply put, America liked Ike.[26] His time in office saw nearly ninety percent of the legislation he deemed "most important," passed, despite having to deal with a Congress that was under Democratic control for most of his two terms.[27]

Ike seemed to master both the role of chief of state and the political head of the executive branch of the federal government. Part of his success had to do with adapting the "staff system" he had been a part of in the military to the White House, complete with a chief of staff to help make sure all the components worked properly and the flow of information to the president and between the branches was smooth and routine. Not only did this mean that Eisenhower received a range of advice from the cabinet secretaries, but it also avoided "impulsiveness" when it came to making decisions and helped foster unity of purpose and action that was dictated by strong planning to guarantee both short- and

---

25 Sherman Adams, *Firsthand Report: The Story of the Eisenhower Administration* (New York: Harper and Brothers, 1961), 47; Irwin F. Gellman, *The President and the Apprentice: Eisenhower and Nixon, 1952–1961* (New Haven: Yale University Press, 2015), ix; Brownell, *Advising Ike*, 129; D.K.R. Crosswell, *Beetle: The Life of General Walter Bedell Smith* (Lexington: The University Press of Kentucky, 2012), 42–45.
26 Robert Wuthnow, *Why Religion is Good for American Democracy* (Princeton: Princeton University Press, 2021), 89. It should also be noted that Ike's popularity was only enhanced on the campaign trail by the presence of Mamie. As one commentator noted, Americans liked Ike, but they loved Mamie. See, Eisenhower, *Mrs. Ike*, 274.
27 Eisenhower, *Mrs. Ike*, 294–295, 302.

long-term success. Cabinet meetings and deliberations became a regular part of the president's agenda. And few who took part in them missed the fact that Ike was a perceptive interlocutor whose strategic thinking skills impressed those around the table.[28]

While Eisenhower's two terms in office were in the midst of the Cold War, his administration was heavily influenced by his experiences during World War II, including the Holocaust. His fight against Nazi Germany had made him (as well as many of the men he had led into battle) a devoted anti-totalitarian.[29] In his first inaugural address, he cast the Cold War in terms of the "forces of good and evil" that clearly echoed the Second World War. There was no doubt about where he saw the United States in that conflict, nor its mission—his mission—in it. America had fought a war "to secure peace in the world," and that "in the presence of God. We are called as a people to give testimony in the sight of the world to our faith that the future shall belong to the free." The new president believed that there was a "moral strength" in America's actions. "Freedom," he told the world in January 1953, "is pitted against slavery; lightness against the dark." In his most obvious reference to the Holocaust, Eisenhower said, "We reject any insinuation that one race or another, one people or another, is in any sense inferior or expendable."[30] America under Eisenhower was to be a "moral force" in the world.[31]

Eisenhower's emphasis on good and evil echoed a newfound religious faith in his own life, perhaps awakened by his service during World War II. Though raised in a religious home, Ike had been rather ambivalent when it came to public professions of faith for much of his adult life. He now gave a "high priority . . . to religion in his personal life and in geopolitical strategy." While he promoted an "ecumenical and inclusive" civic religion, heavy on religious pluralism, for the country, personally, his Christian faith—and the expressions of it—grew while he was in the White House. Eisenhower was baptized and joined National Presbyterian Church in Washington, D.C. during his presidency. As historian Ronit Stahl noted, Eisenhower's insistence on openly advo-

---

28 Greenstein, *The Hidden-Hand Presidency*, 4–5, 15–17, 232–234; Brownell, *Advising Ike*, 132, 288, 296; Eisenhower, *How Ike Led*, 6–7, 149, 158, 171. Greenstein notes that the Kennedy Administration would likely have benefited from following Ike's example.
29 Steven Friess, "A Liberator, But Never Free," https://newrepublic.com/article/121779/liberator-never-free, 15 February 2016.
30 John Gabriel Hunt, editor, *The Inaugural Addresses of the Presidents* (New York: Gramercy Books, 1995), 412–417; Hitchcock, *The Age of Eisenhower*, 93.
31 "Eulogy Delivered at the Capitol During the State Funeral of General Eisenhower," https://www.presidency.ucsb.edu/documents/eulogy-delivered-the-capitol-during-the-state-funeral-general-eisenhower, 19 October 2022.

cating for religion created a "the military-spiritual complex" in the Oval Office as he led the nation during the Cold War.[32]

As president, Eisenhower's latent anti-communism merged publicly with his anti-totalitarianism. But even in the early postwar period, while Ike talked of peace and cooperation with the Soviets, and even counted some Russians as friends, he never doubted that the American way was superior to the communist vision. While serving as Army Chief of Staff, Ike assumed the Soviet Union was the chief threat facing the United States but doubted they would openly seek war so soon after World War II. Once in the White House, he was devoted to halting Soviet expansionism and always sought to negotiate from a position of strength. As he repeatedly told aides, "Munichs win nothing," showcasing one lesson he had learned from the lead up to World War II.[33] Giving in to the demands of a totalitarian dictatorship eventually led to more demands and inevitably, in Ike's opinion, to war. It was for this reason that Ike rejected the isolationism of the Taft-wing of his Republican Party. America being involved in the world was the only way to preserve the nation's freedom in the face of the communist threat. "I have seen that force at close quarters," he wrote of Communism. "It is cunning. It is Godless. It aims to destroy all freedom—most of all ours—because America is its final and chief target."[34]

---

[32] Ronit Y. Stahl, *Enlisting Faith: How the Military Chaplaincy Shaped Religion and State in Modern America* (Cambridge, MA: Harvard University Press, 2017), 134–164; Hitchcock, *The Age of Eisenhower*, 118, 249–252; Ian Johnson, *A Mosque in Munich: Nazis, the CIA, and the Muslim Brotherhood in the West* (New York: Houghton Mifflin Harcourt, 2010), 116; John D. Wilsey, *God's Cold Warrior: The Life and Faith of John Foster Dulles* (Grand Rapids: William B. Eerdmans Publishing Company, 2021), 192–193. See also, Jack M. Holl, *The Religious Journey of Dwight D. Eisenhower: Duty, Honor, Country* (Grand Rapids: William B. Eerdmans Publishing Company, 2021), 150, 206–207. Holl argues that Ike had long, or perhaps always, seen his duty and service to the nation in a religious light but also managed to (largely) keep his personal religious faith private for most of his public life.

[33] Ira Chernus, "Eisenhower and the Soviets, 1945–1947: Rhetoric and Policy," *Rhetoric and Public Affairs*, 2(Spring 1999), 59–60, 63–65, 70–71; Holl, *The Religious Journey of Dwight D. Eisenhower*, 257, 276–277; Richard M. Filipink, Jr., *Dwight Eisenhower and American Foreign Policy during the 1960s* (New York: Lexington Books, 2015), 79–80, 89. The Munich analogy fueled his later critique of John F. Kennedy's position in Southeast Asia and buttressed his support of Lyndon B. Johnson's decisions on Vietnam. See, "President Lyndon Johnson Meeting with Dwight Eisenhower, 2 July 1965," and "Johnson with Eisenhower, 23 July 1965," Presidential Recordings Digital Edition, https://pride.upress.virginia.edu, 19 October 2022; Continetti, *The Right*, 174.

[34] Dwight Eisenhower to Marguerite Courtright Patton, 27 August 1952, Louis Galambos, Editor, *The Papers of Dwight David Eisenhower: NATO and the Campaign of 1952, XIII* (Baltimore: The Johns Hopkins University Press, 1989), 1339–1341.

Ike may not have been an "ideologue," but he did have a "coherent belief system" that he called "the American System." According to historian William I. Hitchcock, Ike's beliefs centered on "self-government based on individual freedom, democracy, faith in God, and the dynamism of free markets." He believed that governments tended to expand if not checked, that America had to "engage and shape the world, not withdraw," and that communism was antithetical to all he held dear. Ike's "conservatism was cautious, gradual, consensus based, and internationalist." He represented a "middle way" in American politics with a mission of advancing the American System against this new totalitarian foe.[35]

In leading the nation in a crusade against Communism, Ike was assisted by his secretary of state, John Foster Dulles. The older brother of former OSS officer (and Eisenhower's choice for director of the Central Intelligence Agency) Allen Dulles, the elder Dulles was seemingly born for the job—having both a grandfather and an uncle who had led State, as well as having worked for previous administrations as part of the diplomatic corps. Like Ike, Dulles believed God had a special mission for the United States, that of spreading and defending freedom from all forms of totalitarianism, and that the country had to employ both spiritual as well as economic, ideological, and military weapons to prevail in the conflict.[36] Ike and the Dulles brothers worked well together.

For the Soviets, Ike's transformation into an ardent Cold Warrior was a shock. After all, they knew that he knew what Germany had done in the camps and that the U.S. and Soviets had been allies in stopping the Nazis. What the Kremlin failed to appreciate was that Eisenhower also now knew what the Soviets had done to facilitate the start of the war, via the Molotov-Ribbentrop treaty, and that they had committed war crimes like the Nazis. While he might have once ignored the pillaging associated with the Great Patriotic War, by 1951 Ike and the rest of the Western world knew that the Soviets had committed war crimes against Poland at the Katyn forest. A House committee, chaired by Indiana Congressman Ray J. Madden, had as its star witness U.S. Army Lieutenant Colonel Donald B. Stewart, who while a prisoner of war, had been taken by the Germans to inspect the mass graves they had uncovered in 1943. While the Soviets held their own investigation after retaking the Smolensk area later that year, Stewart and eventually the Madden committee were convinced that the murder of 22,000 Polish government, military, and cultural leaders was one atrocity that could not

---

[35] Brian Balogh and Bruce J. Schulman, editors, *Recapturing the Oval Office: New Historical Approaches to the American Presidency* (Cornell University Press), 111–113; Continetti, *The Right*, 91; Eisenhower, *How Ike Led*, 141.

[36] Wilsey, *God's Cold Warrior*, 10, 68, 107, 143–154, 172–173.

be blamed on Germany.[37] Furthermore, Ike had witnessed during his time as military governor in Germany that the Soviet Union was often reluctant, which at times bordered on obstruction, to honor very simple inter-Allied requests.[38] Eisenhower's former allies were now very much his enemies, on par with their fellow totalitarians, the Nazis.

Another point of comparison for Eisenhower between the two totalitarian systems was the Soviet gulag prison network, which had a striking similarity to the Nazi concentration camps he had helped to liberate. For Ike, the concentration and gulag camps were merely German and Russian variations of the same theme. Additionally, the knowledge that in the aftermath of the Second World War his Russian allies had kept some 2,000 American POWs that they had liberated from the Germans hostage in their camp system until various demands were met, as well as numerous American civilians caught up in the Red Army's advance rankled Eisenhower. As president, he would not just remember these actions, but work for the release of those who remained prisoners of the Soviet Union. For Ike, "peaceful coexistence" with such a foe was not an option. That Soviet propaganda painted Ike as a warmonger irked him and further soured his opinion of his former allies.[39]

All of these threads were reinforced by what his former chief of staff, Walter Bedell Smith was now arguing. After the war, Smith became the United States ambassador to the Soviet Union. For two years, he watched the old alliance breakdown, culminating in the Berlin Blockade which led to the famed airlift. Smith became convinced, both by the course of events and by his own study of Russian

---

[37] *The Katyn Forest Massacre: Hearings before the Select Committee to Conduct an Investigation of the Fact, Evidence, and Circumstances of the Katyn Forest Massacre, 82nd Congress* (Washington, D.C. Government Printing Office, 1952); Steven J. Brady, *Eisenhower and Adenauer: Alliance Maintenance under Pressure, 1953–1960* (New York: Lexington Books, 2010), 99–101.

[38] For Ike, such obstruction started with organizing the Potsdam Conference in the summer of 1945, when the Soviets had repeatedly denied and delayed the American pre-arrival team from setting up for the delegation on its way from Washington. See, Alfred D. Chandler, Jr. and Louis Galambos, editors, *The Papers of Dwight David Eisenhower: Occupation, 1945: Volume VI* (Baltimore: The Johns Hopkins University Press, 1978), 163–164.

[39] Kenneth Osgood, *Total Cold War: Eisenhower's Secret Propaganda Battle at Home and Abroad* (Lawrence: University of Kansas Press, 2006), 52, 68; Cathal J. Nolan, "Americans in the Gulag: Detention of US Citizens by Russia and the Onset of the Cold War, 1944–1945," *Journal of Contemporary History* 25(October 1990), 523–545. Among those held by the Soviets was John H. Noble, an American who had been caught in Germany at the start of the war and unable to leave, who the Soviets imprisoned after marching into Dresden in 1945. He was not released until 1955, "under pressure from President Eisenhower." See, *Washington Post*, 18 November 2007.

history, that Soviet communism was merely a different version of Nazi fascism.[40] His opinion only aided Ike's take on the duality of twentieth century totalitarianism and made Eisenhower's transformation into a Cold Warrior complete.

Perhaps Eisenhower even saw the hand of Providence in a Cold War development early in his administration. Shortly after his inauguration, in March 1953, the Soviet Union announced the death of Josef Stalin. Personally, Eisenhower was relieved. During the war, despite the trust that Ike, and especially Franklin Roosevelt, had placed in him, the Soviet leader had consistently misled or failed to reciprocate that trust with his allies. Eisenhower doubted if Stalin would have been willing to listen to his, and thus America's, concerns about Soviet policy in either Europe or globally.[41] In some ways then, Stalin's death opened the door potentially for a new page in U.S.-Soviet relations, though without a common enemy in the Nazis, to turn such hopes into reality was going to take a good deal of work and luck. Still, Stalin's death was a "chance for peace" in Ike's estimation.[42]

Despite the war in Korea, which Ike was about to negotiate an armistice to end, the new president understood that the Cold War was going to need to be waged differently than World War II had been. As Supreme Allied Commander, Eisenhower had given orders and approved plans that had led to the deaths of thousands and the reduction of whole cities to rubble. Though he never publicly regretted those decisions, he also did not want to have to repeat them as president. Eisenhower's tours of war-ravaged Germany, including the former concentration camps, made him vow that never again should there be waged a war on such a scale or with so much destruction.[43] His conviction was further strengthened by the development of the atomic bomb. As Eisenhower once explained, "the day that the bomb exploded over Hiroshima our concepts of war were imme-

---

40 Walter Bedell Smith, *My Three Years in Moscow* (New York: J.B. Lippincott Company, 1949); D.K.R. Crosswell, *Beetle: The Life of General Walter Bedell Smith* (Lexington: The University Press of Kentucky, 2012), 17, 22–33, 47–49, 109–111; Astolphe de Custine, *Letters from Russia: The 1843 Translation Edited, Revised, and with Introduction by Anka Muhlstein* (New York: New York Review of Books, 2002), vii; Mircea Platon, "Astolphe de Custine's Letters from Russia and the Defense of the West," *Russian History*, 43(July 2016), 142–180. Smith, who was a native of Indiana, had gone from Moscow to being the Director of Central Intelligence (1950–1953), then Under Secretary of State (1953 to 1954). Even after he retired, he continued to work for the Eisenhower administration.
41 Antony Beevor, *The Fall of Berlin 1945* (New York: Viking Press, 2002), 84–85; Klaus Larres, *Politik der Illusionen: Churchill, Eisenhower, und die deutsche Frage, 1945–1955* (Zurich: Vandenhoeck & Ruprecht, 1995), 71.
42 Eisenhower, *How Ike Led*, 165–167.
43 Thomas, *Ike's Bluff*, 77; Stephen E. Ambrose, *Eisenhower: Soldier and President* (New York: A Touchstone Book, 1990), 216.

diately obsolete."[44] He did not want to see nuclear weapons "normalized" and thought of as the latest conventional weapon, to be employed whenever the nation got into a conflict. That being said, he was more than willing to bluff the use of nuclear weapons—via announcement of a doctrine of massive retaliation—to avoid open war.[45]

The "bluff" did not sit well with all his former and now current subordinates. Generals James Gavin, Matthew Ridgway, and Maxwell Taylor all expressed doubts either publicly or privately about reliance on missile technology (at the budgetary expense of conventional forces) fueled massive retaliation and the related concept of mutually assured destruction to keep the Soviets in check. What all three seemingly missed in the rhetoric was Eisenhower's use of covert operations and commitment to wage war on communism by other means. Diplomat George Kennan understood. Though he may have been famous for articulating the theory of containing communism, Kennan also wrote a position paper advocating for covert action to undermine communism where it existed or threatened to emerge. While Truman had begun to embrace the idea, Eisenhower took it to whole new levels. Ike did not think his predecessor had been aggressive enough in prosecuting the Cold War and he believed there was simply too much at stake to go slow.[46]

---

[44] "Transcript of Interview: Dwight D. Eisenhower and A. Ross Wallen, Friday 27 November 1964, for THE POINTER," DDE Post Presidential Papers, 1965 Signature File, Box 7, PR-3 Public Relations 3, Interview 11-27-64, NAID #12023937, Dwight D. Eisenhower Presidential Library, Abilene, Kansas; Dwight D. Eisenhower, *Crusade in Europe* (New York: Doubleday and Company, 1953), 456.

[45] Ira Chernus, "Eisenhower and the Soviets, 1945–1947: Rhetoric and Policy," *Rhetoric and Public Affairs*, 2(Spring 1999), 71; Richard M. Filipink, Jr., *Dwight Eisenhower and American Foreign Policy during the 1960s* (New York: Lexington Books, 2015), 11; Brownell, *Advising Ike*, 139; Eisenhower, *How Ike Led*, 165, 173, 228; Ambrose, *Eisenhower: Soldier and President*, 224; Jean Edward Smith, *Eisenhower in War and Peace* (New York: Random House, 2013), xiii; Thomas, *Ike's Bluff*, 4, 15–17; Wilsey, *God's Cold Warrior*, 173. His worry about a nuclear war were hammered home by 1957's Gaither Report, which detailed both the likely destruction as well as precautions the United States needed to take in case of a nuclear war.

[46] Bradley Biggs, *Gavin* (Hamden, Connecticut: Archon Books, 1980), 85–87; Johnson, *A Mosque in Munich*, 39–41, 67–69; Nick Cullather, *Secret History: The CIA's Classified Account of Its Operations in Guatemala, 1952–1953* (Stanford: Stanford University Press, 1999); Wilsey, *God's Cold Warrior*, 173, 182 Eisenhower approved covert operations included Iran (1953), Guatemala (1954), and Cuba (1960). He also authorized more military intervention in Vietnam following the French defeat at Dien Bien Phu in 1954. Additionally, Ike approved a destabilization propaganda campaign directed at East Germany in 1953 following anti-government protests in East Berlin. It is hardly surprising that Weiner argues that "covert operations were the pointed end of the spear of American Foreign policy" during the Eisenhower administration. For more see, Tim Weiner, *The Folly and the Glory: America, Russia, and Political Warfare, 1945–2020* (New York: Henry Holt & Company, 2020), 33, 40; "The East German Uprising, 1953," https://history.state.gov/milestones/1953-1960/east-german-uprising, 19 May 2023.

One area of particular concern was West Germany. There was an irony that it was Eisenhower, who as a general led the forces that defeated Germany, now as president oversaw West Germany's integration into the nascent NATO alliance. Yet, the future of Germany was perhaps the one issue upon which the entire Cold War hinged and there was no American who knew better its strategic importance than Ike.[47] As president, Eisenhower was also committed "to preserve the integrity of Berlin and to foster conditions which will eventually permit the German people to be reunited into one free nation."[48] In the years since the end of the war, with West and East Germany being the epicenter of Cold War Europe, Eisenhower sought to foster a strong, democratic West Germany—that could resist not just communism but also a feared revival of the Nazis. As such, Eisenhower stood up to Nikita Khrushchev, in late 1958, when the new leader of the Soviet Union attempted to intimidate the Western Allies out of Berlin. Throughout the 1950s, West Germans came to embrace Ike as their protector as he helped them forge closer ties within the Western alliance.[49]

His experiences in World War II also influenced Eisenhower's domestic agenda in a variety of ways. Thanks to his time running SHAEF, the occupation of the American sector of Germany, and NATO, he knew how to make administering the White House and the federal government look easy and routine. Having seen and used the German Autobahn system, Ike made the Interstate Highway System a reality for the United States.[50] His wartime encounters with African-Americans also eventually made him a quiet, but effective, champion of civil rights. As David A. Nichols reminds us, as president, "Eisenhower desegregated the District of Columbia (including its schools), completed desegregation of the armed forces, appointed progressive federal judges at all levels (including Earl Warren and four other Supreme Court justices), proposed and secured passage of the first civil rights legislation in over eighty years, and took steps to enforce the Supreme

---

[47] Steven J. Brady, *Eisenhower and Adenauer: Alliance Maintenance under Pressure, 1953–1960* (New York: Lexington Books, 2010), 2–3, 14.

[48] "Message to Mayor Brandt of West Berlin: August 28, 1959," http://www.presidency.ucsb.edu/ws/index.php?pid=11484&st=berlin&st1=, 9 March 2018.

[49] John S. D. Eisenhower, *Strictly Personal* (Garden City, NY: Doubleday and Company, 1974), 213, 241. Brownell, *Advising Ike*, 302. As Richard M. Filipink notes, "Khrushchev's aggressive policy and boasts of superiority rankled but did not rattle Eisenhower." See, Filipink, Jr., *Dwight Eisenhower and American Foreign Policy during the 1960s*, 13. Khrushchev, having been foiled in 1958–1959, tested Eisenhower' successor John F. Kennedy by ordering the construction of the Berlin Wall in 1961, which outraged Ike almost as much as Kennedy's timid response to its erection, which Ike described as a "fiasco." See, Filipink, 43–44.

[50] William B. Pickett, *Dwight David Eisenhower and American Power* (Wheeling, IL: Harland Davidson, 1995), 155–157; Eisenhower, *Strictly Personal*, 289–290; Eisenhower, *How Ike Led*, 136.

Court's school desegregation decision in *Brown v. Board of Education*, most dramatically by his military intervention in Little Rock."[51]

International stability, within the shadow of the Cold War and Great Power dynamics, economic prosperity, and moral authority—these were the hallmarks of the Eisenhower Administration according to William Hitchcock.[52] He was, as it turned out, a master politician who was in complete command of his presidency.[53] And as historian Jean Edward Smith notes, "with the exception of Franklin Roosevelt, Dwight Eisenhower was the most successful president of the twentieth century."[54] That success came at a cost, however. For Eisenhower this meant utilizing former Nazis in order to get the American space and ballistic missile programs up and going. While he did not start Operation Paperclip, which brought Nazi scientists and experts to the United States, he certainly utilized it.[55] As Winston Churchill might have told him, defeating totalitarian ideologies and their followers sometimes made for strange bedfellows.

---

51 David A. Nichols, *A Matter of Justice: Eisenhower and the Beginning of the Civil Rights Revolution* (New York: Simon & Schuster Paperbacks, 2007), 1. In addition to Nichols, see Kasey S. Pipes, *Ike's Final Battle: The Road to Little Rock and the Challenge of Equality* (Los Angeles: World Ahead Publishing, 2007), 45, 72–73, 174–175, 296–300; Brownell, *Advising Ike*, 183, 202–217, 266; Hitchcock, *The Age of Eisenhower*, 370–371; Holl, *The Religious Journey of Dwight D. Eisenhower*, 224–225, 232–233, 240–241, 248–249; Mark Stern, "Presidential Strategies and Civil Rights: Eisenhower, the Early Years, 1952–1954," *Presidential Studies Quarterly*, 19 (Fall 1989), 769–795; Jeffrey R. Young, "Eisenhower's Federal Judges and Civil Rights Policy: A Republican 'Southern Strategy' for the 1950s," *The Georgia Historical Quarterly*, 78(Fall 1994), 536–565; Continetti, *The Right*, 127; Eisenhower, *Mrs. Ike*, 286; Eisenhower, *How Ike Led*, 245–263; Carlotta Walls LaNier, *A Mighty Long Way: My Journey to Justice at Little Rock Central High School* (New York: One World Books, 2010), 91–93. LaNier, one of the Little Rock Nine, credits Ike's military background with giving him the resolve to send in the 101st Airborne to allow for the integration of the high school. For a somewhat contra position, see Geoffrey W. Jensen, *The Racial Integration of the American Armed Forces: Cold War Necessity, Presidential Leadership, and Southern Resistance* (Lawrence: University of Kansas Press, 2023). Jensen's argument is that Eisenhower was swept forward by the tide of events more than he was proactive in seeking civil rights/integration and that Truman deserves more credit for setting in motion what Ike saw to fruition. Even then, Jensen admits "Ike did more than most of those who would succeed him on the issue." (289).
52 Hitchcock, *The Age of Eisenhower*, 516–517.
53 Kenneth Strong, *Intelligence at the Top: The Recollections of an Intelligence Officer* (Garden City: Doubleday and Company, 1969), 311; Smith, *Eisenhower in War and Peace*, xv.
54 Smith, *Eisenhower in War and Peace*, xii.
55 Brian E. Crim, *Our Germans: Operation Paperclip and the National Security State* (Baltimore: Johns Hopkins University Press, 2018), 171–192; Johnson, *A Mosque in Munich*, 50; Eisenhower, *How Ike Led*, 271; Peter Caddick-Adams, *Fire and Steel: The End of World War Two in the West* (New York: Oxford University Press, 2022), 517.

Eisenhower then, was never far from his World War II legacy, nor his encounter with the Holocaust. He wrestled with the consequences of victory for the Allies and the defeat of the Nazis throughout his time in the Oval Office. Ike never doubted that what he had done during World War II was not only correct, but came with divine sanction, a feeling buttressed by having come face to face with the Holocaust at Ohrdruf. This faith sustained him throughout his time in the White House, regardless of some of the political compromises that he might have to make along the way.[56]

Ike and the State of Israel

One of the legacies of the Second World War was the ending of several European empires and the creation of new nations around the globe. One of those states was Israel, carved out of the British mandate of Palestine, as a homeland for Jews. The new country played a large role in shaping Eisenhower's presidency both at home and abroad. Ike's relationship with Israel always carried with it the memories of his time at Ohrdruf.

The founding of Israel was a direct result of the Holocaust. European Jews who survived the Nazi genocide generally shifted as far west as they could go, including to the United States.[57] For many survivors, however, their eyes were on Palestine. Americans generally supported Jewish immigration to the area, including Eisenhower and many of the men who had served under him in Europe.[58] In 1947, Ike was asked to give some remarks to the United Jewish Appeal for Refugees and Overseas Needs. In his comments, he mentioned that "I shall never forget my first visit to a concentration camp in Germany in the hour of Allied victory in Europe." He called the "inhuman and bestial treatment meted out by the Nazis to the Jews and others" a "dark chapter in modern history." He regretted that only a "relatively small fraction of survivors" had actually been "liberated by our fighting forces."[59] Later that same year, Secretary of State George Marshall testified before the House

---

[56] Alan Sears and Craig Osten with Ryan Cole, *The Soul of an American President: The Untold Story of Dwight D. Eisenhower's Faith* (Grand Rapids, Michigan: Baker Books, 2019), 97–98, 102, 117–118.

[57] Donald M. McKale, *Nazis after Hitler: How Perpetrators of the Holocaust Cheated Justice and the Truth* (New York: Rowman and Littlefield Publishers, 2014), 10.

[58] Lawrence J. Epstein, *Americans and the Birth of Israel* (New York: Rowman and Littlefield, 2017), 4, 98; Dan Stone, *The Liberation of the Camps: The End of the Holocaust and Its Aftermath* (New Haven: Yale University Press, 2015), 132–133.

[59] "Suggested material for General of the Army Dwight D. Eisenhower for his speech to the United Jewish Appeal, February 23, 1947," Dwight D. Eisenhower Pre-Presidential Papers, Princi-

Committee on the Judiciary arguing that the U.S. had a moral duty to the refugees and displaced persons who had survived the war, including making sure they were resettled in places that were amenable to them.[60] If they wanted to go to Palestine, most Americans believed they should be allowed to do so.

The British, however, were reluctant, even with the Holocaust as recent history, to open immigration to Palestine. They resisted American pressure, starting with President Truman's comments during the Potsdam Conference about allowing more immigrants into the Palestine mandate, for as long as they could. However, Zionists (those Jews intent on creating a Jewish homeland in the mandate) were relentless—both in their political pressure and in preparing for and engaging in armed struggle. On May 14, 1948, Jews proclaimed the formation of the State of Israel. Here, Jews would not be in the minority. Here, Jews could defend themselves.[61] There were some 514,000 Jewish DPs who left Europe after the war–374,000 ended up, eventually, in Israel. The new nation was almost instantly a symbol of hope for the future.[62]

Israel's creation was divisive in the White House. Truman was inclined to recognize the new nation, both because of the Holocaust and because some of his advisors believed it would help him secure the Jewish-American vote in the upcoming 1948 election. Secretary of State George Marshall was against extending recognition to the Jewish state, however. He believed it was domestic political pandering, masquerading as diplomacy. Marshall was merely echoing what he was hearing in the halls of the State Department, where many believed, Israel was going to complicate American foreign policy. Ultimately, for Truman, recognizing Israel was the proper thing to do considering the Holocaust and America not doing more to stop the slaughter of Europe's Jews. With the Harrison Report still fresh in his mind, President Truman made the United States the first nation in the world to recognize the new Jewish state.[63]

---

pal File, Box 194, United Jewish Appeal Feb. 23 1947, NAID#12007653, Dwight Eisenhower Presidential Library, Abilene, Kansas.
60 George C. Marshall Foundation, "Marshall and International Holocaust Remembrance Day," https://www.marshallfoundation.org/blog/marshall-international-holocaust-remembrance-day/, 2 May 2019.
61 Theodore S. Hamerow, *Why We Watched: Europe, America, and the Holocaust* (New York: W. W. Norton & Company, 2008), 470–471, 478. As Truman himself wryly noted, "one of the main problems was that Palestine was not ours [the United States] to depose of." See, Harry S. Truman, *Memoirs of Harry S. Truman: Volume 2, Years of Trial and Hope* (Garden City: Doubleday & Company, 1956), 144.
62 McKale, *Nazis after Hitler*, 10; Epstein, *Americans and the Birth of Israel*, 165.
63 Truman, *Memoirs of Harry S. Truman: Volume 2*, 136–142; Michael Doran, *Ike's Gamble: America's Rise to Dominance in the Middle East* (New York: The Free Press, 2016), 1; Epstein, *Americans and the*

Truman's decision aided both Israel and his re-election bid. Four years later, in the midst of the 1952 campaign, Democrats (including Truman) insinuated that Republicans (including Eisenhower) were anti-Semitic and unsupportive of Israel. Ike quickly met with leading Jewish leaders in New York, who issued public statements denouncing the smear on the Republican nominee's reputation. Writing to one rabbi (and knowing that the letter would be made public), Ike noted that not only was he "in complete and hearty accord with the statement on Israel in the Republican platform," but continued: "As Commander of the Allied Army during the last war I had the fullest opportunity to observe closely the tragic conditions of the war-ravaged and Nazi-decimated Jewish communities of Europe. It will be one of the enduring satisfactions of my life that I was privileged to lead the forces of the free world which finally crushed the brutal regime of Hitler with its responsibilities for all those unspeakable atrocities. Those forces of the free world saved the remnant of the Jewish people of Europe for a new life and a new hope in the reborn land of Israel."[64]

Such rhetoric served Eisenhower well. His opponent in both 1952 and 1956 was the former governor of Illinois, Adlai Stevenson. The grandson of a former Vice President of the United States, Stevenson was well connected and benefited from Franklin Roosevelt's political rise. In addition to holding a variety of minor offices, Stevenson was part of the group delegation that created the United Nations. It was during his time in Washington, that he became a friend to First Lady Eleanor Roosevelt, who later helped convince him to run for elective office. Stevenson was intelligent, had a proven record of governance, and would have likely

---

Birth of Israel, 28–29, 42, 51–52; Harry S. Truman, *Memoirs: Volume 2, Years of Trial and Hope* (Garden City: Doubleday & Company, 1956), 136; Walter Russell Mead, *The Arc of a Covenant: The United States, Israel, and the Fate of the Jewish People* (New York: Knopf, 2022). The first U.S. Ambassador to Israel was James McDonald, who had been an early critic of Hitler and the Nazi Party within American foreign policy circles and had served as the League of Nation's High Commissioner for Refugees in the mid-1930s and then as chair for President Roosevelt's Advisory Committee on Political Refugees. He was frustrated with what he was able to accomplish to help Jews escape the Nazis in both positions. See, "James McDonald Warned the World about the Nazi Threat to Jews," https://medium.com/memory-action/james-mcdonald-warned-the-world-about-the-nazi-threat-to-jews-5cf0cc82244a, 25 May 2023.

64 Dwight Eisenhower to Abba Hillel Silver, 18 October 1952, Louis Galambos, Editor, *The Papers of Dwight David Eisenhower: NATO and the Campaign of 1952, XIII* (Baltimore: The Johns Hopkins University Press, 1989), 1388–1390. The 1952 GOP platform stated that the Republican Party had supported the creation of a Jewish State for thirty years.

been a solid successor to Truman in the White House. But he was no match for Eisenhower, including when it came to winning the so-called "Jewish vote."[65]

Eisenhower admitted that he might not have supported the creation of Israel as quickly as Truman had, but he also was not in favor of the Jewish State disappearing. Though not as vocal of a supporter of Israel on the campaign trail as many Jews, both in the United States and Israel thought proper and surely not as supportive as Truman had been four years before, Ike was perceived to be a "military man" by Jewish leaders in both countries, who would make judgements on foreign policy based on "cold considerations of balance of power and national interest." If there was a "ray of hope," from an Israeli perspective, it was Eisenhower's knowledge of the Holocaust.[66] At a time in which nationally only 10 percent of American Jews identified as Republican, Ike won between 28 to 36 percent of the vote in his elections, about three times the number of Jewish-Americans who voted for the GOP in 1948.[67] Over the course of his presidency, Ike's respect for the State of Israel grew, paralleling what Michelle Mart has argued to be American public opinion that the new Middle Eastern democracy was a reflection of the United States' mythic self.[68] For Ike though, such a reflection started with the stark reality of Ohrdruf.

As president, Eisenhower continued to have the Holocaust as a guide when it came to Israel. In February 1955, Rabbi Philip S. Bernstein wrote to the White House about an upcoming celebration in New York to commemorate the tenth anniversary of the "liberation of Europe's surviving Jews from the concentration camps." Bernstein noted that "in the thoughts of the survivors, and of American Jewry, one man, above all, is associated with liberation—Dwight D. Eisenhower.

---

65 Jules Witcover, *Party of the People: A History of the Democrats* (New York: Random House, 2003), 450–474; C. Stephen Heard, Jr., "Adlai & Eleanor: Progressives Who Shaped the World," https://fdrfoundation.org/publications/adlai-eleanor-progressives-who-shaped-the-world/, 28 February 2023; "Jewish Groups Mourn Death of Stevenson: Was Great Friend of Jews," *Jewish Telegraphic Agency Daily News Bulletin*, July 15, 1965, copy in possession of author.
66 Alteras, *Eisenhower and Israel*, 27–30. Ike had objected to the suggestion, in 1946, that the U.S. takeover or jointly administer, the territory of Palestine alongside the British. See, Joseph W. Bendersky, *The "Jewish Threat": Anti-Semitic Politics of the U.S. Army* (New York: Basic Books, 2000), 378.
67 Ian J. Bickerton, "Dwight D. Eisenhower and Israel: A New Look," *Australasian Journal of American Studies*, 7(July 1988), 10. As Tibor Klopfer, the son of two Holocaust survivors who came to the United States in 1956 put it, while his parents "were not political, but they did like Ike." See, Tibor Klopfer, interview with author, 23 March 2023.
68 *New York Times*, 13 November 1954; Michelle Mart, "Tough Guys and American Cold War Policy: Images of Israel, 1948–1960," *Diplomatic History*, 20(Summer 1996), 357–380; Michelle Mart, *Eye on Israel: How Americans Came to View Israel as an Ally* (Albany: State University of New York Press, 2006).

His historic contribution will forever be remembered and cherished." The organizers wanted to "bring to the President a formal expression of appreciation for his role in liberation," as well as get a letter they could read at the event.[69] Not surprisingly, the White House approved a statement from the president. In the two paragraphs, sent to the American Jewish Congress, Eisenhower said: "To those who believe in human brotherhood, the tenth anniversary of the liberation of Europe's surviving Jews from the concentration camps is a significant occasion. I hope its observance will strengthen in free men the spirit of opposition to totalitarian brutality and persecution, and of devotion to liberty, justice, and good will."[70]

Eisenhower's desire to remember the Holocaust was real, but that did not mean it was his sole guide when it came to foreign policy. One critique he and other members of his administration had of the Truman years was that U.S. foreign policy often seemed improvised, including Truman's decision to recognize Israel. Ike was determined to create a "careful, coherent, and consistent approach" to foreign affairs—one that could be seen as distinct from the previous administration.[71] When it came to the Middle East that meant that Israel and the Arab states that surrounded it needed to be treated as equals. Assistant Secretary of State, and Ike's wartime aide, Walter Bedell Smith assured the Israeli government that while "there has been a change in the administration; there has been no change in U.S policy regarding Israel," in terms of American support and recognition. That said, the Eisenhower Administration's initial goal was to be an impartial arbiter in the area whenever possible.[72]

On this point, it was not the Second World War that was dominating Eisenhower's foreign policy, but the Cold War. The president wanted to cultivate good relationships with the Arab states and saw the Israeli-Arab conflict as something that gave the Soviet Union traction in the area. The Soviets had fashioned considerable propaganda and had diplomatic success in courting the Arab states be-

---

69 Letter, Rabbi Philip S. Bernstein to Maxwell Rabb, February 25, 1955, Dwight D. Eisenhower's Papers as President (WHCF), President's Personal File, Box 921, PPF 53-B-3 Jewish 1955, NAID#12007648, Dwight Eisenhower Presidential Library, Abilene, Kansas. Bernstein had every indication that Ike would respond as the president had spoken at the American Jewish Tercentenary Dinner in October 1954. See, "Address by President Dwight D. Eisenhower," *Publications of the American Jewish Historical Society*, 2(December 1954), 67–74.
70 Letter, President Dwight Eisenhower to Dr. Israel Goldstein, March 21, 1955, Dwight D. Eisenhower's Papers as President (WHCF), President's Personal File, Box 921, PPF 53-B-3 Jewish 1955, NAID#12007645, Dwight Eisenhower Presidential Library, Abilene, Kansas.
71 Bickerton, "Dwight D. Eisenhower and Israel: A New Look," *Australasian Journal of American Studies*, 7(July 1988), 2.
72 Bickerton, "Dwight D. Eisenhower and Israel: A New Look," *Australasian Journal of American Studies*, 7(July 1988), 3.

cause of American support for Israel.[73] Eisenhower turned to Secretary of State John Foster Dulles to craft the broad outlines of U.S. policy, though he retained the last word on any decision. A man of "righteous faith," Dulles was worried that the new Arab states were falling under Soviet influence. As such, while the Secretary of State strove for impartial language, it was not always diplomatic (or friendly) in the minds of Israeli policy makers.[74] Dulles had a "complicated" relationship with Jews. Ike balanced him out.[75] Impartiality, of course, did not extend to the United States old allies from the Second World War, Great Britain and France. But even with them, Eisenhower was wary of the two waning Great Powers and their attempts to maintain portions of their global empires and their desire to continue to exert influence under the banner of American power.[76]

What brought these different strands of foreign policy together was the Suez Canal Crisis. Built by an Anglo-French concern in the late nineteenth century, the Egyptian government now had nominal, formal ownership even if Franco-British investors actually ran the Canal Zone. In the minds of many Egyptians, the arrangement over the canal served as a visible sign of European imperialism. After a successful coup against the Egyptian monarchy in the early 1950s, an anti-British army officer named Gamal Abdel Nasser rose to power in the country. A devoted nationalist and advocate of Pan-Arabism, Nasser wanted to see Egypt independent of any foreign influence and sought to find a middle ground during the Cold War, between the United States and Soviet Union. The British viewed him as a threat to the region. Eisenhower believed Nasser might be a useful, re-

---

[73] Adams, *Firsthand Report*, 245; Alteras, *Eisenhower and Israel*, 31, 55; Daniel C. Williamson, "Understandable Failure: The Eisenhower Administration's Strategic Goal in Iraq, 1953–1958," *Diplomacy and Statecraft*, 17:3 (2006), 597. Williamson argues that Eisenhower's decision to prop up British influence in Iraq ended up contributing to the eventual revolution in that country, and his restrained reaction helped preclude further turmoil. See page 599 and 610–612.

[74] Adams, *Firsthand Report*, 87; Ronald W. Pruessen, *John Foster Dulles: The Road to Power* (New York: The Free Press, 1982), 201; Michael A. Guhin, *John Foster Dulles: A Statesman and His Times* (New York: Columbia University Press, 1972), 47; William Bragg Ewald, Jr., *Eisenhower the President: Crucial Days, 1951–1960* (Englewood Cliffs: Prentice-Hall, 1981), 211–212; Alteras, *Eisenhower and Israel*, 54, 80–85, 124–125; Stephen Kinzer, *The Brothers: John Foster Dulles, Allen Dulles, and Their Secret World War* (New York: Henry Holt and Company, 2013), 244; Wilsey, *God's Cold Warrior*, 199–200; Judah Nadich, *Eisenhower and the Jews* (New York: Twayne Publishers, 1953), 19–23.

[75] Alex von Tunzelmann, *Blood and Sand: Suez, Hungary, and Eisenhower's Campaign for Peace* (New York: Harper, 2016), 230–232.

[76] Michael J. Totten, "We Are Still Living With Eisenhower's Biggest Mistake," http://www.the tower.org/article/we-are-still-living-with-eisenhowers-biggest-mistake-suez-egypt-israel-ikes-gamble-michael-doran/, 6 March 2017.

gional ally, and could not understand the British (and the French) seeing him as some sort of second coming of Adolf Hitler.[77]

In 1956, during his re-election campaign, Eisenhower's entire Cold War foreign policy was put at risk by a series of events in Egypt and Hungary. Unsure of Nasser's motives, the United States in early July decided to not back the funding of the Aswan Dam project on the Nile River. Angry at what he deemed at best as a betrayal and at worse evidence of America succumbing to British pressure about the dam, Nasser nationalized the Suez Canal before the end of the month. As tensions in the Middle East mounted, on October 23, anti-communist Hungarians launched a revolt, believing that the United States would militarily intervene, if necessary, since the Americans had spent the past four years talking about "rolling back" the Iron Curtain, not just containing the spread of Communism. Less than a week later, Israel launched a surprise attack on Egypt, driving across the Sinai Peninsula towards the Nile River. As Egyptian forces attempted to regroup, a joint Anglo-French force landed and took control of the Suez Canal—officially to stop the Israeli advance. What was unbeknownst to Eisenhower, initially, but became clear to the world very quickly, was that the British, French, and Israelis had been planning the operation for some time. And then, just a few days before the election, the Soviet Union launched an invasion of Hungary that crushed the pro-democracy revolt.[78]

Eisenhower was livid. The Anglo-French intervention took diplomatic pressure off the Soviet Union, giving Khrushchev not only an opening to invade Hungary but some diplomatic cover as well. American rhetoric about democracy seemed "hollow" if its allies were invading other nations (just like the Soviets) and it was unable to help those seeking freedom. Furthermore, the Anglo-French actions in trying to retake the Suez Canal nearly sparked an open war in the region, undermining the West in the eyes of many in the Middle East and giving the Soviets an

---

77 Adams, *Firsthand Report*, 246–247; Hamerow, *Why We Watched*, 423; Gellman, *The President and the Apprentice*, 342; Hitchcock, *The Age of Eisenhower*, 309; Alteras, *Eisenhower and Israel*, 189–190; Townsend Hoopes, *The Devil and John Foster Dulles* (Boston: Little, Brown, and Company, 1973), 319. Steven J. Brady, *Eisenhower and Adenauer: Alliance Maintenance under Pressure, 1953–1960* (New York: Lexington Books, 2010), 187. Indeed, West German politicians were more than willing to utilize the comparison between Nazi Germany and Communist Russia to advance their agenda with the United States. See page 189.
78 Adams, *Firsthand Report*, 249–255; Kinzer, *The Brothers*, 212; Eisenhower, *Strictly Personal*, 189; Hitchcock, *The Age of Eisenhower*, 315; Eisenhower, *How Ike Led*, 2, 170–171, 217; Tunzelmann, *Blood and Sand*, 371–373. Continetti, *The Right*, 124. Ike was unwilling to risk or unleash World War III in order to liberate Eastern Europe. Such a conflict would not advance the cause of freedom. It would only bring destruction. As Continetti later notes (156), "it was wrong to say Eisenhower was a Communist just because he did not risk a nuclear war to keep Hungary free."

opportunity make further inroads amongst Arab countries. Additionally, as the U.S. pressured the Anglo-French and Israeli forces to withdraw, Nasser's popularity soared—meaning that Eisenhower had to cancel a proposed C.I.A. operation that would have assassinated the Egyptian leader. Additionally, Ike was upset that U.S. intelligence had missed the Anglo-French build-up, indications that the Israelis were going to join the fray, and the perception that what the British and French were doing was colonialism.[79]

His anger prompted action. Ike was determined to do what was right regardless of what it meant for the election. Faced with the dual crises, as Alex von Tuzelmann put it, Ike "just made it stop."[80] Eisenhower ordered an immediate reevaluation of American involvement in the Middle East. While this process started, he turned his attention to Hungary. In the wake of the Soviet occupation, an estimated 200,000 Hungarians (roughly 2 percent of the population) fled the country. The U.S. estimated some 20,000 Hungarians were killed in the crackdown. Among the refugees were many Hungarian Jews who had survived the Holocaust a decade before, who now feared they would be blamed for the anticommunist uprising by the Soviets and be sent back to concentration camps. Not only did Eisenhower pledge economic assistance to Austria (where the majority of Hungarians fled) but he also promised that the United States would accept refugees immediately. While he dispatched Vice President Richard Nixon to visit the displaced persons camps in Austria, Ike overcame Congressional inaction on speedily bringing Hungarians to America by utilizing, as historian Anita Casavantes Bradford notes, "the parole statute of the 1952 McCarran-Walter Act in order to rapidly admit 38,000 Hungarian refugees" to the country via Operation Safe Haven. The maneuver expanded presidential power in the area of immigration and was coupled with a public relations offensive to win over both the American people and Congress. Not only was the media sent to the DP camps in Austria, but they were also invited to follow the refugees as they journeyed to the United States (mostly to Camp Kilmer in New Jersey) and then across the nation.

---

79 James T. Patterson, *Grand Expectations: The United States, 1945–1974* (Oxford: Oxford University Press, 1996), 305–309; Kinzer, *The Brothers*, 224; Hitchcock, *The Age of Eisenhower*, 319, 329, 336–337; Jeffery C. Livingston, "Ohio Congressman John M. Vorys: A Republican Conservative Nationalist and Twentieth Century American Foreign Policy," (Doctoral Dissertation: University of Toledo, 1989), 292; Alteras, *Eisenhower and Israel*, 195; Gellman, *The President and the Apprentice*, 464; Richard M. Filipink, Jr., *Dwight Eisenhower and American Foreign Policy during the 1960s* (New York: Lexington Books, 2015), 11; Steven J. Brady, *Eisenhower and Adenauer: Alliance Maintenance under Pressure, 1953–1960* (New York: Lexington Books, 2010), 182–185; Holl, *The Religious Journey of Dwight D. Eisenhower*, 223; Tunzelmann, *Blood and Sand*, 373, 436–437, 446–447; Eisenhower, *How Ike Led*, 203, 213, 216, 283. As a result of the Suez Canal Crisis, Ike became focused on using a new spy plane, the U-2, to gather intelligence.
80 Tunzelmann, *Blood and Sand*, 233, 443.

Ike's actions built off his experience publicizing the Holocaust in the wake of visiting Ohrdruf, but also showed he was making sure the way the Roosevelt Administration and Congress had treated the attempted immigration of those fleeing the Nazis twenty years before was not repeated on his watch.[81]

By the time Operation Safe Haven was underway, Ike was prepared to deal with the fallout of the Suez Crisis. Interestingly, the president blamed Israel the least for what had transpired. He believed they had been convinced by Britain and France to take part, with the expectation that if things went bad, the United States would bail their old Allies and Israel out of the mess the Europeans had caused. Ike concluded that the crisis had occurred because he had been timid—and not provided the leadership needed, and Britain and France had attempted to fill the void. He also recognized that there was no "Arab block" that the United States could win over by diplomacy alone. The result of the Suez Crisis was the Eisenhower Doctrine of 1957—in which the United States promised to protect any Middle Eastern nation from Communist aggression, via military and economic aid. He might not be able to liberate Hungary, but he could protect the nation's friends in the Middle East.[82]

The chief friend the United States had in the Middle East, as it turned out, was Israel. The Jewish State, and its military power, now became an "asset" in American Cold War policy. Eisenhower came to understand that Israel was fo-

---

[81] Tibor Klopfer, interview with author, 23 March 2023; *Life Magazine*, 7 January 1957, 20–27; Anita Casavantes Bradford, "'With the Utmost Practical Speed': Eisenhower, Hungarian Parolees, and the 'Hidden Hand' Behind US Immigration and Refugee Policy, 1956–1957," *Journal of American Ethnic History* (2020) 39 (2): 5–35; James P. Niessen (2016). "Hungarian Refugees of 1956: From the Border to Austria, Camp Kilmer, and Elsewhere," *Hungarian Cultural Studies*: e-journal of the American Hungarian Educators Association (AHEA), 9, 122–136, https://doi.org/10.7282/T3P84F4R, 23 March 2023; "Camp Kilmer, " https://www.archives.gov/nyc/exhibit/camp-kilmer, 23 March 2023; "Safe Haven I and II," https://amcmuseum.org/history/safe-haven-i-and-ii/, 23 March 2023; "Operation Safe Haven: The Hungarian Refugee Crisis of 1956," https://www.ucis.gov, 23 March 2023; Tim Weiner, *The Folly and the Glory: America, Russia, and Political Warfare, 1945–2020* (New York: Henry Holt & Company, 2020), 49; Tunzelmann, *Blood and Sand*, 80–81. According to Niessen, of the Jewish Hungarian refugees, two-thirds opted for the United States (the top choice), the United Kingdom, or other Western nations, with the remaining third going to Israel.

[82] Adams, *Firsthand Report*, 271–273; Hitchcock, *The Age of Eisenhower*, 191, 339–340; Bickerton, "Dwight D. Eisenhower and Israel: A New Look," *Australasian Journal of American Studies*, 7 (July 1988), 5, 7; Filipink, Jr., *Dwight Eisenhower and American Foreign Policy during the 1960s*, 9; Eisenhower, *How Ike Led*, 208–211, 220; "The Lebanon Operation," AIRLIFT IN THE DOMINICAN CRISIS (army.mil), 22 August 2021; "The 1958 U.S. Marine Invasion of Lebanon: It was No Day at the Beach," The 1958 U.S. Marine Invasion of Lebanon—It was no day at the beach | Association for Diplomatic Studies & Training (adst.org), 22 August 2021. Ike was chiefly upset with the British, for what he deemed an almost personal betrayal. See, Tunzelmann, *Blood and Sand*, 432–435.

cused on its security. It had no "strategic depth" and seemingly could be overrun by its neighbors. While he never publicly repudiated his decision during the Suez Crisis to support Nasser over Britain, France, and Israel, Eisenhower's estimation for Israel only grew in the coming years, including its use of pre-emptive military power. The American president vowed nothing would happen to Israel while he was in the Oval Office.[83] Some might speculate that Ike's resolve, alongside the doctrine that bore his name, were part of the reason that there was not another Arab-Israeli war after the Suez Crisis until 1967. They might also recognize the legacy of Ohrdruf trumping Cold War fears as well.

The Lingering Nazi Stench

Perhaps Eisenhower would have been less understanding of the Egyptian position during the Suez Crisis had he known the extent to which former Nazis were advising the Nasser government. Johann von Leers, for example, was an anti-Semitic propagandist for the Third Reich, a member of the SS, and by 1956 employed by the Egyptian government to write anti-Jewish/anti-Israeli propaganda. He was, as Joel Fishman describes him, an "unrepentant" Nazi. Nor was he alone. Wilhelm Fahrmbacher, one of Field Marshal Irwin Rommel's staff officers, served as a senior military advisor to the Egyptian government and Oskar Munzel, a former Panzer officer, was also an advisor to Nasser during the Suez Crisis.[84]

Former Nazis were not confined to new lives in Egypt, however. Though the Germans had cultivated Arab and Muslim support during the Second World War, to both destabilize British influence in the Middle East and because some Muslims, including the Grand Mufti of Jerusalem, Amin al-Hussaini, shared the Nazi hatred of Jews, most Germans who fled the destruction of the Reich ended

---

[83] Michael J. Totten, "We Are Still Living With Eisenhower's Biggest Mistake," http://www.the tower.org/article/we-are-still-living-with-eisenhowers-biggest-mistake-suez-egypt-israel-ikes-gam ble-michael-doran/, 6 March 2017; Doran, *Ike's Gamble*, 236–237, 241–243; Alteras, *Eisenhower and Israel*, 170–172, 213, 316; Peter L. Hahn, "Securing the Middle East: The Eisenhower Doctrine of 1957," *Presidential Studies Quarterly*, 36(March 2006), 38–47; Douglas Little, "His Finest Hour? Eisenhower, Lebanon, and the 1958 Middle East Crisis," *Diplomatic History*, 20(Winter 1996), 27–54. Little argues that while Ike could steer the policy effectively, his precedent proved problematic in lesser hands in Vietnam.

[84] Michael Wildt, *An Uncompromising Generation: The Nazi Leadership of the Reich Security Main Office* (Madison: University of Wisconsin Press, 2003), 363–364; Joel Fishman, "The Postwar Career of Nazi Ideologue Johann von Leers, aka Omar Amin, the 'First Ranking German' in Nasser's Egypt," *Jewish Political Studies Review*, 26(Fall 2014), 54–72.

up in South America. Among them was Adolf Eichmann, one of the architects of the Holocaust.[85]

Eichmann was the "ghost of Nuremburg." He and his handiwork were constantly cited and mentioned. Yet, the man himself was not in the courtroom. Though he was not a camp administrator, like the sadistic Rudolf Hoss of Auschwitz, nor a demented doctor like Josef Mengele who performed experiments on prisoners, Eichmann was one of the bureaucrats, perhaps the bureaucrat to listen to hear him tell it, who made the Holocaust happen as it did. And not just in the abstract. Eichmann not only made the work of Hoss and Mengele possible but knew what all the parts were doing. He was the totality of the Final Solution's administrative apparatus; they were merely its parts. It was Eichmann who constructed the plan, beginning with his attendance at the Wannsee conference in 1942 that created the logistical network to "feed" the concentration camp system. He became a master of deportation and never believed it to be anything other than a way to transport Jews to their deaths. Most Nazis had no idea what the bigger picture was or how many people they had in the camps, let alone how many people died there. Eichmann did. He was perhaps the first person to give the figure of six million Jews exterminated. He even claimed, boasted really, to have been the one to coin the phrase "final solution."[86] As Bettina Stangneth put it, his "greed was for death tolls, not for luxury and riches."[87]

Nor was he a faceless or nameless bureaucrat. In 1944, as the tide of the war was turning against the Nazis for good, Eichmann was dispatched to Hungary. A nominal German ally for most of the war, Hungary was home to some 900,000 Jews, virtually all of whom had survived up until Eichmann's arrival. In the final year of the war, Eichmann's administrative genius allowed for the deportation and murder of at least 450,000 Hungarian Jews. Not only that, but Eichmann deftly got around Hungarian reluctance and resistance to the deportation of its citizens by using the Gestapo ruthlessly and working with a newly installed, and adamantly anti-Semitic, Hungarian government. In the span of just two months, Hungary went from being a place of relative safety for its Jewish citizens to a

---

[85] Johnson, *A Mosque in Munich*, 30–31; Quentin Reynolds, Ephraim Katz, Zwy Al Douby, *Minister of Death: The Adolf Eichmann Story* (New York: Viking Press, 1960), 175; Bettina Stangneth, *Eichmann Before Jerusalem: The Unexamined Life of a Mass Murderer* (New York: Vintage Books, 2015), 45–46.

[86] "Wannsee Conference and the 'Final Solution,'" https://encyclopedia.ushmm.org/content/en/article/wannsee-conference-and-the-final-solution, 10 November 2022; Stangneth, *Eichmann Before Jerusalem*, 3, 31, 67, 234, 299–305; Snyder, *Bloodlands*, 144; Laurence Rees, *The Holocaust: A New History* (New York: Viking, 2017), 393–395; McKale, *Nazis after Hitler*, 271–272; Reynolds, Katz, Aldouby, *Minister of Death: The Adolf Eichmann Story*, 90, 137.

[87] Stangneth, *Eichmann Before Jerusalem*, 125.

place that was deporting 10,000 to 20,000 people a day to the camps. Eichmann claimed that one day there would be a statue erected of him in Budapest for the job he had accomplished.[88] He was also prepared, as we have seen, to use his Jewish prisoners as bargaining chips. It was Eichmann (at the behest of Himmler) who attempted to craft a deal with the Allies to release Jews from the camps in exchange for things like soap, coffee, and trucks.[89]

Whether they were in Egypt or, like Eichmann, in Argentina, the consensus among the expatriated Nazis was "that, in time, grass would grow over" the Holocaust. Most expected that they would eventually not just return to Germany, but finish what they had started when it came to the Final Solution. They were, by and large, young men, only in their thirties or forties. They had tasted power and believed they would achieve it again. Eichmann personified this feeling. He did not like living in anonymity, nor working in a factory. He had been someone important after all, who had literally held the power of life and death in his hands.[90]

Eichmann's feelings of wanting to recapture old Nazi glory was palatable among his fellow exiles by the early 1950s. One can view their role in the Suez Crisis as continuing to fight World War II by other means. They routinely downplayed the Holocaust, talking of the "lie of the six million," and spread propaganda throughout the Arab world essentially apologizing for not killing enough Jews to preclude the creation of Israel. Many saw the Cold War as the perfect way to return to power, not just covertly, but overtly, believing that the West's stand

---

[88] Reynolds, Katz, Aldouby, *Minister of Death: The Adolf Eichmann Story*, 171; Raul Hilberg, *The Destruction of the European Jews* (Chicago: Quadrangle Books, 1961), 510–514, 520–530, 544, 547; Yisrael Gutman and Michael Berenbaum, editors, *Anatomy of the Auschwitz Death Camp* (Indianapolis: Indiana University Press, 1994), 456, 461; Timothy Snyder, *Black Earth: The Holocaust as History and Warning* (New York: Tim Duggan Books, 2015), 236–237; Stangneth, *Eichmann Before Jerusalem*, 49.

[89] Rebecca Erbelding, *Rescue Board: The Untold Story of America's Efforts to Save the Jews of Europe* (New York: Anchor Books, 2018), 131–132; The Ambassador in Turkey to the Secretary of State, 25 May 1944, Foreign Relations of the United States, Diplomatic Papers, 1944, Europe, Volume I, accessed on 7 September 2022; Laurence Rees, *The Holocaust: A New History* (New York: Public Affairs, 2017), 397, 409. One of the men Eichmann was negotiating with (via proxy) was the United States' Ambassador to Turkey, Laurence A. Steinhardt, who was the nation's "first Jewish 'career' ambassador." Steinhardt held posts in Sweden, Peru, the Soviet Union (where he downplayed the need to let Jewish refugees enter the United States before the war), Turkey, Czechoslovakia, and Canada. See, Barry Rubin, "Ambassador Laurence A. Steinhardt: The Perils of a Jewish Diplomat, 1940–1945," *American Jewish History*, 70(March 1981), 331–346.

[90] Stangneth, *Eichmann Before Jerusalem*, xviii, xx-xxi, 135; Hannah Arendt, *Eichmann in Jerusalem: A Report on the Banality of Evil* (New York: Penguin, 2006), 235; Rebecca Erbelding, *Rescue Board: The Untold Story of America's Efforts to Save the Jews of Europe* (New York: Anchor Books, 2018), 230.

against Communism would require more Operation Paperclip type accommodations with former members of the Third Reich. They even saw the creation of West Germany, which had largely ended denazification, as a steppingstone to a revival in the heart of Europe itself. Indeed, the West Germans were not only less zealous than the Allies had been in prosecuting offenders, but they also offered amnesty to some imprisoned former Nazis and even allowed many others back into civil service jobs, as a means to leave the past behind and give themselves a fresh start.[91]

Their hopes for a National Socialist second coming vanished, however. West Germany's politics offered no refuge for Nazi thought, or foothold for a return to power. Whatever traction the Suez Crisis may have given them was dashed both by internal Arab state feuding and the continual failure to militarily subjugate Israel, often resulting in stunning Arab defeats. Scholarship on the Holocaust, and the war in general, grew, debunking the claims of the former Nazis. And, to top it off, Dwight Eisenhower was not only reelected as president of the United States in 1956, but his post-Suez initiatives undercut any dreams the Nazis might have had that America would retreat to the sidelines of the international arena as they had through most of the 1930s.[92]

However, that brief period where Eichmann and other Nazis had dared to dream ultimately proved his undoing. By feeling more assured, by shedding some of his anonymity, Eichmann's trail was picked up on by those seeking to bring Nazis to justice, including the Israeli intelligence agency the Mossad. Agents tracked Eichmann to Argentina, observed and documented his movements, and then on May 11, 1960, abducted him off the street. After staying at a safe house for several days, the agents then smuggled Eichmann out of the country, flying him to Israel. On May 23, Israeli Prime Minister David Ben-Gurion announced to the world the capture and planned trial for the architect of the Holocaust.[93]

---

[91] Norbert Frei, *Adenauer's Germany and the Nazi Past: The Politics of Amnesty and Integration*, translated by Joel Golb (New York: Columbia University Press, 2002); Stangneth, *Eichmann Before Jerusalem*, 147–151, 177, 227; "Denazification," http://www.alliiertenmuseum.de/en/topics/denazification.html, 18 June 2021. See also, Kay Schiller, "The Presence of the Nazi Past in the Early Decades of the Bonn Republic," Journal of Contemporary History, 39(April 2004), 285–294.
[92] Stangneth, *Eichmann Before Jerusalem*, 174–175.
[93] Reynolds, Katz, Aldouby, *Minister of Death: The Adolf Eichmann Story*, 3–14. For more on the Mossad operation that brought Eichmann from Argentina to Israel, see, Neal Bascomb, *Hunting Eichmann: How a Band of Survivors and a Young Spy Agency Chased Down the World's Most Notorious Nazi* (New York: Mariner Books 2010) and Peter Z. Malkin and Harry Stein, *Eichmann in My Hands* (NY Grand Central Publishers, 1990). Eichmann had lived in Argentina under the alias Ricardo Klement.

The announcement sent shockwaves around the globe. Public opinion in the United States was somewhat divided over the Israeli operation. No one, at least publicly, came out against Eichmann's capture and the prospect of a trial. But many expressed unease about the legality of the methods that led to the capture.[94] The Eisenhower Administration was a different matter. Ike and his advisors were surprised and impressed by the Israeli operation. The United States had been looking for the Nazi fugitive since the end of the war and Eisenhower made sure that the American government did its part to ensure that justice was rendered now that Eichmann was in an Israeli prison. As it turned out both the Central Intelligence Agency and the Federal Bureau of Investigation had files relating to Eichmann, which they shared with Israel.[95] The legal case against Eichmann suddenly got much stronger.

However, the diplomatic situation was another matter. Eichmann's abduction was an international incident that threatened Israel's relationship with not just Argentina, but virtually every nation in South America. While David Ben-Gurion made a moral case for the action, Argentina saw it as a clear violation of their laws and sovereignty. However, neither side wanted Eichmann to sour what had been a good diplomatic relationship between the two countries. In the end, Argentina got a U.N. resolution passed condemning this sort of covert abduction, but Israel got to keep Eichmann. Argentina then formally expelled Israel's ambassador and the matter was settled.[96]

One reason the diplomatic situation did not escalate was because of Eisenhower. The president threw the United States' diplomatic weight behind Israel's moral case against Eichmann, while making sure that Argentina's concerns were expressed and addressed. The State Department took an active role as did America's United Nations ambassador, Henry Cabot Lodge. The U.N. Security Council held a meeting on June 22, 1960 about the Eichmann incident, at which Lodge argued that while what Israel had done was highly unorthodox, as they had not sought formal extradition, one simply could not separate Eichmann from the Holocaust. While Poland and the Soviet Union abstained from voting, the council eventually passed Resolution 138, which not only acknowledged the need to bring Eichmann to justice but did not condemn Israel for doing so. Instead, it expressed hope that such actions would not be repeated in the future as they caused "friction" between member states, called on Israel to make appropriate reparations to Argentina (which Eisenhower insisted needed to be defined), and called on the two nations to

---

94 Peter Novick, *The Holocaust in American Life* (New York: Houghton Mifflin, 1999), 128.
95 "Uncovering the Architect of the Holocaust: The CIA Names File on Adolf Eichmann," https://nsarchive2.gwu.edu/NSAEBB/NSAEBB150/, 17 June 2021.
96 Reynolds, Katz, Aldouby, *Minister of Death: The Adolf Eichmann Story*, 208–225.

resume their good relations quickly. Among the eight member states on the council who voted for the resolution was Argentina! After the U.N. vote, Israel expressed its "deep appreciation for the position taken by Ambassador Lodge in the Eichmann debate at the Security Council," directly to Eisenhower.[97]

The U.N. resolution all but assured that Eichmann's trial would go ahead. His family held out hope that Argentina might still demand his return from Israel. Eichmann's brother, Otto, sure that Eichmann faced an eventual death sentence, argued that his brother should be spared so that he could tell all he knew about what happened to Jews under Nazi Germany. Even the Vatican tried to put pressure on various governments to demand Eichmann's return to Argentina. The Roman Catholic Church knew all too well that Catholic priests had helped Nazis escape judgement after the war, including providing new identification papers after baptizing fleeing Germans under new names.[98] All these efforts amounted to nothing. Israel had Eichmann in custody. The trial was going to happen.

What became clear in the months leading up to and then during the trial was that Eichmann was not ashamed of what he had done, nor unwilling to share his thoughts if asked. He argued that killing Jews in the Holocaust was merely another front in the war. Harnessing the bureaucracy to kill more of them and doing so more efficiently was much better that exploiting them in some way. He was proud of what he had accomplished.[99] The truly disturbing thing that emerged was not that Eichmann was good at what he did, but rather even if he was just a cog in the Nazi machine, the machine represented not a minority, but a majority, of Germans.

---

[97] Herter, Christian A.: Papers, Box 12, CAH Telephone Calls 3/28/60-6/30/60 (1) [Memoranda of telephone conversations Christian Herter, Ambassador Henry Cabot Lodge and Francis Wilcox, June 23, 1960 regarding Eichmann case at the United Nations], 155. Memorandum of a conversation, Department of State, Washington, June 27, 1960, "Foreign Relations of the United States, 1958–1960, Arab-Israeli Dispute; United Arab Republic; North Africa, Volume XIII; "Resolution 138," http://unscr.com/en/resolutions/138, 14 January 2021; Reynolds, Katz, Aldouby, *Minister of Death: The Adolf Eichmann Story*, 218–219, 221. The Soviet Union and Poland abstained from the vote, though they indicated at least tacit approval of the decision. Both countries had continued war crimes trials, aimed at Nazi collaborators, long after the conclusion of the Nuremberg proceedings. In the case of the Soviets, there were two reasons for their decision not to support Resolution 138: There continued to be a desire not to elevate the suffering of Jews above that of Soviet citizens at the hands of the Nazis and to also curry favor with Arab states by not being supportive of Israel. Deborah Lipstadt gives a good deal of credit for Lodge's position to Richard Nixon. See, Deborah E. Lipstadt, *The Eichmann Trial* (New York: Schocken Books, 2011), 22–23.

[98] Stangneth, *Eichmann Before Jerusalem*, 355; Reynolds, Katz, Aldouby, *Minister of Death: The Adolf Eichmann Story*, 19–20.

[99] Stangneth, *Eichmann Before Jerusalem*, 200–201, 209, 226, 264, 297, 303; Lipstadt, *The Eichmann Trial*, 43, 71.

Whether or not the "obedient clerk" was the brains of the Holocaust or not, he made the machine work.[100]

Eichmann's trial in Jerusalem began on April 11, 1961 and concluded on December 15. He was found guilty and sentenced to death. On June 1, 1962, he was hung, cremated, and his ashes spread beyond Israel's territorial waters. Many of his former compatriots, including Josef Mengele, believed all Germany should be ashamed of allowing Eichmann to be killed by Jews.[101] The rest of the world saw it as closing another chapter in the legacy of the Second World War. This was certainly true in the United States. As Peter Novick relates, "the Eichmann Trial was the first time that the American public was presented with the Holocaust as a distinct-and distinctly Jewish-entity."[102] It cemented Ike's dictum of never allowing such a thing to happen again.

For Eisenhower, the Eichmann capture and trial represented one more victory over the Nazis. American involvement in mitigating the fallout over the Israeli operation was also in line with one of Ike's favorite approaches to foreign policy: working behind the scenes and out of the limelight. If Harry Truman's legacy included presiding over the end of World War II and then recognizing Israel, Ike's legacy was comprised of defeating the Nazis and guaranteeing Israel as a viable state. Americans may not have always wanted to confront the legacy of either the war or the Holocaust during the 1950s, but they had a president in Eisenhower who did.[103]

---

100 Wildt, *An Uncompromising Generation*, 5; Reynolds, Katz, Aldouby, *Minister of Death: The Adolf Eichmann Story*, 202; Arendt, *Eichmann in Jerusalem*, xii–xiv; Lipstadt, *The Eichmann Trial*, 49, 176.
101 "Eichmann Trial," https://encyclopedia.ushmm.org/content/en/article/eichmann-trial, 23 May 2019; Stangneth, *Eichmann Before Jerusalem*, 359–360.
102 Peter Novick, *The Holocaust in American Life* (New York: Houghton Mifflin, 1999), 134.
103 Alteras, *Eisenhower and Israel*, 316; Samantha Power, *"A Problem from Hell": America and the Age of Genocide* (New York: Basic Books, 2002), 72–73.

Epilogue: Never Forgetting

After leaving the White House in 1961, Eisenhower's twin legacies of general and commander-in-chief made him a mythic figure in the United States. They also made him a sought-after advisor to those who followed him into the White House. He was consulted by both John F. Kennedy, whom Eisenhower doubted had the resolve to be an effective president, and Lyndon B. Johnson, whom Eisenhower came to distrust. But he was also the Republican elder statesman, supporting both his own Vice President, Richard Nixon in 1960 and in 1968 (though, as he later lamented, not enough the first time) and Barry Goldwater in 1964, somewhat tepidly, as he never forgave the Arizona Senator for saying the Eisenhower Administration was just a Republican version of the New Deal. He also took a special interest in an actor who decided to enter politics named Ronald Reagan.[1] It was Reagan who, as president, finally saw the United States enter the U.N. Convention on Genocide and who spoke at the cornerstone ceremony of the United States Holocaust Memorial Museum.[2]

---

[1] Jack M. Holl, *The Religious Journey of Dwight D. Eisenhower: Duty, Honor, Country* (Grand Rapids: William B. Eerdmans Publishing Company, 2021), 290, 295; Susan Eisenhower, *Mrs. Ike: Memories and Reflections on the Life of Mamie Eisenhower* (New York: Farrar, Straus and Giroux, 1996), 300; "President John F. Kennedy Meeting with Dwight Eisenhower, 22 October 1962," Presidential Recordings Digital Edition, https://pride.upress.virginia.edu, 19 October 2022; Gene Kopelson, *Reagan's 1968 Dress Rehearsal: Ike, RFK and Reagan's Emergence as a World Statesman* (Los Angeles: Figueroa Press, 2016). The story is told that when Eisenhower was asked by Kennedy to advise him on the aftermath of the Bay of Pigs invasion, he quipped to his son John, "I don't do failed invasions." For more on this meeting, see Gellman, *The President and the Apprentice*, 554–558.

[2] "History of the United States Holocaust Memorial Museum," https://encyclopedia.ushmm.org/content/en/article/history-of-the-united-states-holocaust-memorial-museum, 6 June 2023; Power, "A Problem from Hell," 70. Eisenhower had supported, in principle both the U.N.'s Genocide and Human Rights Conventions, however the treaties ran into Congressional opposition that worried about infringements on U.S. sovereignty. Eisenhower worked behind the scenes to halt what he saw as the Legislative branch's infringements on Executive branch powers—spurred among many Republicans because of their memories of the Roosevelt Administration. See, Duane Tananbaum, *The Bricker Amendment Controversy: A Test of Eisenhower's Political Leadership* (Ithaca: Cornell University Press, 1988), 16–31, 217–219; Hitchcock, *The Age of Eisenhower*, 136; Herbert Brownell, *Advising Ike: The Memoirs of Attorney General Herbert Brownell* (Lawrence: University of Kansas Press, 1993), 269; Matthew Continetti, *The Right: The Hundred-Year War for American Conservatism* (New York: Basic Books, 2022), 125.

During the war, Ike had openly wondered if he would ever "really settle down and live a serene life."[3] During his presidency, he and Mamie had purchased a farm near Gettysburg, Pennsylvania, and it was there that the couple lived starting in 1961. It was also at the farm where they could live as a family and Ike could enjoy being a grandfather unencumbered by official duties. To those outside the family circle, he preferred to be referred to as "general" rather than "president." The military title remained fitting, as the Second World War and the Holocaust were so important to making Eisenhower the public figure he was.[4]

Starting in 1965, a decade after his first heart attack, Ike suffered another one. In the years after, his health slowly started to decline.[5] Dwight David Eisenhower, Supreme Allied Commander and President of the United States, died on March 28, 1969, surrounded by his family. His final words, after ordering the shades to his hospital room at Walter Reed Army Hospital lowered and asking for help sitting up were "I want to go. God take me."[6] Lying in state in Washington, D.C., he was eulogized by both former President Lyndon Johnson and newly inaugurated President Richard Nixon. Johnson said that Ike was the person America needed in both war and peace. Nixon's reminded the nation that Ike came "from the heart of America" and that he was "the right man at the right place at the right time," not just once, but twice, in the nation's history.[7]

Such memorialization is hardly surprising. The Second World War eclipses not just the Great War but also the Cold War when it comes to international conflicts of the twentieth century. And as a part of it, the Holocaust has become perhaps the "axial event of modern history" according to historian Timothy Snyder.[8] What the Nazis were able to unleash continues to remind us just how "shallow . . . the veneer of civilization" actually is and the ease with which human nature can

---

3 John S. D. Eisenhower, editor, *Letters to Mamie* (Garden City: Doubleday & Company, 1978), 157.
4 Eisenhower, *Mrs. Ike*, 304; Susan Eisenhower, *How Ike Led: The Principles Behind Eisenhower's Biggest Decisions* (New York: Thomas Dunne Books, 2020), 1, 319.
5 Eisenhower, *Mrs. Ike*, 310–311.
6 Eisenhower, *Mrs. Ike*, 314.
7 "Eulogy Delivered at the Capitol During the State Funeral of General Eisenhower," https://www.presidency.ucsb.edu/documents/eulogy-delivered-the-capitol-during-the-state-funeral-general-eisenhower, 19 October 2022; "Eisenhower Dies at Age 78, March 28, 1969," https://www.politico.com/story/2018/03/28/eisenhower-dies-at-age-78-march-28-1969-484631, 25 January 2021; Holl, *The Religious Journey of Dwight D. Eisenhower*, 309; Susan Eisenhower, *How Ike Led: The Principles Behind Eisenhower's Biggest Decisions* (New York: Thomas Dunne Books, 2020), 328.
8 Snyder, *Black Earth*, 337.

be persuaded to make the "unthinkable" a horrific reality.[9] Indeed, as Norbert Troller points out, "Most of the Jews who were murdered in the camps of Poland went to their deaths without active resistance, holding on to some slim hope that their murderers were still the humane, civilized people the world had long believed them to be."[10] Lives, community, and a version of European culture was lost as a result.[11] Ike wrestled with the consequences of the war, including what all the death and destruction implied about human nature. In doing so, what he saw at Ohrdruf was always at the forefront of his mind, both in the closing days of the war and as president.[12]

The passage of time, and the deaths of survivors, perpetrators, and liberators have not dampened the event in our collective memories.[13] We know the camp names where Jews and others died almost as well as we know the names of the battlefields where Allied armies fought the Nazis. We fixate on how many died in the Holocaust and at times argue over exact numbers. Rarely do we engage the fact that the Nazis constructed a mechanism to kill that many people and that they did so largely uninterrupted by the Allies. Nor is there much discussion over how those deaths came in more ways than just via gas chambers. Some victims of the Nazis died alone, or with a few others, while many were killed in groups of hundreds or thousands. But each life extinguished was that of an individual. The bodies we see in pictures, the bodies Eisenhower encountered at Ohrdruf; these were all once people like us. Likewise, while we talk of "Nazis" and "Germans," it is good to remember, as Ike did, that they were individuals as well—who made decisions, justifications, and rationalizations for their participation in the war, and for some, the Holocaust.[14]

That the Nazis were able to kill millions of people largely unmolested gnaws at us, as it surely bothered Eisenhower after Ohrdruf.[15] Could the United States

---

9 John C. McManus, *Hell Before Their Very Eyes: American Soldiers Liberate Concentration Camps in Germany, April 1945* (Baltimore: Johns Hopkins University Press, 2015), 128, 150.
10 Norbert Troller, *Theresienstadt: Hitler's Gift to the Jews* (Chapel Hill: The University of North Carolina Press, 1991), xx.
11 Konrad H. Jarausch and Michael Geyer, *Shattered Past: Reconstructing German Histories* (Princeton: Princeton University Press, 2003), 120.
12 Eisenhower, *How Ike Led*, 65.
13 Jarausch and Geyer, *Shattered Past*, 29.
14 Robert H. Abzug, *Inside the Vicious Heart: Americans and the Liberation of Nazi Concentration Camps* (New York: Oxford University Press, 1987), ix; Hilberg, *The Destruction of the European Jews*, 639; Stangneth, *Eichmann Before Jerusalem*, 295; Deborah Dwork and Robert Jan van Pelt, *Auschwitz* (New York: W.W. Norton and Company, 2008), 397; Snyder, *Bloodlands*, x, 111, 406–411; Alvin H. Rosenfeld, *The End of the Holocaust* (Indianapolis: Indiana University Press, 2011), 146.
15 Judah Nadich, *Eisenhower and the Jews* (New York: Twayne Publishers, 1953), 245.

and its allies have done more? It is a haunting question, and one without an easy answer, or at least not one that is easy to accept one way or another. After all, if the answer is "yes," then there is little doubt that the United States and the other Allies failed morally, even as they succeeded on the ground and won the war. If it is "no," then we must admit that the Allies were powerless to stop the greatest crime of the twentieth century. Short of officially making the ending of the Holocaust a war aim, there was likely little that could have been done. The Allies knew, in general, what was happening and opted to pursue victory as the only means to address the evil taking place in the camps. The war had to end with Germany's defeat for the killing to end. But as Theodore Hamerow points out, "the tragedy," with having to win the war to halt the Holocaust, "was that by the time victory came, so few Jews were left to be saved."[16]

However, this should not blind us to the fact that some Jews were saved. The men Eisenhower led became liberators. Along with the camps and the battles, we should remember that men and women stood up and fought against the Nazis. To them, the Holocaust was never "history." How could it be? These crimes and the war they were a part of were not only events they lived through but were committed by people of the same generation as them. If they were the "greatest generation," then the Nazis were the flipside of that generational coin.[17] As former Ambassador William J. van den Heuvel noted, "to say that we are all guilty allows the truly guilty to avoid that responsibility. We must remember for all the days of our lives that it was Hitler who imagined the Holocaust and the Nazis who carried it out. We were not their accomplices. We destroyed them."[18]

Just as Eisenhower led the American liberators, so too did he set the country on the path of never forgetting the Holocaust. And yet remembrance is a complicated concept. The Holocaust continues to spark unease, not just in what might have been done differently to end it, but also with what is the best way to remember the victims. Visiting a camp is a profound experience yet acknowledging that the camp was but one piece of a larger system—like Eichmann was but one cog

---

16 Daniel Jonah Goldhagen, *Hitler's Willing Executioners: Ordinary Germans and the Holocaust* (New York: Vintage Books, 1997), 21; Stangneth, *Eichmann Before Jerusalem*, 295; Hamerow, *Why We Watched: Europe*, 305–307, 330–331, 390–392, 416–418; Richard Breitman, Norman J.W. Goda, Timothy Nafatli, and Robert Wolfe, *U.S. Intelligence and the Nazis* (New York: Cambridge University Press, 2005), 62–63, 444–446; Evelyn Le Chene, *Mauthausen: The History of a Death Camp* (London: Methuen and Company, 1971), 176; Dan Plesch, *Human Rights After Hitler: The Lost History of Prosecuting Axis War Crimes* (Washington, D.C.: Georgetown University Press, 2017), 69; Nadich, *Eisenhower and the Jews*, 52–53, 104–105.
17 McManus, *Hell Before Their Very Eyes*, 17, 142.
18 Keynote Address, Fifth Annual Franklin and Eleanor Roosevelt Distinguished Lecture, Roosevelt University, Chicago, Illinois, 17 October 1996.

in the Nazi bureaucratic machine that made those camps work—is something quite different.[19] Likewise, invoking the Holocaust to apply to other groups and situations, universalizes a particular event and, some have argued, cheapens the meaning and memory of the event itself.[20]

Furthermore, remembrance was difficult even when the events were front page news and fresh in the minds of those who witnessed them. The photographs Eisenhower ordered taken of the camps became important to the war crimes trials as well as to how the camps have been remembered ever since. The images go from literal memories (real people taking pictures of real events) to cultural memories in an instant. Today, they, like documentaries, museum exhibits, and Hollywood films, can give "an impression" of what happened. But only an impression.[21] Many of the liberators themselves struggled with what they saw, opting to stay silent to spare their loved ones the horrors they had ended.[22] While understandable to a degree, their silence was contrasted by Eisenhower's willingness to speak out. For, just as he feared, even in the aftermath of the war, when the accounts were fresh and survivors plentiful, there were people who doubted that the atrocities of the camps had taken place, or that the camps themselves were as bad as the stories claimed.[23] Their numbers have only grown in the decades since.

Along with the deniers has arisen both disillusionment and an attempt to move past the Holocaust. Disillusionment, because no amount of just remembering has prevented further genocides from taking place.[24] Even the power of the

---

[19] Unlike the larger, better-known camps, only small memorials mark Ohrdruf today. Much of the area served as a military training ground for the Bundeswehr until recently. See, "Recollections of a Liberator: The Liberation of Ohrdruf and Buchenwald," https://www.pattonsbestmedics.com/recollections-of-a-liberator-the-liberation-of-ohrdruf-and-buchenwald-part-1-ohrdruf/, 9 September 2022.

[20] Walter Laqueur, *Out of the Ruins of Europe* (New York: Library Press, 1971), 501; Hamerow, *Why We Watched*, 474–475; Rosenfeld, *The End of the Holocaust*, 35–37, 45, 69; Snyder, *Black Earth*, 207–209.

[21] Barbie Zeliger, "La photo de presse et la liberation des camps en 1945: Images et forms de la memoire," *Vingtieme Siecle. Revue d'histoire*, 54(April-June 1997), 62–63; Frank Van Vree, *Performing the Past: Memory, History, and Identity in Modern Europe* (Amsterdam: Amsterdam University Press, 2010), 258.

[22] Leila Levinson, *Gated Grief: The Daughter of a GI Concentration Camp Liberator Discovers a Legacy of Trauma* (Brule, Wisconsin: Cable Publishing, 2011), 119. This is a sentiment that historian Douglas Brinkley noted as well of the men who stormed Normandy's beaches. Douglas Brinkley, *The Boys of Pointe Du Hoc: Ronald Reagan, D-Day, and the U.S. Army Second Ranger Battalion* (New York: Harper Perennial, 2005), 184.

[23] Marcus J. Smith, *Dachau: The Harrowing of Hell* (Albuquerque: University of New Mexico Press, 1972), 242.

[24] Rosenfeld, *The End of the Holocaust*, 277–280.

United States, which Eisenhower wielded so effectively in both war and as president, has not been able to stop it. Indeed, Samantha Power argues that in the decades since the Holocaust, America has crafted a policy of non-intervention in such cases. And as Michael J. Totten has pointed out, even having written this with a chance to change that policy's course, as American ambassador to the United Nations, Power was largely ineffectual, as was the Obama Administration, in stopping the genocidal civil war in Syria.[25]

For Americans, the allure of moving beyond the Holocaust is strong, not just because of the time that has passed but also because of distance.[26] Moving on has taken a different form in Europe, not because of denial but because while the Holocaust is memorialized, liberation has been largely cleansed from the narrative. European resistance against Hitler and Nazism was generally weak; collaboration and acquiescence were far more common. In the end, it took the aid of the United States, in material, manpower, and leadership to end the Third Reich. And that effort was led by Dwight Eisenhower. It was he who led SHAEF. It was Eisenhower who launched Germany on the path to denazification. It was Ike who made sure what he saw at Ohrdruf was publicized not propagandized. And it was Ike who called on his nation to bear witness to the horrors of the Third Reich and to stand, even as their numbers thinned, against those who would deny the truth of the Holocaust.[27]

Those efforts mattered in 1945 and still do today. When he had the power to do so, whether on the battlefront, in the aftermath of his visit to Ohrdruf, as military governor of the American zone of Germany, or as president, Eisenhower focused the nation's resources in combatting the very real evil Nazi totalitarianism represented and unleashed. He did so because it was necessary and dismissing the evil he witnessed was not an option for him or for the United States.[28] He was not perfect, nor did he do everything we might wish he would of, but he did more

---

[25] Power, *"A Problem from Hell,"* xvi, xxi, 69; Michael J. Totten, "Samantha, Powerless: Obama's Problem from Hell in Syria," http://www.thetower.org/article/samantha-powerless-obamas-problem-from-hell-in-syria/, 6 March 2017.

[26] Hilene Flanzbaum, editor, *The Americanization of the Holocaust* (Baltimore: The Johns Hopkins University Press, 1999), 72–80, 149.

[27] McManus, *Hell Before Their Very Eyes*, 152–153; German History Museum, Berlin, Germany; William I. Hitchcock, *The Bitter Road to Freedom: A New History of the Liberation of Europe* (New York: Free Press, 2008), 369.

[28] Al Sommer Jr., letter, 8 April 1945, RG-09.056, United States Holocaust Memorial Museum, Washington, D.C; Smith, *Dachau: The Harrowing of Hell*, 280; Isabel Vincent, *Hitler's Silent Partners: Swiss Banks, Nazi Gold, and the Pursuit of Justice* (New York: William Morrow and Company, Inc., 1997), 4; McManus, *Hell Before Their Very Eyes*, 148; Richard M. Filipink, Jr., *Dwight Eisenhower and American Foreign Policy during the 1960s* (New York: Lexington Books, 2015), 12.

than many of his contemporaries once he knew what the camps and the Holocaust actually was. As Ohrdruf survivor Andrew Rosner put it, "What you, my liberators, did in 1945 represented all that was good and kind in the world. Had it not been for your goodness, and kindness, and compassion, I would have died. A world would have died."[29]

If Eisenhower's quote about encountering the Holocaust is how visitors start their time at the United States Holocaust Memorial Museum, it is equally fitting that his official memorial in Washington, D.C., is just a few blocks away. Both stand as testaments to his charge to the nation to never forget.[30] But the quote does something else important. It reminds us that individual stories matter, both of those who died and those who liberated. Ultimately, the Holocaust is about those stories—stories of what people did to one another and what others did to stop the murders from continuing. One of those stories is Eisenhower's and how walking through the liberated Ohrdruf camp shaped him, the nation he led, and the world in its aftermath. He never forgot and neither should we.

---

29 McManus, *Hell Before Their Very Eyes*, vii.
30 Rosenfeld, *The End of the Holocaust*, 65; *New York Times*, 12 April 2018.

Bibliography

Archives and Museums

Dallas Holocaust and Human Rights Museum, Dallas Texas
Dwight Eisenhower Presidential Library and Museum, Abilene, Kansas
Franklin D. Roosevelt Presidential Library and Museum, Hyde Park, New York
German History Museum, Berlin, Germany
Harry S. Truman Presidential Library and Museum, Independence, Missouri
Memorial to the Murdered Jews of Europe, Berlin, Germany.
University of Southern California Shoah Foundation, Los Angeles, California
United States Holocaust Memorial Museum, Washington, D.C.

Articles

"Address by President Dwight D. Eisenhower," *Publications of the American Jewish Historical Society*, 2 (December 1954), 67–74.
Bauer, Yehuda. "The Death-Marches, January-May, 1945,"*Modern Judaism*, 3(February 1983), 1–21.
Bickerton, Ian. "Dwight D. Eisenhower and Israel: A New Look," *Australasian Journal of American Studies*, 7(July 1988), 1–12.
Bradford, Anita Casavantes. "'With the Utmost Practical Speed': Eisenhower, Hungarian Parolees, and the 'Hidden Hand' Behind US Immigration and Refugee Policy, 1956–1957," *Journal of American Ethnic History* (2020) 39 (2): 5–35.
Chernus, Ira. "Eisenhower and the Soviets, 1945–1947: Rhetoric and Policy," *Rhetoric and Public Affairs*, 2(Spring 1999), 59–82.
Fishman, Joel. "The Postwar Career of Nazi Ideologue Johann von Leers, aka Omar Amin, the 'First Ranking German' in Nasser's Egypt," *Jewish Political Studies Review*, 26(Fall 2014), 54–72.
Friling, Tuvia and Moshe Tlamin, "The New Historians and the Failure of Rescue Operations during the Holocaust," *Israel Studies*, 8(Fall 2003), 25–64.
Hahn, Peter L. "Securing the Middle East: The Eisenhower Doctrine of 1957," *Presidential Studies Quarterly*, 36(March 2006), 38–47.
Hoffmann, Peter. "Colonel Claus von Stauffenberg in the German Resistance to Hitler: Between East and West," *The Historical Journal*, 31(September 1988), 629–650.
Kondoyanidi, Anita. "The Liberating Experience: War Correspondents Red Army Soldiers, and the Nazi Extermination Camps," *The Russian Review*, 69(July 2010), 438–462.
Laczo, Ferenc. "'I could hardly wait to get out of this camp, even though I knew it could only get worse until liberation came': On Hungarian Jewish Accounts of the Buchenwald concentration Camp from 1945–1946," *The Hungarian Historical Review*, 2(Ethnicity, 3, 2013), https://hunghist.org/archive/83-articles/179-2013-3-laczo
Lipstadt, Deborah E. "America and the Holocaust," *Modern Judaism*, 10(October 1990), 283–296.
Little, Douglas. "His Finest Hour? Eisenhower, Lebanon, and the 1958 Middle East Crisis," *Diplomatic History*, 20(Winter 1996), 27–54.
Mart, Michelle. "Tough Guys and American Cold War Policy: Images of Israel, 1948–1960," *Diplomatic History*, 20(Summer 1996), 357–380.

McAuliffe, Mary S. "Eisenhower, the President," *Journal of American History*, 68(December 1981), 625–632.
McCloy, John J. "American Occupation Policies in Germany," *Proceedings of the Academy of Political Science*, 21(January 1946), 80–91.
McCreedy, Kenneth O. "Planning the Peace: Operation Eclipse and the Occupation of Germany," *Journal of Military History*, 65(July 2001), 713–738.
Nolan, Cathal J. "Americans in the Gulag: Detention of US Citizens by Russia and the Onset of the Cold War, 1944–1945," *Journal of Contemporary History* 25(October 1990), 523–545.
Platon, Mircea. "Astolphe de Custine's Letters from Russia and the Defense of the West," *Russian History*, 43(July 2016), 142–180.
Rabe, Stephen G. "Eisenhower Revisionism: A Decade of Scholarship," *Diplomatic History*, 17(Winter 1993), 97–115.
Rubin, Barry. "Ambassador Laurence A. Steinhardt: The Perils of a Jewish Diplomat, 1940–1945," *American Jewish History*, 70(March 1981), 331–346.
Schiller, Kay. "The Presence of the Nazi Past in the Early Decades of the Bonn Republic," *Journal of Contemporary History*, 39(April 2004), 285–294.
Stern, Mark. "Presidential Strategies and Civil Rights: Eisenhower, the Early Years, 1952–1954," *Presidential Studies Quarterly*, 19 (Fall 1989), 769–795.
Williamson, Daniel C. "Understandable Failure: The Eisenhower Administration's Strategic Goal in Iraq, 1953–1958," *Diplomacy and Statecraft*, 17:3 (2006), 597–612.
Young, Jeffrey R. "Eisenhower's Federal Judges and Civil Rights Policy: A Republican 'Southern Strategy' for the 1950s," *The Georgia Historical Quarterly*, 78(Fall 1994), 536–565.
Zeliger, Barbie. "La photo de presse et la liberation des camps en 1945: Images et forms de la memoire," *Vingtieme Siecle. Revue d'histoire*, 54(April-June 1997).
Zink, Harold. "American Occupation Policies in Germany," *The Review of Politics*, 9(July 1947), 284–296.

Books

Abzug, Robert H. *Inside the Vicious Heart: Americans and the Liberation of Nazi Concentration Camps* (New York: Oxford University Press, 1987).
Adams, Sherman Adams. *Firsthand Report: The Story of the Eisenhower Administration* (New York: Harper and Brothers, 1961).
Ahrweiler, Georg, Rainer Rilling, Rolf Schellhase. Editors, *Soziologische Ausfluge: Festschrift fur Hans Jurgen Krysmanski zum 60. Geburtstag* (Westdeutscher Verlag, 1997).
Alteras, Isaac. *Eisenhower and Israel: U.S.-Israeli Relations, 1953–1960* (Gainesville: University Press of Florida, 1993).
Ambrose, Stephen E. *Eisenhower: Soldier and President* (New York: A Touchstone Book,1990).
Ambrose, Stephen E. *D-Day June 6, 1944: The Climactic Battle of World War II* (New York: Simon and Schuster, 1994).
Ambrose, Stephen E. *Citizen Soldiers: The U.S. Army from the Normandy Beaches to the Bulge to the Surrender of Germany, June 7, 1944-May 7, 1945* (New York: Simon & Schuster, 1997).
Ambrose, Stephen E. *The Supreme Commander: The War Years of General Dwight D. Eisenhower* (Jackson: University of Mississippi Press, 1999).
Ambrose, Stephen E. *Ike's Spies: Eisenhower and the Espionage Establishment* (Jackson: University of Mississippi Press, 1999).

Ambrose, Stephen E. *Eisenhower and Berlin, 1945: The Decision to Halt at the Elbe* (New York: W.W. Norton, 2000).
Annual Report of the Superintendent, United States Military Academy 1914.
Arendt, Hannah. *Eichmann in Jerusalem: A Report on the Banality of Evil* (New York: Penguin, 2006).
Atkinson, Rick. *The Guns at Last Light: The War in Western Europe, 1944-1945* (New York: Henry Holt and Company, 2013).
Baier, Bret. *Three Days in January: Dwight Eisenhower's Final Mission* (New York: William Morrow, 2017).
Balogh, Brian and Bruce J. Schulman. Editors, *Recapturing the Oval Office: New Historical Approaches to the American Presidency* (Ithaca: Cornell University Press, 2015).
Bascomb, Neal. *Hunting Eichmann: How a Band of Survivors and a Young Spy Agency Chased Down the World's Most Notorious Nazi* (New York: Mariner Books 2010).
Beevor, Antony. *The Fall of Berlin 1945* (New York: Viking Press, 2002).
Beevor, Antony. *Ardennes 1944: Hitler's Last Gamble* (New York: Viking Press, 2015).
Bellamy, Chris. *Absolute War: Soviet Russia in the Second World War* (New York: Alfred A. Knopf, 2007).
Bendersky, Joseph W. *The "Jewish Threat": Anti-Semitic Politics of the U.S. Army* (New York: Basic Books, 2000).
Beschloss, Michael. *The Conquerors: Roosevelt, Truman and the Destruction of Hitler's Germany, 1941-1945* (New York: Simon and Schuster, 2002).
Betros, Lance. *Carved from Granite: West Point Since 1902* (College Station: Texas A & M Press, 2012).
Biddiscombe, Perry. *Denazification: A History, 1945-1950* (Stroud, UK: Tempus Press, 2007).
Biggs, Bradley. *Gavin* (Hamden, Connecticut: Archon Books, 1980).
Bischof, Gunter and Stephen E. Ambrose, *Eisenhower and the German POWs: Facts Against Falsehood* (Baton Rouge: Louisiana State University Press, 1992).
Blumenson, Martin. Editor, *The Patton Papers, 1940-1945* (Boston: Houghton Mifflin Company, 1974).
Boder, David P. *I Did Not Interview the Dead* (Urbana, IL: The University of Illinois Press, 1949).
Bonhoeffer, Dietrich. *The Cost of Discipleship* (New York: Touchstone, 1995).
Brady, Steven J. *Eisenhower and Adenauer: Alliance Maintenance under Pressure, 1953-1960* (New York: Lexington Books, 2010).
Breitman Richard and Alan M. Kraut. *American Refugee Policy and European Jewry, 1933-1945* (Indianapolis: Indiana University Press, 1987).
Breitman Richard, Norman J.W. Goda, Timothy Nafatli, and Robert Wolfe, *U.S. Intelligence and the Nazis* (New York: Cambridge University Press, 2005).
Breitman Richard, Barbara McDonald Stewart, and Severin Hochberg. Editors, *Refugees and Rescue: The Diaries and Papers of James G. McDonald, 1935-1945* (Indianapolis: Indiana University Press, 2009).
Breitman Richard and Allan J. Lichtman, *FDR and the Jews* (Cambridge: Belknap Press, 2013).
Bridgman, Jon. *The End of the Holocaust: The Liberation of the Camps* (Portland: Areopagitica Press, 1990).
Brinkley, Douglas. *The Boys of Pointe Du Hoc: Ronald Reagan, D-Day, and the U.S. Army Second Ranger Battalion* (New York: Harper Perennial, 2005).
Browne, Blaine T. *Mighty Endeavor: The American Nation and World War II* (New York: Rowman & Littlefield, 2019).
Brownell, Herbert. *Advising Ike: The Memoirs of Attorney General Herbert Brownell* (Lawrence: University of Kansas Press, 1993).
Burleigh, Michael. *Moral Combat: Good and Evil in World War II* (New York: Harper Collins Publishers, 2011).
Butcher, Harry C. *My Three Years with Eisenhower: The Personal Diary of Captain Harry C. Butcher, USNR, Naval Aide to General Eisenhower, 1942 to 1945* (New York: Simon and Schuster, 1946).

Caddick-Adams, Peter. *Fire and Steel: The End of World War Two in the West* (New York: Oxford University Press, 2022).
Celinscak, Mark. *Distance from the Belsen Heap: Allied Forces and the Liberation of a Nazi Concentration Camp* (Toronto: University of Toronto Press, 2015).
Chandler, Jr., Alfred D. Editor, *The Papers of Dwight David Eisenhower: The War Years,Volume I* (Baltimore: The Johns Hopkins University Press, 1970).
Chandler, Jr. Editor, *The Papers of Dwight David Eisenhower: The War Years, Volume II* (Baltimore: The Johns Hopkins University Press, 1970).
Chandler, Jr. Editor, *The Papers of Dwight David Eisenhower: The War Years, Volume IV* (Baltimore: The Johns Hopkins University Press, 1971).
Chandler, Jr., and Louis Galambos. Editors, *The Papers of Dwight David Eisenhower: Occupation, 1945, Volume VI* (Baltimore: The Johns Hopkins University Press, 1971).
Chapoutot, Johann. *The Law of Blood: Thinking and Acting as a Nazi* (Cambridge, Massachusetts: The Belknap Press of Harvard University Press, 2018).
Churchill, Winston S. *The Second World War: Volume I, The Gathering Storm* (Boston: Houghton Mifflin, 1948).
Citino, Robert M. *The Wehrmacht's Last Stand: The German Campaigns of 1944–1945* (Lawrence: University Press of Kansas, 2017).
Clark, Christopher. *Iron Kingdom: The Rise and Downfall of Prussia, 1600–1947* (Cambridge: Harvard University Press, 2006).
Clark, Douglas E. *Eisenhower in Command at Columbia* (New York: Lexington Books, 2013).
Clendinnen, Inga. *Reading the Holocaust* (New York: Cambridge University Press, 1999).
Continetti, Matthew. *The Right: The Hundred-Year War for American Conservatism* (New York: Basic Books, 2022).
Cox, Graham B. *Seeking Justice for the Holocaust: Herbert C. Pell, Franklin D. Roosevelt, and the Limits of International Law* (Norman: University of Oklahoma Press, 2019).
Crim, Brian E. *Our Germans: Operation Paperclip and the National Security State* (Baltimore: Johns Hopkins University Press, 2018).
Crosswell, D.K.R. *Beetle: The Life of General Walter Bedell Smith* (Lexington: The University Press of Kentucky, 2012).
Cullather, Nick. *Secret History: The CIA's Classified Account of Its Operations in Guatemala, 1952–1953* (Stanford: Stanford University Press, 1999).
Davis, George B. *The Elements of International Law* (New York: Harper and Brothers, 1915).
Davis, George B. *A Treatise on the Military Law of United States Together with the Practice and Procedure Courts-Martial and Other Military Tribunals*, (1916).
De Custine, Astolphe. *Letters from Russia: The 1843 Translation Edited, Revised, and with Introduction by Anka Muhlstein* (New York: New York Review of Books, 2002).
DeFelice, Jim. *Omar Bradley: General at War* (Washington, D.C.: Regnery Publishing, 2014).
Department of the Army Field Manual, FM 19–40: Handling Prisoners of War (Washington: United States Government Printing Office, 1952).
Donaldson, Gary A. *When America Liked Ike: How Moderates Won the 1952 Presidential Election and Reshaped American Politics* (New York: Rowman & Littlefield, 2017).
Doran, Michael. *Ike's Gamble: America's Rise to Dominance in the Middle East* (New York: The Free Press, 2016).
Douglas, R.M. *Orderly and Humane: The Expulsion of the Germans after the Second World War* (New Have: Yale University Press, 2012).
Dulles, Allen Welsh. *Germany's Underground* (New York: The Macmillan Company, 1947).

Dwork, Deborah and Robert Jan van Pelt, *Auschwitz* (New York: W.W. Norton and Company, 2008).
Edsel, Robert M. *The Monuments Men: Allied Heroes, Nazi Thieves, and the Greatest Treasure Hunt in History* (New York: Center Street, 2009).
Erbelding, Rebecca. *Rescue Board: The Untold Story of America's Efforts to Save the Jews of Europe* (New York: Anchor Books, 2018).
Eisenhower, David. *Eisenhower: At War, 1943-1945* (New York: Random House, 1986).
Eisenhower, Dwight D. *Crusade in Europe* (New York: Doubleday and Company, 1953).
Eisenhower, Dwight D. *At Ease: Stories I tell to Friends* (New York: Doubleday and Company, 1967).
Eisenhower, John S. D. *Strictly Personal* (Garden City, NY: Doubleday and Company, 1974).
Eisenhower, John S. D. Editor, *Letters to Mamie* (Garden City: Doubleday & Company, 1978.
Eisenhower, Susan. *Mrs. Ike: Memories and Reflections on the Life of Mamie Eisenhower* (New York: Farrar, Straus and Giroux, 1996).
Eisenhower, Susan. *How Ike Led: The Principles Behind Eisenhower's Biggest Decisions* (New York: Thomas Dunne Books, 2020).
Ephraim, Frank. *Escape to Manila: From Nazi Tyranny to Japanese Terror* (Chicago: University of Illinois Press, 2003).
Epstein, Lawrence J. *Americans and the Birth of Israel* (New York: Rowman and Littlefield, 2017).
Evans, Richard J. *The Third Reich at War* (New York: Penguin Press, 2010).
Ewald, Jr., William Bragg. *Eisenhower the President: Crucial Days, 1951-1960* (Englewood Cliffs: Prentice-Hall, 1981).
Fest, Joachim. *Inside Hitler's Bunker: The Last Days of the Third Reich* (New York: Farrar, Straus and Giroux, 2002).
Filipink, Jr., Richard M. *Dwight Eisenhower and American Foreign Policy during the 1960s* (New York: Lexington Books, 2015).
Flanzbaum, Hilene. Editor, *The Americanization of the Holocaust* (Baltimore: The Johns Hopkins University Press, 1999).
Frei, Norbert. *Adenauer's Germany and the Nazi Past: The Politics of Amnesty and Integration*, translated by Joel Golb (New York: Columbia University Press, 2002).
Friedlander, Saul. *Nazi Germany and the Jews, 1933-1945 - Abridged Edition* (New York: Harper Perennial, 2009).
Fritz, Stephen G. *Ostkrieg: Hitler's War of Extermination in the East* (Lexington: University Press of Kentucky, 2015).
Fritzsche, Peter. *An Iron Wind: Europe Under Hitler* (New York: Basic Books, 2016).
Galambos, Louis. Editor, *The Papers of Dwight David Eisenhower, Columbia University, XI* (Baltimore: The Johns Hopkins University Press, 1984).
Galambos, Louis. *The Papers of Dwight David Eisenhower: NATO and the Campaign of 1952, XII* (Baltimore: The Johns Hopkins University Press, 1989).
Galambos, Louis. *The Papers of Dwight David Eisenhower: NATO and the Campaign of 1952, XIII* (Baltimore: The Johns Hopkins University Press, 1989).
Galambos, Louis. *Eisenhower: Becoming the Leader of the Free World* (Baltimore: Johns Hopkins University Press, 2018).
Gavin, James M. *On To Berlin: Battles of an Airborne Commander, 1943-1945* (New York: The Viking Press, 1978).
Gienow-Hecht, Jessica C.E. *Transmission Impossible: American Journalism as Cultural Diplomacy in Postwar Germany, 1945-1955* (Baton Rouge: Louisiana State University Press, 1999).
Gelb, Norman. *Ike and Monty: Generals at War* (New York: William Morrow and Company, 1994).

Gellately, Robert. Editor, *The Nuremberg Interviews: An American Psychiatrist's Conversations with the Defendants and Witnesses, Conducted by Leon Goldensohn* (New York: Vintage Books, 2005).

Gellman, Irwin F. *The President and the Apprentice: Eisenhower and Nixon, 1952–1961* (New Haven: Yale University Press, 2015).

Gilbert, Martin. *Auschwitz and the Allies* (New York: Pimlico, 2001).

Gilbert, Martin. *Churchill and the Jews: A Lifelong Friendship* (New York: Henry Holt and Company, 2007).

Goldhagen, Daniel Jonah. *Hitler's Willing Executioners: Ordinary Germans and the Holocaust* (New York: Vintage Books, 1997).

Gould, Lewis L. *Grand Old Party: A History of the Republicans* (New York: Random House, 2003).

Greenstein, Fred I. *The Hidden-Hand Presidency: Eisenhower as Leader* (New York: Basic Books, 1982).

Grossmann, Atina. *Jews, Germans and Allies: Close Encounters in Occupied Germany* (Princeton, N.J.: Princeton University Press, 2007).

Guhin, Michael A. *John Foster Dulles: A Statesman and His Times* (New York: Columbia University Press, 1972).

Gun, Nerin E. *The Day of the Americans* (New York: Fleet Publishing Corporation, 1966).

Gutman, Yisrael and Michael Berenbaum. Editors, *Anatomy of the Auschwitz Death Camp* (Indianapolis: Indiana University Press, 1994).

Hackett, David A. Editor, *The Buchenwald Report* (Boulder: Westview Press, 1995).

Hamerow, Theodore S. *Why We Watched: Europe, America, and the Holocaust* (New York: W. W. Norton & Company, 2008).

Hamilton, Nigel. *Monty: The Battles of Field Marshal Bernard Montgomery* (New York: Random House, 1994).

Hamilton, Nigel. *War and Peace: FDR's Final Odyssey, D-Day to Yalta: 1943–1945* (New York: Houghton Mifflin Harcourt, 2019).

Hastings, Max. *Inferno: The World at War, 1939–1945* (New York: Alfred A. Kopf, 2011).

Hauenstein Ralph W. with Donald E. Markle, *Intelligence Was My Line: Inside Eisenhower's Other Command* (New York: Hippocrene Books, 2005).

Hearing Before the Committee on Military Affairs, House of Representatives, Sixty-Second Congress, Second Session on H.R. 23628: Being a Project for the Revision of the Articles of War (Washington: Government Printing Office, 1912).

Heefner, Wilson Allen. *Dogface Soldier: The Life of General Lucian K. Truscott, Jr.* (Columbia: University of Missouri Press, 2010).

Helm, Sarah. *Ravensbruck: Life and Death in Hitler's Concentration Camp for Women* (New York: Nan A. Talese Doubleday, 2014).

Hilberg, Raul. *The Destruction of the European Jews* (Chicago: Quadrangle Books, 1961).

Hirsh, Michael. *The Liberators: America's Witnesses to the Holocaust* (New York: Bantam Books, 2010).

Hitchcock, William I. *The Bitter Road to Freedom: A New History of the Liberation of Europe* (New York: Free Press, 2008).

Hitchcock, William I. *The Age of Eisenhower: American and the World in the 1950s* (New York: Simon and Schuster, 2018).

Holl, Jack M. *The Religious Journey of Dwight D. Eisenhower: Duty, Honor, Country* (Grand Rapids: William B. Eerdmans Publishing Company, 2021).

Holland, James. *Together We Stand: America, Britain and the Forging of an Alliance* (New York: Hyperion, 2005).

Holland, James. *Normandy '44: D-Day and the Epic 77-Day Battle for France* (New York: Atlantic Monthly Press, 2019).

Hoopes, Townsend. *The Devil and John Foster Dulles* (Boston: Little, Brown, and Company, 1973).
Hughes, Daniel J. and Richard L. Dinardo, *Imperial Germany and War, 1871–1918* (Lawrence: University Press of Kansas, 2018).
Hunt, John Gabriel. Editor, *The Inaugural Addresses of the Presidents* (New York: Gramercy Books, 1995).
James, D. Clayton. *The Years of MacArthur: Volume I: 1880–1941* (Boston: Houghton Mifflin Company, 1970).
Jarausch, Konrad H. and Michael Geyer, *Shattered Past: Reconstructing German Histories* (Princeton: Princeton University Press, 2003).
Jensen, Geoffrey W. *The Racial Integration of the American Armed Forces: Cold War Necessity, Presidential Leadership, and Southern Resistance* (Lawrence: University of Kansas Press, 2023).
Johnson Eric A. and Karl-Heinz Reuband, *What We Knew: Terror, Mass Murder, and Everyday Life in Nazi Germany, An Oral History* (New York: Basic Books, 2005).
Johnson, Ian. *A Mosque in Munich: Nazis, the CIA, and the Muslim Brotherhood in the West* (New York: Houghton Mifflin Harcourt, 2010).
Kahn, David. *Hitler's Spies: German Military Intelligence in World War II* (New York: Macmillan Publishing Company, 1978).
The Katyn Forest Massacre: Hearings before the Select Committee to Conduct an Investigation of the Fact, Evidence, and Circumstances of the Katyn Forest Massacre, 82nd Congress (Washington, D.C. Government Printing Office, 1952).
Kennedy, David M. *Freedom From Fear: The American People in Depression and War, 1929–1945* (New York: Oxford University Press, 1999).
Kershaw, Ian. *The End: The Defiance and Destruction of Hitler's Germany, 1944–1945* (New York: The Penguin Press, 2011).
Kinzer, Stephen. *The Brothers: John Foster Dulles, Allen Dulles, and Their Secret World War* (New York: Henry Holt and Company, 2013).
Kopelson, Gene. *Reagan's 1968 Dress Rehearsal: Ike, RFK and Reagan's Emergence as a World Statesman* (Los Angeles: Figueroa Press, 2016).
Kotlowski, Dean J. *Paul V. McNutt and the Age of FDR* (Indianapolis: Indiana University Press, 2015).
LaNier, Carlotta Walls. *A Mighty Long Way: My Journey to Justice at Little Rock Central High School* (New York: One World Books, 2010).
Laoiselee, Marcel. *Ohrdruf, le camp oublie de Buchenwald: Un Survivant Temoigne* (Madison: The University of Wisconsin Press, 2010).
Laqueur, Walter. *Out of the Ruins of Europe* (New York: Library Press, 1971).
Larson, Erik. *In the Garden of Beasts: Love, Terror, and an American Family in Hitler's Berlin* (New York: Broadway Paperbacks, 2011).
Larres, Klaus. *Politik der Illusionen: Churchill, Eisenhower, und die deutsche Frage, 1945–1955* (Zurich: Vandenhoeck & Ruprecht, 1995).
Le Chene, Evelyn. *Mauthausen: The History of a Death Camp* (London: Methuen and Company, 1971).
Levinson, Leila. *Gated Grief: The Daughter of a GI Concentration Camp Liberator Discovers a Legacy of Trauma* (Brule, Wisconsin: Cable Publishing, 2011).
Libbey, James K. *Alben Barkley: A Life in Politics* (Lexington: University Press of Kentucky, 2016).
Lipstadt, Deborah E. *The Eichmann Trial* (New York: Schocken Books, 2011).
Logan, Ben. *Lest We Forget: Ben Harrison Logan, Jr.: An American Soldier in World War II* (Independently Published, 2021).
Longerich, Peter. *Holocaust: The Nazi Persecution and Murder of the Jews* (New York: Oxford University Press, 2010).

MacDonald, Charles B. *United States Army in World War II: The European Theater of Operations, the Last Offensive* (Washington, D.C.: Center of Military History United States Army, 1984).

MacDonogh, Giles. *After the Reich: The Brutal History of the Allied Occupation* (New York: Basic Books, 2007).

MacDonogh, Giles. *1938: Hitler's Gamble* (New York: Basic Books, 2009).

MacGregor, Neil. *Germany: Memories of a Nation* (New York: Vintage Books, 2014).

Malinowski, Stephan, *Nazis & Nobles:The History of a Misalliance* (New York: Oxford University Press, 2020).

Malkin, Peter Z. and Harry Stein, *Eichmann in My Hands* (NY Grand Central Publishers, 1990).

Manchester, William. *American Caesar: Douglas MacArthur, 1880–1964* (New York: Little, Brown and Company, 1978).

Mart, Michelle. *Eye on Israel: How Americans Came to View Israel as an Ally* (Albany: State University of New York Press, 2006).

Mason, David S. *A Concise History of Modern Europe: Liberty, Equality, Solidarity* (New York: Rowman and Littlefield, 2011).

McCullough, David. *Truman* (New York: Simon & Schuster, 1992).

McKale, Donald. *Hitler's Shadow War: The Holocaust and World War II* (New York: Cooper Square Press, 2002).

McKale, Donald. *Nazis after Hitler: How Perpetrators of the Holocaust Cheated Justice and the Truth* (New York: Rowman and Littlefield Publishers, 2014).

McKeogh, Michael James and Richard Lockridge, *Sergeant Mickey and General Ike* (San Francisco: Lucknow Books, 2016).

McManus, John C. *Hell Before Their Very Eyes: American Soldiers Liberate Concentration Camps in Germany, April 1945* (Baltimore: Johns Hopkins University Press, 2015).

McMeekin, Sean. *Stalin's War: A New History of World War II* (New York: Basic Books, 2021).

Mead, Walter Russell. *The Arc of a Covenant: The United States, Israel, and the Fate of the Jewish People* (New York: Knopf, 2022).

Mendelsohn, John. Editor, *The Holocaust: Volume 3, The Crystal Night Pogrom* (New York: Garland Publishing, Incorporated, 1982).

Mendelsohn, John. Editor, *The Holocaust: Selected Documents, Volume 9, Medical Experiments on Jewish Inmates of Concentration Camps* (Clark, New Jersey: The Lawbook Exchange, Ltd., 2010).

Merridale, Catherine. *Ivan's War: Life and Death in the Red Army, 1939–1945* (New York: Metropolitan Books, 2006).

Miller, Merle Miller. *Ike the Soldier: As They Knew Him* (New York: Perigee Books, 1987).

Morin, Relman. *Dwight D. Eisenhower: A Gauge of Greatness* (New York: The Associated Press, 1969).

Morris, Sylvia Jukes. *The Price of Fame: The Honorable Clare Boothe Luce* (New York: Random House, 2014).

Nadich, Judah. *Eisenhower and the Jews* (New York: Twayne Publishers, 1953).

Naimark, Norman M. *Genocide: A World History* (New York: Oxford University Press, 2017).

Nazi Conspiracy and Aggression: Volume 1 (Washington, D. C.: United States Government Printing Office, 1946).

Neiberg, Michael. *Potsdam: The End of World War II and the Remaking of Europe* (New York: Basic Books, 2015).

Nichols, David A. *A Matter of Justice: Eisenhower and the Beginning of the Civil Rights Revolution* (New York: Simon & Schuster Paperbacks, 2007).

Novick, Peter. *The Holocaust in American Life* (New York: Houghton Mifflin, 1999).

Official Register of the Officers and Cadets of the United States Military Academy for 1911.

Official Register of the Officers and Cadets of the United States Military Academy for 1912.
Official Register of the Officers and Cadets of the United States Military Academy for 1913.
Official Register of the Officers and Cadets of the United States Military Academy for 1914.
Official Register of the Officers and Cadets of the United States Military Academy for 1915.
Osgood, Kenneth. *Total Cold War: Eisenhower's Secret Propaganda Battle at Home and Abroad* (Lawrence: University of Kansas Press, 2006).
Ousby, Ian. *The Road to Verdun: World War I's Most Momentous Battle and the Folly of Nationalism* (New York: Doubleday, 2002).
Overy, Richard. *Blood and Ruins: The Last Imperial War, 1931-1945* (New York: Viking, 2021).
Patterson, James T. *Mr. Republican: A Biography of Robert A. Taft* (Boston: Houghton Mifflin Company, 1972).
Patterson, James T. *Grand Expectations: The United States, 1945-1974* (Oxford: Oxford University Press, 1996).
Patton, Jr., George S. *War as I Knew It* (Boston: Houghton Mifflin Company, 1947).
Perret, Geoffrey. *Eisenhower* (New York: Random House, 1999).
Perisco, Joseph E. *Piercing the Reich: The Penetration of Nazi Germany by American Secret Agents during World War II* (New York: Viking Press, 1979).
Perisco, Joseph E. *Roosevelt's Secret War: FDR and World War II Espionage* (New York: Random House, 2001).
Petersen, Neal H. Editor, *From Hitler's Doorstep: The Wartime Intelligence Reports of Allen Dulles, 1942-1945* (University Park, PA: The Pennsylvania State University Press, 1996).
Pickett, William B. *Dwight David Eisenhower and American Power* (Wheeling, IL: Harland Davidson, 1995).
Pipes, Kasey S. *Ike's Final Battle: The Road to Little Rock and the Challenge of Equality* (Los Angeles: World Ahead Publishing, 2007).
Plesch, Dan. *Human Rights After Hitler: The Lost History of Prosecuting Axis War Crimes* (Washington, D.C.: Georgetown University Press, 2017).
Plokhy, S.M. *Yalta: The Price of Peace* (New York: Viking, 2010).
Power, Samantha. *"A Problem from Hell": America and the Age of Genocide* (New York: Basic Books, 2002).
Pringle, Heather. *The Master Plan: Himmler's Scholars and the Holocaust* (New York: Hyperion, 2006).
Pruessen, Ronald. *John Foster Dulles: The Road to Power* (New York: The Free Press, 1982).
Rapport, Aaron. *Waging War, Planning Peace: U.S. Noncombat Operations and Major Wars* (Ithaca: Cornell University Press, 2015).
Read, Anthony. *The Devil's Disciples: Hitler's Inner Circle* (New York: W.W. Norton & Company, 2003).
Rees, Laurence. *The Holocaust: A New History* (New York: Public Affairs & Viking, 2017).
Reilly, Joanne. *Belsen: The Liberation of a Concentration Camp* (New York: Routledge, 1998).
Reynolds, Quentin, Ephraim Katz, Zwy Al Douby, *Minister of Death: The Adolf Eichmann Story* (New York: Viking Press, 1960).
Rosenfeld, Alvin H. *The End of the Holocaust* (Indianapolis: Indiana University Press, 2011).
Ryan, Cornelius. *The Last Battle* (New York: Simon and Schuster, 1966).
Sears, Alan and Craig Osten with Ryan Cole, *The Soul of an American President: The Untold Story of Dwight D. Eisenhower's Faith* (Grand Rapids, Michigan: Baker Books, 2019).
Sebald, W.G. *On the Natural History of Destruction* (New York: Modern Library Classics, 2004).
Seillier, Andre. *A History of the Dora Camp* (Chicago: Ivan R. Dee, 2003).
Shapiro, Robert Moses. Editor, *Why Didn't the Press Shout?: American and International Journalism During the Holocaust* (Newark: KTAV Publishing House, 1995).

Schultz, Duane. *Patton's Last Gamble: The Disastrous Raid on POW Camp Hammelburg in World War II* (New York: Stackpole Books, 2018).

Shephard, Ben. *After Daybreak: The Liberation of Bergen-Belsen, 1945* (New York: Schocken Books, 2005).

Simmons, Gerald and the editors of Time-Life Books. *World War II: Victory in Europe* (Alexandria: Time-Life Books, 1982).

Smith, Bradley F. *Sharing Secrets with Stalin: How the Allies Traded Intelligence, 1941–1945* (Lawrence: University Press of Kansas, 1996).

Smith, Jean Edward. Editor, *The Papers of General Lucius D. Clay: Germany, 1945–1949, Volume I* (Bloomington: Indiana University Press, 1974).

Smith, Jean Edward. *Eisenhower in War and Peace* (New York: Random House, 2013).

Smith, Bradley F. *Sharing Secrets with Stalin: How the Allies Traded Intelligence, 1941–1945* (Lawrence: University Press of Kansas, 1996).

Smith, Marcus J. *Dachau: The Harrowing of Hell* (Albuquerque: University of New Mexico Press, 1972).

Smith, Walter Bedell. *My Three Years in Moscow* (New York: J.B. Lippincott Company, 1949).

Snyder, Timothy. *Bloodlands: Europe Between Hitler and Stalin* (New York: Basic Books, 2010).

Black Earth: The Holocaust as History and Warning (New York: Tim Duggan Books, 2015).

Stahl, Ronit. *Enlisting Faith: How the Military Chaplaincy Shaped Religion and State in Modern America* (Cambridge, MA: Harvard University Press, 2017).

Stander, Manfred. *Ohrdruf im Dritten Reich* (Sutton Verlag, 2012).

Stangneth, Bettina. *Eichmann Before Jerusalem: The Unexamined Life of a Mass Murderer* (New York: Vintage Books, 2015).

Stargardt, Nicholas. *The German War: A Nation Under Arms, 1939–1945, Citizens and Soldiers* (New York: Basic Books, 2015).

Steinert, Marlis G. *Hitler's War and the Germans: Public Mood and Attitude During the Second World War* (Athens, OH: Ohio University Press, 1977).

Steinweis, Alan E. and Robert D. Rachlin. Editors, *The Law in Nazi Germany: Ideology, Opportunism, and the Perversion of Justice* (New York: Berghahn, 2013).

Stone, Dan. *The Liberation of the Camps: The End of the Holocaust and Its Aftermath* (New Haven: Yale University Press, 2015).

Stromer, Marvin E *The Making of a Political Leader: Kenneth S. Wherry and the United States Senate* (Lincoln: University of Nebraska Press, 1969).

Strand, Ginger. *The Brothers Vonnegut: Science and Fiction in the House of Magic* (New York: Farrar, Straus and Giroux, 2015).

Strong, Kenneth. *Intelligence at the Top: The Recollections of an Intelligence Officer* (Garden City: Doubleday and Company, 1969).

Sutton, Robert K. *Nazis on the Potomac: The Top Secret Intelligence Operation that Helped Win World War II* (Philadelphia: Casemate, 2021).

Szybicki, Edmund. *To Hope or Die: From Warsaw Uprising to Sachsenhausen Concentration Camp and After, Memoirs of a Survivor* (London: Athena Press, 2007).

Tananbaum, Duane. *The Bricker Amendment Controversy: A Test of Eisenhower's Political Leadership* (Ithaca: Cornell University Press, 1988).

Taylor, Telford. *The Anatomy of the Nuremberg Trials: A Personal Memoir* (Boston: Back Bay Books, 1992).

Thomas, Evan. *Ike's Bluff: President Eisenhower's Secret Battle to Save the World* (New York: Back Bay Books, 2012).

Tiergartenstrasse 4: Memorial and Information Point for the Victims of National Socialist Euthanasia Killings (Berlin: The Foundation Memorial to the Murdered Jews of Europe, 2016).

Trachtenberg, Barry. *The United States and the Nazi Holocaust: Race, Refuge and Remembrance* (New York: Bloomsbury, 2018).

Troller, Norbert. *Theresienstadt: Hitler's Gift to the Jews* (Chapel Hill: The University of North Carolina Press, 1991).

Truman, Harry S. *Memoirs: Volume 2, Years of Trial and Hope* (Garden City: Doubleday & Company, 1956).

Vincent, Isabel. *Hitler's Silent Partners: Swiss Banks, Nazi Gold, and the Pursuit of Justice* (New York: William Morrow and Company, Inc., 1997).

Van Vree, Frank. *Performing the Past: Memory, History, and Identity in Modern Europe* (Amsterdam: Amsterdam University Press, 2010).

Von Hildebrand, Dietrich. *My Battle Against Hitler: Faith, Truth, and Defiance in the Shadow of the Third Reich* (New York: Image Books, 2014).

Von Tunzelmann, Alex. *Blood and Sand: Suez, Hungary, and Eisenhower's Campaign for Peace* (New York: Harper, 2016).

Vollmer, Anje and Lars-Broder Keil. *Stauffenbergs Gefahrten: Das Schicksal der unbekannten Verschworer* (Berlin: Hanser, 2013).

Wachsmann, Nikolaus. *KL: A History of the Nazi Concentration Camps* (New York: Farrar, Straus and Giroux, 2016).

Wagner, Elisabeth. Editor, *Der General-Quartiermeister: Briefe und Tagebuchaufzeichnungen des General Quartiermeisters des Heeres General der Artillerie Eduard Wagner* (Munich: Gunter Olzog Verlag, 1963).

Weigley, Russell F. *Eisenhower's Lieutenants: The Campaign of France and Germany, 1944–1945* (Bloomington: Indiana University Press, 1981).

Weinberg, Gerhard L. *World in the Balance: Behind the Scenes of World War II* (Hanover: University Press of New England, 1981).

Weiner, Tim. *The Folly and the Glory: America, Russia, and Political Warfare, 1945–2020* (New York: Henry Holt & Company, 2020).

Wildt, Michael. *An Uncompromising Generation: The Nazi Leadership of the Reich Security Main Office* (Madison: University of Wisconsin Press, 2003).

Wiley, Robert S. *Dewey Short: Orator of the Ozarks* (Cassville, MO: Litho Printers and Bindery, 1985).

Wilsey, John D. *God's Cold Warrior: The Life and Faith of John Foster Dulles* (Grand Rapids: William B. Eerdmans Publishing Company, 2021).

Witcover, Jules. *Party of the People: A History of the Democrats* (New York: Random House, 2003).

Witt, John Fabian.*Lincoln's Code: The Laws of War in American History* (New York: Free Press, 2012).

Wuthnow, Robert. *Why Religion is Good for American Democracy* (Princeton: Princeton University Press, 2021).

Wyman, David S. *The Abandonment of the Jews: America and the Holocaust, 1941–1945* (New York: The New Press, 2007).

Wyman, Mark. *DPs: Europe's Displaced Persons, 1945–1951* (Ithaca: Cornell University Press, 1998).

Ziemke, Earl F. *The U.S. Army in the Occupation of Germany, 1944–1946: Army Historical Series* (Washington, D.C., Center of Military History United States Army, 1975).

Dissertations and Theses

Lindsey, Benjamin A. "Organized Crime Against Civilization: The Congressional Investigation of Liberated Concentration Camps in 1945," (Master's Thesis, University of Vermont, 2012).
Livingston, Jeffery C. "Ohio Congressman John M. Vorys: A Republican Conservative Nationalist and Twentieth Century American Foreign Policy," (Doctoral Dissertation: University of Toledo, 1989).

Newspapers and Periodicals

Christian Science Monitor
Daily Mail
Indianapolis News
Jewish Telegraphic Agency Daily News Bulletin
Life Magazine
New York Times
Times of Israel
Washington Post

Oral Histories and Interviews

Adler, Jacob. 28 February 2014, USC Shoah Foundation, accessed on 13 September 2022.
Andres, David. Oral History, Dallas Holocaust and Human Rights Museum.
Baum, Rudy. Oral History, Dallas Holocaust and Human Rights Museum.
Brosseau, Charles. Oral History, Dallas Holocaust and Human Rights Museum.
Calabrase Zero. Testimony, 23 October 1992, RG-09.019.01, United States Holocaust Memorial Museum, Washington, D.C.
Canafax, Wilson. Oral History, Dallas Holocaust and Human Rights Museum.
Cohen, David. Oral History, USC Shoah Foundation, Visual History Archive, accessed 2 August 2017.
Erzell, Bert. Oral History, Dallas Holocaust and Human Rights Museum.
Fitzgerald, Bill. Oral History, Dallas Holocaust and Human Rights Museum.
Flynn, Larry. Oral History, USC Shoah Foundation, Visual History Archive, accessed 2 August 2017.
Katz, Ernest Katz. 28 March 1995, USC Shoah Foundation, accessed on 13 September 2022.
Kohn, Rose. Oral History, USC Shoah Foundation, Visual History Archive, accessed 2 August 2017.
Garrick, Richard. 15 May 1998, USC Shoah Foundation, accessed on 13 September 2022.
Klopfer, Tibor. Interview with author, 23 March 2023.
McCool, William. Holocaust Testimony 2002, Gratz College Holocaust Oral History Archive, accessed on 8 September 2022.
Moszenberg, Mina. Oral History, USC Shoah Foundation, Visual History Archive, accessed 2 August 2017.
Sakheim, George. Oral History, USC Shoah Foundation, Visual History Archive, accessed 2 August 2017.

Stricoff, Lester. Oral History, USC Shoah Foundation, Visual History Archive, accessed 2 August 2017.
Wise, Sam. Oral History, USC Shoah Foundation, Visual History Archive, accessed 2 August 2017.
Zuidema, James. 1 December 1996, USC Shoah Foundation, accessed on 13 September 2022.

Websites

"Buchenwald," https://encyclopedia.ushmm.org/content/en/article/buchenwald, 17 March 2017.
C. Stephen Heard, Jr., "Adlai & Eleanor: Progressives Who Shaped the World,"
https://fdrfoundation.org/publications/adlai-eleanor-progressives-who-shaped-the-world/,
    28 February 2023.
"Camp Kilmer," https://www.archives.gov/nyc/exhibit/camp-kilmer, 23 March 2023.
"Casablanca Conference," https://avalon.law.yale.edu/wwii/casablan.asp, 15 December 2020.
"Cecilienhof," https://en.potsdam.de/content/cecilienhof-palace, 17 September 2022. Author visit,
    18 May 2022 and 13 May 2023.
"Confronting General Eisenhower Over Allies Refusal to Bomb Auschwitz," http://www.aish.com/ho/
    i/Confronting-General-Eisenhower-Over-Allies-Refusal-to-Bomb-Auschwitz.html, 5 July 2018.
"Dachau," https://encyclopedia.ushmm.org/content/en/article/dachau, 17 March 2017.
"Death Mills," http://www.camps.bbk.ac.uk/testimonies/death-mills.html, 20 May 2023.
"Denazification," http://www.alliiertenmuseum.de/en/topics/denazification.html, 18 June 2021.
"Dwight D. Eisenhower," http://c250.columbia.edu/c250_celebrates/remarkable_columbians/dwight_
    d_eisenhower.html, 9 January 2021.
"Dwight Eisenhower," https://www.nato.int/cps/en/natohq/declassified_137961.htm, 9 January 2021.
"Eichmann Trial," https://encyclopedia.ushmm.org/content/en/article/eichmann-trial, 23 May 2019.
"Eisenhower Dies at Age 78, March 28, 1969," https://www.politico.com/story/2018/03/28/eisen
    hower-dies-at-age-78-march-28-1969-484631, 25 January 2021. "Esther and Malka Deutch,"
    Auschwitz Twins, CANDLES, Inc., https://candlesolocaustmuseum.org, 7 December 2016.
"Eulogy Delivered at the Capitol During the State Funeral of General Eisenhower," https://www.presi
    dency.ucsb.edu/documents/eulogy-delivered-the-capitol-during-the-state-funeral-general-
    eisenhower, 19 October 2022.
"Exit the Fatherland," https://aeon.co/essays/germany-became-a-tolerant-nation-only-by-painful-
    small-steps, 7 June 2021.
"Flossenburg," https://encyclopedia.ushmm.org/content/en/article/flossenbuerg,
    25 September 2022.
"Folder 9, Statement by General Eisenhower," http://www.fdrlibrary.marist.edu/_resources/images/
    wrb/wrb1467.pdf, 26 June 2018.
"Franklin D. Roosevelt's D-Day Prayer," http://docs.fdrlibrary.marist.edu/odddayp.html,
    3 December 2015.
"Franklin D. Roosevelt: Statement on Axis Crimes in Occupied Countries," http://www.presidency.
    ucsb.edu/ws/index.php?pid=16293&st=&st1=; 28 June 2018.
"Franklin D. Roosevelt: Statement on the Plan to Try Nazi War Criminals," http://www.presidency.
    ucsb.edu/ws/index.php?pid=16174&st=&st1=, 28 June 2018.
"Genocide 1915: Armenian Genocide Information: Popular Quotes," http://www.genocide1915.info/
    quotes/, 6 March 2017.

George C. Marshall Foundation, "Marshall and International Holocaust Remembrance Day, https://www.marshallfoundation.org/blog/marshall-international-holocaust-remembrance-day/, 2 May 2019.

"Harrison Report," https://www.ushmm.org/exhibition/displaced-persons/resourc1.htm, 29 June 2017.

"History of the United States Holocaust Memorial Museum," https://encyclopedia.ushmm.org/content/en/article/history-of-the-united-states-holocaust-memorial-museum, 6 June 2023.

"Home," http://voices.iit.edu/, 22 May 2018.

"How the World Discovered Nazi Death Camps," https://news.yahoo.com/world-discovered-nazi-death-camps-020933983.html?guccounter=1&guce_referrer=aHR0cHM6Ly9kdWNrZHVja2dvLmNvbS8&guce_referrer_sig=AQAAAGX8LgECX5YQonmt1TB5eJJu7vf5EvuiqVoR3wmdEDdhRXnPrC2E8WeaPDpDwJqAPpu87GFxaro-aOTb8C_qIneKSKdTBVo_bjiQ_-UN6YnHdjR0ykmCumRKDx37FvOZLfUHuVG3YdGp9UnK-ZlH2J172Krdf_TJtZZ3u8bj-geP, 18 June 2021.

"Isaak and Tzvi Klein," Auschwitz Twins, CANDLES, Inc., https://candlesolocaustmuseum.org, 7 December 2016.

"James McDonald Warned the World about the Nazi Threat to Jews," https://medium.com/memory-action/james-mcdonald-warned-the-world-about-the-nazi-threat-to-jews–5cf0cc82244a, 25 May 2023.

John Q. Barrett, "Meeting Ike (May 1945)," https://thejacksonlist.com/wp-content/uploads/2015/07/20150526-Jackson-List-Eisenhower.pdf, 8 January 2021.

"Last Stand at Volkerschlachtdenkmal: The Battle of Leipzig, 1945," https://warfarehistorynetwork.com/article/last-stand-at-volkerschlachtdenkmal-battle-of-leipzig–1945/, 7 September 2022.

"Mamie Geneva Doud Eisenhower," https://www.whitehouse.gov/about-the-white-house/first-families/mamie-geneva-doud-eisenhower/, 31 January 2021.

Marc G. Desantis, "The Court-Martial of Colonel Billy Mitchell," https://www.historynet.com/the-court-martial-of-colonel-bill-mitchell/, 20 November 2022.

"Mauthausen," https://encyclopedia.ushmm.org/content/en/article/mauthausen, 25 September 2022.

"Menashe and Leah Lorenzi" Auschwitz Twins, CANDLES, Inc., https://candlesolocaustmuseum.org, 7 December 2016.

"Message to Mayor Brandt of West Berlin: August 28, 1959," http://www.presidency.ucsb.edu/ws/index.php?pid=11484&st=berlin&st1=, 9 March 2018.

Michael J. Totten, "Samantha, Powerless: Obama's Problem from Hell in Syria," http://www.thetower.org/article/samantha-powerless-obamas-problem-from-hell-in-syria/, 6 March 2017.

Michael J. Totten, "We Are Still Living With Eisenhower's Biggest Mistake," http://www.thetower.org/article/we-are-still-living-with-eisenhowers-biggest-mistake-suez-egypt-israel-ikes-gamble-michael-doran/, 6 March 2017.

"Munich Documentation Center For the History of National Socialism," https://www.nsdoku.de/en/, 20 May 2023. Author visit 17 May 2023.

"Museum Berlin-Karlshorst," https://www.museum-karlshorst.de/en/, 5 May 2023.

"Ohrdruf," https://encyclopedia.ushmm.org/content/en/article/ohrdruf, 10 March 2017.

"Opening Statement Before the International Military Tribunal," https://www.roberthjackson.org/speech-and-writing/opening-statement-before-the-international-military-tribunal/, 8 January 2021.

"Operation Safe Haven: The Hungarian Refugee Crisis of 1956," https://www.ucis.gov, 23 March 2023.

"President John F. Kennedy Meeting with Dwight Eisenhower, 10 September 1962," Presidential Recordings Digital Edition, https://pride.upress.virginia.edu, 19 October 2022.

"President John F. Kennedy Meeting with Dwight Eisenhower, 22 October 1962," Presidential Recordings Digital Edition, https://pride.upress.virginia.edu, 19 October 2022.

"President Lyndon Johnson Meeting with Dwight Eisenhower, 2 July 1965," and "Johnson with Eisenhower, 23 July 1965," Presidential Recordings Digital Edition, https://pride.upress.virginia.edu, 19 October 2022.

"Press Conference #842," http://www.fdrlibrary.marist.edu/_resources/images/pc/pc0138.pdf, 27 June 2018.

"Recollections of a Liberator: The Liberation of Ohrdruf and Buchenwald," https://www.pattonsbestmedics.com/recollections-of-a-liberator-the-liberation-of-ohrdruf-and-buchenwald-part-1-ohrdruf/, 9 September 2022.

"Resolution 138," http://unscr.com/en/resolutions/138, 14 January 2021.

"Runde Ecke," https://www.runde-ecke-leipzig.de/, 17 September 2022; Author visit, 20 May 2022.

"Safe Haven I and II," https://amcmuseum.org/history/safe-haven-i-and-ii/, 23 March 2023.

"Sermon on Yom Kippur by the Klausenberger Rebbe," https://www.yadvashem.org/yv/en/exhibitions/rosh_hashana/rabbi_yekutiel_yehuda_halberstam.asp, 16 June 2021.

Steven Friess, "A Liberator, But Never Free," https://newrepublic.com/article/121779/liberator-never-free, 15 February 2016.

"Summary of Bermuda Conference Recommendations," https://perspectives.ushmm.org/item/summary-of-bermuda-conference-recommendations, 5 May 2023.

"Surrender of Germany (1945)," https://www.archives.gov/milestone-documents/surrender-of-germany, 25 February 2023.

"The 1958 U.S. Marine Invasion of Lebanon: It was No Day at the Beach," The 1958 U.S. Marine Invasion of Lebanon – It was no day at the beach | Association for Diplomatic Studies & Training (adst.org), 22 August 2021.

"The Battle for Berlin," https://www.historylearningsite.co.uk/world-war-two/world-war-two-and-eastern-europe/the-battle-for-berlin/, 8 April 2018.

"The Battle over FDR's Record on Saving Jews from the Nazis," https://www.haaretz.com/jewish/holocaust-remembrance-day/2019-01-06/ty-article/.premium/u-s-holocaust-museum-accused-of-whitewashing-fdrs-record-on-saving-jews/0000017f-e3e6-df7c-a5ff-e3fe137e0000, 31 August 2022.

"The Berlin Airlift, 1948–1949," https://history.state.gov/milestones/1945–1952/berlin-airlift; 9 January 2021.

"The Bermuda Conference," https://www.pbs.org/wgbh/americanexperience/features/holocaust-bermuda/, 11 April 2023.

"The Black Book," https://collections.yadvashem.org/en/search-results/black%20book?page=1&subjects_search_en=The%20Black%20Book, 20 November 2022.

"The East German Uprising, 1953," https://history.state.gov/milestones/1953–1960/east-german-uprising, 19 May 2023.

"The Frontier Between Armenia and Turkey as Decided by President Woodrow Wilson," http://asbarez.com/151022/the-frontier-between-armenia-and-turkey-as-decided-by-president-woodrow-wilson/, 6 March 2017.

The German Resistance Memorial Center, https://www.gdw-berlin.de/en/home/, 17 December 2020. Author visits, 17 March 2018, 14 March 2019, 12 May 2022, 12 May 2023.

"The July 20, 1944 Plot to Assassinate Adolf Hitler," https://www.ushmm.org/wlc//en/article.php?ModuleId=10008294, 23 March 2018.

"The Holocaust," https://cla.umn.edu/chgs/holocaust-genocide-education/resource-guides/holocaust, 20 June 2021.

"The Lebanon Operation," AIRLIFT IN THE DOMINICAN CRISIS (army.mil), 22 August 2021.

"The Soviet Liberation of Auschwitz: Firsthand Memories and Photos," https://www.rbth.com/history/331599-auschwitz-liberation-soviet, 18 June 2021.

"The Truman Doctrine, 1947," https://history.state.gov/milestones/1945–1952/truman-doctrine, 9 January 2021.

"The United States and the Holocaust, 1942–45," https://encyclopedia.ushmm.org/content/en/article/the-united-states-and-the-holocaust–1942–45, 5 May 2023.

"Theodore Roosevelt – Statement on the Armenian Genocide," http://www.armenian-genocide.org/roosevelt.html, 6 March 2017.

"Treaties, States Parties and Commentaries: Geneva Convention III, Commentary 1960," https://ihl-databases.icrc.org/applic/ihl/ihl.nsf/Comment.xsp?action=openDocument&documentId=E34CAB7D3C60B986C12563CD00425C11, 12 July 2017.

"Treaties, States Parties and Commentaries: Geneva Convention I, Commentary 1952," https://ihl-databases.icrc.org/applic/ihl/ihl.nsf/Comment.xsp?action=openDocument&documentId=24EDDBDE44E33800C12563CD00420907, 12 July 2017.

"Treaties, States Parties and Commentaries: Hague Convention (II)," https://ihl-databases.icrc.org/applic/ihl/ihl.nsf/Treaty.xsp?documentId=CD0F6C83F96FB459C12563CD002D66A1&action=openDocument, 12 July 2017.

"Treblinka," https://muzeumtreblinka.eu/en/informacje/commemoration/, 22 September 2022.

"Uncovering the Architect of the Holocaust: The CIA Names File on Adolf Eichmann," https://nsarchive2.gwu.edu/NSAEBB/NSAEBB150/, 17 June 2021.

"United Nations Relief and Rehabilitation Administration," https://encyclopedia.ushmm.org/content/en/article/united-nations-relief-and-rehabilitation-administration, 18 September 2022.

"Wannsee Conference and the 'Final Solution,'" https://encyclopedia.ushmm.org/content/en/article/wannsee-conference-and-the-final-solution, 10 November 2022.

"War Refugee Board," https://encyclopedia.ushmm.org/content/en/article/the-war-refugee-board, 7 September 2022.

"We Trudged Through an Unknown, Unexperienced Evil – Unaware How that Evil Took Hold in Us," https://thewarhorse.org/nazi-concentration-camp-liberation-soldier-recalls-ohrdruf/, 9 September 2022.

"What is the Shoah?," http://www.memorialdelashoah.org/en/archives-and-documentation/what-is-the-shoah.html, 20 June 2021.

Index

Aachen, Germany 69
Armenian Genocide 92
Anti-Semitism 15–16, 18–19, 32, 38, 57, 121
Arabs 21, 32, 162–163, 167
Atomic Bomb 154–155
Auschwitz KZ 3, 40, 43, 56, 73–74, 84

Barkley, Alben 101
Beck, Ludwig 65
Bergen-Belsen KZ 93–94
Bermuda Conference 58, 60
Black Book 76
Bonhoeffer, Dietrich 95
Bradley, Omar 2, 6–8, 110
Buchenwald KZ 2, 84–88, 100, 123
– Edward R. Murrow and 87
– U.S. Army report and 87–88
Butcher, Harry 6, 105

Casablanca Conference 54–55, 66
Clay, Lucius D. 141, 145
Cold War 142, 145, 153, 157, 162, 176
– and denazification 125
– and Eisenhower's Moral View of 150, 158
Concentration camps 178 See also, individual camps by name.
– Death camps 40, 43–44, 72–73
– Death marches 3, 78–79
– Prisoners as workforce 42–44, 80, 123
– Liberation of XIII, 3–4, 92, 95, 98–99, 107, 113
– Medical experimentation in 45
– Reactions to 2–9, 99
– Sadism in 44–45, 79
– System of 40–42, 46, 53, 78, 122
– Survivors of 123
Conner, Fox 14–15, 28
Churchill, Winston 18, 29–30, 49, 103, 108, 111, 157
Cronkite, Walter 52

Dachau KZ 82, 88–91, 93, 125
– Murder of Camp Guards at 90
Darlan, Jen-Francois 31
De Gaulle, Charles 31

Displaced Persons 126–134 See also, Refugees
Doenitz, Karl 113
Dulles, Allen 152
Dulles, John Foster 152, 163

Egypt 30, 163 See also, Suez Canal Crisis
– Former Nazis and 167
– Suez Canal and 30, 32
Eichmann, Adolf 41, 168–173
– Hopes for a Nazi Revival and 170
Einsatzgruppen 35, 122
Eisenhower, Dwight XIII–XIV, 144, 176, 180–181
– Anticommunism of 151–152
– As Military Governor of Germany 114–119, 124–126, 135, 142
– As Political Candidate 147–149, 160
– As Supreme Allied Commander 48–50, 59, 77, 111
– Background of 10–11
– Battle of the Bulge and 69–70, 78
– Berlin and 108–114
– Columbia University and 144–145
– Covert Operations and 155
– Death of 176
– Displaced Persons and 131–132, 134
– Eichmann Trial and 171, 173
– Eisenhower Doctrine and 166
– Harrison Report and 130, 132–133
– Hungarian Refugees and 165
– Knowledge of the Holocaust 57, 81
– Marriage of 13–14
– Military service of 14, 28–29
– Military strategy of XII, 68, 155
– Postwar Return to the Army of 145–146
– Presidency of 149–150, 152, 156–157, 162, 167, 175
– Publicizing the Holocaust by 76, 82, 98, 100–107
– Reaction to Holocaust by XIV–XV, 1–2, 5–6, 8, 10, 76, 83, 100, 177
– Reaction to Kristallnacht by 24
– Religion and 150–151
– Remembering D-Day by 52
– State of Israel and 143, 161–163, 166

200 — Index

- View of totalitarianism of XV, 63, 154
- War Refugee Board and 62–63
- War Crimes Trials and 136–137
- West Germany and 156

Eisenhower, Mary "Mamie" Doud (wife) XIII, 13, 117
Eisenhower, John (son) XIII, 13, 51, 100
Ethnic cleansing 34
Europe First Strategy 28–30

Final Solution 37, 39–41
Flossenberg KZ 95
France 116, 164–166
- North African colonies 30–32, 61, 68
- Vichy Government 31–32, 68
Frank, Anne 93
Frieder, Alex 24–25, 120–121
Frieder, Philip 24–25

Gavin, James 95, 155
Germany 17, 23, 29 See also, Nazi Germany
- Postwar Conditions 115, 122, 124
- Denazification 119–126, 140–142
Giraud, Henri H. 31
Goebbels, Joseph 19, 140–141
Goering, Hermann 39–40, 92, 140–141
Goldwater, Barry 175
Gotha 8–9
Great Britain 21, 23, 62, 93–94, 103, 164–166

Harrison, Earl G. 128–129
- Harrison Report 129–130, 133–134, 159
Hauenstein, Ralph 82
Heydrich, Reinhard 39, 55
Himmler, Heinrich 35, 37, 41, 45, 78, 88, 93, 96, 140
Hitler, Adolf 17–19, 21, 23–24, 26, 33–34, 36–37, 47, 55, 63, 67, 78, 141
- Death of 91–92
Holocaust 23, 33, 37, 42, 80, 106, 168, 172
- Disbelief of Allied governments 46, 54, 59, 83, 93
- How to end 55–56, 63
- In American politics 53
- In Memory 177–180
- Knowledge of within Germany 80, 91, 97, 105

- Survivors of 123
Hungary 81, 168–169
- 1956 Revolt 164–165

Immigration 21–23, 61, 129
Israel 143, 158–166
- Eichmann Trial and 170–173

Jackson, Robert 137–139
Japan 26, 29
Jews 17, 19–23, 32, 34–38, 41–42, 52–54, 60–61, 65, 78, 121–123, 127, 158
Jodl, Alfred 113
Johnson, Lyndon B. 175–176

Karski, Jan 54
Katyn Massacre 152
Kennan, George 155
Kennedy, John F. 149, 175
Kesselring, Albert 3
Konev, Ivan 77
Korean War 146–147, 154
Kristallnacht 19–21, 23–25, 27, 37, 53
Krueger, Walter 28

League of Nations 20, 160
Lemkin, Ralph 140
Lodge, Henry Cabot 171
Luce, Clare Boothe 103–104

MacArthur, Douglas 15, 17, 26, 146
Majdanek 72–73
Marshall, George 1, 9, 28, 31, 49, 58, 101, 105, 114, 144, 158–159
Mauthausen 96–97
McNutt, Paul V. 16, 25
Merkers, Germany 2
Montgomery, Bernard 49, 68–69, 94, 111
Morgenthau, Jr., Henry 60, 68, 128
- Morgenthau Plan 116, 118
Moseley, George Van Horn 15–16

Nadich, Judah 130
Nasser, Gamal Abdel 163–164, 167
Nazi Germany 8, 17–20, 22, 24, 26, 34–38, 42, 45, 52–53, 55, 63

- Internal Resistance 64
- July 20 Plot 64–67, 95
Nixon, Richard 165, 175–176

Ohrdruf XIV, 1–10, 32, 48, 70, 74, 82–84, 93, 98, 102, 108, 113, 158, 181
Office of Strategic Services 55, 81–82
Operation Anthropoid 55
Operation Barbarossa 33–34, 71
Operation Bolero 30
Operation Eclipse 118
Operation Husky 49
Operation Market Garden 68–69, 111
Operation Overlord (D-Day) XI–XIII, 48, 50–53, 56, 64, 66–67
Operation Paperclip 157, 170
Operation Roundup 30
Operation Safe Haven 165–166
Operation Sledgehammer 30
Operation Torch 30–31, 47, 49

Patton, George 2–3, 6–9, 57, 61, 67, 86, 104, 110, 125, 131
Pearl Harbor XII, 26, 28, 32
Pehle, John 60
Pershing, John 14–15, 27, 49
Philippines 15–17, 23–26, 28–29, 120
Pister, Hermann 85
Poland 29, 33, 37, 116
Potsdam Conference 136, 149, 153
Prisoners of War 57, 74, 124–125, 135–136, 146, 153

Quezon, Manuel 16, 24–26

Reagan, Ronald XI, 175
Refugees 57–60, 126, 132
Roosevelt, Franklin XII, 21–23, 26, 30, 47, 49, 53–56, 60–62, 68, 92, 102, 108, 116, 118, 149, 160
Roosevelt, Theodore 92

Sawkowsky, Gustav 17, 25
Schneider, Albert 8
Smith, Walter Bedell 31, 105, 153, 162

Stalin, Joseph 33, 75, 108, 111, 119, 154
Stauffenberg, Claus von 66
Stevenson, Adlai 160
Suez Canal Crisis 163–167, 170

T-4 Euthanasia Program 38
Taft, Robert 148
Tehran Conference 49
Truman, Harry 128, 134, 136, 144–149, 155, 159–162
Truscott, Lucian 131

Unconditional Surrender doctrine 55, 66, 111
United Nations Relief and Rehabilitation Administration 127
Union of Soviet Socialist Republics 33–35, 116, 134, 139, 171
- Gulag camps and 71, 153
- Liberating Concentration Camps and 70–75
- Red Army and 71–72, 74–75, 108, 113, 152
United States Army Intelligence 8, 59, 81
- Lack of knowledge on the camps 60, 82–83
United States Congressional Delegation Camp Visit 101–103
United States Holocaust Memorial and Museum 1, 46, 175, 181
United States Military Academy (West Point) XIII, 11–13

Vengeance Weapons 48, 84
Vorys, John 61, 101

Wallenberg, Raoul 60
Wannsee Conference 39–41, 55
War Crimes Trials 135, 138–141
- Investigating Potential Allied Crimes 124
- Need for 136
- Selection of Nuremberg 139
War Refugee Board 60–62
Wilson, Woodrow 63, 92
Wishnyatskaya, Judith 47
Wise, Stephen 53
World War I 14, 17, 63, 115, 117

Yalta Conference 108–109, 111–114, 149

www.ingramcontent.com/pod-product-compliance
Lightning Source LLC
Chambersburg PA
CBHW020231170426
43201CB00007B/389